T0390667

Asia's High Performing Education Systems

Education officials, specialist leaders and teachers have all been involved in different ways to bring about school reform in Hong Kong. This book is a very current and relevant analysis of this reform, highlighting the way in which agencies have cooperated in bringing about change over the last several decades. Through a process of wide-ranging decision-making, collaboration and consensus among key bodies and agencies of change, some important developments have occurred. The reforms collectively have had, and are continuing to have, a major impact upon schooling in Hong Kong.

This volume represents a range of authors and specialists involved in a number of different reforms, covering themes such as historical policy contexts, new curriculum approaches, changing pedagogies, school leadership, implementation and change, and assessment and evaluation. This is a very topical book which provides a probing analysis of how an Asian education system has been able to reach and maintain a very high performing level.

Colin Marsh was an Adjunct Professor at Curtin University, Perth, Western Australia. He published many books in education, including *Key Concepts for Understanding Curriculum* (Routledge), currently in its fourth edition. He passed away in 2012.

John Chi-Kin Lee is the Vice-President (Academic) and Chair Professor of Curriculum and Instruction, the Hong Kong Institute of Education (HKIEd). He has served also as Co-Director of the Centre for Small Class Teaching (CSCT) and Co-Director of Centre for Education in Environmental Sustainability (CEES) at the HKIEd. He has been awarded as Chang Jiang Chair Professor to serve at Southwest University, China. Recently, he co-edited two books, *Changing Schools in an Era of Globalization* (with Prof. Brian Caldwell, Routledge, 2011) and *New Understandings of Teacher's Work: Emotions and Educational Change* (with Prof. Chris Day, Springer, 2011).

Routledge Series on Schools and Schooling in Asia

SERIES EDITOR: KERRY J. KENNEDY

1 **Minority Students in East Asia**
Government Policies, School
Practices and Teacher Responses
*Edited by JoAnn Phillion, Ming
Tak Hue and Yuxiang Wang*

2 **A Chinese Perspective on
Teaching and Learning**
Edited by Betty C. Eng

3 **Language, Culture, and Identity
Among Minority Students in
China**
The Case of the Hui
Yuxiang Wang

4 **Citizenship Education in China**
Preparing Citizens for the
"Chinese Century"
*Edited by Kerry J. Kennedy,
Gregory P. Fairbrother, and
Zhenzhou Zhao*

5 **Asia's High Performing
Education Systems**
The Case of Hong Kong
*Edited by Colin Marsh and John
Chi-Kin Lee*

Asia's High Performing Education Systems
The Case of Hong Kong

Edited by
Colin Marsh and John Chi-Kin Lee

NEW YORK   LONDON

First published 2014
by Routledge
711 Third Avenue, New York, NY 10017

and by Routledge
2 Park Square, Milton Park, Abingdon, Oxon OX14 4RN

*Routledge is an imprint of the Taylor & Francis Group,
an informa business*

© 2014 Taylor & Francis

The right of Colin Marsh and John Chi-Kin Lee to be identified as the
authors of the editorial material, and of the authors for their individual
chapters, has been asserted in accordance with sections 77 and 78 of the
Copyright, Designs and Patents Act 1988.

All rights reserved. No part of this book may be reprinted or reproduced or
utilised in any form or by any electronic, mechanical, or other means, now
known or hereafter invented, including photocopying and recording, or in
any information storage or retrieval system, without permission in writing
from the publishers.

Trademark Notice: Product or corporate names may be trademarks or
registered trademarks, and are used only for identification and explanation
without intent to infringe.

Library of Congress Cataloging-in-Publication Data

Asia's high performing education systems : the case of Hong Kong /
edited by Colin Marsh, John Chi-Kin Lee.
  pages cm. — Includes bibliographical references and index.
1. Education—Asia. 2. Educational change—Asia. 3. Academic
achievement—Asia. 4. Education—China—Hong Kong—Case
studies. 5. Educational change—China—Hong Kong—Case studies.
  I. Marsh, Colin. II. Li, Zijian, 1960–
  LA1051.A77 2014
  370.95—dc23
  2013050679

ISBN13: 978-0-415-83487-2 (hbk)
ISBN13: 978-0-203-49963-4 (ebk)

Typeset in Sabon
by IBT Global.

Contents

Dedication		ix
JOHN CHI-KIN LEE		
List of Figures		xi
List of Tables		xiii
List of Appendices		xv
Series Editor's Note		xvii
KERRY J. KENNEDY		

1 Asia's High-Performing Education System: The Case of Hong Kong — 1
COLIN MARSH AND JOHN CHI-KIN LEE

PART I
Policy Context

2 Curriculum Reforms in Hong Kong: Historical and Changing Socio-Political Contexts — 17
JOHN CHI-KIN LEE

3 Centralization and Decentralization: An Historical Analysis of School-Based Curriculum Development Initiatives in Hong Kong — 33
COLIN MARSH, PAUL MORRIS AND JOE TIN-YAU LO

vi *Contents*

PART II
Curriculum for New Times

4 Ideology and Priorities of School Curriculum in Hong Kong   51
   SHIRLEY SZE YIN YEUNG

5 "Learning to Learn" Basic Curriculum   70
   ANTHONY WAI-LUN LEUNG

6 Liberal Studies in Hong Kong:
   Teachers' Space, Place and Fusion of Horizons   84
   JOHN TAK-SHING LAM

7 National Identity and Patriotism
   in Hong Kong's Educational Reform:
   Student Attributes and Contested Curriculum Structures   102
   KERRY J. KENNEDY AND XIAOXUE KUANG

PART III
Changing Classrooms

8 The Impact of the Learning Study Approach on
   Chinese Classrooms: The Hong Kong Experience   117
   PO-YUK KO

9 Small Class Teaching in Hong Kong:
   Seizing the Opportunities   132
   KWOK-CHAN LAI, KAM-WING CHAN AND JOHN CHI-KIN LEE

PART IV
School Leadership

10 Transformational School Leadership: Principals'
   Strategic Vision and Teacher Development Practices   151
   JAMES KO AND ALLAN WALKER

Contents vii

11 Curriculum Leadership Developments:
Lessons Learned and Achievements Made 175
KWOK-TUNG TSUI

PART V
Curriculum Change and Implementation

12 Initiating Change and Innovations 195
EDMOND HAU-FAI LAW

13 Curriculum Reform Implementation at the
Classroom Level: Impacts and Challenges 207
JACQUELINE KIN-SANG CHAN AND PING-KWAN FOK

14 Changes in English-Language Education:
Ideology and Reform Strategies 221
ALICE W.K. CHOW

PART VI
Assessment

15 Assessment for Learning in Hong Kong:
Conceptions, Issues and Implications 255
RITA BERRY

16 School-Based Assessment in Secondary Schools 274
ZI YAN

17 Accountability and Improvement:
Lessons from Studying Hong Kong
Teachers' Conceptions of Assessment 288
SAMMY KING-FAI HUI

viii *Contents*

PART VII
Quality Assurance and School Evaluation

18 **The Role of Quality Assurance System in the Implementation of Curriculum Reform**
CHI CHUNG LAM
307

19 **The Effectiveness of the Quality Assurance Mechanism for School Improvement**
ERIC CHI-KEUNG CHENG AND JOHN CHI-KIN LEE
320

20 **Curriculum and Teaching Reforms: Challenges and Prospects**
JOHN CHI-KIN LEE
338

Contributors 355
Index 361

Dedication

I have come across the scholarly works of the late Professor Colin Marsh for a long time, and have been inspired by not only his academic papers on curriculum studies but also his co-edited book *Curriculum Development in East Asia* (Marsh and Morris, 1991) and his two classic books, *Perspectives: Key Concepts for Understanding the Curriculum* (Marsh, 1997a) and *Planning, Management and Ideology* (Marsh, 1997b). I was later honoured to write a review on the third edition of Colin's book *Key Concepts for Understanding Curriculum* (Lee, 2005) and occasionally maintained contact with him.

After I moved from the Chinese University of Hong Kong to the Hong Kong Institute of Education (HKIEd) in August 2010, I had the privilege of meeting Colin more often as he had served as the adjunct professor at the Department of Curriculum and Instruction of HKIEd. In early January 2012, we started our dialogue of co-editing a book involving chapters contributed by current and former colleagues at HKIEd. Colin suggested to me in an email on 9 March 2012 the tentative book be entitled *Hong Kong: Curriculum Achievements and Issues* and remarked, "I think there could be a market for such a book which provides a very detailed analysis of curriculum developments, some dead ends and a number of promising achievements over the last decade in Hong Kong. Other recent books take a wider sweep of education in Asia and so therefore I consider that this proposal might have some merit". On 25 April 2012, we submitted our book proposal to Professor Kerry Kennedy, series editor of Routledge Series on Schools and Schooling in Asia. This is by far almost the quickest book proposal I have worked out with a world-renowned scholar like Colin. We obtained the book contract in July 2012 and started to communicate with contributors about the details and their deadlines of submission. I was devastated when I received the email from Mrs. Glenys Marsh about the passing of Colin on 6 August 2012. She hoped that I would be able to continue this project.

After more than a year's concerted efforts, the book comes to the final stage. I would like to thank Mrs. Glenys Marsh and Mr. Ross Marsh, Colin's wife and son, respectively, as well as Professor Kerry Kennedy,

x *Dedication*

Mr. Michael Chau, Ms. Noto and Ms, Lauren M. Verity of Routledge and the HKIEd for their sincere and great support to our book project, which shows our last tribute to Professor Colin Marsh, our curriculum scholar, friend and colleague, who has made significant impacts on the scholarship of curriculum studies.

John Chi-Kin Lee
August 2013

REFERENCES

Lee, J.C.K. (2005). Review on Key concepts for understanding curriculum (3rd ed.) by C.J. Marsh. *Curriculum Perspectives*, 25(1), 69–70.
Marsh, C.J. (1997a). *Perspectives: Key concepts for understanding the curriculum*. London: Routledge.
Marsh, C.J. (1997b). *Planning, management and ideology*. London: Routledge.
Marsh, C.J. & Morris, P. (Eds.) (1991). *Curriculum development in East Asia*. London: Falmer Press.

Figures

5.1	"Learning to Learn" curriculum in Hong Kong.	81
10.1	Comparison of the conditions of schools with the highest and lowest leadership scores.	161
15.1	The AfL PDP.	260

Tables

1.1	Hong Kong Students' Performance in TIMSS 2007 and 2011	5
1.2	Hong Kong Students' Performance in PISA 2006, 2009 and 2012	6
4.1	Analytical Framework of the Present Study: Seven Kinds of Curriculum Ideologies/Conceptions	52
4.2	Curriculum Ideologies of the Five Curriculum/Curriculum-Related Policies in Hong Kong	60
8.1	Pre and Post-Test Comparison of the Number of Students Using the Three Components of 'Introduction', 'Topic Raising' and 'Transition' in the Opening Paragraph at the Same Time	126
10.1	Descriptive Information on the Participating Principals	155
10.2	Demographics of the Key Staff	156
10.3	Maximum, Minimum and Mean Overall and Specific Leadership Practice Scores in the Missing Link Project	157
10.4	Correlations of Specific Leadership Practices and the School Condition Alignment, Coherence and Structure	159
10.5	Overall and Specific Leadership Practice Scores of Principal Kay and their Ranks in the Missing Link Project	162
10.6	Overall and Specific School Condition Scores of Great Hope Secondary School Compared with the Scores of All Schools in the Missing Link Project	163
11.1	Performance Evaluation of PSCLs after Completion of the Professional Development Programme	187
12.1	Characteristics of Leadership Styles and Their Impacts on Team Interactions	200
13.1	The Development Strategies Adopted by the Government at Different Stages of Implementation	209
13.2	'Soft' Methods Used in the "Learning to Learn" Reform	210

xiv *Tables*

14.1	Focus of QEF Projects on Improvement of English Language Learning	236
15.1	AfL Indicators	261
16.1	Weighting and Implementation Timetable for SBA in HKDSE	276
17.1	Features of Assessment *of, for* and *as* Learning	290
17.2	Differences between the Assessment Purposes of Accountability and Improvement	296
19.1	Comparing the Key Characteristic of First and Second Cycle ESR	324
19.2	Summary of the Findings from the Case Studies	335

Appendices

14.1	English-Language Curriculum Aims in the 1975, 1983, 1999 and 2002 Syllabuses	244
14.2	An Overview of the Hierarchy of Learning Targets and Objectives for the Subject of English Language	245
14.3	Subject and Dimension Targets for the Subject of English Language	246
14.4	Comparison of Teacher Roles and Skills	247
14.5	Characteristics of the Secondary English-Language Curriculum (New versus Old and Existing)	248

Series Editor's Note

The so-called Asian century provides opportunities and challenges for both the people of Asia as well as in the West. The success of many of Asia's young people in schooling often leads educators in the West to try and emulate Asian school practices. Yet these practices are culturally embedded. One of the key issues to be taken on by this series, therefore, is to provide Western policymakers and academics with insights into these culturally embedded practices in order to assist better understanding of them outside specific cultural contexts.

There is vast diversity as well as disparities within Asia. This is a fundamental issue, and it will be addressed in this series by making these diversities and disparities the subject of investigation. The 'tiger' economies initially grabbed most of the media attention on Asian development, and more recently China has become the centre of attention. Yet there are also very poor countries in the region and their education systems seem unable to be transformed to meet new challenges. Pakistan is a case in point. Thus the whole of Asia will be seen as important for this series in order to address questions relevant to not only developed countries but also developing countries. In other words, the series will take a 'whole of Asia' approach.

Asia can no longer be considered in isolation. It is as subject to the forces of globalization, migration and transnational movements as other regions of the world. Yet the diversity of cultures, religions and social practices in Asia means that responses to these forces are not predictable. This series, therefore, is interested to identify the ways tradition and modernity interact to produce distinctive contexts for schools and schooling in an area of the world that has impacts across the globe.

Against this background, I am pleased to welcome this book to the Routledge Series on Schools and Schooling in Asia.

Kerry J. Kennedy
Series Editor
Routledge Series on Schools and Schooling in Asia

1 Asia's High-Performing Education System
The Case Of Hong Kong

Colin Marsh and John Chi-Kin Lee

INTRODUCTION

Hong Kong Special Administrative Region (SAR) became part of the People's Republic of China (PRC) in 1997 when Hong Kong, a former British colony, returned to the Chinese sovereignty. At the end of 2011, it had a population around 7.15 million (Census and Statistics Department, Hong Kong SAR Government, 2013, p.4) in an area of about 1,104 km² ('Hong Kong', n.d., 'Geography and Climate', para. 1). In the 2011–2012 financial year, the approved estimate for recurrent government expenditure on education was HK$54.5 billion (about US$ 7.03 billion), accounting for about 22.5% of all recurrent government expenditure, while the total estimate for government expenditure on education made up about 18.2% of total government expenditure (Information Services Department, Hong Kong SAR, 2012c, p.150). As regards the number of educational institutions from the pre-primary, primary to secondary levels, there were 861 local and 96 non-local kindergartens; 455 local, government and aided primary schools; 394 local, government and aided secondary schools; 73 other local primary schools (e.g., Direct Subsidy Scheme and private schools); 96 other local secondary schools (e.g., Direct Subsidy Scheme and private schools); 61 local and international special schools; 41 international primary schools; and 29 international secondary schools in 2012 (Census and Statistics Department, Hong Kong SAR Government, 2013, pp.341, 359). In terms of student enrolment in 2012, there were 164,764 kindergarten students; 317,442 primary school students; 418,787 secondary school students; and 8,021 students enrolling in schools of special education and special classes in ordinary schools (Census and Statistics Department, Hong Kong SAR Government, 2013, pp.341, 359). For the number of teachers in the teaching profession in 2012, there were an overall 11,817 kindergarten teachers comprising 3,907 trained and 362 untrained kindergarten teachers with university graduate or equivalent qualification, as well as 7,328 trained and 220 untrained teachers, respectively, who were non-university graduates. There were 22,173 primary day school teachers, which included 20,221 trained and 777 untrained

2 Colin Marsh and John Chi-Kin Lee

teachers with university graduate or equivalent qualification, as well as 1,053 trained and 122 untrained teachers, respectively, who were non-university graduates. There were 29,981 secondary day school teachers, which included 27,968 trained and 1,456 untrained teachers with university graduate or equivalent qualification, as well as 488 trained and 69 untrained teachers, respectively, who were non-university graduates (Census and Statistics Department, Hong Kong SAR Government, 2013, p.349). As regards pupil-teacher ratio in 2012, kindergarten was 9.3, while the overall ratio for primary day school and secondary day school was 14.4 and 14.2, respectively (Census and Statistics Department, Hong Kong SAR Government, 2013, p.351).

The Education Commission (EC) has its terms of references for advising the government via the secretary for education, on "the overall education objectives and policies; and the priorities for implementation of its recommendations having regard to resources available" (EC, n.d.[b], para. 1). In the EC, there are the chairman and the permanent secretary for education, as well the vice-chairman, 11 non-official members, the secretary and eight ex officio members (EC, n.d.[a]).

In 2000, the EC announced the education blueprint for the education system in Hong Kong in the 21st century. In the foreword of the document, *Learning for Life Learning through Life: Reform Proposals for the Education System in Hong Kong*, Mr. Antony K.C. Leung, the then chairman of the EC, remarked:

> Learning is the key to one's future, and Education is the gateway to our society's tomorrow . . . 'Students' are the focal point of the entire reform, 'life-long learning' and 'all round development' the spirit. At the basic education level, the goal is to ensure that every student attain the basic competencies, while those with greater potentials be allowed to further excel. At the senior secondary and post-secondary level, a diversified and multi-channel education system will be introduced to provide more opportunities and choices. (EC, 2000, p.i)

The overall aims of education for the 21st century are stated as follows (EC, 2000, p.30):

> To enable every person to attain all-round development in the domains of ethics, intellect, physique, social skills and aesthetics according to his/her own attributes so that he/she is capable of lifelong learning, critical and exploratory thinking, innovating and adapting to change; filled with self-confidence and a team spirit; willing to put forward continuing effort for the prosperity, progress, freedom and democracy of their society, and contribute to the future well-being of the nation and the world at large.

In addition, the priorities are to enable Hong Kong students to enjoy learning, enhance their effectiveness in communication and develop their creativity and sense of commitment. As regards the vision of the education reform, it is hoped that a lifelong learning society will be built, the overall quality of students will be raised, a diverse school system will be constructed, an inspiring learning environment will be created, the importance of moral education will be acknowledged and an education system that is rich in tradition but cosmopolitan and culturally diverse will be developed (EC, 2000, p.35). In addition, the principles of "student-focused", "no-loser", "quality", "life-wide learning" and "society-wide mobilisation" (EC, 2000, p.36) were adopted.

The Curriculum Development Council (CDC) (2001) announced the curriculum reform document *Learning to Learn: Lifelong Learning and Whole-Person Development*, which proposed a ten-year plan, with 2001–2002 to 2005–2006 as the short-term phase, and 2006–2007 to 2010–2011 as the medium-term phase. It was suggested: "By 2006, schools will be ready to use their professional autonomy to strike a balance between the recommendations of the CDC's new curriculum guides and school-based curriculum development [SBCD], in matters such as choice of options, contents, flexible use of time and life-wide learning opportunities". And "by 2011, we hope that our students will possess life-long learning qualities such as resourcefulness, resilience, motivation, collaboration, critical mindedness and creativity" (p.13).

For many years, the education system in Hong Kong followed the British system, exemplified by the 6–5-2–3: six years of primary school (primary 1–primary 6), five years of secondary schools (secondary 1–5, leading to a certificate examination), two years of pre-university or sixth form study (secondary 6–7, leading to an advanced level examination) and three years of normative university study. Recently, the education system for secondary and higher education became a 334 academic structure consisting of three years of junior secondary, three years of senior secondary and a four-year normative undergraduate degree.

In 2005, the Education and Manpower Bureau (now the Education Bureau [EDB]) issued the document *The New Academic Structure for Senior Secondary Education and Higher Education: Action Plan for Investing in the Future of Hong Kong.* From the 2008–2009 school year, the government launched a 12-year free education comprising nine years of basic education and three years of senior secondary education for students in public sector schools. Starting in 2009, the New Senior Secondary (NSS) curriculum, comprising four core subjects (Chinese Language, English Language, Mathematics and Liberal Studies) and a flexible, coherent and diversified curriculum, was implemented for secondary 4 to secondary 6 students who sit for the only one public examination leading to the Hong Kong Diploma of Secondary Education (HKDSE) at secondary 6.

4 Colin Marsh and John Chi-Kin Lee

There have been systematic arrangements for the continuing professional development (CPD) of principals and teachers since the late 1990s. In 2003, the Advisory Committee on Teacher Education and Qualifications (ACTEQ) (2003) proposed a generic teacher competencies framework with four domains: teaching and learning; student development; school development; and professional relationships and services. In addition, it was suggested that "all teachers, irrespective of their rank and capacity, should engage in CPD activities of not less than 150 hours in a three-year cycle" and "time spent on the 3 school-organised staff development days will be fully recognized and counted towards the CPD requirement" (ACTEQ, 2003, p.13). The ACTEQ has been renamed the Committee on Professional Development of Teachers and Principals (COTAP), effective 1 June 2013, to broaden its mission of promoting the professional development of teachers and principals. The new COTAP may carry out educational research and professional development programmes for both teachers and principals (ACTEQ, n.d.).

Another unique feature of the education system is that many schools in Hong Kong are supported by School Sponsoring Bodies (SSBs). In 2005, the government implemented the school-based management (SBM) governance framework and with the amendment of the Education Ordinance required the SSBs of an aided school to submit a draft incorporated management committee (IMC) constitution before 1 July 2011 so that an IMC could be established to manage the school. An IMC involves SSB managers, the principal (an ex officio manager), elected teacher manager(s), elected parent manager(s), alumni manager(s)and independent manager(s) (EDB, School Management Section, 2010b).

ASIA'S HIGH-PERFORMING EDUCATION SYSTEM: THE CASE OF HONG KONG

Over the last decade, there has been a prevailing trend of international comparison and benchmarking of educational systems. Comparative tests, such as Progress in International Reading Literacy Study (PIRLS) (Tse, 2012); Trends in International Mathematics and Science Study (TIMSS) (Leung, 2012); and the Programme for International Student Assessment (PISA) display a growing emphasis on benchmarking the performance of different systems. Taking the PIRLS, for example, the overall mean score of Hong Kong grade 4 students' reading performance was 564 (ranked second) in 2006 and 571 (ranked first) in 2011. The average score for informational reading was 568 (ranked first) in 2006 and 578 (ranked first) in 2011. The average score for literary reading was 557 (ranked fourth) in 2006 and 565 (ranked fourth) in 2011 (Information Services Department, Hong Kong SAR, 2012a).

In TIMSS, Hong Kong students also demonstrated remarkable performance. Table 1.1 shows Hong Kong students' performance in TIMSS 2007 and 2011 (Information Services Department, Hong Kong SAR, 2012b).

Asia's High-Performing Education System 5

Table 1.1   Hong Kong Students' Performance in TIMSS 2007 and 2011

	TIMSS 2007	*TIMSS 2011*
Grade 4 Mathematics	607 (ranked 1st)	602 (ranked 3rd)
Grade 8 Mathematics	572 (ranked 4th)	586 (ranked 4th)
Grade 4 Science	554 (ranked 3rd)	535 (ranked 9th)
Grade 8 Science	530 (ranked 9th)	535 (ranked 8th)

According to the EDB spokesman:

> The outstanding performance of Hong Kong students in PIRLS 2011 should be attributed to the continuous efforts made by schools and teachers. They have taken up the new Chinese Language curriculum and engaged in targeted professional development. All education professionals know the importance of reading for better learning. As for TIMSS, Hong Kong students on the whole had an outstanding performance in TIMSS 2011. It is indeed a great challenge to maintain a high ranking in various international studies. It is normal for the ranking to have minor fluctuations over time, but Hong Kong students have sustained an excellent performance continuously. The achievement is indeed encouraging. (Hong Kong Special Administration Region Government, 2012b)

As for the PISA in 2009, Hong Kong 15-year-old students ranked fourth in reading and third in both mathematics and science. The PISA 2009 results also showed that the difference in student performance between schools was smaller than that in 2002, suggesting that Hong Kong is moving towards a quality school system with equality. However, the within-school difference of student performance had increased significantly, highlighting the possibility of having more diverse academic ability of students within the school (Chinese University of Hong Kong, 2010).

The latest results of the PISA 2012, released on 3 December 2013, indicate that Hong Kong students' performance continues to rank among the world's best. Table 1.2 presents Hong Kong students' performance in PISA 2006, 2009 and 2012 (Hong Kong SAR Government, 2013).

International agencies such as the McKinsey & Company and the Organisation for Economic Co-operation and Development (OECD) have also published influential reports, such as *How the World's Most Improved School Systems Keep Getting Better* (Mourshed, Chijioke and Barber, 2010) and *Lessons from PISA for the United States, Strong Performers and Successful Reformers in Education* (OECD, 2011), where Hong Kong was included as an example of successful reformers in education.

6 Colin Marsh and John Chi-Kin Lee

Table 1.2 Hong Kong Students' Performance in PISA 2006, 2009 and 2012

	Reading Literacy	Mathematical Literacy	Scientific Literacy
PISA 2006	536 (ranked 3rd)	547 (ranked 3rd)	542 (ranked 2nd)
PISA 2009	533 (ranked 4th)	555 (ranked 3rd)	549 (ranked 3rd)
PISA 2012	545 (ranked 2nd)	561 (ranked 3rd)	555 (ranked 2nd)

In *How the World's Most Improved School Systems Keep Getting Better* (Mourshed, Chijioke and Barber, 2010), Hong Kong is considered as having an improvement from "good" to "great" from around 1990 to 2000 (p.15) and since then taking up an improvement journey from "great" to "excellent". In particular, it was mentioned in that report that Hong Kong has put forward a "strongly recommended" stipulated number of professional development hours over certain time period as part of teacher and principal capacity building (pp.63–64). In addition, the creation of the Quality Education Fund for supporting school improvement and action research (pp.41, 44), the emphasis on a flexible medium of instruction (MOI) policy (p.68) and the recognition of the importance of both English, for future employability of students, and Chinese, for "cultural cohesion and identity" (p.66), as well as the uniqueness of the school system "being privately operated and publicly funded" were highlighted (p.68).

In a recent report, *The Learning Curve*, on a global index of cognitive skills and educational attainment published by Pearson (Economist Intelligence Unit, 2012, p.40), Finland and South Korea were ranked first and second with z-scores at least one standard deviation above the mean, while Hong Kong was ranked third as one of the countries in group two with z-scores within half to one standard deviation above the mean.

Hong Kong is considered as having one of the best school systems in East Asia. As remarked by Jensen (2012, p.2):

> Success in high-performing education systems in East Asia is not always the result of spending more money . . . Only 11 years ago, Hong Kong ranked 17th in assessments of reading literacy (PIRLS) and Singapore was ranked 15th. Just five years later (in 2006) they ranked 2nd and 4th. However, Hong Kong, Shanghai, Korea and Singapore all focus on the things that are known to matter in the classroom, including a relentless, practical focus on learning, and the creation of a strong culture of teacher education, research, collaboration, mentoring, feedback and sustained professional development.

In that report, Chapter 6 entitled, 'Best Practice Reform: Hong Kong', Hong Kong experiences were discussed as illustrations of "a prime example of successful education strategy and implementation", including four education strategy steps: (1) "improving learning: choosing a strategic objective(s)"; (2) "reforming teaching to improve learning: prioritising policy levers"; (3) "implementation"; and (4) "allocating resources (and continually reallocating following continual feedback and evaluation" (p.24). For reforms in Hong Kong from 1999 to 2012, school education has encountered structural reform exemplified by NSS academic structure and curriculum and pedagogy reforms, including school-based curriculum development; assessment reform comprising introduction of "Assessment for Learning" (AfL) and low stakes competency assessments; SBM reform; and languages education reform, such as promoting of reading (p.26).

Education and curriculum reforms in Hong Kong, like reforms elsewhere, were not free from critics as these quality-oriented reforms were seen, from a critical perspective, as filled with the ideologies of managerialism and performativity with corresponding regulatory mechanisms, such as quality assurance (QA) consisting of School Self-Evaluation (SSE), External School Review (ESR) and SBM. As Choi (2005, p.248) lamented, "Ultimately, state-induced reforms . . . are what Ball called 'policy technologies' that reform the social relationships and subjectivities of the teachers. The basic, misguided assumption that underlies managerialism—namely, that all conflicts within various levels of the education system can be resolved through good management—amounts to a denial of value differences and structurally embedded conflicts of interests (Tse, 2002). This denial, in turn, leads to compliance with the hegemonic notions of 'efficiency', 'quality', and 'choice'".

Moreover, despite the sustained high performance of the Hong Kong educational system, there had been setbacks and educational reform syndrome that led to the phenomenon of "bottle-neck effect" during the reform journey (Cheng, 2009). There may still exist some challenges or areas for improvement. Based on the results of the reading performance in PIRLS 2001 and 2006, for example, Lam, Cheung and Lam (2009) suggested that more support is needed to help the weaker student readers; more measures are needed to help families with relatively low socio-economic backgrounds to enhance their home reading environment; and more resources, training and support are needed to help teachers handle students with reading difficulties and to communicate with parents.

The *QA Inspection Annual Report 2009/10* (Quality Assurance Division [QAD], 2011) highlighted:

> the use of assessment for learning in classroom teaching is at the exploratory stage. Although questioning and small group discussion have been the major and common teaching methods employed, the use of these two teaching methods has much room for improvement. Teachers are often unable to point out the strengths and weaknesses of student learning, nor can they provide specific feedback to inform learning and make improvement. More attention should be given to assessment for learning in adjusting teaching content and methods. (pp.46–47)

8   Colin Marsh and John Chi-Kin Lee

SYNOPSIS OF CHAPTERS

This book is divided into seven parts. The first, including Chapters 2 and 3, is concerned with policy contexts. The second part, including Chapters 4, 5, 6 and 7, refers to a curriculum for new times. The third part, encompassing Chapters 8 and 9, concentrates on changing classrooms. The fourth part, including Chapters 10 and 11, highlights school leadership, while the fifth, comprising Chapters 12–14, discusses curriculum change and implementation. The sixth part, encompassing Chapters 15, 16 and 17, concentrates on assessment related issues. The seventh part, including Chapters 18 and 19, touches upon QA and school evaluation. The book is concluded with Chapter 20 on challenges and prospects of curriculum reforms.

Lee, in Chapter 2 of Part I, on policy context, analyzes the historical and socio-political contexts of curriculum contexts in Hong Kong on or before its return to the Chinese sovereignty in 1997. He examines the tensions/balance considerations in curriculum review as espoused by the CDC's (2000) consultation document entitled *Learning to Learn: The Way Forward in Curriculum Development*: globalization and localization; academic, personal, social and economic goals of the curriculum; central development and school-based development; specialist development and whole-person development; uniformity, diversity and flexibility; co-operation and competition; knowledge transmission and knowledge creation; assessment for selection and AfL; and urgency and feasibility. In Chapter 3, Marsh, Morris and Lo offer an historical analysis of SBCD initiatives in Hong Kong based on the perspectives of centralization and decentralization. They observe that the SBCD initiatives are loosely coupled and non-coherent in structure, and implemented on an ad hoc basis. Nonetheless, the SBCD as an example of "centralized decentralization" (Lee and Gopinathan, 2004; Mok, 2004) fostered a significant change in the overall culture in schools and the role of teachers.

In Chapter 4 of Part II, on curriculum for new times, Yeung discusses the ideologies and priorities of school curriculum. She remarks that the ideology of social efficiency was dominant in the new senior curriculum reform document (Education and Manpower Bureau, 2005), the policy of ESR and SSE (QAD, 2006, 2009) and fine-tuning of MOI policy, while the ideology of political orthodoxy was revealed in the language policy in the school and the recent controversial Moral and National Education (MNE) curriculum (CDC, 2012). Leung in Chapter 5 echoes the introductory chapter and focuses on the "Learning to Learn" basic curriculum, examining the following aspects: the overall aims, curriculum framework, areas of action; recognition and achievement, challenges and concern; and the "Learning to Learn" curriculum beyond 2011. Lam in Chapter 6 discusses the implementation of Liberal Studies as one of the four core subjects in the NSS curriculum. Kennedy and Kuang in Chapter 7 analyze the National Education agenda in Hong Kong through the transformation of "civic and moral education" under Chinese sovereignty.

Ko, in Chapter 8 of Part III, on changing classrooms, discusses the impact of teaching innovations in the Chinese classroom through the experiences of Learning Study as an approach to classroom research based at the Hong Kong Institute of Education (HKIEd). Through the illustration of a case study, the impact of this approach on student learning is discussed with a view to enriching our pluralistic understanding of Chinese classrooms. Lai, Chan and Lee, in Chapter 9, review the policies and related issues of Small Class Teaching (SCT) in Hong Kong from 1950 to 2000. They also use two cases to illuminate how SCT could bring impact to schools based on the partnership of the HKIEd and the schools.

Ko and Walker examine, in Chapter 10 of Part IV, on school leadership, the role and effectiveness of professional teacher development (PTD) in Hong Kong secondary schools. In addition, empirical evidences from a recent large-scale study that attempted to identify the links between principal leadership practices with student outcomes is discussed. Tsui, in Chapter 11, discusses the unique scheme aimed to develop teachers into Primary School Curriculum Leaders (CLs) in Hong Kong and its effectiveness and points to future ways of sustaining the positive impact of CLs.

In Chapter 12 of Part V, on curriculum change and implementation, Law discusses teacher curriculum leadership through projects of "Accelerating School-Based Curriculum Development" with three stages of planning and reviewing, implementation and trial, and reflection to reveal how leadership styles, teacher curriculum development skills, teachers' situational and deep learning are shaped.

Chan and Fok, in Chapter 13, highlight in the context of curriculum reform how teachers perceived their work and related changes, the impacts of the curriculum reforms on teachers' classrooms and issues arising from the classroom implementation. In Chapter 14, Chow examines curriculum changes in English-language education. She highlights strategies such as "from centre periphery initiation to rational-empirical persuasion" and "a normative-re-educative approach to sustaining reforms". In addition, she notes the ongoing tensions between emphasis on external examinations coupled with didactic pedagogy and learner-centred philosophy of education and advocacy of AfL and practice of assessment of learning. She calls for reform in public examinations and introduction of portfolio assessment to address learners' diversity. Chapters 15 to 17 then shift to assessment as an integral part of curriculum change and implementation. Berry, in Chapter 15, discusses the developments of AfL (used interchangeably with formative assessment) in Hong Kong and illustrates a model with 50 AfL indicators aiming to empower teachers with knowledge and skills of using AfL for teaching and student learning. Yan, in Chapter 16, highlights the implementation of school-based assessment (SBA) in secondary schools and examines the challenges. He attempts to provide insights through cases on how the development of SBA practices in Chinese Language, Liberal Studies and Physical Education could

10 *Colin Marsh and John Chi-Kin Lee*

help reconcile the formative and summative purposes of assessment. In Chapter 17, Hui discusses teachers' conceptions of assessment, whether assessment is linked with accountability or associated with improvement of student learning. He draws on Brown et al.'s (2011) model, which revealed the three inter-correlated core purposes of assessment in the Chinese contexts—accountability, improvement and irrelevance. His studies on perceptions of CLs also illustrated that non-examination/test formats and assessments with a formative, improvement-oriented purpose were still strongly associated their tasks with improvement as well as accountability and examination purposes.

In Chapter 18 of Part VII, on quality assurance and school evaluation, Lam examines the new school review system as one of the key strategies to promote the curriculum reform formally launched in 2001. While the school review system was seen as controversial, its implementation over a decade appeared to help establish a self-evaluation culture in many schools as well as ensure the implementation of the major curriculum reform initiatives in schools. In Chapter 19, Cheng and Lee discuss possible effects of institutionalizing SSE for improving strategic planning capacity through two in-depth case studies in an aided primary school and an aided secondary school. It is concluded that despite challenges encountered, embedding SSE into strategic planning process not only helped school leaders analyze the organizational environment of their schools but also supported the implementation of strategic management for improving the quality of curriculum plans, teaching and learning, as well as for achieving school objectives for sustainable development.

In Chapter 20, Lee suggests we consider sustainability issues or future curriculum development. At the policy level, it is argued that it is better to relieve teachers' workloads and anxiety and to enhance a participative process in which the languages of appreciation and co-operation as well as an integration of self-evaluation and external support are highlighted. At the practice/implementation level, it is desirable to consider issues such as planning for leadership succession and developing school capacity, broadening and deepening student learning, nurturing professional learning communities and conserving the merits of the educational system under the influence of Chinese culture. In particular, it is highlighted to preserve the essence of Chinese pedagogy and explore ways of assimilating it with those of Western approaches to learning and teaching. As regards student learning, more attention could be paid to explore ways of enhancing students' self-directed learning and socio-emotional learning.

ACKNOWLEDGEMENT

This chapter was written by John Chi-Kin Lee, but the idea and structure of the book was jointly prepared by Colin Marsh and John Chi-Kin Lee.

REFERENCES

Advisory Committee on Teacher Education and Qualifications (2003). *Towards a learning profession: The teacher competencies framework and the continuing professional development of teachers.* Hong Kong: Government Logistics Department.

Advisory Committee on Teacher Education and Qualifications (n.d.). *Renaming ACTEQ as COTAP.* Retrieved 27 June 2013, from http://www.acteq.hk/category.asp?pid=39&cid=434&lang=en.

Brown, G.T.L., Hui, S.K.F., Yu, W.M., & Kennedy, K.J. (2011). Teachers' conceptions of assessment in Chinese contexts: A tripartite model of accountability, improvement, and irrelevance. *International Journal of Educational Research, 50*(5–6), 307–320.

Census and Statistics Department, Hong Kong Special Administrative Region Government (2013). *Hong Kong annual digest of statistics (2013 ed.).* Hong Kong: Printing Department. Retrieved 16 December 2013, from http://www.statistics.gov.hk/pub/B10100032013AN13B0100.pdf.

Cheng, Y.C. (2009). Hong Kong educational reforms in the last decade: Reform and syndrome and new developments. *International Journal of Educational Management, 23*(1), 65–86.

Chinese University of Hong Kong (2010). *CUHK releases the results of Programme for International Student Assessment.* 7 December. Retrieved 10 January 2013, from http://www.fed.cuhk.edu.hk/~hkpisa/events/2009/files/PISA2009_Results_e.pdf.

Choi, P.K. (2005). A critical evaluation of education reforms in Hong Kong: Counting our losses to economic globalization. *International Studies in Sociology of Education, 15*(3), 237–256.

Curriculum Development Council (2000). *Learning to Learn: The way forward in curriculum development.* Retrieved 3 November 2012, from http://www.edb.gov.hk/FileManager/EN/Content_4079/overview-e.pdf.

Curriculum Development Council (2001). *Learning to Learn: Life-long learning and whole-person development.* Hong Kong: Printing Department.

Curriculum Development Council (2012). *Moral and National Education: Curriculum guides (primary 1 to secondary 6).* Hong Kong: Education Bureau.

Economist Intelligence Unit (2012). *The learning curve: Lessons in country performance in education.* London: Pearson. Retrieved 10 January 2013, from http://thelearningcurve.pearson.com/content/download/bankname/components/filename/FINALLearningCurve_Final.pdf

Education and Manpower Bureau (2005). *The new academic structure for senior secondary education and higher education: Action plan for investing in the future of Hong Kong.* Retrieved 10 January 2013, from http://334.edb.hkedcity.net/doc/eng/report_e.pdf.

Education Bureau, School-Based Management Section (2010a) *Introduction of school-based management.* Retrieved 11 January 2013, from http://www.edb.gov.hk/FileManager/EN/Content_1951/introduction10_e.pdf.

Education Bureau, School Management Section (2010b). *School-based management and school-based management governance framework.* Retrieved 20 January 2013, from http://www.edb.gov.hk/index.aspx?nodeID=1937&langno=1.

Education Commission. (2000). *Learning for life—learning through life: Reform proposals for the education system in Hong Kong.* Retrieved January 11, 2013, from http://www.e-c.edu.hk/eng/reform/annex/Edu-reform-eng.pdf.

Education Commission (n.d.[a]). *Terms of reference.* Retrieved 11 January 2013, from http://www.e-c.edu.hk/eng/reference/index_e.html.

12   Colin Marsh and John Chi-Kin Lee

Education Commission (n.d.[b]). *Membership*. Retrieved 11 January 2013, from http://www.e-c.edu.hk/eng/memship/index_e.html.

Hong Kong. (n.d.). *Wikipedia*. Retrieved 10 January 2013, from http://en.wikipedia.org/wiki/Hong_Kong.

Hong Kong Special Administrative Region Government (2012a). *Hong Kong yearbook 2012*. Hong Kong: Government Printer.

Hong Kong Special Administrative Region Government (2012b). *International study shows Hong Kong students' outstanding performance in reading literacy, mathematics and science* [Press Release]. Retrieved 11 January 2013, from http://www.info.gov.hk/gia/general/201212/12/P201212120332.htm.

Hong Kong Special Administrative Region Government (2013). *International study shows Hong Kong students' reading, mathematical and scientific literacy continue to rank among the world's best* [Press Release and Annex]. Retrieved 4 December 2013, from http://www.info.gov.hk/gia/general/201312/03/P201312030421.htm and http://gia.info.gov.hk/general/201312/03/P201312030421_0421_121314.pdf.

Information Services Department, Hong Kong Special Administrative Region (2012a). *Annex 1: PIRLS 2011 background information and key statistics*. Retrieved 4 December 2013, from http://gia.info.gov.hk/general/201212/12/P201212120332_0332_104254.pdf.

Information Services Department, Hong Kong Special Administrative Region (2012b). *Annex 2: TIMSS 2011 background information and key statistics*. Retrieved 4 December 2013, from http://gia.info.gov.hk/general/201212/12/P201212120332_0332_104255.pdf.

Information Services Department, Hong Kong Special Administrative Region (2012c). *Hong Kong 2011*. Hong Kong: Printing Department.

Jensen, B. (2012). *Catching up: Learning from the best school systems in East Asia*. Carlton, Australia: Grattan Institute. Retrieved 10 January 2013, from http://grattan.edu.au/static/files/assets/00d8aaf4/130_report_learning_from_the_best_detail.pdf.

Lam, J.W.I., Cheung, W.M., & Lam, R.Y.H. (2009). Learning to read: The reading performance of Hong Kong primary students compared with that in developed countries around the world in PIRLS 2001 and 2006. *Chinese Education and Society, 42*(3), 6–32.

Lee, M.H., & Gopinathan, S. (2004). Centralized decentralization of higher education in Singapore. In K.H. Mok (Ed.) *Centralization and decentralization: Educational reforms and changing governance in Chinese societies* (pp.117–136). Hong Kong: Comparative Education Research Centre, University of Hong Kong.

Leung, F.K.S. (2012). Hong Kong SAR. In I.V.S. Mullis, M.O. Martin, C.A. Minnich, G.M. Stanco, A. Arora & V.A.S. Centurino (Eds.) *TIMSS 2011 encyclopedia: Education policy and curriculum in mathematics and science, Vol 1:A-K*, (pp.367–380). TIMSS & PIRLS International Study Center. Boston: Lynch School of Education, Boston College. Retrieved 4 December 2013, from http://timssandpirls.bc.edu/timss2011/downloads/TIMSS2011_Enc-v1.pdf

Mok, K.H. (2004) Centralization and decentralization: Changing governance in Education. In K.H. Mok (Ed.) *Centralization and decentralization: Educational reforms and changing governance in Chinese societies* (pp.3–17). Hong Kong: Comparative Education Research Centre, University of Hong Kong.

Mourshed, M., Chijioke, C., & Barber, M. (2010). *How the world's most improved school systems keep getting better*. New York: McKinsey & Company. Retrieved 8 January 2012, from http://mckinseyonsociety.com/downloads/reports/Education/How-the-Worlds-Most-Improved-School-Systems-Keep-Getting-Better_Download-version_Final.pdf.

Organisation for Economic Co-operation and Development (2011). *Lessons from PISA for the United States, strong performers and successful reformers in education*. Paris, France: OECD Publishing. Retrieved 10 January 2013, from http://www.oecd.org/pisa/46623978.pdf.

Quality Assurance Division (2006). *Handbook of External School Review for schools*. Hong Kong: Education and Manpower Bureau.

Quality Assurance Division (2009). *External School Review: Information for schools*. Hong Kong: Education Bureau.

Quality Assurance Division (2011). *QA inspection annual report 2009/10*. Retrieved 10 January 2013, from http://www.edb.gov.hk/FileManager/EN/Content_756/qa_annual_report0910_e.pdf.

Tse, K.C. (2002). A critical review of the quality education movement in Hong Kong. In J.K.H. Mok & D.K.K. Chan (Eds.) *Globalisation and education: The quest for quality education in Hong Kong* (pp.143–170). Hong Kong: Hong Kong University Press.

Tse, S.K. (2012). Hong Kong SAR. In I.V.S. Mullis, M.O. Martin, C.A. Minnich, K.T. Drucker & M.A. Regan (Eds.) *PIRLS 2011 encyclopedia: Education policy and curriculum in reading* (pp.287–299). TIMSS & PIRLS International Study Center. Boston: Lynch School of Education, Boston College.

Part I
Policy Context

2 Curriculum Reforms in Hong Kong
Historical and Changing Socio-Political Contexts

John Chi-Kin Lee

INTRODUCTION

In 2000, the Education Commission (EC) issued the document *Learning for Life—Learning through Life: Reform Proposals for the Education System in Hong Kong* and the Curriculum Development Council (CDC) announced the consultation document *Learning to Learn: The Way Forward in Curriculum Development* (2000b), which later led to the *Learning to Learn: Life-Long Learning and Whole-Person Development* (2001). This chapter is divided into four sections. The first briefly discusses the trends of curriculum development and the status of the school system on or before the return of Hong Kong to Chinese sovereignty in 1997. The second section highlights the socio-cultural background and changing socio-political, post-colonial contexts since the late 1990s, which are illustrated by fluctuating demographic changes, increasing emphasis on national education and building up a knowledge-based and lifelong learning society. The third section gives a snapshot of the implementation of the four key tasks as illustrated examples of curriculum reforms, and the final section analyzes the tensions/balance considerations in curriculum review.

The subtitle of this chapter is historical and changing socio-political contexts. For "contexts", McLaughlin and Talbet (1990) refer to the socio-cultural context as well as those organizational and policy contexts, including the school context, that shape teaching and student learning. For Mourshed, Chijioke and Barber (2010, p.62), "context" embraces two forms: "current education's performance (poor, fair, good, great, excellent) and its impact . . . [and] . . . the influence of history, culture, values, system structure, politics, etc. upon how the system implements the common interventions in their improvement journey".

THE TRENDS OF CURRICULUM DEVELOPMENT AND THE STATUS OF THE SCHOOL SYSTEM ON OR BEFORE THE RETURN OF HONG KONG TO CHINESE SOVEREIGNTY IN 1997

Hong Kong, as a British colony before 1997, had a unified centralized education system before the 1990s and both the government and the School

18   John Chi-Kin Lee

Sponsoring Bodies (SSBs) have played a dominant role in school governance and the aided school sector which has occupied a large proportion of primary and secondary schools.

Nine-year compulsory education was introduced in 1978 and the early 1980s were primarily the "quantitative era of educational development" (Cheng, 2002, p.41). Educational agendas were given a higher priority of attention until the formation of the EC in 1984 to advise the government on educational policies (Kwan, 2011). To understand the impact of curriculum reforms on schools and teachers in Hong Kong, we should not ignore the broad context of educational reforms, which could be categorized into first and second waves in the last two decades. The first waves of educational reforms took place in the 1980s, which could be reflected by the EC reports nos. 1 to 6 (1984–1996). These reforms covered areas such as school education, language teaching and learning, teacher quality, improvements of private schools, curriculum development, teaching and learning conditions and special education. As remarked by Cheng (2009, p.66), these reform initiatives tended to adopt "a top-down approach with an emphasis on external intervention or increasing resources input".

Kennedy (2005, p.101; 2011, p.95) elaborated that the pre-1997 curriculum was "traditional, elitist, competitive, examination-dominated and bureaucratic" based on the British grammar school model with an underlying Eisner's "academic rationalist" ideology and Bernstein's "collection code" curriculum (Morris and Chan, 1998, p.249). There were few large-scale curriculum changes until the launch of Targets and Target Related Assessment (TTRA) and Target Oriented Curriculum (TOC) as a territory-wide curriculum reform in the context of a political transition before and after the return of Hong Kong to Chinese sovereignty in 1997 (Morris, 2002). The TTRA/TOC reform could be classified into three phases: phase 1 (1989–1993) initiation and decision; phase 2 (1993–1997) adjustment and resourcing; and phase 3 (1997–2000) flexibility to abandonment (p.15). Morris (2002, p.27) remarked that the TOC experiences revealed the following characteristics:

> the pitfalls of a top-down strategy of curriculum innovation; the clash between policy intentions and the grammar of schooling; the barriers and frame factors which inhibit change; the process of mutual adaptation; the unintended impact of reform; the legitimatory roles which reforms can play in supporting school improvement; the dangers of transferring or importing innovations across cultures, and so on.

THE CHANGING SOCIO-POLITICAL, POST-COLONIAL CONTEXTS SINCE THE LATE 1990S

In addition to some inherent design problems and implementation difficulties of TOC, Morris (2002, p.21) explained that after 1997, the newly

Curriculum Reforms in Hong Kong 19

established government wanted to establish its own legitimacy and agenda of reform and so turned TOC into a problem. Attention was then shifted to prepare the new curriculum reform around the new century. Law (2004) echoed that, similar to Taiwan, Hong Kong adopted a pincer, top-down approach to educational reform in which the EC basically initiated and set the agenda for public consultation.

The call for comprehensive education and curriculum reform partly arose from the public dissatisfaction with the quality of schooling, dissatisfaction with excessive competition for better schools and excessive homework, for example, as well as employers' dissatisfaction with the quality of graduates from local institutions (Organisation for Economic Co-operation and Development [OECD], 2011, p.101). Kennedy (2005; 2011, p.92) emphasized that the post-1997 or post-colonial education and curriculum reforms under "new progressivism" echoed the need of the knowledge economy in Hong Kong for flexible, responsive and innovative workers. As he succinctly put it:

> the state has co-opted progressive principles to support an economic instrumentalism as the basis of the school curriculum . . . integrated curriculum, assessment for learning, and engaging teaching strategies do not just represent a particular ideology: they are seen by governments to advance the development of the knowledge economy through stimulating problem solving, creativity and critical thinking. (2011, p.93)

The education and curriculum reforms in Hong Kong since the late 1990s were largely driven by the need for economic globalization, which calls for learning English and information and technology as transnational skills (Law, 2004, p.507). Taking information technology as an example, the importance of building up a digital culture and a knowledge-based economy coupled with economic globalization has led to the development of information technology in education (ITEd) in Hong Kong school education since the 1990s (Kong, 2008, p.130). In 1997, the chief executive in his policy address promised to invest in ITEd, which then spurred the emergence of the first ITEd strategic development document, *Information Technology for Learning in a New Era: Five-Year Strategy—1998/99 to 2002/03* (Education and Manpower Bureau, 1998) and the promulgation of *Information Technology Learning Targets* in 2000 (Kong, 2008, p.130; CDC, 2000a). Law (2006, p.167) further explained the context for ITEd, which is integral to the reform in Hong Kong:

> An important contextual background that impinged on the implementation and impact of the first five-year IT in Education strategy in Hong Kong was the lack of an overall education reform initiative at the time the plan was launched. It was not until 2000 that the blueprint for education reform of the entire education system *Learning for Life, Learning*

20   John Chi-Kin Lee

through Life (Education Commission, 2000), was launched. The reform was again motivated by the perceived economic imperative that Hong Kong needs a flexible and reflexive workforce that can serve emerging industries founded on knowledge, technology and innovation.

Concomitant with the curriculum reform is the second wave of educational reform exemplified by the EC report No. 7 in 1997, which required all schools to implement school-based management (SBM) as an internal quality assurance (QA) mechanism and recommended that the Education Department (ED) adopt a whole-school approach to QA inspection. That report also recommended the establishment of the "Quality Education Development Fund", which later became the Quality Education Fund (QEF). In 2000, the EC announced the reform blueprint *Learning for Life—Learning through Life: Reform Proposals for the Education System in Hong Kong*, which adopted the principles of student-focused, "no-loser", quality, life-wide learning and society-wide mobilization. The promotion of quality education, notwithstanding its desirable aims and intentions, has been seen as adopting "the managerialist and market-oriented approach to education reform" (Tse, 2005, p.103), highlighting accountability of schools to the public, the establishment of a private school sector, and increasing choices and information to the parents and the public. It is notable that Hong Kong is not alone in educational and curriculum reforms. Cheng (2009, p.75) explained that Hong Kong and other countries in the Asia-Pacific region exhibit the features of reform syndrome: educational reforms mutually influencing each other and displaying some common patterns; implementing multiple initiatives coupled with achievement of targets within a short time span; paying inadequate attention to the cultural and contextual conditions of their own countries; being over-worried about losing their competitive edges and urging for reforms; and having chaos and painful failures owing to too many parallel reforms.

Regarding socio-political changes, the development of national/nationalistic, civic and citizenship education has generated heated debate in curriculum development. Leung and Yuen (2009, p.36) pointed out that there are three stages of civic education: "Stage 1 (From World War II to mid-1980s): depoliticization by the state and the schools"; "Stage 2 (mid-1980s–1997): the politicization of the intended curriculum" and "Stage 3 (1997 to present): re-depoliticization and official affirmation of nationalistic education". They suggested that as Hong Kong is a cosmopolitan city, there is a need to address issues of cultural diversities and multi-culturalism, political and human rights, democratic principles and values (p.39). Recently, in the light of the huge public controversy and outcry against national education, the government has shelved the introduction of Moral and National Education (MNE) curriculum guide.

According to Morris and Scott (2005, p.94), Hong Kong's post-handover government has inherited "both the structural and legitimacy problems and the symbolic policies of the colonial regimes". This is further exacerbated by two major tensions: "a disarticulated political system" and "the highly destructive nature of Hong Kong's political culture" (pp. 94–97). Different political parties have different agendas and viewpoints and different stakeholders sometimes have competing priorities on educational agenda. Consensus is often easier said than done. The debates on Small Class Teaching (SCT) and national education are some of the vivid examples for illustrating tensions and difficulties in communication and building up mutual trust among stakeholders. The transformation of "civic and moral education" into the controversial "national education" agenda in curriculum reform under Chinese sovereignty will be examined in Chapter 7, while the issue of SCT will be discussed in Chapter 9.

From a socio-cultural perspective and apart from the impact of economic globalization and "new progressivism" to build up a knowledge economy, Hong Kong is still under the influence of Confucian Heritage Culture (CHC) (Lee and Dimmock, 1998). This is reflected by the EC's (2000, p.5) document on the blueprint of educational reform, which adopted a balanced approach and acknowledged the value of moral education and the education system with both local tradition and cosmopolitan and culturally diverse characteristics (Kennedy, 2011, p.95). In addition, Hong Kong as a Chinese community tends to display a collectivist culture and high power–distance culture, where school leaders and teachers command respect from the community, parents, peers and students (Kwan, 2011). There are strong traditions of teacher-directed instruction, rote learning and centralized administrative structures that are distinct from the Western societies (Hallinger, 2011, p.402). In the progress report on the New Academic Structure Review (CDC, Hong Kong Examinations and Assessment Authority, Education Bureau, 2013, p.34), it is mentioned that the Hong Kong education system is backed up by a strong family culture that "values education" and "support diligence in studying". In addition, there is a hardworking professional culture of school teachers and principals which is conducive to the enhancement of curriculum leadership and professional development.

It is also imperative to note that educational governance and implementation of educational reform in Hong Kong after 1997 primarily adopted an approach of "combination of centralised design, school-based implementation and professional support" (OECD, 2011, p.104). In addition, compared with school districts in some Western countries and city districts in Shanghai that co-ordinate and monitor educational policies and practices in schools, Hong Kong adopts a more centralized and effective approach as follows (OECD, 2011, p.108):

A single government organ, the Education Bureau, co-ordinates all matters concerning education in Hong Kong and administers more than 1,000 schools. This centralised set up has the advantage of equal distribution of research funding and equal student unit expenditures.

22   *John Chi-Kin Lee*

Schools are also not left on their own or in small clusters where reforms might not be straightforward.

Another remarkable contextual change during the new century is the fluctuating demographic changes and reduction of school-age population. The primary school enrolment decreased from about 493,979 in the 2000 school year to 446,618 in 2004 and 317,442 in 2012. The secondary school enrolment changed from 456,693 in 2000 to 474,049 in 2004 and 418,787 in 2012 (Secretary for Education and Manpower, 2005, pp.31–32; Secretary for Education, 2013, p.188). This has led to school closures and has also created severe competition for students among schools. At the same time, the schools and teachers are under high anxiety and stress to implement education and curriculum reforms so as to maintain their own survival (Cheng, 2009, p.78).

For curriculum development, Morrison (2003) suggested that Hong Kong has moved from a modernist curriculum towards a complexity-based curriculum which is in line with the society highlighting "openness, diversity, difference and change" (p.288). Yeung (2012b, p.19) argued that the curriculum reform in Hong Kong adopts a postmodernist perspective exemplified by "student-centred" approach, "whole-person development" and "Learning to Learn".

IMPLEMENTATION OF THE FOUR KEY TASKS AND THE NEW SENIOR SECONDARY CURRICULUM

The curriculum reform, as advocated by the CDC, involves the implementation of four key tasks: project learning, reading to learn, moral and civic education and information technology for interactive learning. In a study of the implementation of four key tasks, Cheung and Wong (2011) found that the primary schools had increased the implementation of project learning from only 20% before the initiation of the curriculum reform to more than 60% in 2006–2007. For reading to learn, the secondary schools had increased the implementation from less than 20% in 2001–2002 to more than 60% in 2006–2007. It is notable that moral and civic education had the smallest increase among the four tasks, amounting to about 21% and about 10% for primary and secondary schools, respectively. More in-depth analysis will be given in Chapter 5, on the "Learning to Learn" basic curriculum.

In addition to the reform of the basic curriculum, there has been a reform for the New Academic Structure. In 2012, it was witnessed the completion of the New Senior Secondary (NSS) education and the Hong Kong Diploma of Secondary Education (HKDSE) for the first batch of secondary six students.

TENSIONS AND BALANCES FOR CURRICULUM DEVELOPMENT

In the CDC's (2000b, pp. 12–14) consultation document, the following tensions and balances were considered: globalization and localization; academic, personal, social and economic goals of the curriculum; central development and school-based development; specialist development and whole-person development; uniformity, diversity and flexibility; co-operation and competition; knowledge transmission and knowledge creation; assessment for selection and Assessment for Learning (AfL); and urgency and feasibility.

Globalization and Localization; Central Development and School-Based Development

Some scholars argue that neoliberal globalization may lead to denationalization, deterritorialization, marketization and universalization (Beck, 2000, p.9; Lo, 2010, p.63). While there is increasing impact of globalization, different nation-states may react differently and have local adaptations through, for example, various forms of educational decentralization.

For Hong Kong, there has been educational decentralization related to administrative reform with the pursuit for diversity and innovation (Lo, 2010). Schools have been driven to become self-governing and accountable units monitored by the QA mechanism. The emphasis is not on how individual stakeholders are empowered in their participation in the decentralization process, including the decision-making processes of curriculum development. Similar to Singapore, Hong Kong tends to adopt a state-steering or controlled approach, on the one hand, and reflect decentralized centralism or recentralization through decentralization, on the other (Lee, 2006; Lo, 2010). Ho (2006), based on the 2000–2001 PISA study, analyzed the nature and extent of educational decentralization in three Asian societies: Japan, Korea and Hong Kong. The findings revealed that about 45% of the secondary schools were operated on a "school-driven model" (featured by high levels of school autonomy but low levels of teacher participation), while about 35% were a decentralized model (characterized by both high levels of school autonomy and teacher participation) (p.595). This suggests that the authority tends to be delegated to the upper administrative levels in many schools in Hong Kong. Areas such as decision making, "curriculum and instruction" and "student affairs" tend to be more decentralized, while "staffing" and "salary setting" remain much less decentralized (p.598).

As regards the interaction between globalization and localization and their influence on curriculum content, Lee and Lam (2006) adapted Chen et al.'s (2003) framework of localization to analyze the curriculum structure and themes of primary General Studies, secondary Geography, History and Liberal Studies. The initial findings revealed that some

24   *John Chi-Kin Lee*

curriculum contents tended to highlight the subjectivity and contextual characteristics of local society and environments, while there was less attention given to critical thinking and multiplicity, as well as opportunities given to students for recognizing their possible roles and contributions through practical activities.

Moreover, as regards citizenship education in Hong Kong as a cosmopolitan city shifting from a British colony to a special autonomous region of the People's Republic of China, there have been interactions not only between the processes of globalization and localization but also involving nationalization. How these triple processes (globalization, localization and nationalization) interact with, complement and contradict each other remains to be seen (Tse, 2007).

In some Asian countries and places, including Hong Kong, there has been a tension between centralized curriculum control and localized curriculum development. As remarked by Kennedy (2010, p.9), "the common feature of all these Asian cases is that none of them indicates centralized curriculum decision-making has in any sense been abandoned in favour of SBCD. Rather, SBCD is seen to be an adjunct to current reform efforts". This is to some extent reflected by the official position of the government that "a school-based curriculum is therefore the outcome of a balance between guidance from the CDC and the autonomy of the school and teachers. It is jointly owned by schools and the government" (CDC, 2001, p.70).

School-based curriculum development (SBCD) remains a Western construct, and it is argued that while the curriculum approach is appropriate by Western standards, it may be culturally inappropriate and infeasible by local standards. In addition, curriculum studies in Hong Kong tend to focus on practical issues and have drawn heavily from the scholarship and work undertaken elsewhere, especially in the United Kingdom, Australia and the United States. There is still a need to define and build up a distinctive Hong Kong approach to curriculum planning, curriculum implementation and curriculum research and achieve a balance between theories and practices (Lee, 2009, p.113). This may be attributable to the situation that some teachers in Hong Kong tend to consider SBCD as small-scale innovations or theme-based or subject-based projects partly because of teachers' conceptions of curriculum and low sense of ownership to implement SBCD owing to heavy workloads. More importantly, while the Curriculum Development Institute of the government has the good intention to offer on-site professional support, officials' visits may be seen as a kind of intervention with "quality assurance measure in disguise" (Lam and Yeung, 2010, p.78). More discussion about the examples of successful melding of centralized and decentralized curriculum decision making will be provided in Chapter 3. As the school review system has been refined, coupled with feedback from school practitioners, how the school review system serves as a means to promote School Self-Evaluation (SSE) and curriculum reform will be dealt with in Chapter 18.

Uniformity, Diversity and Flexibility;
Co-Operation and Competition

Morrison (2003) applied complexity theory to analyze Hong Kong curriculum reform, and he argued that several elements of curriculum are in "dynamic balance", such as co-operation/competition and central development/school-based development (p.287). The emphasis on flexible learning through the use of information technology (p.294) and the flexible use of timetabling and learning time for life-wide learning (CDC, 2001, pp.75–76), to some extent, echo the features of complexity-based curriculum.

Under the NSS curriculum education system, there is a removal of a major examination and, in terms of school banding, there is a change from the five to three bands with the intentions of reducing competition for students with good academic abilities among schools and examination pressure. However, Ng (2009) opined that the drastic change of the overall goal of an educational system such as Hong Kong, which is a based on a long history of selection and influence of Chinese cultural heritage emphasizing achievement, may be unrealistic. Despite the government's good intentions of introducing project learning, life-wide learning and SBCD, the schools, teachers and parents may not be convinced that these new measures will lead to as good achievements as before. He therefore proposes from a socio-cultural perspective "learning for achievement" as a collective motive for schooling and re-culturing teaching and learning with a mastery orientation for different students in Hong Kong (Ng, 2009, pp.270–271).

From a socio-cultural perspective, Leung (2004, p.11) highlighted the importance of integration and harmony as well as the concepts of uniformity (*dayitong* or a "unified domain") and conformity in East Asian culture. The promotion of flexibility and innovations through decentralization from the Western perspective may be at odds with uniformity in the context of East Asian culture. Leung (2004, p.11) also elaborated the influence of pragmaticism on educational decentralization:

> If we view the decentralization movement in the context of wider movement of the pursuit of democracy, we may begin to understand why it is difficult for decentralization to take root in East Asia. For Westerners, ideological ideals such as democracy are pursued for its own sake. But for the East Asians, they are perceived as means to serve the purpose of efficiency rather than an end in itself . . . For East Asian economies, centralization is for control and decentralization is for efficiency (without losing the control). So decentralization is a pragmatic rather than an ideological move.

While some scholars emphasized the notion of "dynamic balance" (Morrison, 2003), some others pointed to the dilemmas and tensions. Competition and co-operation have been a dilemma of education reform in Hong

26 John Chi-Kin Lee

Kong. Tse (2005, p.119) pointed to the example of Quality Education Fund (QEF), which has been cited as a good example of infrastructure for stimulating curriculum innovation, school improvement projects and action research (Mourshed, Chijioke and Barber, 2010, pp.42, 44) "but competition among schools for funding becomes increasingly divisive".

Specialist Development and Whole-Person Development; Academic, Personal, Social and Economic Goals of the Curriculum; Knowledge Transmission and Knowledge Creation

The basic education curriculum reform advocated by the CDC highlighted whole-person development (Cheung, 2011), while the senior secondary curriculum attempted to provide a flexible and diversified curriculum and broaden the curriculum by introducing Other Learning Experiences, Applied Learning and Liberal Studies as one of four compulsory subjects, along with Chinese Language, English Language and Mathematics. While there are good intentions to promote whole-person development in basic education, different schools used various school-based activities, such as school assemblies, talks, case studies in classroom teaching and voluntary service experience. Teachers found it difficult to cultivate positive values and attitudes in their students in the face of constraints such as time and influence from the society (Yuen, Cheung and Wong, 2012, p.724). More systematic and longitudinal studies, however, may be needed to understand the progress of students' whole-person development under the context of curriculum reform.

As regards the academic, personal, social and economic goals of the curriculum, while there is a clear attempt to achieve balanced curriculum goals, the CDC's (2000b, p. 14) consultation document refers to "examinations embedded in Chinese culture" as a reflection of local culture and environments which tend to highlight the realization of academic and economic goals rather than personal and social goals.

With reference to knowledge creation of students, which is an important direction of the curriculum reform, it is paradoxical that "skilful knowledge transmission in Chinese classrooms has been successful in knowledge scaffolding of students" (CDC, 2000b, p.14). This poses challenges to students, in terms of their shift towards self-regulated learning, and to teachers' change of pedagogy towards facilitating students' learning and fostering their thinking skills. In the progress review of the NSS curriculum implementation, there are signs of a better balance between direct teaching and enquiry learning. Of teachers in a survey, 84% perceived that they tended to "develop reflective ability by guiding them to think in depth", while 80% of teacher respondents "encourage students to actively engage in discussion" in most/some lessons (CDC, Hong Kong Examinations and Assessment Authority, Education Bureau, 2013, p.39). From the students' perspective, 82% and 80% of them in the survey considered that their teachers tended to "use a lot of examples to help us understand the lesson

Curriculum Reforms in Hong Kong   27

content" and "teach us how to find the main points or ideas". In addition, only 52% of students responded that their teachers "use a variety of teaching strategies (e.g. lecturing, group activities or games/competition)" in most/some lessons (CDC, Hong Kong Examinations and Assessment Authority, Education Bureau, 2013, p.40).

Assessment for Selection and Assessment for Learning (AfL)

Chinese people have a long history of seeing pubic examinations as channels for gaining social mobility and prestige. Berry (2011, p.58) has succinctly described the assessment culture and practices as follows:

> The assessment practices at schools are often teacher-led with a strong emphasis on getting students to demonstrate factual knowledge Scholars generally found these kinds of assessment practices problematic and argued that they narrowed teaching, encouraged rote-memorization and restrained students from achieving their full potential.

In the curriculum reform, AfL is promoted with an intention to "provide information for both students and teachers to improve learning and teaching" (CDC, 2001, p.80). Nonetheless, there seems to be a persistent emphasis on good examination results, which are still essential entrance requirements for university education. Yeung (2012a, p.257) comments:

> the central education authority (the Education Bureau) is inconsistent in repeatedly enforcing different forms of curriculum change while simultaneously doing little to convert the performance-oriented and examination-driven focus of local education. This, in turn, discourages a sheer reform in curriculum and pedagogy in classrooms.

To some extent, this necessitates in the future concerted efforts among parents, universities, schools and students who take a broader and more liberal view of quality in education and educational achievements (other than merely examination results).

Adamson (2011, pp.200–202) suggested a pragmatic approach to AfL which is context-sensitive, integrative and accommodating. This approach assesses features of the policy in a particular context and then synthesis and adaptation are applied to align compatible features of the policy in that context with salient features of appropriation subcontexts and at various levels (e.g., implemented, adopted, resourced and policy levels). This implies that in contexts where teacher-centred pedagogy is still the norm, some features of AfL, such as peer and self–assessment, may not be implemented, while other features, such as timely and comprehensive feedback to students and assessment tasks for informing learning and teaching, could be introduced. In the NSS curriculum, there is an introduction of school-based assessment (SBA) for some subjects in the 2012 HKDSE. The initial

28 John Chi-Kin Lee

feedback from students revealed that SBA could enhance their learning (CDC, Hong Kong Examinations and Assessment Authority, Education Bureau, 2013, pp.11–12). More discussion on AfL and assessment-related issues is provided in Chapters 15, 16 and 17.

Urgency and Feasibility

In the CDC's (2000b) consultation document, it was mentioned that "the feasibility of any measure is actually dependent on many intriguing factors such as teacher readiness, competence, commitment, physical conditions in schools, evidence to inform practice, resources, and other systemic features (e.g., assessment, school place allocation" (p.14). Morrison (2003, p.296) also noted that anyone moving towards a complexity-based curriculum in Hong Kong needs to be aware of some concerns, such as practicality (whether there is the appropriate class size and time for student learning), superficiality (whether there is a lack of specialized and in-depth knowledge), uncertainty (whether curricula becoming too diversified and unpredictable), sensitivity (whether introduction of controversial knowledge will pose threats to conventional curriculum and pedagogy), changing mentalities (how to enhance buy-ins from key stakeholders), teacher expertise (whether they have innovation fatigue and work overload), resources (whether there is adequate resources and manpower support) and assessment (how to address the balance between external assessments and school-based formative assessments).

While there are good intentions behind the educational and curriculum reforms, the implementation of multiple parallel and demanding initiatives within a short time created "bottle-neck effect", leading to serious teacher and school resistance. Such "bottle-neck" effect could be partly attributed to structural constraints, such as high teacher workload and large class size before the second wave of reform and increasing student diversity owing to change of school bandings from five to three and introduction of inclusive education. With the implementation of curriculum reform, teachers spent extra time outside school hours engaging in professional training and development and relatively much less time on caring for students (Cheng, 2009, pp.76–77). As regards the early implementation of the NSS curriculum, it is unsurprising to note that the prime concern is heavy teacher workloads and the key challenges for schools are "catering for the much greater diversity of students . . . managing time to cover the full breadth and depth of the new curriculum; implementing SBA; and attending to non-teaching duties" (CDC, Hong Kong Examinations and Assessment Authority, Education Bureau, 2013, p.42).

CONCLUSION

It is noteworthy that in many Asian countries and places, including Hong Kong, there has been strong advocacy for developing a knowledge-based

Curriculum Reforms in Hong Kong   29

and lifelong learning society and for cultivating future knowledge workers who are innovative, creative, flexible, capable of resolving problems independently and collaboratively, and who think critically and are committed to lifelong learning (Kennedy and Lee, 2010). This has generated a call for curriculum and assessment reforms towards SBCD and AfL, as well as devolution of decision-making authority and responsibility to teachers and students, which are broadly in line with the trend of educational decentralization and SBM in schools (Adamson, 2011, p.197). Nonetheless, Hong Kong, like some Asian countries, may share an Asian way in educational reform with the following characteristics (Hallinger, 2011, p.413): "hierarchical structure of the system; Ministry power; key role of human capital in national development; explicit link of education reform to globalization; persistence of effort; pushing responsibilities to schools; and wide media coverage of educational reform policies and programs".

From an international perspective, Hong Kong's experience is considered to be an example of strong performance and successful reform (OECD, 2011) despite local and vocal criticisms and concerns. The following seems to capture the essence of Hong Kong's reform experience (p.105):

> Hong Kong is almost the opposite. Its reform provides schools with a platform, supports them with resources and modifies the public examination as well as university admissions, but leaves the process of reform to the schools.
>
> Teachers may find this difficult because changes in the curriculum and examinations have made their familiar paths invalid. But the reform has pushed schools and teachers to take a professional stand, exercise professional autonomy and adapt the changes to best fit their respective student bodies.

Curriculum reform is not a matter for schools and teachers only. If we could practically engage and respect the interests of different social groups and stakeholders in Hong Kong (Hallinger, 2011) as a cosmopolitan, collectivist, partially democratic society under Chinese sovereignty and the influences of globalization and the CHC/East Asian culture in future educational and curriculum changes, there will be even greater potential and momentum for positive change and outcomes.

REFERENCES

Adamson, B. (2011). Embedding assessment for learning. In R. Berry & B. Adamson (Eds.) *Assessment reform in education: Policy and practice* (pp.197–203). New York, NY: Springer.

Beck, U. (2000). *What is globalization?* (Trans. P. Camiller). Cambridge: Polity Press.

Berry, R. (2011). Educational assessment to Mainland China, Hong Kong and Taiwan. In R. Berry & B. Adamson (Eds.) *Assessment reform in education: Policy and practice* (pp.49–61). New York, NY: Springer.

30   John Chi-Kin Lee

Chen, Li-hua, Jheng, Y.Q., Syu, S.Y., Syu, P.Y., Jhan, B.Q., Shen, Y.R., . .., Hong, L.. (2003). *Final report on research on localization of social studies learning area in the nine-year articulation curriculum.* National Institute for Compilation and Translation thematic research report. Taiwan: Taipei Municipal University of Education. (In Chinese)

Cheng, K.M. (2002). The quest for quality education: The quality assurance movement in Hong Kong. In J.K.H. Mok & D.K.K. Chan (Eds.) *Globalisation and education: The quest for quality education in Hong Kong* (pp.41–66). Hong Kong: Hong Kong University Press.

Cheng, Y.C. (2009). Hong Kong educational reforms in the last decade: Reform syndrome and new developments. *International Journal of Educational Management, 23*(1), 65–86.

Cheung, A.C.K., & Wong, P.M. (2011). Effects of school heads' and teachers' agreement with the curriculum reform on curriculum development progress and student learning in Hong Kong. *International Journal of Educational Management, 25*(5), 453–473.

Cheung, K.W. (2011). Curriculum reform in Hong Kong: Preparing students for lifelong learning and whole-person development. *College & University, 87*(1), 55–57.

Curriculum Development Council (2000a). *Information technology learning targets.* Hong Kong: Curriculum Development Council. Retrieved 10 November 2012, from http://www.edb.gov.hk/index.aspx?langno=1&nodeID=3700.

Curriculum Development Council (2000b). *Learning to Learn: The way forward in curriculum development.* Retrieved 3 November 2012, from http://www.edb.gov.hk/attachment/en/curriculum-development/cs-curriculum-doc-report/learn-learn-1/overview-e.pdf

Curriculum Development Council (2001). *Learning to Learn: Life-long learning and whole-person development.* Hong Kong: Printing Department.

Curriculum Development Council, Hong Kong Examinations and Assessment Authority, Education Bureau (2013). *The new senior secondary learning journey—moving forward to excel.* Retrieved 26 June 2013, from http://334.edb.hkedcity.net/doc/eng/FullReport.pdf

Education & Manpower Bureau. (1998). *Information Technology for Learning in a New Era: Five-year strategy–1998/99 to 2002/03.* Hong Kong: Education & Manpower Bureau. Retrieved 4 December 2013, from http://www.edb.gov.hk/en/about-edb/publications-stat/major-reports/consultancy-reports/it-learning-1998–2003/index.html

Education Commission (2000). *Learning for life—learning through life: Reform proposals for the education system in Hong Kong.* Hong Kong: Printing Department.

Hallinger, P. (2011). Making education reform happen: Is there an 'Asian' way? *School Leadership and Management, 30*(5), 401–418.

Ho, E.S.C. (2006). Educational decentralization in three Asian societies: Japan, Korea and Hong Kong. *Journal of Educational Administration, 44*(6), 590–603.

Kennedy, K. (2005). *Changing schools for changing times—new directions for the school curriculum in Hong Kong.* Hong Kong: Chinese University Press.

Kennedy, K. (2010). School-based curriculum development for new times. In E.H.F. Law & N. Nieveen (Eds.) *Schools as curriculum agencies: Asian and European perspectives on school-based curriculum development* (pp.3–18). Rotterdam, The Netherlands: Sense Publisher.

Kennedy, K. (2011). Transformational issues in curriculum reform: Perspectives from Hong Kong. *Journal of Textbook Research, 4*(1), 87–113.

Kennedy, K.J. & Lee, J.C.K. (2010). *The Changing Role of Schools in Asian Societies—Schools for the Knowledge Society.* London: Routledge.

Kong, S.C. (2008). A curriculum framework for implementing information technology in school education to foster information literacy. *Computers & Education, 51*, 129–141.

Kwan, P. (2011). Development of school leaders in Hong Kong: Contextual changes and future challenges. *School Leadership and Management, 31*(2), 165–177.

Lam, C.C., & Yeung, S.S. (2010). School-based curriculum development in Hong Kong: An arduous journey. In E.H.F. Law & N. Nieveen (Eds.) *Schools as curriculum agencies: Asian and European perspectives on school-based curriculum development* (pp.61–82). Rotterdam, The Netherlands: Sense Publisher.

Law, N. (2006). Leveraging technology for educational reform and pedagogical innovation: Policies and practices in Hong Kong and Singapore. *Research and Practice in Technology Enhanced Learning, 1*(2), 163–170.

Law, W-W. (2004). Translating globalization and democratization into local policy: Educational reform in Hong Kong and Taiwan. *International Review of Education, 50*(5–6), 497–524.

Lee, J.C.K. (Tz-Chien Lee) (2006). Curriculum policy in Hong Kong: Approaches, strategies and contexts. In Department of Education and Graduate Institute of Curriculum and Instruction, National Taichung University (Eds.) *Constructing Taiwan's thematic curriculum and teaching: Taiwan and international education* (pp.293–317). Taiwan: Great Scholar Publishing. (In Chinese)

Lee, J.C.K. (2009). The landscape of curriculum studies in Hong Kong from 1980–2008: A review. *Educational Research Journal, 24*(1), 95–133.

Lee, J.C.K., & Dimmock, C. (1998). Curriculum management in secondary schools during political transition: A Hong Kong perspective. *Curriculum Studies, 6*(1), 5–28.

Lee, J.C.K. (Tz-Chien Lee), & Lam, K.K. (2006). Hong Kong curriculum reform: Analysis from the perspectives of globalization and localization. In Association for Curriculum and Instruction, ROC. (Ed.) *Localization and globalization of curriculum and instruction* (pp.193–212). Taiwan: Fuwen Publisher. (In Chinese)

Leung, F.K.S. (2004). *Educational centralization and decentralization in East Asia.* Paper presented at the APEC Educational Reform Summit, Beijing, China, January.

Leung, Y.W., & Yuen, W.W. (2009). A critical reflection of the evolution of civic education in Hong Kong schools. *Pacific-Asian Education, 21*(1), 35–50.

Lo, W.Y.W. (2010). Educational decentralization and its implication for governance: Explaining the differences in the four Asian newly industrialized economies. *Compare, 40*(1), 63–78.

McLaughlin, M.W., & Talbert, J.E. (1990). The contexts in question: The secondary school workplace. In M.W. McLaughlin, J.E. Talbert & N. Bascia (Eds.) *The contexts of teaching in secondary schools: Teachers' realities* (pp.1–14). New York: Teachers College Press.

Morris, P. (2002). Promoting curriculum reforms in the context of a political transition: An analysis of Hong Kong's experience. *Journal of Education Policy, 17*(1), 13–28

Morris, P., & Chan, K.K. (1998). Cross-curricular themes and curriculum reform in Hong Kong: Policy as discourse. *British Journal of Educational Studies, 45*(3), 248–262.

Morris, P., & Scott, I. (2005). Education reform and policy implementation in Hong Kong. In L.S. Ho, P. Morris & Y.P. Chung (Eds.) *Education reform and the quest for excellence: The Hong Kong Story* (pp.83–97). Hong Kong: Hong Kong University Press.

Morrison, K. (2003). Complexity theory and curriculum reforms in Hong Kong. *Pedagogy, Culture & Society, 11*(2), 279–302.

32 John Chi-Kin Lee

Mourshed, M., Chijioke, C., & Barber, M. (2010). *How the world's most improved school systems keep getting better.* New York, NY: McKinsey & Company. Retrieved 4 November 2012, from http://mckinseyonsociety.com/downloads/reports/Education/How-the-Worlds-Most-Improved-School-Systems-Keep-Getting-Better_Download-version_Final.pdf.

Ng, C.H. (2009). 'Learning for achievement' as a collective goal in re-culturing teaching and learning in Hong Kong classrooms. In C-H C. Ng & P.D. Renshaw (Eds.) *Reforming learning: Concepts, issues and practice in the Asia-Pacific region* (pp.255–275). Springer.

Organisation for Economic Co-operation and Development (2011). Shanghai and Hong Kong: Two distinct examples of reform in China. In OECD (Ed.), *OECD lessons from PISA for the United States, strong performers and successful reformers in education.* Paris: OECD Publishing. DOI :10.1787/2220363x. Retrieved 11 November 2011, from http://www.oecd.org/countries/hong-kongchina/46581016.pdf.

Secretary for Education (2013). *Replies to initial written questions raised by Finance Committee Members in examining the Estimates of Expenditure 2013–14.* Hong Kong: Legco. Retrieved 8 June 2013, from http://www.legco.gov.hk/yr12–13/english/fc/fc/w_q/edb-e.pdf.

Secretary for Education and Manpower (2005). *Replies to supplementary questions raised by Finance Committee Members in examining the Estimates of Expenditure 2005–06.* Hong Kong: Legco. Retrieved 8 June 2013, from http://www.legco.gov.hk/yr04–05/english/fc/fc/sup_w/s-emb-e.pdf.

Tse, K.C. (2005). Quality education in Hong Kong: The anomalies of managerialism and marketization. In L.S. Ho, P. Morris & Y.P. Chung (Eds.) *Education reform and the quest for excellence: The Hong Kong story* (pp.99–123). Hong Kong: Hong Kong University Press.

Tse, K.C. (2007). Whose citizenship education? Hong Kong from a spatial and cultural politics perspective. *Discourse: Studies in the Cultural Politics of Education, 28*(2), 159–177.

Yeung, S.S. (2012a). Conclusions and future direction. In S.S.Y. Yeung, J.T.S. Lam, A.W.L. Leung & Y.C. Lo (Eds.) *Curriculum change and innovation* (pp.255–268). Hong Kong: Hong Kong University Press.

Yeung, S.S. (2012b). Critical problems of contemporary society and their influence on the curriculum. In S.S.Y. Yeung, J.T.S. Lam, A.W.L. Leung & Y.C. Lo (Eds.) *Curriculum change and innovation* (pp.1–25). Hong Kong: Hong Kong University Press.

Yuen, T.W.W., Cheung, A.C.K., & Wong, P.M. (2012). A study of the impact of the first phase of the curriculum reform on student learning in Hong Kong. *International Journal of Educational Management, 26*(7), 710–728.

3 Centralization and Decentralization
An Historical Analysis of School-Based Curriculum Development Initiatives in Hong Kong

Colin Marsh, Paul Morris and Joe Tin-yau Lo

INTRODUCTION

In August–September 2012, there was an outburst of protests and hunger strikes against the Hong Kong government's attempt to enforce Moral and National Education as a compulsory subject in primary and secondary schools (Education Bureau [EDB], 2012c). The policy was seen as a brainwashing attempt by the Chinese Communist Party in Beijing to control the thinking of Hong Kong people through education and schooling. Under strong public pressure to withdraw the subject, the Hong Kong government gave way and announced that:

> school-sponsoring bodies and schools can exercise their discretion to decide whether to implement the subject, whether the subject should be introduced as an independent subject and . . . determine the modes and schedule for its implementation. (EDB, 2012b)

Delegation of decision-making power and responsibility to schools, as a form of decentralization (Bray, 1999) was, once again, used by the government as a convenient strategy to cope with the crisis arising from the highly centralized approach to policy making. In fact, the decentralization of school governance, and specifically school-based curriculum development (SBCD), has been advocated as an effective means to implement central educational/curriculum reform initiatives since the 1970s. And greater school-based decision making and autonomy has been used as a form of policy rhetoric or symbolic policy throughout the history of curriculum development in Hong Kong (Morris and Adamson, 2010).

This chapter examines the ways in which SBCD has emerged and evolved in Hong Kong since the 1970s. It is argued that SBCD, portrayed in policy rhetoric as a vehicle for enhancing teacher empowerment and school autonomy, has had limited impact on schools. The primary effect has been to introduce more teachers to the ethos and practical skills necessary to implement or improve the national curriculum and other central initiatives in their respective schools. Yet, paradoxically, the use of SBCD to support centrally initiated, systemic reforms has had a far greater impact—it has

34   Colin Marsh, Paul Morris and Joe Tin-yau Lo

created an environment conducive to teachers' professional engagement or enhancement in ways that go beyond the specific intentions of the centre.

THEORETICAL AND CONCEPTUAL RESOURCES

In general, educational centralization involves the concentration of power, authority, resources and expertise at the centre that seeks to maintain uniformity and efficiency in policy/programme implementation (Hanson, 1998). Under such a system, teachers are positioned as technicians implementing the centrally prescribed documents/policies (Kennedy, 1992).

However, teachers might need to decide on the time allocations, sequences and resources of individual lessons as well as the modes of assessment and evaluation in their implementation of the central curriculum, especially when the curriculum guides are not prescribed by standardized tests/exams and the diverse needs/abilities of students are to be catered for. In these aspects, the top-down mode of curriculum development has been portrayed as ignoring classroom teachers' incentives, involvement and job satisfaction (Marsh, 1992).

In principle, SBCD can be viewed as an initiative directed towards achieving greater decentralization. According to Skilbeck (1998), 'school-based' means that the major decisions about the design, content, organization and presentation of the curriculum, as well as pedagogy and Assessment of Learning (AfL), are made at the school level. The assumption was that SBCD as a decentralizing measure would encourage teachers' involvement and participation, develop their professionalism and make the curriculum more sensitive or relevant to local needs (Hawkins, 2000; Lo, 1999).

Hanson (1998) and Bray (1999) have identified three modes of decentralization:

1. Deconcentration (transfer of tasks and work but not authority)
2. Delegation (transfer of decision-making authority to lower levels, but authority can be withdrawn by the centre)
3. Devolution (transfer of authority to an autonomous unit, which can act independently without permission from the centre)

From a practical viewpoint, SBCD without any central planning/input is also found to be problematic and unfeasible. As Marsh (1992) points out, teachers would experience difficulties in the lack of time, lack of expertise, lack of finance, external restrictions (from employers and parents) and threatening school climate (e.g., lack of effective leadership). Morris (1990) also indicates that students in different schools could potentially have very different curricula leading to different learning outcomes. These practical problems might have resulted in some teachers' preference to use central curriculum guides rather than working on SBCD (Kennedy, 1992).

Indeed, some scholars have also noticed that there are no clear examples of completely decentralized educational systems, but rather there are mixtures of centralization and decentralization (Bray, 1999; Hanson, 1998). Kennedy (1992) observes that SBCD could cover both centrally prepared curriculum frameworks and locally implemented curricula (with pedagogical decisions made by teachers). Lo (1999) also delineates how locally produced materials were tightly linked to the central curriculum and how SBCD could be subjected to bureaucratic and centralized control to meet the expectations of the authorities. In the light of the above, this chapter seeks to: (1) trace the development of the major SBCD initiatives in Hong Kong since the 1970s; (2) analyze the nature and features of these initiatives; and (3) discuss the implications for the future development.

CHANGING POLICY CONTEXTS FOR SBCD IN HONG KONG

In the 1950s, the Hong Kong government faced a tumultuous political situation generated by the Communist take-over in China. It began to exert strong central control over schools and school curricula in an attempt to ensure that they were not used to destabilize the colonial government. A highly centralized system emerged in which pupils' progress through the stages of schooling was determined by their performances in highly competitive public examinations. This system did not allow or encourage teacher involvement in the process of curriculum development as the government controlled the key elements which defined the curriculum, namely, the content of subjects, the textbooks and the examinations (Morris and Adamson, 2010). SBCD was mentioned in passing in the rhetoric of curriculum documents, especially from the early 1970s, but there were no systematic attempts at promoting it. When SBCD was referred to, it was designed to distance the government from the responsibility for implementation by arguing that in the final analysis, the success of curriculum policy was in teachers' hands, as they decided what to do in the classrooms. In reality, whilst the government tightly controlled the key determinants of the curriculum, it took a laissez-faire position on matters of implementation. The outcome was what UNESCO described as a centralized curriculum with a non-organized implementation structure (UNESCO, 1980).

During the 1970s, and especially since the introduction of nine-year compulsory education in 1978, there was growing public criticism of the centralized control of curriculum decision making as the government was not able to cater for students' diverse needs and abilities (Lam and Yeung, 2010). This concern, inter alia, eventually led the Secretary for Education (Education Department [ED]) in 1982 to invite an overseas visiting panel to review the educational policies. The outcome was the Llewellyn Report (Llewellyn et al., 1982) that has exerted a long-term impact on the development of SBCD.

In the 1990s, various SBCD initiatives were introduced into a context that was dominated by three system-wide reforms. These were: (1) the School Management Initiative (SMI) introduced in 1991, which attempted to encourage schools to take greater responsibility for decision making and

36   Colin Marsh, Paul Morris and Joe Tin-yau Lo

to be generally less reliant on the government; (2) the Target Oriented Curriculum (TOC) for primary schools in 1992, which was essentially Hong Kong's version of outcomes-based education; and (3) the decision in 1993 to move all primary schools from bi-sessional operation to whole-day schooling (Lo, 2000; Morris and Adamson, 2010). Whilst these central reforms were not perceived by schools to be part of a coherent and connected reform package, they each in different ways were seen to benefit from schools and teachers taking a more active role in implementing the curriculum. However, these had not been accompanied by any transfer of decision-making power and authority from the centre to schools.

After Hong Kong's reintegration with China in 1997, the government began to embark on educational reforms that preserved national traditions while enhancing students' global outlook (Education Commission [EC], 2000). The government was increasingly aware of the need to implement curriculum reform that could keep Hong Kong abreast of global trends and empower students to learn beyond the confines of the classroom in order to cope with the challenges of the 21st century. The global neoliberal agenda was evident in the goals of helping the younger generations to develop an international outlook, to learn how to learn, to master lifelong skills and to cultivate positive values and attitudes to achieve the educational aims of whole-person development and lifelong learning (Curriculum Development Council [CDC], 2001). In the reform document, the government encouraged schools to "have the flexibility to design their school-based curricula to satisfy the needs of their students, *so long as the requirements set out in the central curriculum framework are fulfilled*" (CDC, 2001, p.ii, italics added). Hence, SBCD has been, and remains, a means to reify the central curriculum reform initiatives by making them more relevant to and therefore more feasible in local (school) contexts. Herein lies the perennial tension between central design, control and legitimacy, on the one hand, and local implementation, autonomy and participation, on the other.

This tension has been addressed in Hong Kong, where the government both operates through a highly centralized system of governance and in parallel promotes different forms of short-term site-based development or SBCD as the primary means of supporting centralized reforms (Lam and Yeung, 2010). Below we illustrate the continuities and changes in the evolution of SBCD through analysing the major initiatives.

AN HISTORICAL ANALYSIS OF THE MAJOR INITIATIVES THAT PROMOTED SBCD IN HONG KONG

Llewellyn Report (1982)

As mentioned, SBCD was first explicitly identified as a strategy to be actively promoted by the Visiting Panel in 1982. The report called for "periphery-centred", "school-based" and "teacher-oriented" approaches to curriculum development (Llewellyn et al., 1982). However, these approaches seemed to promote a degree of decentralisation that was not readily acceptable to the centre at this stage.

The report (Llewellyn, et al., 1982) criticized the curriculum development practices in Hong Kong as not professional enough and recommended that:

> A genuine drive towards school–based curriculum selection and adaptation, together with school–based programme and pupil evaluation, could open up new horizons for teacher participation . . . Every effort must be made to encourage innovation at the school level which, after all, is where the real work is being done. (p.56)

It is noteworthy that the explicit rationale for promoting SBCD was based on the desire to create a more professional and empowered teaching service and to reduce what it described as an over-administered education system. The government's response to the report was initially muted and confined to restating the importance of teachers as the key people who decided what to do in their classrooms. The report also recommended the creation of an EC to advise on education policy. This was endorsed and the subsequently created body was asked to consider the Visiting Panel's recommendations. The Llewellyn Report, however, did have long-term impact on the subsequent development of SBCD in Hong Kong.

The School-Based Curriculum Project Scheme (1988–1999)

The School-Based Curriculum Project Scheme (SBCPS) was introduced in 1988 following the recommendations of the EC in its first report. This was a direct, if delayed, response to the proposals of the Visiting Panel (EC, 1992). It is notable that the basic goal of and rationale for introducing the SBCPS were, in contrast to those of the Visiting Panel, to allow schools to better cater for the diverse needs and interests of pupils. The enhancement of teacher professionalism and the development of a sense of curriculum ownership by teachers were viewed as means to achieve that end rather than as ends in themselves.

In terms of its implementation, the SBCPS was subject to extensive criticism. Lam and Yeung (2010) contended that SBCPS was viewed only as a channel of producing teaching materials that could replace commercially developed school textbooks. Morris (1990) argued that the SBCPS failed, as many of its critical features were designed to ensure compliance with the highly bureaucratic model, which the Visiting Panel had critiqued, and this undermined any sense of teacher professionalism. For example, the government specified what types of projects would be supported; required teachers to state that their proposed projects did not interfere with their normal duties and involve work undertaken outside normal working hours; and

38 *Colin Marsh, Paul Morris and Joe Tin-yau Lo*

required a massive expansion of the educational bureaucracy to approve and monitor the projects in schools. The whole scheme was therefore criticized as bureaucratically and administratively rather than educationally driven (Lo, 1999).

School-Based Curriculum Tailoring Scheme (1994–2005)

In 1994, the School-Based Curriculum Tailoring Scheme (SBCTS) was launched in those schools admitting the bottom 10% of students at junior secondary level to address the learning and behavioural problems arising from the gap between the compulsory mass education and the centralized academic-oriented curriculum (EC, 1990). Compared with the SBCPS, in which individual teachers were merely encouraged to develop teaching resources under the central curriculum, SBCTS was a measure to address social and educational issues in Hong Kong. However, to avoid upsetting the central curriculum, student disaffection with the central curriculum was merely defined as a form of special education needs that could be addressed by those schools taking students with learning and behavioural problems. This is consistent with deviance theories that argue that problems of disaffection can be contained in ways which do not destabilize the system of mainstream schooling as a whole (Tattum, 1986).

To support this group of schools in tailoring their school-based curriculum, a Central Curriculum Development Support (Secondary) Team, comprising six curriculum officers on a contract basis and six seconded teachers, was set up in the ED to provide on-site curriculum tailoring strategies to these schools (CDC, 1993). However, the school-based curriculum was only confined to the junior secondary level. The public examination, which closely followed the central curriculum, rendered the tailoring scheme futile and difficult to sustain. There was a gradual decline in the number of participating schools and the Scheme eventually faded out and died in 2005. Once again, the scheme was characterized by school-based curriculum tailoring (development) with central guidance and management. It was meant to avoid destabilizing the mainstream schooling system by providing remediation for those students who were struggling with the central curriculum. The decentralization was thus merely a transfer of problems and tasks, but not authority, to schools.

School-Based Curriculum Support Teams (1998–Ongoing)

In addition to the above-mentioned initiatives, the first Policy Address of the Chief Executive, Tung Chee Hwa, announced in 1997 the setting up of the Central Curriculum Development Support Team (Primary) in the ED to support schools with large intakes of academically low achievers in implementing the central curriculum in primary schools (Tung, 1997). Teacher deficiency was still seen as an impediment to curriculum implementation

(Morris, Lo and Adamson, 2000). Teacher empowerment was not seen to reside in the teachers' autonomy to make curriculum decisions but in the enhancement of their technical skills to implement the central curriculum.

Under the subsequent holistic curriculum review and the consultation conducted by the Curriculum Development Institute (CDI) of the ED in 1998, the relationship between SBCD and teacher development in making classroom decisions was articulated more explicitly (CDI, 1999). In the official document on curriculum reform (CDC, 2001), the two support teams were renamed as School-Based Curriculum Development (Secondary) Section and School-Based Curriculum Development (Primary) Section, respectively. While the re-naming of the two support teams revealed the government's intention to emphasize SBCD, this still had to be achieved under the requirements of the central curriculum in terms of the learning time, learning targets and essential content. School-based curriculum was described as "the outcome of a balance between the guidance from the CDC and the autonomy of the school and teachers" (CDC, 2001, p.70).

The basis for all the activities of both support sections was to help promote students' "Learning to Learn" capabilities and was strongly linked to the ongoing system-wide curriculum reform. The recognition of the provision of on-site support as "effective" in helping teachers develop school-based curriculum by the Board of Education (1997), and the increasing demand from schools for support services, motivated the government to use external support agents as important measures to implement the centralized reform. In 2004, another school-based support section, the Language Learning Support Section, was set up by the Education and Manpower Bureau (EMB, which was renamed from the previous ED in 2003) to provide on-site support to help teachers raise the standard of their students' language proficiency. The site-based support was used by the centre to support teachers, through the delivery of workable instrumental strategies, in achieving the goals and objectives set in the education and curriculum reform documents (EMB, 2004).

However, the uncertain and dynamic complexities in the classroom (Darling-Hammond, 1997; Fullan, 2001) forced the external support agents to reflect critically on the feasibility and impact of the "delivery" model on classroom practices (SBCDP, 2002, 2005, 2009). The interplay of the intended, enacted and lived curriculum (Marton and Tsui, 2004) in the authentic context led the external support agents, in collaboration with the teachers, to delve more deeply into understanding how students think and learn. Classroom and assessment data were used not only to measure the standard of the students but to discern their learning difficulties and reflect on the gap between teaching and learning (SBCDP, 2011, 2012). The learning experience of students and the evidence on how they learn have become the centrepieces of curriculum and pedagogical practices. Accordingly, there has been a fundamental and unplanned change in the direction of SBCD emphasizing responsible freedom, responsiveness and accountability

40   *Colin Marsh, Paul Morris and Joe Tin-yau Lo*

by all members of the school community (Skilbeck, 1998). In this way, the unintended outcomes of this initiative seem to have outweighed the intended ones that focused on enhancing teachers' skills in implementing the central curriculum and making the curriculum reform work.

Collaborative Research and Development— "Seed" Projects (2001–Ongoing)

These projects were introduced as part of the ongoing actions designed to support the curriculum reform. The intentions were to: (1) generate useful knowledge and experiences for schools; (2) develop a critical mass of curriculum change agents to enhance the reform; and (3) serve as an impetus to SBCD (EDB, 2012a). These intentions were achieved by seconding teachers from schools to conduct the "Seed" Projects with CDI and expert consultants on topics related to the curriculum reform.

Undoubtedly, the scale and scope of the "Seed" Projects are more extensive than those of the previous SBCD initiatives. They cover a wide range of key learning areas (KLAs) and involve many different schools. The collaboration among CDI officials, seconded teachers and curriculum experts (university staff in some projects) was designed to enrich the repertoire for the new curriculum initiatives. However, most of the funded "Seed" Projects have been centrally selected and decided by CDI officials. School participants have been solicited to develop and try out the materials or learning frameworks of these centrally selected projects for dissemination (EDB, 2012a). Though the development of the projects is school-based and there is an intention to provide impetus for SBCD, the products/resources are meant to complement and supplement the central curriculum reform. Albeit the "Seed" Projects are portrayed as collaborative research and development projects that facilitate the putting of theories into practice, there is little or no evidence to show whether and how the collaborative research has really informed and improved curriculum development in school contexts. Despite these deficiencies, the "Seed" Projects still mark a partial delegation of decision-making authority from the centre to schools in lieu of a mere transfer of task/responsibility, although the influence of the centre is still dominant in the process of collaboration.

Primary School Masters/Mistresses (Curriculum Development) (2002–Ongoing)

This innovative measure was launched as part of a number of strategies to bring about significant changes to primary schools. It was realized that teachers with expertise in curriculum development were needed "on the ground" in their respective schools to encourage other teachers to embark upon school-based activities. The government then created a senior career post, known as Primary School Masters/Mistresses (PSM) (Curriculum

Development [CD]), in each primary school to support the principal to lead curriculum development strategies and implement curriculum reform initiatives.

The results of this PSM (CD) initiative were viewed by the government as encouraging, on the grounds that it had promoted diversified school-based curriculum programmes, collaborative lesson planning, discussions on how students learn and new attempts at AfL in primary schools, as reported in the External School Reviews (ESRs) (EDB, 2009). Lo (2007) also argues that the scheme has changed curriculum leaders (CLs) from perceiving the new job cynically as an administrative post to enthusiastically committing themselves to being professional agents who worked with fellow teachers to discern, discriminate and decide on their own teaching and learning.

Through various attempts at SBCD (e.g., collaborative lesson planning and action research), this PSM (CD) initiative has spearheaded a different mode of decentralization—it encourages teachers as curriculum developers to emancipate themselves in developing curriculum for themselves and students through collaborative research that enhances their professional competency and systematically collects data/evidence to inform and improve pedagogical practices. Greater professional autonomy and responsibility have been devolved to schools, though the centre still controls the resources and holds the authority (e.g., screening participating schools, monitoring and evaluating). The focus of curriculum development is not solely designed to supplement and complement the central curriculum through local adaptations. Rather, teachers can creatively develop their own resources, pedagogies and assessments that make the central curriculum more relevant to local needs (Lo, 2007).

Education Development Fund (2004–Ongoing)

In 2004, a substantial Education Development Fund (EDF) of $550 million was set up to provide differentiated school-based professional support for building up school capacity and taking education reform initiatives further (EMB, 2004). Five programmes, namely, Principal Support Network (PSN), School Support Partners Scheme (SSP), Professional Development Schools Scheme (PDS), University–School Support Programmes (USP) and Collegial Participation in ESRs were set up and monitored. In the external review (Wong, Yip and Ko, 2009), which focused on the evaluation of the effectiveness of the EDF in supporting schools to implement the education reform, it was found that schools participating in the school-based professional programmes were more ready to promote the generic skills, the "five essential learning experiences" and AfL proposed in the reform document than those which did not participate in the programme.[1] Teachers and principals from the participating schools also considered that promoting SBCD, facilitating lifelong learning experience and integrated learning and

42 *Colin Marsh, Paul Morris and Joe Tin-yau Lo*

working in collaboration with peers were more important and related to their work than those who did not join the programme.

Overall, the EDF has supported a wide variety of programmes that could (1) enable schools and teachers to build up learning communities for experience sharing that facilitates curriculum reform; (2) engage teachers in evidence-based and evidence-informed enquiry for improving teaching and learning with the support of university staff, for example, the Variation for Improvement of Teaching and Learning (VITAL) programme in the USP; and (3) encourage teacher collaborations in developing school-based resources and bringing about pedagogical change (Elliott, 2008; Lo, Pong and Chik, 2005). An independent evaluation on VITAL conducted by Elliott (2008), which used quantitative and qualitative data, argues strongly that:

> Learning Studies had the power when injected into the system to effect sustainable improvements in the capabilities of teachers to bring about worthwhile curriculum and pedagogical change. (p.185)

Although the EDF in general and the USP in particular seem to have enhanced teachers' professional competency and literacy in SBCD, they do not deviate much from the previous modes of decentralisation that tried to secure local support and participation through teacher development and tap locally developed resources to strengthen and substantiate the central reform initiatives. There is no devolution of power and authority, and the centre continues to decide what schools focus on through its control of resource allocation, monitor the quality of outcomes, conduct periodic evaluations and set the programme foci or directions. Though the strategy seems to be liberating teachers for reforms, the kind of professional autonomy and democratic participation required for really emancipating teachers is not clearly visible.

DISCUSSION AND IMPLICATIONS

From the above, it is evident that the early forms of SBCD were designed to supplement student resource materials in subjects not considered to be of major importance and to ameliorate the situation of students with lower academic ability. Examples of this include SBCPS and others which had a very short lifespan and were only piloted in a small number of schools.

Since the 1980s, SBCD activities have shifted away from symbolic gestures, in which schools and teachers are portrayed as responsible for developing site-based curricula, to closer alignment with central policies to bring about curriculum reform. However, whilst the promotion of SBCD has appropriated the discourse of democratic engagement and teacher empowerment, the nature of the multitude of schemes introduced suggests that neither the democratic nor the neoliberal agenda adequately explains the role of SBCD as it has developed in Hong Kong. SBCD has primarily been developed as a means by which the government has introduced a range of activities in schools either to address critical problems in the education system or to support major system-wide education reforms. Thus in the early period, schemes such as the SBCTS were introduced to address the problem of disaffected pupils in Band 5 (lower ability) schools. From the early 1990s, most of the schemes were designed to provide schools with additional resources to support reforms and/or to help teachers develop the skills and competencies to implement system-wide curriculum reforms.

Essentially, whilst SBCD was initially portrayed as a tool to empower teachers or as a means to decentralize governance or locate power in schools, it has exerted little impact in these aspects. It has evolved as a centralized and closely monitored system to initiate school-based activities to support central reforms. It has also been promoted at times to deal with crises arising from unpopular central initiatives. Whilst the government has been willing to employ the language of decentralization, it has in practice neither delegated nor abdicated its responsibility for determining the nature and purposes of schooling. It is evident that the EDB is still monitoring very closely who initiates SBCD, the scope of the activities, and the personnel involved. The central office retains a monopoly over the curriculum knowledge and practices, sets the goals and directions of the policy and trains teachers via SBCD activities, such as the "seed" teachers and PSM (CD) initiatives, to reify the central policies.

Nonetheless, like most of the educational reforms initiated by the centre, the SBCD initiatives are loosely coupled; they are fragmented in design, non-coherent in structure and implemented on an ad hoc basis in response to contextual needs or public pressure. There is little or no evidence from the evaluations of and reflections on the SBCD initiatives that they have generated ongoing and sustained improvement in schools in the specific areas they were designed to focus on. A sense of historical amnesia tends to prevail as the focus is on constantly introducing new initiatives which hinder the development of SBCD in a holistic, coherent and sustainable way (Morris, Lo and Adamson, 2000).

However, the range of SBCD activities that involved teachers, the resources/posts and support that were provided for teachers, and the cross fertilization and sharing which were encouraged, have nurtured a significant change in the overall culture in schools and the role of teachers, intentionally or unintentionally. As the findings of the external review reveal, "participation in the SBPS Programmes has a beneficial impact on teachers' performance, as perceived by teachers, in respect of knowledge and skills, assessment and evaluation, student development, school development" (Wong, Yip and Ko, 2009, p.xii). Lo's study also shows how the engagement of teachers in collaborative reflection has helped them develop the courage "to critique the structures which shaped their practices and the power to

44 Colin Marsh, Paul Morris and Joe Tin-yau Lo

negotiate change within the system which maintained them" (2007, p.312). Teachers have become more enabled, if not empowered, as they no longer see themselves as mere implementers of the central curriculum, and the space that has been created for teacher engagement is no longer amenable to the close monitoring and administrative surveillance which character-ized early attempts to promote SBCD (Lo, 2007). Similarly, Elliott (2008) concluded, with regard to one of the projects, that it made a significant dif-ference in schools in respect of effecting changes in the professional culture and in the capabilities of teachers.

Furthermore, there are more opportunities and resources within school environments for keen teachers to find space to plan and deliver new and innovative teaching approaches. The generic nature of the holistic reform, especially its focus on improving pedagogy, places few limitations on the range of activities which teachers can initiate. The increasing use of net-works is also facilitating communication between central office personnel and active teachers in schools. It is clear that more and more teachers are becoming involved through such multiplier initiatives as "seed" teachers, PSM (CD) teachers and central office's innovative programmes, especially at the primary school level. In addition, even at the secondary school level, the new secondary certificate examination (known as the Hong Kong Diploma of Secondary Education Examination [HKDSE]), with an empha-sis on school-based assessments (SBAs) in most subjects, is indicative of more decentralized activities at this level. It can be anticipated that more and more teachers, who see the professional need to ride the tide of cur-riculum reform and satisfy the expectation for professional accountability (e.g., preparing students for SBAs), are keen to utilize the resources and spaces available to them to develop their own pedagogies, assessments and resources. If the centre could allow more spaces and provide more resources and professional development platforms, teachers' participation as curricu-lum developers could make the reforms more relevant to diverse local needs and would therefore be conducive to the sustainable development of vari-ous reforms initiated from the centre.

All in all, since the creation of a system of mass schooling in Hong Kong in the late 1970s, there has never been a high degree of autonomy through the devolution of power and authority from the centre to schools. Schools have only been given greater power to decide how to implement the central-ized policies of the government, which include a common vision, a central curriculum, government-approved textbooks and a highly centralized system of public examinations. Instead of moving towards greater decentralization, it is discernible that the trend of SBCD in Hong Kong has been one of "cen-tralized decentralization"—using decentralization as a means or strategy to achieve the centre's goals and ends (Lee and Gopinathan, 2004; Mok, 2004).

Despite this, the SBCD initiatives seem to have narrowed, if not bridged, the gap between the intentions of the policymakers and their implementa-tion in schools, even though it might take time for both sides to develop a transactional approach that encourages mutual consultation and negotiation (Morris and Scott, 2003). In the long run, SBCD can be an effective channel for promoting teachers' professionalism that is relatively more rooted in local culture and relevant to local needs rather than being driven solely by central policies.

ACKNOWLEDGEMENT

Colin Marsh, who initiated this chapter, passed away on 6 August 2012 whilst still working on it. He is missed by the many people who benefitted from his collegiality and friendship.

NOTE

1. The five essential learning experiences are: moral and civic education, intellectual development, community service, physical and aesthetic development and career-related experiences (CDC, 2001, p.20).

REFERENCES

Board of Education (1997). *Review of 9-year compulsory education*. Hong Kong: Government Printer.

Bray, M. (1999). Control of education: Issues and tensions in centralization and decentralization. In R.F. Arnove & C.A. Torres (Eds.) *Comparative education: The dialectic of the global and the local* (pp.207–232). Lanham, MD: Rowman and Littlefield.

Curriculum Development Council (1993). *Report of the working group on support services to schools with band 5 students*. Hong Kong: Education Department.

Curriculum Development Council (2001). *Learning to Learn: The way forward in curriculum development*. Hong Kong: Government Printer.

Curriculum Development Institute (1999). *Draft report of the working group on the holistic review of curriculum development in Hong Kong*. Hong Kong: Government Printer.

Darling-Hammond, L. (1997). *The right to learn: A blueprint for creating schools that work*. San Francisco, CA: Jossey-Bass Publishers.

Education and Manpower Bureau (2004). *Implementation of the school-based professional support (SBPS) programmes* (Circular Memorandum No. 239/2004). Hong Kong: Education and Manpower Bureau.

Education Bureau (2009). *2008/09 Annual inspection report*. Retrieved 3 November 2012, from http://www.edb.gov.hk/FileManager/EN/Content_756/qa_annual_report0809.

Education Bureau (2012a). Collaborative research and development ("seed") projects. Retrieved 26 October 2012, from http://www.edb.gov.hk/ index. aspx?langno =1&node ID=2370.

Education Bureau (2012b). EDB's statement on moral and national education subject. Retrieved 20 October 2012, from http://www.info.gov.hk/gia/general/201209/10/ P2012 09100606.htm.

46 Colin Marsh, Paul Morris and Joe Tin-yau Lo

Education Bureau (2012c). *Implementation, support measures and grant for the moral and national education subject (primary 1 to secondary 6)* (EDB Circular Memorandum 73/2012). Hong Kong: Education Bureau.

Education Commission (1990). *Education Commission report No.4: The curriculum and behavioural problems in schools.* Hong Kong: Government Printer.

Education Commission (1992). *Education Commission report No.5: The teaching profession.* Hong Kong: Government Printer.

Education Commission (2000). *Learning for life—learning through life: Reform proposal for the education system in Hong Kong.* Hong Kong: Printing Department.

Elliott, J. (2008). *An independent evaluation of the 'Variation for the Improvement of Teaching and Learning' (VITAL) project.* Hong Kong: School Partnership and Field Experience Office, the Hong Kong Institute of Education.

Fullan, M. (2001). *Leading in a culture of change.* San Francisco, CA: Jossey-Bass.

Hanson, E.M. (1998). Strategies of educational decentralization: Key questions and core issues. *Journal of Educational Administration, 36*(2), 111–128.

Hawkins, J.N. (2000). Centralization, decentralization, recentralization: Educational reform in China. *Journal of Educational Administration, 38*(5), 442–454.

Kennedy, K.J. (1992). School-based curriculum development as a policy option for the 1990s: An Australian perspective. *Journal of Curriculum and Supervision, 7*(2), 180–195.

Lam, C.C., & Yeung, S.S.Y. (2010). School-based curriculum development in Hong Kong: An arduous journey. In E.H.F. Law & N. Nieveen (Eds.) *Schools as curriculum agencies: Asian and European perspectives on school-based curriculum development* (pp.61–83). Rotterdam: Sense Publishers.

Lee, M.H., & Gopinathan, S. (2004). Centralized decentralization of higher education in Singapore. In K.H. Mok (Ed.) *Centralization and decentralization: Educational reforms and changing governance in Chinese societies* (pp.117–136). Hong Kong: Comparative Education Research Centre, University of Hong Kong.

Llewellyn, J., Hancock, G., Kirst, M., & Roeloffs, K. (1982). *A perspective on education in Hong Kong: Report by a visiting panel.* Hong Kong: Government Printer.

Lo, B.Y.M. (2007). *Who's supporting whom? Learning to become curriculum leaders together in the context of curriculum support services in Hong Kong.* Unpublished doctoral dissertation, University of East Anglia, UK.

Lo, M.L. (2000). Learning without tears? The relativity of a curriculum reform and its impact. In B. Adamson, T. Kwan & K.K. Chan (Eds.) *Changing the curriculum: The impact of reform on primary schooling in Hong Kong* (pp.47–79). Hong Kong: Hong Kong University Press.

Lo, M.L., Pong, W. Y., & Chik, P.P.M. (Eds.) (2005). *For each and everyone: Catering for individual differences through learning studies.* Hong Kong: Hong Kong University Press.

Lo, Y.C. (1999). School-based curriculum development: The Hong Kong experience. *Curriculum Journal, 10*(3), 419–442.

Marsh, C.J. (1992). *Key concepts for understanding curriculum.* London: Falmer Press.

Marton, F., & Tsui, A.B.M. (2004). *Classroom discourse and the space of learning.* Mahwah, NJ: Lawrence Erlbaum Associates.

Mok, K.H. (2004). Centralization and decentralization: Changing governance in education. In K.H. Mok (Ed.) *Centralization and decentralization: Educational reforms and changing governance in Chinese societies* (pp.3–17). Hong Kong: Comparative Education Research Centre, University of Hong Kong.

Morris, P. (1990). Bureaucracy, professionalization and school centred innovation strategies. *International Review of Education (UNESCO), 36*(1), 21–41.

Morris, P., & Adamson, B. (2010). *Curriculum, schooling and society in Hong Kong.* Hong Kong: Hong Kong University Press.

Morris, P., Lo, M. L., & Adamson, B. (2000). Improving schools in Hong Kong—lessons from the past. In B. Adamson, T. Kwan & K. K. Chan (Eds.) *Changing the curriculum: The impact of reform on primary schooling in Hong Kong* (pp.245–262). Hong Kong: Hong Kong University Press.

Morris, P., & Scott, I. (2003). Educational reform and policy implementation in Hong Kong. *Journal of Educational Policy, 18*(1), 71–84.

School-Based Curriculum Development (Primary) Section (2002). *Crystallization of knowledge—letter to principals* (Released 30 May 2002). Retrieved 1 November 2012, from http://www.edb.gov.hk/FileManager/ tc/Content_3911/2002may.pdf. (In Chinese)

School-Based Curriculum Development (Primary) Section (2005). *Extraordinary experience in the past five years—Review on the development of school-based action research* (Released May 2005). Retrieved 3 Novemver 2012, from http://www.edb.gov.hk/FileManager/tc /Content_3911/newsletter_may2005.pdf (In Chinese)

School-Based Curriculum Development (Primary) Section (2009). *Journey on learning in action: Innovation and cognition.* Hong Kong: Education Bureau. (In Chinese)

School-Based Curriculum Development (Primary) Section (2011). Reading skills—taught, not caught. In School-Based Curriculum Development (Primary) Section (Ed.) *Journey on learning in action: Learning and teaching* (pp.36–45). Hong Kong: Education Bureau. (In Chinese)

School-Based Curriculum Development (Primary) Section (2012). Learning path of non-Chinese-speaking students—From counting to addition and subtraction. In School-Based Curriculum Development (Primary) Section (Ed.) *Journey on learning in action: Learning and teaching* (pp.57–60). Hong Kong: Education Bureau. (In Chinese)

Skilbeck, M. (1998). School-based curriculum development. In A. Hargreaves, A. Lieberman, M. Fullan & D.W. Hopkins (Eds.) *International handbook of educational change* (pp.121–44). London: Kluwer Academic Publishers.

Tattum, D.P. (1986). Introduction. In D.P. Tattum (Ed.) *Management of disruptive pupil behaviour in schools* (pp.1–12). Chichester: John Wiley and Sons.

Tung, C.H. (1997). *Chief executive's policy address 1997.* Retrieved 5 February 2012, from http://www.policyaddress.gov. hk/pa97/english/patext.htm.

UNESCO (1980). *National strategies for curriculum design and development.* Bangkok: UNESCO/APEID.

Wong, K.C., Yip, H.K., & Ko, Y.L. (2009). *External review of school-based professional support (SBPS) programmes financed by Education Development Fund.* Hong Kong: Policy 21 Limited, the University of Hong Kong.

Part II
Curriculum for New Times

4 Ideology and Priorities of School Curriculum in Hong Kong

Shirley Sze Yin Yeung

INTRODUCTION

When educators design and construct curricula, they bring with them various conceptions or orientations about curriculum (e.g., Eisner and Vallance, 1974; Schiro, 2008; Glatthorn, Boschee and Whitehead, 2009). 'Curriculum ideology' is an alternative term for this idea. Authors categorize the variety of curriculum conceptions by various classifications.

Striving hard to sustain its status as an international city, Hong Kong is not immune from the impact of worldwide trends and phenomena, including globalization, the shift to a knowledge society and the development of information technology. These forces articulate with each other and lead to a shift in the orientation and design of the school curriculum. On the other hand, Hong Kong has emerged from colonization, and its sovereignty reverted to the People's Republic of China (PRC) in 1997. Inevitably, such political and economic changes have some impact on the local school curriculum. In fact Hong Kong's school curriculum has been undergoing various reforms since 1997, intertwined with changes in education policy. The curriculum ideology of the local society is inevitably affected by changes in social, political and economic forces.

This chapter focuses on the implicit values of Hong Kong's official curriculum, from 1997 to the present. By means of documentary analysis, the author traces the curriculum ideology underlying the key influential curriculum and curriculum-related policies. Building on the analysis of the findings, the strengths, weaknesses, threats and opportunities of the school curriculum are explored. The chapter concludes by considering the ideology of social reconstruction as an orientation for future planning of the school curriculum in Hong Kong.

CURRICULUM IDEOLOGIES AND CONCEPTIONS

When people make decisions about school curriculum, they carry with them their own values, beliefs and philosophy about education. Hence, 'ideology' can be defined as the underlying belief and philosophy of any curriculum.

52 Shirley Sze Yin Yeung

Table 4.1 Analytical Framework of the Present Study: Seven Kinds of Curriculum Ideologies/Conceptions

Curriculum Conceptions/Ideologies	Proposers
1. Academic rationalism	Eisner & Vallance (1974); Dukacz & Bacbin (1980); McNeil (2009); Schiro (2008); Ornstein & Hunkins (2009)
2. Curriculum as technology	
3. Social efficiency	
4. Development of cognitive processes	
5. Learner-centred ideology, or Humanistic approach	
6. Social reconstruction	
7. Religious/political orthodoxy	Eisner (1992); Adamson and Morris (2010)

Different authors categorize the variety of curriculum ideologies in various classifications. Besides curriculum ideologies, some use the terms 'curriculum conceptions', 'curriculum orientations', or 'curriculum values'. For instance, Eisner and Vallance (1974) categorize curriculum orientations into five kinds; they are *development of cognitive processes, curriculum as technology, humanistic approach, social reconstruction* and *academic rationalism*. Eisner (1992) suggests six curriculum ideologies, which are referred to as *rational humanism, progressivism, cognitive pluralism, religious orthodoxy, critical theory* and *reconceptualism*. Adamson and Morris (2010) rename 'religious orthodoxy' as 'political orthodoxy'. Schiro (2008) proposes four curricular ideologies: *the social efficiency ideology, the scholar academic ideology, the child study ideology* and *the social reconstruction ideology*. Commonalities or overlaps exist among the above proposals. In the real world, some curriculum conceptions appear more often than others. This author found that seven ideologies or conceptions affected the design of school curriculum in many cases (see Table 4.1). The seven ideologies or conceptions became the analytical framework for data analysis in a recent research project (Yeung, 2011–2012).[1]

This chapter summarizes the meaning of the seven curriculum conceptions as follows.

Academic Rationalism

This is the most traditional ideology. In this conception, schooling is thought to bear the function of cultural transmission. The school curriculum is therefore responsible for passing on what is most worthwhile from the great scholars of the past to the next generation. A curriculum that reflects the view of academic rationalism will emphasize the classic disciplines.

Curriculum as Technology

In this view, the procedures of curriculum planning are most important. Curriculum is thought to be a technology of systematic design that includes key procedures including setting up of objectives, selecting and organizing teaching content and learning experiences, and planning for tests and assessments.

Social Efficiency

Advocates of this ideology believe that the purpose of school curriculum is to "train youth to function as future mature contributing members of society" (Schiro, 2008, p.4). To them, the goal of school education is to equip students with the knowledge, skills and procedures they will need in the workplace so as to perpetuate the functioning of the society. Hence, the design of school curriculum, with regard to its aims, choice of content and so on should adapt to changing social needs.

Development of Cognitive Processes

In this view, 'how' rather than 'what' a student learns is believed to be the key for curriculum development. Schooling must be concerned with the 'process' and the general intellectual or cognitive skills that should be learned by students. Curriculum should be developed in ways that foster students' curiosity and higher-order thinking skills, such as critical thinking, creativity and problem solving.

Learner-Centred Ideology, or Humanistic Approach

This conception focuses on the needs and concerns of individual learners. In this view, each student is considered as a whole child unique in intellectual, social, psychological and physical aspects. The job of educators is to carefully create those contexts, environments or curriculum materials which will stimulate growth in learners as they construct meaning, learning and knowledge for themselves. Students' interest is the guiding premise of the school curriculum. Dewey's (1938) philosophy of progressivism is central to this ideology.

Social Reconstruction

This orientation holds that schools are called upon to serve as agents for social change. In this view, the purpose of curriculum is to orient learners to current social issues or problems of living, such as pollution, human

54   Shirley Sze Yin Yeung

rights, multi-culturalism, racial discrimination, life problems, community affairs, real world problems and so forth. This is a reformist vision which believes that schools should educate students to be critical towards social change. Students should be better equipped, through the school curriculum, to intervene actively in shaping social changes.

Religious/Political Orthodoxy

Eisner (1992) explains that the aim of an orthodoxy is "to shape the views of others so that they match the views of those who have already discovered the truth contained in the orthodoxy" (p.307). This orientation views the primary role of school curriculum as to pass on to students the existing values and beliefs of a society. Usually it is the government which decides what students should learn, including the culture, the nation's history, language and so on. The extreme form of this view involves shaping the beliefs of students so that they match the prevailing orthodoxy, which could be the beliefs of a given religion or of a political ideology.

THE PREVAILING IDEOLOGY/CONCEPTION OF HONG KONG SCHOOL CURRICULUM BEFORE 1997

Before 1997, academic rationalism characterized the design of school curriculum in Hong Kong. The design of the subjects was basically discipline-based, with strict subject boundaries and little consideration of students' learning needs. The teaching approach was teacher-centred and expository with little teacher–student or student–student interaction. Various attempts were made to adjust the school curriculum so as to cater better for the needs of all students within a system of mass education. In the 1980s, the Curriculum Development Council (CDC) introduced the Activity Approach (AA) (CDC, 1995) and curriculum integration in the forms of the cross-curricular themes (civic, moral, sex and environmental education) from 1981. Yet studies show that changes have not occurred in schools and that these progressive ideas were for the most part implemented at a superficial level. Researches indicated that these initiatives were not properly implemented (for AA, see Chan, 1997; Fung et al., 1997; for curriculum integration, see Yeung and Lam, 2006). Evidence consistently implies that the learner-centred approach is mere rhetoric and has not been successfully applied in Hong Kong (see also Yeung, 2009).

DOCUMENTARY ANALYSIS OF LOCAL CURRICULUM POLICY

Using the analytical framework (Table 4.1), the author of this chapter conducted a study.[1] The purpose of this study was to look into the implicit

Ideology and Priorities of School Curriculum in Hong Kong   55

values of Hong Kong's current key official curriculum or curriculum-related policies (from 1997 to present). The study concentrated on the level of the ideal and planned curriculum.

To achieve this purpose, the research method of documentary analysis was used. Documentary methods are "the techniques used to categorize, investigate, interpret and identify the limitations of all related written documents" (Payne and Payne, 2004, p.60). The sample studied included all curriculum or curriculum-related policies proposed or launched by the Education Bureau (EDB) from 1997 to 2012 (the present). 1997 was a critical year for Hong Kong because it was when the territory emerged from colonialism and returned to the sovereignty of the PRC. Important curriculum and education policies started to be formulated around this year. Hence, policy documents issued by the EDB from 1997 to the present were reviewed and analyzed.

Altogether 89 official documents were collected for analysis. They included official guidelines, memoranda, circulars, letters, reports and online resources. The researcher then analyzed the text in these documents in light of the seven curriculum conceptions. The procedure was basically qualitative, though with some counting of the number of instances that fell into each category of the seven ideologies (Silverman, 2006). To enhance the reliability of the study, the author invited a colleague to follow the same procedure of textual investigation. We made independent decisions. Afterwards, we compared and discussed to ensure inter-rater reliability.

Key Curriculum and Curriculum-Related Policy 1997–2012

After analyzing more than 89 official documents, seven key curriculum or curriculum-related policies were identified as most influential and significant. The following items are the curriculum priorities of Hong Kong government from 1997 to the near future:

1. Comprehensive Curriculum Reform (CDC, 2001)
2. New Senior Secondary (NSS) curriculum (CDC, 2009)
3. Liberal Studies as a core subject in NSS (Curriculum Development Council and Hong Kong Examinations and Assessment Authority [CDC & HKEAA], 2007)
4. External School Review (ESR) and School Self-Evaluation (SSE) policy (Quality Assurance Division [QAD], 2006, 2009)
5. Medium of instruction (MOI) language policies (EDB, 2009a)
6. Moral and National Education (MNE) curriculum policy (CDC, 2012)
7. Pilot Scheme on e-learning in schools (EDB, 2009b)

The following sections analyze briefly the key premises of each of the seven curriculum or curriculum-related policies.

56 Shirley Sze Yin Yeung

Comprehensive Curriculum Reform

This is a curriculum reform for all levels of schools in Hong Kong (CDC, 2001). It followed a review of local education aims after the handover of Hong Kong's sovereignty to Mainland China in 1997 (Education Commission [EC], 2000).

As indicated in the document, the rationale behind this round of curriculum reform was to prepare the next generation to meet the challenges of a knowledge-based society, globalization and the blossoming of information technology in an interdependent but competitive world. Hence, the guiding principles of this curriculum reform included developing students' generic skills, providing a broad and balanced curriculum for students, widening students' perspectives to attain whole-person development and providing alternatives to conventional modes in teaching and learning. Students were to be helped to possess a breadth and foundation of knowledge in eight key learning areas (KLAs), which were Chinese/English Language, Mathematics, Science, Technology, Personal, Social and Humanities, Arts and Physical Education. Nine generic skills (including collaboration, communication, creativity, critical thinking, IT skills and others), five essential learning experiences, and values education were incorporated in the curriculum. Higher-level thinking capacities and interpersonal skills became important components in the overall curriculum framework. All the school subjects were planned according to this framework.

New Senior Secondary (NSS) Curriculum

This round of curriculum reform focused on a revision of the academic structures as well as a change in the curriculum of senior secondary education in Hong Kong (EMB, 2005). It was proposed as a follow-up to the comprehensive curriculum reform (CDC, 2001). The previous academic structure of senior education had changed from '5+2+3' to '3+3+4'. The NSS curriculum laid emphasis on diversifying and broadening the senior secondary curriculum in Hong Kong (CDC, 2009); as well as introducing new learning experiences and applied subjects. As mentioned in the document, the curriculum goal was to enhance the knowledge and competence of all students so that they could contribute as a productive workforce for society in future. The curriculum consists of four core subjects (Chinese, English, Mathematics and Liberal Studies), two to three elective subjects (e.g., History, Biology, Chemistry) and other learning experiences (OLEs), including moral and civic education, community service, aesthetic and physical activities.

Liberal Studies as a Core Subject in the NSS Curriculum

Liberal Studies is one of the core subjects in the NSS curriculum. It is a compulsory subject for all senior secondary students. The subject is an

Ideology and Priorities of School Curriculum in Hong Kong   57

integrated subject which was designed "to broaden students' knowledge base and enhance their social awareness through the study of a wide range of issues" (CDC & HKEAA, 2007, p.1). An 'issue-enquiry approach' was adopted for learning and teaching Liberal Studies (p.4). In place of a conventional expository teaching approach, students would be led by teachers to study issues related to selected themes. The issues are to be contemporary ones which affect students, their society, nation, the human world and the physical environment. There were altogether six modules under three areas of study. Through these areas of study plus an Independent Enquiry Study (IES), students would learn to see the connections of knowledge among different themes and disciplines, as well as the interconnectedness of personal, local, national and global issues.

External School Review (ESR) and School Self-Evaluation (SSE)

The EC put forward a number of recommendations in its report no. 7 to improve school accountability and performance towards provision of "quality school education" in Hong Kong (EC, 1997). Along with the report, the Education Department (ED) introduced a quality assurance (QA) framework. In this framework, Quality Assurance Inspection (QAI) served as an external QA mechanism while schools were required to conduct SSE as an internal QA process. The QAI continued until 2003, when the EDB developed a school development and accountability (SDA) framework, which comprised SSE and ESR (QAD, 2006, 2009). SSE forms in part a systematic and SDA framework. ESR simultaneously acts as an official measure to help scrutinize the validity and objectivity of the SSE process. To help schools to perform self-evaluation, a framework of performance indicators (PIs) was prepared. The framework of PIs, as revised recently, comprises four domains, with eight areas which are subcategorized into 23 PIs. The four domains are management and organization, learning and teaching, student support and school ethos, and student performance. Correspondingly, the EDB has developed key performance measures (KPM) and measurement tools, such as Standard Stakeholder Survey questionnaires. Schools are expected to use these instruments to assess their own performance.

Medium of Instruction (MOI) Language Policies

English was a key MOI of secondary education in Hong Kong when it was a British colonial city. Shortly after 1997 (the year of handover of Hong Kong's sovereignty to Mainland China), the Hong Kong government passed an ordinance to adopt the mother-tongue language—Chinese—as the official MOI (CMI) in secondary classrooms. From then, only around 120 secondary schools were to be allowed to retain English as the MOI (EMI). After years of implementation of the mother-tongue as MOI policy, there

58 *Shirley Sze Yin Yeung*

was strong popular pressure for a review of the policy. As a consequence, the EDB proposed a new policy—the fine-tuning policy of the MOI—for secondary schools in 2009.

The fine-tuning policy (EDB, 2009a) took effect from September 2009. Under the new fine-tuning framework, schools were no longer divided into CMI and EMI schools. Secondary schools were given greater autonomy and room for development in selecting the appropriate MOI with regard to students' learning ability, teachers' capability and the requirements of individual subjects.[2] EDB officials explained this fine-tuning MOI policy as an effort to foster proficiency in English, which was essential for Hong Kong's prospects as a global financial centre.

Moral and National Education (MNE) Curriculum

Recently, the government of Hong Kong announced the launching of a MNE programme in schools. The implementation of the MNE curriculum was on a "subject" basis. The MNE Curriculum Guide (primary 1 to secondary 6) was prepared for use in primary and secondary schools implementing the MNE curriculum (CDC, 2012). As stated in the curriculum guide, the MNE was intended to help students to "recognize their roles and responsibilities as members in the family, the society, and the nation" and to help them "understand their national identity and commit to contributing to the nation and society" (CDC, 2012, p.6). Starting from the new school term in September 2012, primary to junior secondary (primary 1 to secondary 3) schools were recommended to allocate 3%–5% of their total lesson time (around one to two periods per week) in the school timetable to implement the MNE subject. In senior secondary it was suggested that about 5% of the lesson time should be devoted to the MNE curriculum in the form of OLEs and civic education.

However, the proposal to launch the MNE curriculum did not have the full support of the educational community or the public. Public apprehension about the programme was provoked by the contents of the curriculum guide and two EDB moves: the provision of subsidy for the publication of the *Chinese Model: National Conditions Teaching Manual (National Education Services Center, 2012)*, and the preparation of a "Patriotism Evaluation" questionnaire for evaluation of the programme's efficacy in schools. As a consequence, tens of thousands of citizens, including parents and students, took to the streets on 29 July 2012 in opposition to the National Education programme as launched. Strikes and protests followed. The government announced on 8 October 2012 that it had formally shelved the curriculum guide, adding that it would no longer "request schools to adopt the Curriculum Guide and the Education Bureau would not use it as the basis for school inspection" (Information Services Department, 2012). From then on, the government said, schools could make their own decision whether or not to introduce the MNE subject.

Ideology and Priorities of School Curriculum in Hong Kong 59

Pilot Scheme on E-Learning in Schools

Developing students' IT skills and the ability to use electronic learning resources to support independent learning have been a focal policy of EDB (EC, 2000; CDC, 2001). The government considers this as in line with an important global trend to establish students' self-regulated learning ability, to address learner diversity and to sustain lifelong education. With a view to enhance learning through the use of electronic media, the Working Group on Textbooks and e-Learning Resources Development recommended the EDB launch a pilot scheme to look into how e-learning equipment, such as e-books could be implemented in different school contexts (EDB, 2009b). The pilot scheme has commenced with 21 projects running in the coming three years (from 2012 to 2014). Sixty-one schools are involved in these projects, through which school teachers and principals will have the opportunity to better understand the impact of the e-book and other e-learning methods/ resources on students' learning, teacher development, school culture and so on. The government expects that the research findings will shed light on strategic development of e-learning in Hong Kong. Considering that the scheme is a prelude for a major reform in the use of learning resources in schools in Hong Kong, it was identified as one item to be investigated in the study.

ANALYZING THE OFFICIAL VALUES IN CURRICULUM BY THE CATEGORIES OF CURRICULUM IDEOLOGIES

In this study, documentary analysis was used to study the official values implied in curriculum policies. Textual investigation (Silverman, 2006) of the seven key official curriculum or curriculum-related policies by the analytical framework (Table 4.1) shows that these policies hold six types of curriculum ideology/conceptions, apart from the ideology of academic rationalism (see Table 4.2).

Comprehensive Curriculum Reform and NSS Curriculum— Learner-Centred/ Development of Cognitive Processes

Before the launch of the comprehensive curriculum reform and the NSS curriculum, academic rationalism characterized the design of school curriculum in Hong Kong.

The two rounds of curriculum reform (CDC, 2001, 2009) have put into the planned curriculum the educational ideal of Dewey (1938). These curriculum reforms show the following features:

1. A student-centred approach that stresses active acquisition of knowledge through experiences, enquiry-based learning and problem-solving activities.

60 *Shirley Sze Yin Yeung*

Table 4.2 Curriculum Ideologies of the Five Curriculum/Curriculum-Related Policies in Hong Kong

Year of Launching	Related Policy	Curriculum Ideology/ Conception	Controlling/Influencing Parties
2001, 2005	Curriculum reform: I. Comprehensive Curriculum Reform (CDC, 2001) II. New Senior Six curriculum (EMB, 2005)	Development of cognitive processes/learner-centred Social efficiency	The bureaucrats (EDB)
2007	Liberal Studies as a core subject in NSS (CDC & HKEAA, 2007)	Development of cognitive processes/learner-centred Social reconstruction	The bureaucrats (EDB)
2004, 2008	ESR/SSE (QAD, 2006, 2009)	Social efficiency	The bureaucrats (EDB)
1999	Language policy in school curriculum: mother-tongue as medium of instruction for nearly all secondary schools in Hong Kong	Political orthodoxy	The bureaucrats (EDB); politicians
2009	Language policy: fine-tuning of MOI policy (EDB, 2009a)	Social efficiency	The bureaucrats (EDB); the commercial sectors, parents and schools
2012	MNE curriculum (CDC, 2012)	Political orthodoxy	The bureaucrats (EDB); politicians the state (PRC)
2012	Pilot Scheme on e-learning in schools (EDB, 2009b)	Social efficiency Curriculum as technology	The bureaucrats (EDB); The commercial sector

2. A curriculum and pedagogy capable of developing students' higher-order thinking skills and other capacities that are pertinent to lifelong learning.
3. A curriculum that is not merely about content but is developed with a process approach; the experience and interest of students are used as the bases for content selection or for designing learning activities.

Compared with the past, the literal descriptions of these two reforms show advancement in curriculum ideology. All the features demonstrate that both

Ideology and Priorities of School Curriculum in Hong Kong   61

curriculum policies embody an orientation of *development of cognitive processes* and *learner-centredness*. Instead of focusing heavily on transmission of subject knowledge, equal emphasis is given in both proposals to procedural knowledge (such as an emphasis on generic skills) and experiential knowledge (such as the OLEs). Besides, personal learning needs and individual differences are respected. The new curricula also promote group processes in the classroom, so that children can learn with their peers to use collective intelligence to solve problems.

Liberal Studies in NSS Curriculum—Learner-Centred/ Development of Cognitive Processes and Social Reconstruction

The intention of the Liberal Studies curriculum is to develop students' intellectual capabilities such as critical and analytical skills, problem-solving skills and creative-thinking skills. By means of IES, the subject hopes to cater for students' individual interests and learning needs. Indeed, Liberal Studies is by nature a problem-centred subject that motivates students to enquire into social issues, and thus fulfils Dewey's (1910) ideal of "complete act of thought"—the movement from purpose to experimental treatment to assessment of results. This is a model toward which social constructionist curricula should aspire. Morris and Chan (1997, p.257) also consider that Liberal Studies reflects a social reconstruction ideology which sees a need for social and political awareness and critical thinking.

SSE/ESR—Social Efficiency

The QAD (2009) claims that SSE and ESR aim to achieve quality school education through school improvement and accountability. The officials affirm that the ultimate aim of SSE and ESR is to enhance school development and generate improvement in students' learning performance. By means of this pair of curriculum-related policies, the EDB's power to mandate school curriculum and direct officially designed curriculum change is expanded (Yeung, 2010). Hence, this policy directly influences the content and the design approach of school curriculum. By aligning the school assessment criteria to centrally set curriculum standards, teachers and schools are made to become more accountable to the public. Obviously, the policy is characterized by the conception of *social efficiency*. The school curriculum is thus shaped to suit the needs of the society.

Two Rounds of Change in Language Policy— Political Orthodoxy, Social Efficiency

The initial proposal of the change of language policy in school education after 1997 originated from an ideology of *political orthodoxy*. It stated in the document that it aimed at promoting patriotism and Chinese cultural identity in the next generation in Hong Kong. The political considerations

62 Shirley Sze Yin Yeung

over-shadowed the purely educational ones. After that, the fine-tuning policy of the MOI for secondary schools in 2009 inclined back to an orientation of *social efficiency*. The social concern to uphold the English standards of the young, to retain Hong Kong's status as an international city and to respond to the demands of parents and the schools were found to be influencing factors for this change in curriculum policy.

Moral and National Education Curriculum—Political Orthodoxy

In many ways, the MNE curriculum was intended to play a strong role in creating a sense of national identity and patriotism in the next generation. As specified in the curriculum guide, the overall learning objective was to "encourage them (students) to stay closely connected with the motherland, stand together in adversity, and contribute to the development and betterment of the country and its people" (CDC, 2012, p.21). Hence, it stressed cultivating a "sense of affection for the country". To scrutinize the implementation of MNE in schools, the EDB stated in the curriculum guide that it would gather information through various channels, including regular school visits, SSE, ESR, questionnaire surveys and so on. This made the proposal look threatening to the local educational community. Moreover, the slogan quoted in *The Chinese Model: National Conditions Teaching Manual* (National Education Services Center, 2012), that "the PRC is an ever-improving, selfless and united governing authority (of China and Hong Kong)", was widely criticized as disclosing an official intention to indoctrinate the young into uncritical patriotism with regard to the PRC. Apparently it intended to promote a sense of "extreme nationalism" (Audi, 2009, p.366) in the next generation. Hence, the ideology of *political orthodoxy* characterized this newly launched curriculum.

As mentioned, the proposed curriculum aroused a public struggle and private anxiety in the minds of Hong Kong citizens. After a series of student-led and parent-led strikes and petitions, the government finally announced it would shelve the MNE curriculum guide on 8 October 2012. Some critics were sceptical about this move of the government—suspecting that the decision to shelve the curriculum was a temporary measure to sooth public emotions. The official policy to re-launch the curriculum endured, they believed.

Pilot Scheme on E-Learning in Schools—Social Efficiency and Curriculum as Technology

This scheme, as described in the official document (EDB, 2009b), was a response to a global trend in which e-learning was becoming an effective learning mode inside and outside the classroom. Moreover, e-learning resources/e-books were viewed as one way to deal with the ever-increasing price of printed textbooks in Hong Kong. The use of e-learning resources will increase in the foreseeable future, though they may not completely replace printed textbooks. Hence, the scheme and the initiation of e-books are oriented toward *social efficiency* ideology.

The design of e-learning resources usually aims at "a programmed curriculum that consists of a carefully sequenced set of learning experiences, each representing a behavior to be learned" (Schiro, 2008, p.55). The process of e-learning design usually engages in "behavioral engineering" that involves clear basic tasks, such as planning of educational objectives, selection of content, choice of learning activities and assessment methods—steps parallel to Tyler's (1949) four questions about curriculum development. Hence, this innovation also holds an ideology of *curriculum as technology*.

DISCUSSION

Documentary analysis showed that the curriculum in Hong Kong is largely influenced by four types of ideology, namely, *the development of cognitive processes, learner-centred, social efficiency* and *political orthodoxy*. The ideology of *social reconstruction* and *curriculum as technology* are also found underlying two of the recent curriculum innovations. However, these ideologies are essentially inconsistent and contradictory. In most cases, curriculum which is oriented toward social construction will certainly go against the ideology of political orthodoxy. It is unusual for a society to have a common curriculum that has such conflicting conceptions. This interesting phenomenon may be unique to Hong Kong and can be explained by analysis of its social, political and economic changes from pre- to post-1997. At any rate, in conjunction with this diverse curriculum ideology in various policies and innovations, there exist certain strengths and weaknesses. Besides, potential threats and opportunities were found. A SWOT analysis (an analysis of Strength, Weakness, Opportunity and Threat) may help continued advancement in the local curriculum.

Strength (S) Found in the Curriculum Reform and Innovation— Student-Centred/Development of Cognitive Processes

To help schools cope with the challenges of globalization, technological development and social change in the 21st century, many scholars have made noteworthy recommendations to improve the existing curriculum. Among them, Young (1998) and Kress (2000) have similar suggestions about the characteristics of the *curriculum of the future*; they see that curriculum most useful in the near future ought to be:

64 Shirley Sze Yin Yeung

- Student-centred, with learners as full agents in the process of learning
- Orienting learners' disposition toward innovation, transformation and change
- Emphasizing the use of knowledge to solve everyday problems
- Stressing the interdependence of knowledge areas (instead of maintaining rigid subject boundaries)
- Focusing on the creation of new knowledge by learners

This study showed that local school curriculum has been reformed to hold an orientation of *development of cognitive processes* and *learner-centredness*. The two consecutive curriculum reforms (CDC, 2001, 2009) along with Liberal Studies for NSS (CDC & HKEAA, 2007) stressed the importance of helping students to learn how to learn by developing students' higher-order thinking, collaboration and problem-solving skills; they adopt a learning-focused approach in teaching and an integrated approach in curriculum construction. These changes, in actual fact, demonstrate some important features proposed by Young (1998) and Kress (2000) about the *curriculum of the future*. This advancement in curriculum ideology is highly positive for future development of education in Hong Kong.

Weaknesses (W) of Local Curriculum and Education—the Thrust of Social Efficiency

Besides its positive impact, globalization also brings a negative impact to school curriculum: marketization and managerialism are two influential forces. Evidence in the study showed that the local curriculum policies hold a value of 'social efficiency'. For instance, the aim of 'sustaining Hong Kong's economic status in the world' or 'as a global financial city' is often used to rationalize the various curriculum policies. The elementary and NSS curricula were reformed to equip students with competences for coping with challenges brought by globalization. By means of SSE and ESR, officials mandate school curriculum through formulation of standards and measurement of performance. School curriculum is thus made to be more accountable to the public. The shift of MOI policy from purely CMI to 'fine-tuning policy' proves that the local curriculum policy has to give way to market-oriented accountability. After all, the main purpose of the curriculum is to provide the knowledge and skills appropriate to future producers and consumers in a market economy. The recent experimentation with e-textbooks is another example. Any uncritical implementation of e-learning will probably reduce curriculum deliberation to a mundane matter of technical expertise. Then schools would become more similar and more committed to a standard and monocultural curriculum.

This weakness would discourage a blanket reform in curriculum and pedagogy in classrooms. Schools have become "factories" (Bobbitt, 1913) and curriculum has become dominated by the ideology of economic efficiency. Thus, certain aspects in need in current decades have been neglected

Ideology and Priorities of School Curriculum in Hong Kong   65

in the school curriculum. They include: global literacy and global awareness, environmental studies, values, civic and moral issues of all relevant kinds, multi-cultural issues, differences in gender, intelligences and other kinds of diversity in the classroom.

These aspects should be conscientiously dealt with in our curriculum and pedagogy.

Shifting the Locus of Influence on Curriculum—an Opportunity(O) for Hong Kong

From the study, it was also found that there was a change of 'locus of influence/control' (Adamson and Morris, 2010) in the change process of curriculum policy making. The recent controversy over the MNE curriculum was a good example. Student-led or parent-led anti-brainwashing movements ultimately forced the government to shelf the MNE curriculum guide. This incident showed that in Hong Kong the list of groups who influence the deliberation of policy was extending from the bureaucrats to the politicians, and then to other stakeholders in the community like parents, students and the public (see the last column on Table 4.2). The process of campaigning against MNE by politicians, policymakers, teachers and other participants (even students) can be taken as an opportunity for the future democratic development of Hong Kong. Evidence shows that the curriculum debate in which these different groups took part helped to determine the end result of the MNE curriculum policy. As a consequence, social awareness of the kinds of education needed for our community was aroused because of the MNE curriculum. In fact, it shaped the story of the MNE curriculum, from its launching to its being put on hold. We have to be clear that without the educational and political struggle to promote a 'curriculum for democracy', the further democratization of society is unlikely to occur (Carr, 1998). This kind of collective movement could become a positive kind of social discourse over the sort of education and school curriculum needed by this community. This is because curriculum policy and practice is always "the subject of disagreements and conflicts within and between parties holding different views about the nature of society and the role of education in its reproduction and transformation" (Carr, 1998, p.326). Perhaps we could take this crisis as an opportunity for progress in the democratic education of our society. More important, this incident demonstrates how the curriculum is reconceptualized (Eisner, 1992) by the public. In any case, it is indeed a positive achievement and a worthy cause for the city to celebrate.

A Threat (T) against the Key Curriculum Trend—Political Orthodoxy

The introduction of MNE curriculum shows the intention and tendency of officials to infuse patriotism and nationalism into the school curriculum—a

66 *Shirley Sze Yin Yeung*

tendency toward *political orthodoxy*. This shift of curriculum ideology may tighten the frame of the local curriculum (Bernstein, 1977), thus limiting its ability to cope with the key forces brought by globalization, for instance, the force of democratization (Gardner, 1999). Democratization is inevitably a global trend of political change. As an international city, the curriculum in Hong Kong also faces demands for change in the political ecology. Nonetheless, in addition to the MNE curriculum, the introduction of e-textbooks can be a way for officials to manipulate the ideology of school curriculum by gradually infusing the notion of nationalism or patriotism. One has to be aware of the reproductive role of curriculum and that pre-set teacher-proof curricula (Apple, 2012) in forms of printed or e-textbook can be an effective tool to perform this role. The officials in Hong Kong and the PRC need to consider carefully whether this tendency is good for the future development of Hong Kong (political, social and educational) and thus that of Mainland China.

CONCLUSION

This chapter investigates the curriculum ideologies of several curriculum priorities in Hong Kong. The list of curriculum or curriculum-related policies is certainly not exhausted. As time goes by, priorities of curriculum innovations may change. The analytical framework proposed in this chapter, and the strategy used for analyzing the policies, could serve as one means to analyze and identify the emergence of ideologies for school curriculum in the new century. Besides, we need to assess the effects of curriculum ideologies on the processes and outcomes of schooling.

Local officials should sustain their efforts to reform the curriculum and teaching in Hong Kong. They should consider the weaknesses, threats and opportunities for advancing to future excellence. Current conceptions of curriculum must be reconceptualized so as to prepare our next generation to live in and to transform our current society into the envisioned future society. For this to be accomplished, the social reconstructionist approach to curriculum and education is promising (Gardner, 1999). To be sure, a curriculum oriented towards social reconstruction is more promising and effective in developing democracy, social participation, civic and citizenship education than in teaching academic knowledge. To accomplish the ideal of social reconstruction, Ornstein and Hunkins (2009) suggest that the propositions of critical pedagogy be infused in the curriculum (Giroux, 1985; Yeung, 2012). All in all, the curriculum oriented towards social reconstruction should be based on social issues and social services and could lead students to critically examine controversial issues, the cultural heritage of society and the entire civilization. Teachers should be fearless in challenging the outdated structures of society. In Hong Kong, Liberal

Ideology and Priorities of School Curriculum in Hong Kong 67

Studies in NSS can be a starting point for achieving this ideal. Further evaluation of its actual implementation would be useful.

Lastly, the curriculum ideology shapes a society's curriculum, which plays a major role in initiating students into the culture, practices and development of all aspects of a society. The relationship between curriculum and society is always reciprocal: each serves to reproduce and transform the other (Carr, 1998). Educational practitioners have the role and responsibility to shape the curriculum to make a better future for coming generations.

NOTES

1. S.Y. Yeung (principal investigator), *Value and Value Conflicts in Curriculum: A Critical Analysis of Official Curriculum in Hong Kong* (Individual Research Project, Department of Curriculum and Instruction, HKIEd; budget approved: HK$16,000; September 2011–July 2012).
2. If the average proportion of secondary 1 intake of a school admitted to a class belonging to the 'top 40%' group in the previous two years reaches 85% of the size of a class, the school is allowed to have full flexibility in determining the MOI arrangement in the class concerned. The school may exercise such flexibility in the form of 'by class', 'by group', 'by subject' and 'by session' arrangements. For other classes, students will mainly learn in their mother-tongue. But schools are allowed to increase the percentage of total lesson time (excluding the lesson time for the English Language subject) allowed for English-medium extended learning activities from the original 15%, 20% and 25% for secondary 1, 2 and 3, respectively.

REFERENCES

Adamson, B., & Morris, P. (2010). *Curriculum, schooling and society in Hong Kong.* Hong Kong: Hong Kong University Press.

Apple, M.W. (2012). *Education and power* (2nd ed.). New York: Routledge.

Audi, R. (2009). Nationalism, patriotism, and cosmopolitanism in an age of globalization. *Journal of Ethics, 13,* 35–381.

Bernstein, B. (1977). *On the classification and framing of educational knowledge.* London: Routledge and Kegan Paul.

Bobbitt, E. (1913). Some general principles of management applied to the problems of city school systems. In S.C. Parker (Ed.) *Twelfth yearbook of the National Society for the Study of Education* (pp.365–381). Chicago: University of Chicago Press.

Carr, W. (1998). The curriculum in and for a democratic society. *Curriculum Studies, 6*(3), 323–340.

Chan, S.M. (1997). Is there a real Activity Approach? In Education Department (Ed.) *Journal of Activity Approach in Primary Schools* (p.12). Hong Kong: Printing Department. (In Chinese)

Curriculum Development Council (1995). *Guide to the Activity Approach.* Hong Kong: Government Printer. (In Chinese)

Curriculum Development Council (2001). *Learning to Learn: The way forward in curriculum development.* Hong Kong: Government Printer.

68 Shirley Sze Yin Yeung

Curriculum Development Council (2009). *Senior secondary curriculum guide : the future is now : from vision to realisation : (secondary 4–6)*. Hong Kong : Government Logistics Department.

Curriculum Development Council (2012). *Moral and National Education: Curriculum guides (primary 1 to secondary 6)*. Hong Kong: Education Bureau.

Curriculum Development Council and the Hong Kong Examinations and Assessment Authority (2007). *Liberal Studies curriculum and assessment guide (secondary 4 to 6)*. Hong Kong: Government Logistics Department.

Dewey, J. (1910). *How we think*. Boston: Heath.

Dewey, J. (1938). *Experience and education*. New York: Norton.

Dukacz, A.S., & Bacbin, P. (1980). Perspective in curriculum. In F.M. Connelly, A.S. Dukacz & F. Quinlan (Eds.) *Curriculum planning for the classroom* (pp.13–22). Toronto: Ontario Teachers' Federation OISE Press.

Education and Manpower Bureau (2005). *The New Academic Structure for senior secondary education and higher education*. Hong Kong: Government Logistics Dept. Retrieved 18 August 2013, from http://334.edb.hkedcity.net/EN/index.php.

Education Bureau (2009a). *Fine-tuning of medium of instruction for secondary schools*. Education Bureau Circular No.6/2009. Retrieved 18 August 2013, from http://www.edb.gov.hk/index.aspx?nodeID=1900&langno=1.

Education Bureau (2009b). *Working group on textbooks and e-learning resources development: Main report*. Hong Kong: Education Bureau.

Education Commission (1997). *Education Commission report no.7: Quality school education*. Hong Kong: Printing Department.

Education Commission (2000). *Learning for life, learning through life: Reform proposals for the education system in Hong Kong*. Hong Kong: Printing Department.

Eisner, E.W. (1992). Curriculum ideologies. In P.W. Jackson (Ed.) *Handbook of research on curriculum* (pp.302–366). New York: Macmillan.

Eisner, E.W., & Vallance, E. (1974). *Conflicting conceptions of curriculum*. Berkeley, CA: McCutchan.

Fung, Y.Y., Wong, H.W., Leung, S.Y., Wu, S.W., Chan, S.Y., & Chow, P.M. (1997). An evaluation of the Activity Approach in primary schools in Hong Kong. In H.W. Wong (Ed.) *Universal education and curriculum* (pp.197–223). Hong Kong: Chinese University Press. (In Chinese).

Gardner, H. (1999). *The disciplined mind: What all students should understand*. New York: Simon and Schuster.

Giroux, H.A. (1985). Critical pedagogy, cultural politics and the discourse of experience. *Journal of Education, 167*(2), 22–41.

Glatthorn, A.A., Boschee, F., & Whitehead, B.M. (2009). *Curriculum leadership: Strategies for development and implementation* (2nd ed.). Thousand Oaks, CA: Sage Publications.

Information Services Department (2012). *Curriculum guide of Moral and National Education subject formally shelved* [Press Release]. Retrieved 18 August 2013, from http://www.info.gov.hk/gia/general/201210/08/P201210080622.htm.

Kress, G. (2000). A curriculum for the future. *Cambridge Journal of Education, 30*(1), 133–145.

McNeil, J.D. (2009). *Contemporary curriculum in thought and action* (7th ed.). Hoboken, NJ: Wiley.

Morris, P. & Chan, K.K. (1997). The Hong Kong school curriculum and the political transition: Politicisation, contextualisation and symbolic action. *Comparative Education, 33*(2), 247–264.

Ideology and Priorities of School Curriculum in Hong Kong 69

National Education Services Center (2012). *The Chinese Model: National Conditions Teaching Manual.* Hong Kong: Center of Contemporary China Studies, Baptist University of Hong Kong. (in Chinese)

Ornstein, A.C., & Hunkins, F.P. (2009). *Curriculum: Foundations, principles, and issues* (5th ed.). Hong Kong: Pearson/Allyn and Bacon.

Payne, G., & Payne, J. (2004). *Key concepts in social research.* London: Sage Publications.

Quality Assurance Division (2006). *Handbook of External School Review for schools.* Hong Kong: Education and Manpower Bureau.

Quality Assurance Division (2009). *External School Review: Information for schools.* Hong Kong: Education Bureau.

Schiro, M.S. (2008). *Curriculum theory: Conflicting visions and enduring concerns.* Los Angeles, CA: Sage Publications.

Silverman, D. (2006). *Interpreting qualitative data: Methods for analyzing talk, text and interaction* (3rd ed.). London: Sage Publications.

Tyler, R. (1949). *Basic principles of curriculum and instruction.* Chicago: University of Chicago Press.

Yeung, S.Y.S. (2009). Is student-centered pedagogy impossible in Hong Kong? The case of inquiry in classrooms. *Asia Pacific Education Review, 10*(3), 377–386.

Yeung, S.Y.S. (2010). Using school evaluation policy to effect curriculum change? A reflection on the SSE and ESR exercise in Hong Kong. *Educational Research Journal, 25*(2), 187–210.

Yeung, S.Y.S. (2012). Conclusion and future direction. In S.Y.S. Yeung, T.S. Lam, W.L. Leung & Y.C. Lo (Eds.) *Curriculum change and innovation* (pp.255–268). Hong Kong: Hong Kong University Press.

Yeung, S.Y.S., & Lam, C.C. (2006). The malfunctioning of the curriculum policy-making system in Hong Kong: A case study of curriculum integration. *International Journal of Educational Reform, 15*(3), 400–423.

Young, M.F.D. (1998). *The curriculum of the future: From the 'new sociology of education' to a critical theory of learning.* London: Falmer Press.

5 "Learning To Learn" Basic Curriculum

Anthony Wai-Lun Leung

INTRODUCTION OF "LEARNING TO LEARN" CURRICULUM REFORM

The chief executive of the Hong Kong Special Administrative Region (SAR) of China, Mr. Tung Chee-Hwa, in his October 1999 policy address (Chief Executive, 1999), highlighted the need to cultivate talents for an innovative and knowledge-based society through lifelong learning and all-round development of children. During 1999 and 2000, the Curriculum Development Council (CDC) conducted a holistic review of the Hong Kong school curriculum so as to introduce a quality school curriculum that helps students meet the challenges from a knowledge-based and changing society, as well as globalization, high-speed technological growth and a competitive economy. The guidelines and recommendations highlighted in the "Learning to Learn" curriculum reform are based on the idea and overall aims of education for the 21st century indicated in the Education Commission's (EC's) report (Education Commission, 2000), public responses to the consultation documents, genuine experiences of schools, local research and policy contexts and different viewpoints of global development. Therefore, the "Learning to Learn" curriculum introduced in 2001 established the blueprint and guidelines for Hong Kong school curriculum development in the subsequent years, and included the introduction of the New Senior Secondary (NSS) curriculum in 2009. According to CDC (2001, p.v), the overall aims of the "Learning to Learn" curriculum are as follows:

- The school curriculum should provide all students with essential lifelong learning experiences for whole-person development in the domains of ethics, intellect, physical development, social skills and aesthetics, according to individual potential, such that all students can become active, responsible and contributing members of the society, the nation and the world.
- The school curriculum should help students learn how to learn through cultivating positive values, attitudes and commitment to lifelong learning, and through developing generic skills to acquire,

"Learning To Learn" Basic Curriculum 71

construct and communicate knowledge. These qualities are essential for whole-person development to cope with the challenges of the 21st century.

- A quality curriculum for the 21st century should set the directions for learning and teaching through a coherent and flexible framework that can be adapted to changes and the different needs of students and schools.

The curriculum reform has also introduced the following interconnected components of curriculum framework:

- *Eight Key Learning Areas* (KLAs): Chinese Language Education; English Language Education; Mathematics Education; Personal, Social and Humanities Education; Science Education; Technology Education; Arts Education; and Physical Education.
- *Nine generic skills*: collaboration skills, communication skills, creativity, critical thinking skills, information technology skills, numeracy skills, problem-solving skills, self-management skills and study skills.
- *Values/attitudes*: values are qualities that students should develop as principles underlying conduct and decision making, while attitudes are personal dispositions needed to perform a task well (CDC, 2001).

Moreover, the curriculum highlights the following areas of action for effective learning, teaching and assessment.

Actions via School Structure, Processes, and Management

- Learning opportunity and learning environment for whole-person development
- School-based curriculum development (SBCD) by flexible use of time, space, various teaching and learning environments and resources available within and external to school
- Collaborative lesson preparation as an important means to enhance the professional development of teachers
- Learning time and timetable management for whole-person development

Actions with Direct Impact on Learning and Teaching within and outside Classrooms

- Effective learning and teaching approaches for motivating students
- Assessment for Learning (AfL) to improve learning and adjust teaching
- Four key tasks (moral and civic education, reading to learn, project learning for generic skills and building knowledge, and applying

72 Anthony Wai-Lun Leung

information technology for interactive learning) and effective use of textbooks and learning/teaching resources for student learning inside and outside classrooms
- Catering for learner differences by using different assessment modes and varying the methods of learning and teaching
- Quality homework for encouraging independent learning

Actions via Partnership with Organizations and Partners

- Lifelong learning for whole-person development
- Smooth transition between kindergarten and primary school and primary and secondary schools
- Home-school co-operation for maximizing the potential of students (CDC, 2001)

Meanwhile, the resources and supportive measures to support schools and teachers for curriculum implementation are as follows:

- Curriculum resources and support materials
- Collaborative research and development 'Seed' projects
- Teacher and principal development programmes
- Library development
- School-based support to curriculum development
- Creating time and space for teachers and learners
- Dissemination strategies and networks
- Involvement of experts (CDC, 2001)

The "Learning to Learn" curriculum reform that aims at lifelong learning and all-round development of students has been implemented for more than ten years since its introduction. The reform programme has strong indications of systematic curriculum planning in terms of aims, curriculum framework and areas of action, resources and supportive measures. However, the public in Hong Kong frequently asks how good the "Learning to Learn" curriculum is. To some, this question may seem difficult to answer. To others, the answer is obvious.

RECOGNITION AND ACHIEVEMENT

With reference to several international assessments (e.g., Trends in International Mathematics and Science Study [TIMSS], Programme for International Student Assessment [PISA] and Progress in International Reading Literacy Study [PIRLS]), Mourshed, Chijioke and Barber (2010) reported the findings of a large-scale international study, entitled *How the World's*

Most Improved School Systems Keep Getting Better, published by McKinsey & Company. This study examines 20 improved school systems from all parts of the globe, including Hong Kong, during the past 15 to 25 years. The findings are based on interviews with system leaders and educators in addition to statistical exercises. The Hong Kong school system is regarded as 'sustained improver', which is a system that has sustained improvement over five or more years, according to the report. In addition, the Hong Kong school system is classified as having a 'good to great' performance stage from 2001 to 2010. This classification reveals that the school system focuses on encouraging teaching and school leadership is a full-fledged profession. It should be emphasized that the introduction of the "Learning to Learn" curriculum reform in Hong Kong also started within this period.

Local studies indicate their findings on the impact of the "Learning to Learn" curriculum reform on student learning. To determine the views and responses of stakeholders, including school leaders, teachers, parents and students, regarding the curriculum reform, the Education Bureau (EDB) conducted studies in association with tertiary institution and other government departments from 2003 onwards by means of questionnaires and interviews. In the mid-term report on curriculum reform to school heads and teachers (EDB, 2008b), the positive responses brought by the curriculum reform on students are as follows:

- Teachers played multiple roles as reported by students.
- Students improved their generic skills as perceived by teachers.
- Students improved their values/attitudes as perceived by school heads and teachers.
- Students performed generic skills and values/attitudes as reported by students themselves.

According to the studies on local teacher involvement in the implementation of the "Learning to Learn" curriculum (Leung, 2009a, 2009b, 2012b), some typical examples of "Learning to Learn" practice are identified:

- Teachers are willing to integrate student learning, within and beyond subject boundaries, with real-life experiences although there are various challenges.
- Teachers, in general, have positive attitudes towards providing students with integrated learning such as project learning.
- Teachers recognize the importance of motivating student enquiry from different perspectives by means of elaboration learning.

Furthermore, according to the major findings of the *Inspection Annual Report* (EDB, 2009–2010) regarding the External School Review (ESR) conducted by the government, the following areas indicate positive evidence.

School's Sustainable Development

- The performance of primary, secondary and special schools regarding the sustainable development of students is generally good.
- Schools show a good grasp of the School Self-Evaluation (SSE) concept, and implement the planning-implementation-evaluation cycle to sustain their continuous development.

School-Based Curriculum

- Rich and diversified school-based curricula that are implemented inside and outside the classroom provide sufficient emphasis on student learning. These programmes extend student learning in lifelong learning and whole-person development.
- Schools promote various professional development activities for teachers to enhance the quality and effectiveness of teaching and learning.

Catering for Learner Diversity

- Schools greatly emphasize catering for learner diversity by means of exploring various strategies and devoting considerable amount of human and financial resources to meet the diversified learning needs of students.

By referring to the aforementioned international and local studies on the implementation of the "Learning to Learn" curriculum reform, clear and substantial evidences are seen in the recognitions and achievements. These proofs include continuous improvement in the school system that focuses on encouraging teaching and school leadership, the multiple roles of teachers in nurturing the all-round development of students, sustainable SBCD and catering to learner diversity.

CHALLENGE AND CONCERN

Building on the existing strengths and experiences developed during the curriculum reform, the EDB (2008b), in its mid-term report on curriculum reform to school heads and teachers, highlighted the following five aspects for future development identified by most school heads and teachers. These actions are regarded as the challenges for the "Learning to Learn" curriculum implementation in the future:

1. Continue to develop school-based curriculum.
2. Continue to improve learning, teaching and assessment strategies.

3. Strengthen the implementation of moral and civic education in different KLAs/subjects.
4. Reinforce catering for learner diversity.
5. Strengthen generic skills of students.

Furthermore, the EDB (2009–2010), in the *Inspection Annual Report* on assessing school performance by the ESR, highlighted the following major concerns.

School's Sustainable Development

- Schools should consider being more focused and specific in the formation of major concerns by consistently implementing the major concerns with concrete plans and avoiding too many aims.
- More attention should be given to formulating appropriate strategies from the evaluation stage for school development.

School-Based Curriculum

- The implementation and monitoring stages show significant variations.
- Effectiveness varies.
- Assessment data of students are not analyzed regularly and sufficiently to inform effectively teaching, learning and assessment at school levels.

Catering for Learner Diversity

- Diversified teaching and assessment strategies are needed in remedial classes.
- The effectiveness of curriculum adaptation varies.
- The effectiveness of co-operative learning varies.

According to the findings of the studies on the involvement of local teachers in the implementation of the "Learning to Learn" curriculum initiatives (Leung, 2009a, 2009b, 2012b), some critical teacher concerns are summarized as follows:

- Teachers have diversified interpretations of the key initiatives of the curriculum reform.
- Teachers are uncertain whether they are able to manage the multiple roles in curriculum implementation.
- Limited resources, lack of collaboration among staff, strong subject boundaries and learner diversity limit the motivation of teachers to apply innovative teaching strategies.

76 Anthony Wai-Lun Leung

- Teachers tend to teach by individual effort and there is a genuine need for more teacher involvement in the practice of collaborative teaching.
- Teachers have doubts about the quality and sufficiency of professional development, and they have diversified concerns and worries about school-based professional development.

On the adoption-implementation-sustainability of K–12 common core curriculum standard in the United States, the Association for Supervision and Curriculum Development (ASCD) (2012) recommends several crucial priorities. The features concerned with the "Learning to Learn" curriculum in Hong Kong are adapted as follows.

Interpretation of Initiatives

- Make sure educators deeply understand the standards and the key instructional shifts they require.
- Vet instructional resources for quality and alignment with the standards.
- Understand and plan for the coming common assessments.
- Align initiatives into comprehensive reforms.

Resources and Support

- Engage higher-education partners.
- Adopt technology with the priority in meeting teaching and learning needs, and work with new assessments.
- Transform principals into instructional leaders.
- Listen to educators about their professional learning needs.
- Maximize opportunities for collaboration and capacity building through professional learning.

Furthermore, several good common practices in the global school systems (Mourshed, Chijioke and Barber, 2010) are identified in the aforementioned international study, *How the World's Most Improved School Systems Keep Getting Better.* By referring to the study, the following common practices of intervention and sustainability, especially those efforts in close relation with curriculum issues, are worthy of further reflection and concern by the policymakers and educators in Hong Kong for the future "Learning to Learn" curriculum development:

Intervention

1. Advance the school systems from 'good to great' and to 'great to excellent' performance stages through the introduction of:

"Learning To Learn" Basic Curriculum 77

- Peer-based learning through school-based and system-wide interaction
- System-sponsored innovation and experimentation
2. Implement the continuous revisions of the curriculum and standards.

Sustainability

1. Establishing collaborative practices between teachers within and across schools by:
   - Working together of teachers and school leaders
   - Coaching their peers
   - Sharing their pedagogical skills
   - Self-sustaining improvements at the frontlines of schools
2. Developing a mediating layer between the schools and the centre by means of school clusters/districts/regions or subject-based groups to provide:
   - Hands-on support
   - A buffer between the school and the centre
   - Channels to share and to integrate improvements across schools
3. Architecting tomorrow's leadership by:
   - Fostering the continuity of the system's leadership from within

After examining the findings and suggestions of the abovementioned international and local studies, the challenges and concerns about the "Learning to Learn" curriculum are incorporated by referring to the good common practices in the global school systems.

ADVANCING THE SCHOOL SYSTEMS FOR EXCELLENCE

Since the connection with the wider environment is critical for success (Fullan, 1993), complacency has no room in the Hong Kong education community on the recognition received and the achievement identified. Therefore, the programme still needs continuous improvement. In addition to the local quality assurance (QA) in school curriculum, such as school development and accountability (SDA), SSR and ESR, the Hong Kong education community should connect with the wider environment by referring to the exemplar practices of the improved school systems around the world. Among those practices, undertaking successful SBCD is a long-term process involving additional resources; otherwise, it may produce little effects. However, promising examples exist in the school-based curriculum despite the tightening controls exercised by the central authorities (Marsh, 2009).

The central authorities, especially in the incorporation of the resources and supportive measures (CDC, 2001) should continuously support school-based innovations and experimentations on learning, teaching and

78 *Anthony Wai-Lun Leung*

assessment through peer groups of teachers. For example, some of these measures should consider the latest instructional technology in teaching, learning and assessment. Some basic lessons of the new paradigm of change (Fullan, 1993) were determined, as well. The paradigm highlights the equal importance of top-down versus bottom-up strategies, as well as centralization versus decentralization. If the education community in Hong Kong intends to strive for excellence in school curriculum based on what has been achieved, then resources and supportive measures, effective communications and collaborations between schools and the central authorities should be enhanced.

CONTINUOUS REVISIONS ON CURRICULUM ORGANIZATION

The implementation of the "Learning to Learn" curriculum genuinely needs to revisit regularly the interconnected components of the curriculum framework (CDC, 2001) and the curriculum documents with response to changes in the society. On the revision of the curriculum guides, curriculum organization is an important aspect of curriculum development because it affects the teaching, learning and assessment brought about by curriculum change.

Vertical (sequence/continuity) and horizontal (scope/integration) relations for organizing learning experiences are indicated in the areas of actions for effective learning, teaching and assessment (CDC, 2001). For example, the actions via partnership with organizations and partners (smooth shift between kindergarten and primary schools, primary and secondary schools) indicate the quality of vertical organization of the "Learning to Learn" curriculum. Moreover, the actions with direct impact on learning and teaching inside and outside classrooms (four key tasks and effective use of textbooks and learning/teaching resources for learning and teaching inside and outside classrooms) could represent the horizontal organization of learning experiences for students.

In the decision-making process of organizing the school-based curriculum at the frontiers, teachers may encounter dilemmas in prioritizing subject matter, the needs of society/culture and learner diversity in response to the ever-changing society. Hence, teachers need to realize that no unique model for curriculum organization exists, and that different approaches could supplement each other. From time to time, teachers should be aware of the characteristics of different practices and the challenges encountered in organizing the school curriculum for guiding students in "Learning to Learn". The continuous professional development of teachers, collaborative effort, awareness, judgement and the sharing of experiences need to be nurtured, as these aspects are critical factors to success (Leung, 2012a).

ESTABLISHING SELF-SUSTAINING COLLABORATIVE PRACTICES BETWEEN TEACHERS WITHIN AND ACROSS SCHOOLS

According to an independent study on the effectiveness of ESR led by Professor John MacBeath from the University of Cambridge (EDB, 2008a), the implementation of SSE and ESR as complementary processes has served as a significant catalyst to change and to school improvement. The impact of ESR in validating and supporting SSE, which in turn, facilitates continuous school improvement, is categorized into the following areas:

- Giving impetus to nurturing the culture of the self-evaluation of the school
- Promoting the use of data and evidence as a basis for the self-evaluation of the school
- Creating a greater sense of openness, transparency and collaboration within schools
- Enhancing a sense of ownership and team spirit
- Creating a positive impact on learning and teaching

Owning the improvement process and enhancing the internal accountability of schools should ensure that the process does not become mechanical or inhibit spontaneous and creative approaches to the self-improvement of the school. For the substantial improvement of school curriculum, the areas of action for effective teaching, learning and assessment (CDC, 2001) should be addressed. These areas include actions via school structure, processes and management, such as SBCD, collaborative lesson preparation, learning opportunity and environment for the all-round development of students. On strengthening the post-ESR support, the EDB should strengthen the facilitation of collegial networking, provision of opportunities for the school leaders, school improvement team and teachers to learn from and with their peers.

Since changes cannot be mandated, the more complex the change, the less people can force it to happen (Fullan, 1993), and, thus, the self-sustaining improvement at the frontiers of schools depends on the school effort from the bottom together with system support from the top. Change is a complex process affected by a number of factors, while the implementation of curriculum change involves focusing on the enactment of the curriculum plan. The decision making of teachers and the fidelity and adaptation of curriculum implementation of schools are subject to challenges. The critical issue now is how schools and teachers respond to the planned reform in the "Learning to Learn" curriculum and implement these changes into classroom practice by considering the school or individual factors. The process can vary between individual schools as well as individual teachers.

80 Anthony Wai-Lun Leung

The application and ongoing cycles of planning-implementation-evaluation could be the solution to the self-sustaining of the programme. Educators, however, should be aware that the critical underlying issues in curriculum reform still rest on the fidelity and adaptation of implementation (Leung, 2012c). Hence, the ultimate goals for self-sustaining collaborative practices by teachers rest on the focused and specific formation of major concerns and the effectiveness of SBCD for learner diversity.

DEVELOPING A MEDIATING LAYER BETWEEN
SCHOOLS AND CENTRAL AUTHORITIES

Change is a journey and not a blueprint; problems are inevitable for lessons to be learned (Fullan, 1993). Several challenges face the implementation and effectiveness of SBCD and catering for learner diversity. Hence, schools in Hong Kong should consider strengthening the engagement with higher education partners for collaboration and professional learning. Professional development and sharing of effective learning, teaching and assessment strategies of teachers for learner diversities, such as advanced questioning techniques, co-operative learning, group work and mastery learning, could help establish collaborative practices to sustain curriculum reform. In designing the structure and hands-on content of collaboration and professional development programmes with individual schools, higher education institutions could consider assuming the role of the mediating layer or buffer between the schools and the central authorities by means of setting up school clusters or subject-based groups.

In the planning of the programmes for teacher development, the critical concerns on local teacher involvement in the implementation of the "Learning to Learn" curriculum initiatives should be addressed. The concerns of teachers include their diversified interpretations of the key initiatives of the curriculum reform, uncertainty in their multiple roles in curriculum implementation, their weak motivation to apply innovative teaching strategies for learner diversity and their doubts concerning the quality of professional development.

ARCHITECTING TOMORROW'S
LEADERSHIP AT DIFFERENT LEVELS

Individualism and collectivism are of equal importance, and every person is a change agent (Fullan, 1993). The enhanced nurturing of leadership at different levels of individual schools is crucial for the continuity of leadership for sustaining the curriculum reform. The enhancement could be done in fostering leadership at different levels of the school systems. More in-depth discussions are illustrated in the chapter on school leadership.

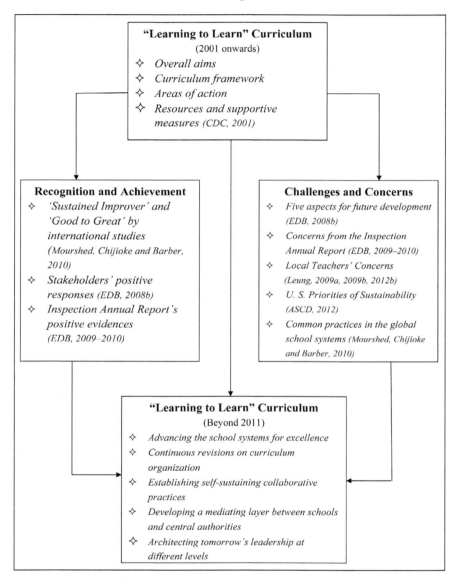

Figure 5.1 "Learning to Learn" curriculum in Hong Kong.

In sum, the implementation of the "Learning to Learn" curriculum has various challenges and concerns that are highlighted in several studies from international and local perspectives. Interventions and sustainability regarding the striving for excellence in terms of curriculum development and implementation are the key issues of challenges and concerns. Improvement is needed in school's sustainable development; school-based curriculum for

82 Anthony Wai-Lun Leung

learner diversity and all-round development; teachers' collaborative involvement and leadership in curriculum implementation; and resources, support and professional learning for teachers. Figure 5.1 illustrates the "Learning to Learn" curriculum regarding its introduction, recognition and achievement, challenges and concerns, and future development.

CONCLUDING REMARKS

To put in place the "Learning to Learn" curriculum reform by means of a gradual approach, the long-term plan beyond 2011 put forward by CDC (2001, p.iii) highlights the following:

Government

- Continues to update and improve the curriculum framework according to the needs of society and students.
- Continues to work in partnership with schools and various concerned parties to generate and accumulate successful experiences with a view to helping schools further improve the quality of education.

Schools

- Make good use of effective learning and teaching strategies to help students attain all-round development and lifelong learning.
- Develop school-based curricula that suit the needs of their students, on the basis of the central curriculum framework.

Apart from the abovementioned long-term schedules for the government and schools, some would ask about teacher involvement at the frontier. Specifically, what are their responding roles now and where should they go beyond the current stage to sustain the curriculum reform? Therefore, teachers should grasp a substantial interpretation of the curriculum reform and cater to their various concerns with continuous quality professional development to sustain what has been achieved.

The "Learning to Learn" curriculum has been implemented for more than ten years since 2001, and the overall implementation has been recognized and well received to a certain extent, according to a number of studies. Challenges and concerns have also been identified for future development. With reference to the existing achievements and accumulated experiences developed during curriculum reform, the Hong Kong education community needs continuous reflection, review and improvement on its future directions, especially in the aspects concerning the role of teachers at the frontier. While there is no unique and perfect approach to get the curriculum reform done, the discussion and analysis in this chapter could provide the policymakers and educators in Hong Kong with the insights to evaluate seriously whether the "Learning to Learn" curriculum reform is on its path to success and whether alternatives to implementation are available for the future.

REFERENCES

Association for Supervision and Curriculum Development (2012). *Fulfilling the promise of the common core state standards: Moving from adoption to implementation to sustainability.* Retrieved 5 November 2012, from http://www.ascd.org.

Chief Executive (1999). *Address by the Chief Executive at the Legislative Council meeting.* Hong Kong: Government Printer.

Curriculum Development Council (2001). *Learning to Learn: The way forward in curriculum development.* Hong Kong: Government Printer.

Education Bureau (2008a). *The impact study on the effectiveness of External School Review in enhancing school improvement through School Self-Evaluation in Hong Kong—final report.* Hong Kong: Quality Assurance Division, EDB.

Education Bureau (2008b). *Improving learning, teaching and the quality of professional life in schools: A mid-term report on curriculum reform to school heads and teachers.* Hong Kong: Government Printer.

Education Bureau (2009–2010). *Inspection annual report (primary, secondary, special schools and kindergartens).* Hong Kong: Quality Assurance Division, EDB.

Education Commission (2000). *Learning for life—learning through life: Reform proposal for the education system in Hong Kong.* Hong Kong: Government printer.

Fullan, M. (1993). *Change forces.* London: Falmer Press.

Leung, W.L.A. (2009a). Curriculum integration for Liberal Studies in Hong Kong. *Curriculum and Teaching, 24*(1), 75–98.

Leung, W.L.A. (2009b). Curriculum reform: Hong Kong primary school teachers' insight into curriculum integration. *International Journal of the Humanities, 6*(10), 97–104.

Leung, W.L.A. (2012a). Change in models and practice of curriculum organization. In S.Y. Yeung, T.S. Lam, W.L. Leung & Y.C. Lo (Eds.) *Curriculum change and innovation* (pp.149–170). Hong Kong: Hong Kong University Press.

Leung, W.L.A. (2012b). Integrated curriculum: Elaboration learning for students. *International Journal of Learning, 18*(10), 29–47.

Leung, W.L.A. (2012c). Strategies for change and curriculum implementation. In S.Y. Yeung, T.S. Lam, W.L. Leung & Y.C. Lo (Eds.) *Curriculum change and innovation* (pp.171–188). Hong Kong: Hong Kong University Press.

Marsh, C. (2009). *Key concepts for understanding curriculum.* New York: Routledge.

Mourshed, M., Chijioke, C., & Barber, M. (2010). *How the world's most improved school systems keep getting better.* New York: McKinsey & Company.

6 Liberal Studies in Hong Kong
Teachers' Space, Place and Fusion of Horizons

John Tak-shing Lam

INTRODUCTION

Liberal Studies was recently introduced into the new Hong Kong secondary school curriculum in 2009 as a core subject and an examination subject in the new Diploma of Secondary Education Examination (DSE) in 2012. One of its unique roles to play in the new secondary curriculum lies in its espoused articulation of three learning outcomes, which are known as the 'ABCs'—raising students' awareness (A) to the world around them, broadening their knowledge base and horizons (B) and connecting knowledge of different disciplines and strengthen their critical mindedness (Cs). There are some inhibiting and facilitating factors at the classroom, school and societal levels that are seen to play a crucial role to the success of achieving these desirable outcomes. In this chapter the author would like to argue that learning and teaching Liberal Studies calls for multiple perspectives, awakening of consciousness/sensitivity and projection of possibilities. In this case, teachers as the teaching practitioners of this subject should be given the space and place for nurturing such kinds of curriculum consciousness and competencies. For achieving the 'ABCs' outcomes and for the goodness of students, teachers and society at large, a kind of community of philosophical hermeneutic enquiry both within and outside the school context should be established in the fashion of Gadamer's (1989) notion of 'fusion of horizons'. This chapter will also include a few recommendations for revamping the local teacher education programmes for Liberal Studies teachers, teachers' networks and the public examination issue.

LIBERAL STUDIES AS A CORE SUBJECT

Liberal Studies was introduced as a core subject in the new secondary school curriculum reform, and it was not without some heated debate and controversies from the public and the academia. Two of the major curriculum objectives in the new secondary school curriculum reform are, firstly, to strike a balance between depth and breadth and, secondly, to

Liberal Studies in Hong Kong 85

achieve greater coherence in students' learning between the various subjects. They are in response to the call for all-roundedness and connectedness in students' learning in the new curriculum to prepare for this age of globalization and knowledge society. And Liberal Studies is foregrounded as the subject to play this pivotal role. The old discipline-based curriculum framework is critiqued as being skewed towards a premature mandatory screening of students into the Arts or Science stream at the end of the junior secondary education. This is seen as defeating the desirable postmodern notion of helping students to see the connectedness of things in the world and to broaden their horizons through seeing things from various different perspectives. There is a wild cry in the 2005 Education and Manpower Bureau (EMB) document *The New Academic Structure for Senior Secondary Education and Higher Education—Action Plan for Investing in the Future of Hong Kong* that Liberal Studies as a new subject will play the important role of incorporating elements of Arts into Science and Science into Arts in the new secondary curriculum. The following remark from the document bears witness to the unique nature of Liberal Studies in enacting the curriculum notion of connectedness and multiplicity in perspectives:

> Liberal Studies plays a unique role in the NSS curriculum by helping students to connect concepts and knowledge across different disciplines, to look at things from more than one single perspective, and to study issues not covered by any single disciplines. (2005, p.36)

Nevertheless even though the 2005 document and the subsequent consultation documents repeatedly state that the new subject has met with a majority support from various curriculum stakeholders, the intended curriculum outcomes of the new subject are not without any challenges from the teachers and the academia. The following section reveals one of the many concerns teachers have in teaching the subject.

THE ABCS OF LIBERAL STUDIES

In the subject's Curriculum and Assessment Guide, the aims of the subject are spelt out as follows:

> Liberal Studies aims to broaden students' knowledge base and enhance their social awareness through the study of a wide range of issues. The modules selected for the curriculum focus on themes of significance to students, society and the world, designed to enable students to make connections across different fields of knowledge and to broaden their horizons. The learning experiences provided will foster students' capacity for life-long learning, so that they can face the challenges of the future with confidence. (Curriculum Development Council and

86 John Tak-shing Lam

the Hong Kong Examinations and Assessment Authority [CDC & HKEAA], 2007, p.1)

Some education practitioners and academics, such as Hui (2006), see in this statement the espousal of the subject's three learning goals which distinguish it from other subjects, they are, namely: *awareness of social and global issues, broadening of one's horizon* and *cultivating one's critical mindedness*, the so-called 'ABCs' of the subject's learning outcomes. The rationale of embedding these three goals into the subject's overall aim is commendable. When examining the degree of alignment between the objectives of the different subjects offered on the plate and the overall curriculum aims of the new secondary curriculum, one can easily find that the three goals of Liberal Studies handsomely fill up the void left by the departmentalized curriculum. An informal personal observation of the stakeholders' views of the subject seems to portray the three goals as recommendable and not at all unattainable. The Education Bureau (EDB) had in one session of the Panel on Education reported to the Legislative Council that its first and second consultation exercise in 2004 and 2005 had recorded more than 90% of schools expressing approval and support for the rationale and goals of the subject. And more than 80% of them supported the overall curriculum design, objectives and themes and enquiry questions of all units. Nevertheless another survey done by the Hong Kong Professional Teachers' Union in 2010 showed that teachers of Liberal Studies rank teaching these desirable outcomes third, after 'catering for students' diversity' and 'lesson preparation' in terms of difficulty level. In other words, Liberal Studies teachers find the 'ABCs' outcomes of the subject difficult to achieve if not insurmountable. Recently Hong Kong saw a series of social and political movements actively and admirably led by local adolescents and students. Some critics even informally attribute this to the success of the teaching of Liberal Studies for teaching the adolescents to enact the three desirable outcomes. While we should contemplate this statement with caution and should suggest that further studies need to be done to correlate youths' active political involvement with the learning of Liberal Studies, it seems that the majority of the Liberal Studies teacher community still does not refute the importance of enculturation of such noble character traits in the younger generation. Perhaps the following remark by Hui (2006) might serve as a gentle reminder of where the three guiding principles should *not* lead us to:

In face of the misleading concepts found in our local Liberal Studies text, the Education Bureau, the Curriculum Development Institute, local universities offering LS teacher-prep programmes, veteran teachers and principals should take a more proactive role in delving into a discourse that would clarify the wrongs and illuminate the right directions. Otherwise, the Independent Education Study (IES)

Liberal Studies in Hong Kong 87

will merely be reduced to a few data-collection methods and principles and the ABC of the new subject Liberal Studies will become like thus: Awareness = social mannerism and attitudes, Broadening = broadening the knowledge base without knowing how to associate, integrate and apply the different bodies of knowledge, Critical/Creative Thinking = producing mental conflict. Is this what we teachers would like to see? (literal translation, Ming Pao, 2006)

Hui's (2006) statement alerts us of the importance of engaging Liberal Studies teachers and other stakeholders of the subject in an in-depth and continual dialogue lest the new subject should deviate from its original path of paving the way to making our next generation more globalized, more sensitive to the world around us and more mindful of our citizens' rights and obligations. For students to achieve the ABC traits, their teachers must be the role models. Then comes the corollary questions: "Can our Liberal Studies teachers model the 'what', 'why' and 'how' of achieving ABCs to their students?" and "If not, where can we find the source of input or inspirations for these teachers?" Ben-Peretz (1975) opines that teachers have the 'potential' to make curriculum with their wealth of professional and contextual knowledge. McCutcheon (1995) and Paris (1993) also talk about teachers, if given the space and place to do curriculum, can execute their curriculum roles in the most professional of manners. In the following sections, the importance of nurturing teachers' curriculum space and place will be highlighted. Also the whole chapter would be premised on the assumption that Liberal Studies teachers can, just like any other teachers, be made aware of their curriculum consciousness and competencies to achieve the subject curriculum objectives by a kind of hermeneutic dialogue either between their peers or with academics. The outcome of this will be a 'hermeneutic circle' in which both parties would contribute to the dialogue and in the end their original thinking will be mediated in a consensual way to become the 'fusion of horizons' (Gadamer, 1989). This will also be elaborated in the following sections.

TEACHERS' CURRICULUM SPACE AND PLACE
AND TEACHERS' CURRICULUM POTENTIALS

MacDonald (1981) and Greene (1971, 1974) are two of the several pioneering scholars in the United States to draw the notions of 'curriculum' and 'consciousness' together. In the eyes of Greene (1974), curriculum must be conceived in terms of possibilities for individuals, all kinds of individuals. For teachers and students, the curriculum must enable them to raise their consciousness and perceive themselves as 'subjects' rather than passive objects of control. The word 'consciousness', Greene reminds us, means a thrusting toward the things of the world. It refers to the multiple ways in

88   John Tak-shing Lam

which the individual comes in touch with objects, events and other human beings. It involves our "perceiving, judging, believing, remembering and imagining" (p.71). In talking about the 'space' and 'place' of teachers in doing curriculum work, Paris extrapolates the dimensions and realms of meanings of teachers' agency in curriculum matters as follows:

> Initiating the creation or critique of curriculum, an awareness of alternatives to established curriculum practices, the autonomy to make informed curriculum choices, an investment of self, and ongoing interaction with the others. (1993, p.16)

All these resonate well with what Ben-Peretz said about teachers' 'potentials' of interpreting and enacting the curriculum goals of a subject inside the classroom. This kind of interpreting curriculum materials for curriculum potentials requires a careful analysis and unpacking of the meanings and significance of the content contained in the materials (Deng, 2009). In contrast to the *Didaktik* tradition which construes teaching as merely delivering a body of objectified knowledge and skills to learners, Deng reminds us that, as a kind of 'fruitful encounter' between content and the learner, teachers are required to analyze and unpack content in a way that opens up its educational meaning and significance. In other words, Paris, Ben-Peretz and the like all point to the desirability of teachers to accomplish the space and place to interpret, critique, review and enact the refined curriculum inside/outside the classroom for the well-being of the students, schools and the world at large. Here, the 'space' and 'place' are defined as the room or autonomy for teachers to innovate, experiment with and to try out in their classroom new curriculum and pedagogical practice to meet the needs of their students.

'The space' can vary from school to school, from subject to subject, and even from primary to secondary sector. In Hong Kong, there is a dearth of large-scale empirical studies that investigate the space and place of teachers' curriculum making in schools; instead most of the research done in this realm adopted the case study approach (Lam, 2011; Law, Van Den Akker and Wan, 2010; Lam and Yeung, 2010; Ko and Lee, 2012; Tam, 2010; Lee, Dimmock and Au-yeung, 2009) An educational case study is a study of a singularity conducted in-depth in natural settings (Bassey, 1999). Its essential features are that sufficient data are collected for researchers to be able to explore significant features of the case and to put forward interpretations for what is observed. It is an ideal methodology to study human interpretations of such kind of vague and personal concepts of 'space' and 'place' in a certain context, but it has the limitations of poor generalizations. The methodological and epistemological complexities involved in studying such a phenomenon in case study method are exacerbated by the fact that schools in Hong Kong, just like schools in any part of the world, show a spectrum of variations in various factors, such as school factors (e.g., school's curriculum leadership and school culture); teacher factors (e.g., teachers' culture and curriculum competencies); parents' support and external factors, such as public examination pressure. There are evidences that these factors play a vital role in framing either an enabling or an inhibiting environment for teachers' curriculum space and place in school (Cheung and Wong, 2012; Brown and McIntye, 1978; Tam, 2010). There are some case studies that reveal that space can be found in the local classroom (Lam, 2011; Law, Van Den Akker and Wan, 2010; Ko and Lee, 2012), but there are also other studies that tell a different story (Tam, 2010; Lee, Dimmock and Au-yeung, 2009). While harmony, co-operation and joint efforts are still the prevailing norms in most of the case study schools, Lee, Dimmock and Au-yeung observe that the school curriculum development context would be better served if there existed a non-threatening and co-operative teacher–principal partnership. Nevertheless, there are signs that Hong Kong teachers' professional space and place are beginning to be confined by competition in the schooling market, government evaluations and chores of non-teaching duties (Lai and Lo, 2007). Painting a rosier picture, after studying five cases of school-based curriculum development (SBCD) initiatives in Hong Kong that extended from 1980s to 2001, Lam and Yeung (2010) observe that Hong Kong has seen an increase in the room for teachers' to do curriculum over the recent decades. The following section also shows that teachers' space and place will be further elevated because of the recent systemic and contextual incentives laid down by the central education authority and the curriculum reforms.

TEACHERS' CURRICULUM MAKING IN A CONTEXT OF HIGH-PERFORMING EDUCATION SYSTEM

As one of the top high-performing education systems in the world, Hong Kong has been extensively researched by world-renowned researching organizations (for example, the McKinsey & Company report in 2007 and the Grattan Institute report in 2012) in an attempt to understand the critical factors behind the success of the former British colony in terms of students' achievements in international testing systems such as Programme for International Student Assessment (PISA) and Trends in International Mathematics and Science Study (TIMMS) in the areas of language and mathematical literacy, problem solving and scientific reasoning. Both the McKinsey & Company report and Grattan Institute report point out that the high-performing success of Hong Kong, as well as some other Asian countries such as Singapore, Shanghai and Korea, lies in the space and place given to teachers in improving the curriculum and teaching in their school context. The two reports also explicitly attribute the top-performing success of Hong Kong to its hardworking teaching force (Grattan Institute, 2012, p.29) and the teachers' 'potential' in enacting the new curriculum.

90 John Tak-shing Lam

The McKinsey research identified four approaches high-performing school systems used to help teachers improve instruction and curriculum, including (1) building practical skills during the initial training, (2) placing coaches in schools to support teachers, (3) selecting and developing effective instructional leaders in schools and (4) enabling teachers to learn from each other. These kinds of enabling factors that empower teachers' curriculum competencies and consciousness are in place in the local context. These in turn generate space and place for local teachers to do curriculum. The curriculum space and place given to local teachers come from various sources like the EDB, the school management and higher education/ teacher education institutions. The EDB provides grants for schools and teachers to implement the new secondary curriculum. It also gives out "academic research funds for academics to work with schools and teachers to implement reforms in learning and teaching" (Grattan Institute, 2012, p.20). Teacher professional development and in-school support are also incentives used by the EDB in collaboration with local universities to nurture teachers' curriculum consciousness and competencies. The above measures can be seen as the 'soft' and 'hard' policy drives done by the EDB (see Kennedy, Chan and Fok, 2011) to facilitate the implementation of the new curriculum. On the 'soft' side, they gave increased resources, school autonomy, incentives and extensive consultations for school principals and teachers to create a sense of ownership over the changes. On the 'hard' side, the systemic External School Review (ESR) and the Territory-Wide Assessment System have been used by the EDB as the needed instruments to monitor the implementation of the new curriculum reform in schools. One of the guiding principles of the recent curriculum reform is that schools have the flexibility to design their school-based curricula to satisfy the needs of their students, so long as the requirements set out in the central curriculum framework are fulfilled (Curriculum Development Council [CDC], 2001, p.ii).

In those successful school cases, the school has also provided a favourable climate and space for teachers to learn from each other and reflect on their own practice by various means, including scheduling one afternoon in the week for team planning, peer observations, sharing sessions and innovative try-outs. Nevertheless the writer opines that while it is easier to reframe and enhance teachers' curriculum competencies through the above means, it is not so easy to change teachers' mind-sets and their consciousness overnight. Fullan (Fullan and Stiegebauer, 1991) argues that it is impossible to change 'on the surface' of any curriculum reform by "endorsing certain goals, using specific materials, and even imitating the behavior without specifically understanding the principles and rationale of the change" (p.40). In other words, for any curriculum reform to take root, teachers as the front-line practitioners of the curriculum reform need to change not only their technical roles (gaining the knowledge and skills required) but also their dispositional roles, beliefs and consciousness

Liberal Studies in Hong Kong

toward the new curriculum. He goes on to cite Werner (1980) to remind us that "(curriculum) implementation is an on-going construction of a shared reality among group members through their interaction with one another within the program" (pp.62–63). For teachers who are mostly free-thinking individuals, there are specific ways to ensure they will acquire the kind of teacher learning that espouses such kinds of consciousness awakeness, deconstruction and re-construction between 'I' and 'Others'. The 'hermeneutic enquiry' (van Manen, 1997) is one such effective avenue for change. The following section will elaborate on the significance of this method.

HERMENEUTIC ENQUIRY AND FUSION OF HORIZONS

Cochran-Smith and Lytle (1999) postulate three kinds of conceptions of teacher learning, namely: (1) knowledge-for-practice, (2) knowledge-in-practice and (3) knowledge-of-practice. The first one refers to teachers learning the 'formal knowledge' from teachers education programmes or the like. The second one means that there is knowledge in practice and teachers are to seek it out either through self-reflection or from expert teachers. The third one ' knowledge-of-practice' is different from the first two in that there is no distinction between formal and practical knowledge, and also there is no distinction between expert or novice teachers. In other words, 'knowledge-of-practice' implies that all teachers can learn and generate knowledge in their own way, drawing reference from different social contexts and sources of inspiration. The source of knowledge can originate from collective enquiry within schools and broader communities, such as in the form of dyadic oral enquiry (Hollingsworth et al., 1994; McDonald, 1992); teachers' enquiry communities or networks (Lieberman, 1992); action research projects (Elliott, 1998); and hermeneutic interviewing (van Manen, 1997). Clandinin (1986), Greene (1978) and Noddings (1984) all point to the important findings that teachers require a stronger and better understanding of the self in relationship to 'Others', including students, pedagogical practice and curriculum.

In order to breed in a collaborative manner the kind of awareness, extended horizons and critical-mindedness in students and teachers of Liberal Studies, it is important to bring in a few notions related to hermeneutics, namely: 'bracketing', 'projection of multiple possibilities' and 'fusion of horizons' of Gadamer (1989). To the hermeneutists, every person has his or her own prejudices shaped by our history and traditions. This kind of variance may work to his or her own advantage or disadvantage. There are in the world different interpretations and understanding toward an object of interest which are framed by one's own ethnic, cultural and sectoral origin and context. This multi-dimensional horizon will inevitably breed a polyphony of voices and interpretations. Rather than seeing this variance as a kind of tension, the hermeneutists have turned it into an advantage.

92 John Tak-shing Lam

They posit that there will never be *better* or *worse* answers, but it is always beneficial to let us know of the existence of and the rationales behind these differences. Awareness and sensitivity towards these variances would bring us to a new 'horizon' in seeing the object of interest. That is what Gadamer (1989) meant when he wrote, "The hermeneutic task consists in not covering up this tension by attempting a naïve assimilation of the two but in consciously bringing it out" (p.306).

On the other hand, hermeneutics asks us to 'bracket' out (or forsake temporarily) our previous conceptions and understandings and come to a multiple interpretation of meanings and imaginative possibilities. Liberal Studies, with its inherent nature of multiplicity and interpretability, will find this a good tool to help students and teachers in raising their awareness, projecting multiple ways of 'reading into' and addressing issues and problems at hand. This will inevitably involve a kind of dialogue in which the 'Others' would help us to see our blind spots or our partiality and we see theirs. In the end, our horizons will thus be mediated by the others and a kind of 'fusion of horizons' (Gadamer, 1989) will emerge. Nevertheless, this does not mean that 'I' will become 'the Other' and 'the Other' will become 'I' for the resultant 'I' will be a different constituent 'I'. This kind of genuine dialogue with 'the Other' can alter us by making us discard the very prejudices that we are made up of and reconstituting the truth that we have established in our daily connection to the rest of the world. It is vital that Liberal Studies teachers gain these kinds of consciousnesses and competencies—the consciousness to (1) engage in hermeneutical conversations with peers or academics to broaden their horizons, (2) be socially and politically aware of the world around us and (3) be critical-minded enough to critique and address issues and objects of interest. The competencies are to (1) 'bracket out' one's own prejudices to engage in genuine dialogue, (2) autonomously voice one's own ideas and (3) mediate one's own views with others to arrive at 'a fusion of horizons'. This kind of hermeneutic phenomenological research into the relational mediation of Liberal Studies curriculum consciousness and conceptual interpretations between "I' and 'Others' will edify the personal insights (Benson, 2006).

THE PRESENT STATE OF LIBERAL STUDIES AT THE MICRO AND MESO LEVELS

At the classroom (micro) level, it is discerned that the subject has given the teachers adequate space for teachers to experiment with the new subject. Teachers are required to be trained from Curriculum Development Institute's (CDI's) workshops for teachers (which are composed of 'curriculum interpretation' elements) to interpret and enact it in their own classrooms in the best way they deem fit. Nevertheless, one survey by the Professional Teachers Union and Lingnan University in 2012 shows that teachers feel constrained by the following factors in teaching the subject: (1) the class size is too big (30 to 40 students), (2) students' poor academic standards, (3) students' lack of interest in the subject, (4) the lack of clarity in the subjects' public assessment requirement (no graded exemplars), (5) lack of good teaching materials and (6) lack of clarity in parts of the curriculum guide (especially the part on how to translate the objectives into clear teaching content). The subject's breadth and depth also baffles most of the teachers and students, with 94% of the former and 82.2% of the latter agreeing to this statement. What is most striking is that despite all the perceived constraints and difficulties, more than 50% of the teacher respondents state they still like to teach the subject. The report opines that given that the curriculum guide and assessment criteria will be made more explicit to the public in the near future, it sees a good prospect that the majority of Liberal Studies teachers will continue to support teaching the subject.

At the school (meso) level, there is a dearth of large-scale research evidence that can tell us whether local schools are coping with the new subject successfully or not. Curriculum matter is a complicated exercise inside a school. It involves many parties and individuals, such as the principal, the middle managers, the panel heads and the front-line teachers. Different individuals would perceive the merit or value of or show concern about a curriculum differently. Research literature shows that school practitioners are the major curriculum decision makers at the school level (Marsh and Willis, 2003). The success or failure of a curriculum hinges on the perceptions of the principal (Ornstein and Hunkins, 1994), the middle managers (Leung, 2001; Holt, 1981) and the front-line teachers (Marsh and Willis, 2003) toward the curriculum. Locally, Yu (2007) in a case study found that the successful preparation for the Liberal Studies in the case school hinged very much on the favourable and proactive attitudes and perceptions of the principal, the two middle managers and the majority of the Liberal Studies teachers. One observation in Yu's study merits our attention on the importance of cultivating a kind of ideational platform between Liberal Studies colleagues in the school. One of the teachers in the study remarked that:

> the development of the collaborative culture in exchanging and sharing ideas can be seen as a means of curriculum preparation. Teachers can certainly be benefited from participating in constructive discussions among the panel. By pooling together the expertise and various views of the panel of teachers, more enlightenment and inspirations on different issues can be obtained. (p.118)

The author in another article (Lam, 2007) argued that a whole-school kind of hermeneutical dialogue among different education practitioners in the school, not only limited to Liberal Studies teachers, will be conducive to the professional development of the latter. In that article, the author used Gadamer's (1989) notion of 'fusion of horizons' and Bakhtin's (1981) 'heteroglossia'

94 John Tak-shing Lam

(Bakhtin defined 'heteroglossia' as a blending of worldviews through language that creates complex unity from a hybrid of utterances) as the premise for the transformation of the school into a hermeneutical learning community. It is postulated that a community of teachers engaged in multi-vocality and multi-faceted interpretation and projection of multiple possibilities will lend itself to becoming a nice ground of fusion of horizons. Not only Liberal Studies teachers but every teacher has his or her own beliefs, prejudices and dispositions toward an object of interest. Bringing together and collating the pool of individual ideas, thinking and prejudices from all education practitioners in a school maximizes the dialogical potential of the whole-school learning community. This will definitely strengthen Liberal Studies teachers' consciousnesses and competencies in interpreting, mediating, enacting and re-envisioning their Liberal Studies goals and practices in the classroom and the school. Some possible avenues can be in the form of formal and informal school organizational meetings, sharing sessions and intranet debate. The school thus provides a breeding ground for multi-vocality and cacophony and for cross-fertilization of ideas and perspectives for teachers at the micro level.

IN THE FUTURE—ENHANCING TEACHERS' SPACE AND PLACE AT THE MACRO LEVEL

Curriculum in the postmodern era has become a search for deeper understanding and aesthetic awareness. Slattery (2013) maintains that in Deweyan terms, aesthetics provides us with the interpretive tool that allows us to envision alternative scenarios and a multiple of possibilities to conceiving and engaging in future problematic situations. Interpretation should emphasize 'possibility' and 'becoming' because human consciousness can never be static. In a postmodern world, organic, non-linear and holistic approaches of adaptation and development override simple cause-and-effect models and linear ways of thinking and monolithic approach of understanding phenomena around us. Complexity theory is one kind of meaning-making theory that arises amid such a postmodern craving for flexibility, diversity, adaptability, complexity and connectedness. Complexity theory is a theory of adaptation and development in the interests of survival in a changing environment (Morrison, 2002). Systems, under the tenet of complexity theory, learn and develop into the next higher-order system through self-organization, feedback and learning. Seeing the awakening and enhancement of Liberal Studies teachers' curriculum consciousness as a kind of learning system, such a system (or a school) must look for connectedness. Connectedness is required if a system is to survive. In this case, connectedness through communication is vital.

> This requires a distributed knowledge system, in which knowledge is not centrally located in a command and control centre or a limited set

Liberal Studies in Hong Kong 95

of agents . . . rather it is dispersed, shared and circulated throughout the organization and its members. (Morrison, 2003, p.285)

Same for Liberal Studies teachers, their horizons and consciousness should always be on an ever evolving stance in order to grow professionally and personally. The process of evolvement and growth in reconceptualizing the curriculum of Liberal Studies and personal perspectives must include forms of hermeneutical enquiry that open to the shifting vantage points among various stakeholders and among competing voices.

To accomplish this constant reconceptualizing of Liberal Studies vantage points and mediation with others' voices, the following avenues should be seriously considered:

- Sharing inside and outside teachers' network
- Thematic talks organized by CDI and universities
- Intra- and inter-schools' community of learners
- School–university partnership (collaborative hermeneutic enquiry)
- EDB establishment of a collusion or platform of worldviews in collaboration with local universities for all Liberal Studies stakeholders to exchange their worldviews
- The revamping of Liberal Studies teacher education programmes

Here the author would like to give a more in-depth extrapolation to the last point of recommending the local Liberal Studies teacher education programmes to be revamped. The proposed change in the local teacher education programmes for Liberal Studies is in line with the modern fast-moving and complex needs of a knowledge society. Grant and Wieczorek (2000) see that the modern knowledge society necessitates a new way of conceptualizing teacher education programmes that include openings to "consider knowledge as multiple, shifting yet moored to social, historical and cultural movements" (p.914).

In fact, Liberal Studies as a new subject in local secondary school curriculum has captured the attention of some academics abroad. Gal (2011) from the United States commends the introduction of the subject of Liberal Studies in the Hong Kong school curriculum and the kind of teacher education programme that nurtures it. Situating the subject against the present background of Hong Kong's changing social, political and economic situations, Gal contrasts it with the didactic approach of teaching and learning by highlighting the uniqueness of the subject:

The nature of the liberal studies curriculum and enquiry approach for Hong Kong students and teachers is an opportunity for them to engage in a constructivist epistemology of teaching and learning. It expects a relational dynamic among teachers, students, and their peers. (p.254)

96   John Tak-shing Lam

Both the United States and Hong Kong are committed to the view that education should support the viability of their economic futures, Gal argues. She points out that the advantages of Hong Kong's recent educational system change over that of the United States lie in the autonomy given to teachers to learn along with their students through personal meaning making of contemporary issues, the alternative assessment strategies employed in measuring students' achievements (referring to the Student Learning Profile) and the value of Liberal Studies as a subject in helping students create meaning based on their situated experiences and through peer deliberation. While there is some truth in Gal's statement in highlighting the teacher education, the education system and the student assessment methods as the successful factors that the United States should follow, the author would like to point out that further reforms need to be made in the areas of teacher education and public assessment format in order for Liberal Studies to achieve its unique curriculum roles.

There is a need to revamp the teacher education programmes for Liberal Studies in Hong Kong by incorporating the essence of self-reflexivity, collaborative and dialogical examination of worldviews and critical discourse. Most of the local teacher education programmes are marked by a pedagogical and technical orientation that focus mainly on studying the nature of Liberal Studies, the issue-based enquiry, the teaching of the Independent Enquiry Study (IES) and the planning/designing/assessment of Liberal Studies curriculum. These kinds of programmes will no doubt prepare the teachers well for a fidelity approach of delivering the Liberal Studies curriculum but will in no way enhance teachers' consciousness and their focus on multi-vocality. Up to the present, the author observes that the most viable and effective mode of enhancing Liberal Studies teachers' dialogical and critical discourse is through the teachers' network. A teacher professional network is defined by Adams (2000, p.19) as one that:

> consists of the linkages and voluntary, reciprocal interactions among teachers, their colleagues, and professional referents that are instrumental in shaping teachers' beliefs, knowledge, and practice.

Very often a teachers' network will provide similar or different source of perceptions, beliefs and actions for its members when viewing a curriculum implementation, thus manifesting its supportive or constraining reaction to that particular curriculum policy. Locally the two teachers' networks for Liberal Studies have done a substantial job primarily in helping member teachers in acquiring the needed pedagogical skills and content knowledge and secondarily in sharing and exchanging Liberal Studies teachers' worldviews, concepts and beliefs.[1] Nevertheless, there is still a lot of room for expanding and mediating Liberal Studies teachers' horizons in the teacher community when we notice that the exchange is still on a closed membership status without wider interaction between teachers and academics and also it is usually on a personal initiative basis that individual Liberal

Studies teachers turn to the network for inspiration or enrichment. The author would like to propose a conglomerated effort to be spearheaded by the EDB in pooling together expertise from universities, teacher education institutions, teacher communities and society at large in providing a more systematic context for dialogue and interflow of ideas. Extra government resources should be put into helping Liberal Studies teachers raise their consciousness to the point of becoming a good model for their students in achieving the 'ABCs' outcomes. A more systematic central planning of forums, e-forums, seminars and special theme talks for the general Liberal Studies teachers should go hand in hand with school–university partnership schemes or research projects that help make Liberal Studies teachers conscious of the strengths and limitations of their personal beliefs, conceptual schemata and worldviews and the impact on their pedagogical practices. Teachers should be encouraged to document the kind of professional and personal growth they experience through such kinds of hermeneutic enquiry approaches. Such narratives should be celebrated, disseminated and held up for further scrutiny in the avenue of teacher journals, network forums and sharing sessions. In such a conglomerated and concerted effort, it is hoped that the EDB, academia, the Liberal Studies teacher community and the local society at large would benefit in such a melding of beliefs, perspectives and worldviews—Gadamer's notion of 'fusion of horizons'.

Another front we should pay attention to is the subject's public and school-based assessment (SBA) issue. Some teachers had serious concerns in the beginning stage about the subject's public examination format, which consists of three parts:

1. Paper I in the public examination on answering data-response questions
2. Paper II in the public examination on answering extended-response questions
3. SBA (on doing an IES project)

Teachers and academics were worried that the pen-and-paper format would induce memorization of facts and provision of 'politically correct' answers, which would defeat the subject's curriculum objectives. There were even worries that there was some hidden agenda in introducing this subject in the secondary curriculum. They were afraid these worries might bring a negative 'washback effect' on their teaching and assessment. Fairness and reliability issue in script marking and SBA is also another pestering factor that kept many Liberal Studies teachers anxiously waiting on the side-line for the first public examination result of the new subject to come out. In the end when the first DSE result came out recently in 2012, their fears had been slightly alleviated. The Hong Kong Examination and Assessment Authority in a way had kept their promise to make the Liberal Studies marking free of bias and supporting students' multiple perspectives

98 John Tak-shing Lam

and critical argumentation that were rationally grounded. Nevertheless, the Liberal Studies teacher community at present still wants more assurance from the Examination Authority that the grading criteria will not change from year to year and those samples of candidates' grading be made open and accessible to teachers' scrutiny. The author would like to support these demands. It would be wise for the EDB to continuously send out clear signals to the Liberal Studies teacher community that there is no hidden agenda in the implementation of this subject and LS teachers are really given the space and place in the planning, teaching and assessment of this subject to achieve the desirable learning outcomes of the 'ABCs'.

CONCLUSION

Slattery (2013) portrays the modern world as having an awareness and sensitivity toward the environments, be they physical, psychological, social and spiritual. It is also marked by a sense of liberation and synthesis (of ideas). This would bring for the individuals a process for growing and becoming and for the school an opportunity for seeing alternatives and expanded possibilities for the future.

The main aim of this chapter is to ultimately argue for the establishment of a Gadamer 'fusion of horizons' for all Liberal Studies stakeholders, namely, the parents, the teachers, the students, the school administrators, the EDB officials and the academics. For the well-being of students, teachers and society at large, the EDB has the obligation of and the advantage (with its resources and expertise) in establishing a platform for the fruitful exchange and mediation of the worldviews of all Liberal Studies stakeholders. The platform can utilize the multiple channels of collating teachers' worldviews as well as from the 'significant others' in the community through teachers' networks, school–university partnership schemes, intra- and inter-school sharing sessions, special theme talks and e-platforms. Education is "the construction and reconstruction of personal and social stories; teachers and learners are storytellers and characters in their own and others' stories" (Connelly and Clandinin, 1990, p.2). In his study of teachers' narratives of curriculum application, Shkedi (2009) using Elbas-Luswisch (2005) statement adds that, "According to this interpretation, education is a narrative of experience that grows and strengthens a person's ability to cope with life" (p.834).

The argument in this chapter for a platform is to provide the teachers (the storytellers) with an ideational space for their professional and personal growth in life, which will ultimately benefit the students and society at large. This chapter hopes to provide useful insights and future signposts for Liberal Studies teachers as well as other professional referents who care about the subject and are willing to go on a co-journeying passage together in the development of this subject so that it can ultimately achieve its valuable and unique curriculum objectives.

NOTES

1. There are at present two Liberal Studies teacher associations. One is the Hong Kong Liberal Studies Association and the other is the Hong Kong Liberal Studies Teachers' Association.

REFERENCES

Adams, Jr., J.E. (2000). *Taking charge of curriculum: Teacher networks and curriculum implementation*. New York: Teachers College Press.

Bakhtin, M.M. (1981). *The dialogic imagination: Four essays* (Trans. C. Emerson & M. Holquist). Austin: University of Texas Press.

Bassey, M. (1999). *Case study research in educational settings*. Buckingham: Open University Press.

Ben-Peretz, M. (1975). The concept of curriculum potential. *Curriculum Theory Network, 5*(2), 151–159.

Benson, K.M. (2006). *Conversations of curriculum reform: Students' and teachers' voices interpreted through autobiographical and phenomenological texts*. New York: Peter Lang Publishers.

Brown, S., & McIntyre, D. (1978). Factors influencing teachers' responses to curriculum innovations. *British Education Research Journal, 4*(1), 19–23.

Cheung, C.K. Alan, & Wong, P.M. (2012). Factors affecting the implementation of curriculum reform in Hong Kong: Key findings from a large-scale survey study. *International Journal of Educational Management, 26*(1), 39–54.

Clandinin, D.J. (1986). *Classroom practice: Teachers images in action*. Barcombe Lewes: Falmer Press.

Cochran-Smith, M., & Lyttle, S.L. (1999). Relationships of knowledge and practice: Teaching learning in communities. *Review of research in education, 24*, 249–305.

Connelly, F.M., & Clandinin, D.J. (1990). Stories of experience and narrative inquiry. *Educational Researcher, 19*(5), 2–14.

Curriculum Development Council (2001). *Learning to learn: Life-long learning and whole-person development*. Hong Kong: Government Logistics Department.

Curriculum Development Council and the Hong Kong Examinations and Assessment Authority (2007). *Liberal Studies: Curriculum and assessment guide (secondary 4 to 6)*. Hong Kong: Government Logistics Department.

Deng, Z.Y. (2009). The formation of a school subject and the nature of curriculum content: An analysis of Liberal Studies in Hong Kong. *Journal of Curriculum Studies, 41*(5), 585–604.

Education and Manpower Bureau (2005). *The New Academic Structure for senior secondary education and higher education—Action plan for investing in the future of Hong Kong*. Hong Kong: Education and Manpower Bureau.

Elbas-Luwisch, F. (2005). *Teachers' voices: Storytelling and possibility*. Greenwich, CT: Information Age Publishing.

Elliott, J. (1998). *The curriculum experiment: Meeting the challenge of social change*. Oxford University Press.

Fullan, M.G., & Stiegebauer, S. (1991). *The new meaning of educational change* (2nd ed.). London: Cassell Educational Limited.

Gadamer, H.G. (1989). *Truth and method* (revised 2nd Ed.) (Trans. J. Weinsheimer & D.G. Marshall). New York: Crossroad Press.

Gal, D. (2011). New opportunities for change in American teacher education: Insights from Hong Kong. *Educational Studies, 47*, 240–259.

100 John Tak-shing Lam

Grant, C.A., & Wieczorek, K. (2000). Teacher education and knowledge in 'the Knowledge Society'? The need for social moorings in our multicultural schools. *Teachers College Record, 102,* 913–935.

Grattan Institute (2012). *Catching up: Learning from the best school systems in East Asia.* Victoria, Australia: Grattan Institute.

Greene, M. (1971). Curriculum and consciousness. *Teachers College Record, 73*(2), 253–269.

Greene, M. (1974). Cognition, consciousness, and curriculum. In W. Pinar (Ed.) *Heightened consciousness, cultural revolution, and curriculum theory* (pp.69–84). Berkeley, CA: McCutchan.

Greene, M. (1978). *Landscape of learning.* New York: Teachers College Press.

Hollingsworth, S., Cordy, A., Davis-Smallwood, J., Dybdahl, M., Gallagher, P., Gallego, M., Maestre, T., Minarik, L., Raffle, L., Standerford, N.S., & Teel, K. (1994). *Teacher research and urban literacy education: Lessons and conversations in a feminist key.* New York: Teachers College Press.

Holt, M. (1981). The head of department and the whole curriculum. In M. Marland & S. Hill (Eds.) *Departmental management.* (pp.9–24).London: Heinemann.,

Hong Kong Professional Teachers' Union (2012). *The results of a survey study on Liberal Studies subject in Hong Kong.* Hong Kong: Hong Kong Professional Teachers' Union. Retrieved 3 Aug 2013, from http://www.hkptu.org/ptu/director/pubdep/ptunews/576/p02a.htm. (In Chinese)

Hui, P.K. (2006). *How to achieve the 'ABC' outcomes of Liberal Studies subject?* Hong Kong: Ming Pao Publication. (In Chinese)

Kennedy, K.J., Chan, K., Jacqueline, S., & Fok, P.K. (2011). Holding policy-makers to account: Exploring 'soft' and 'hard' policy and the implications for curriculum reform. *London Review of Education, 9*(1), 41–54.

Ko, M.L., & Lee, C.K.J. (2012). Chinese Language curriculum reform and the change of teacher working culture: Case studies of curriculum decision-making of Chinese Language teachers. *Hong Kong Teachers' Centre Journal, 11,* 25–44. (In Chinese)

Kwan Fong Cultural Research and Development Centre of the Lingnan University, the Hong Kong Professional Teachers' Union, the Hong Kong Liberal Studies Teachers' Association and the New Territories West Liberal Studies Professional Network (2012). *A survey study on the curriculum content of Liberal Studies.* Hong Kong: Kwan Fong Cultural Research and Development Programme of Lingnan University. (In Chinese)

Lai, M.H., & Lo, N.K.L. (2007). Teacher professionalism in educational reform: The experiences of Hong Kong and Shanghai. *Compare: A Journal of Comparative and International Education, 37*(1), 53–68.

Lam, C.C., & Yeung, S.Y. Shirley (2010). School-based curriculum development in Hong Kong: An arduous journey. In H.F. Edmond Law & N. Nieveen (Eds.) *Schools as curriculum agencies: Asian and European perspectives on school-based curriculum development* (pp.61–82). Boston: Sense Publishers.

Lam, T.S. (2007). Fusions of horizons: Implications for a whole-school hermeneutical community approach for implementing Liberal Studies. *Education Journal, 35*(1), 39–62.

Lam, T.S. (2011). Deliberation and school-based curriculum development: A Hong Kong case study. *New Horizons in Education, 59*(2), 69–82.

Law, H.F. Edmond, Van Den Akker, J., & Wan, S. (2010). Implementation of a school-based curriculum development project in Hong Kong. In H.F. Edmond Law & N. Nieveen (Eds.) *Schools as curriculum agencies: Asian and European perspectives on school-based curriculum development* (pp.83–98). Boston: Sense Publishers.

Lee, C.K. John, Dimmock, C., & Au-yeung, T.Y. (2009). Who really leads and manages the curriculum in primary schools? A Hong Kong case study. *Curriculum Journal, 20*(1), 3–26.

Leung, W.K. (2001). *Curriculum decision-making within the hierarchy of aided secondary schools during a period of curriculum change: The case of Advanced Supplementary level in Hong Kong.* Unpublished PhD dissertation, University of Hong Kong.

Lieberman, A. (1992). The meaning of scholarly activity and the building of community. *Educational Researcher, 21*(6), 5–12.

Marsh, C., & Willis, G. (2003). *Curriculum: Alternative approaches, ongoing issues* (3rd ed.). Englewood Cliffs, NJ: Merrill.

MacDonald, J.B. (1981). Curriculum, consciousness and social change. *Journal of Curriculum Theorizing, 3*(1), 143–153.

McCutcheon, G. (1995). *Developing the curriculum: Solo and group deliberation.* NewYork.: Longman Publishers.

McDonald, J.P. (1992). *Teaching: Making sense of an uncertain craft.* New York: Teachers College Press.

McKinsey & Company (2007). *How the world's best-performing schools come out on top?* New York: McKinsey & Company.

Morrison, K. (2002). *School leadership and complexity theory.* London: Routledge Falmer.

Morrison, K. (2003). Complexity theory and curriculum reforms in Hong Kong. *Pedagogy, Culture & Society, 11*(2), 279–302.

Noddings, N. (1984). *Caring: A feminine approach to ethics and moral education.* Berkeley: University of California Press.

Ornstein, A.C., & Hunkins, F.P. (1994). *Curriculum: Foundations, principles, and issues* (4th ed.). Boston: Allyn and Bacon.

Paris, C. L. (1993). *Teacher agency and curriculum making in classrooms.* New York: Teachers College Press.

Shkedi, A. (2009). From curriculum guide to classroom practice: teachers' narratives of curriculum application. *Journal of Curriculum Studies, 41*(6), 833–854.

Slattery, P. (2013). *Curriculum development in the Postmodern era: Teaching and learning in an age of accountability.* New York: Routledge.

Tam, C.F. (2010). An investigation of teachers' decision-making on school-based curriculum and its contributing factors: A case study of Hong Kong. *Journal of Educational Research and Development, 6*(2), 2–32. (In Chinese)

van Manen, M. (1997). *Researching lived experience: Human science for an action sensitive pedagogy* (2nd ed.). London: Althouse Press.

Werner, W. (1980). *Implementation: The role of belief.* Unpublished paper, Centre for Curriculum Studies, University of British Columbia, Vancouver.

Yu, H.W. (2007). *Preparation for the New Senior Secondary Liberal Studies curriculum: The perception of school practitioners in a Direct Subsidy Scheme school in Hong Kong.* Unpublished MEd dissertation, University of Hong Kong.

7 National Identity and Patriotism in Hong Kong's Educational Reform
Student Attributes and Contested Curriculum Structures

Kerry J. Kennedy and Xiaoxue Kuang

When the Curriculum Development Council (CDC) (2012, p.i) introduced a proposed new school subject of Moral and National Education (MNE) to schools and the Hong Kong community, it noted that "since the return of sovereignty, promoting national education and enhancing students' understanding of their country and national identity have become a common goal of primary and secondary schools". The secretary of education responsible for implementing the new subject had no doubts about its importance as he indicated in a television interview (Ng, 2012):

> After 15 years of Hong Kong returning to the homeland, and I believe everyone actually at this point of time would realize it. Even a lot of people who said opposite to the programme these days, but if you ask them are you Chinese, they would categorically tell you, I am Chinese. *This is the national pride, this is identity, this is the one we're not shy, we're not implicit to say, this is the one we're looking for, identity, number one.* (Emphasis added)

This spirited defence of national identity building by the secretary did not save the new school subject that was eventually "shelved" by the government, with implementation encouraged but not mandatory for schools in Hong Kong. The reasons for this action by the government are not the subject of this chapter. There is a more important issue to pursue here, and it is that of national identity. Even though the school subject may have gone away, identity issues remain for individuals, for schools and for the society as a whole. What is more, such issues have been subject to much speculation (Lau, 1997, 2000; Brewer, 1999; Lee and Chan, 2005; Ma and Fung, 2007) and there is a need for greater clarification.

Because the development of national identity has been a curriculum objective in Hong Kong since 2001, the purpose of this chapter is to examine a range of evidence that has the potential to contribute to a better understanding of how Hong Kong students regard their national identity more than a decade after Hong Kong's return to China. At the same time some consideration will also be given the related concept of patriotism since there has been considerable debate and discussion about it as new curriculum objective in the context of national education. Finally, there is the issue of how the school curriculum is meant to cope with these contested concepts. In order to address these issues, this chapter will address the following questions:

- What is meant by 'national identity' in the Hong Kong context?
- Does national identity influence patriotism?
- How should the school curriculum cater for these social and political constructs?

NATIONAL IDENTITY IN THE HONG KONG CONTEXT

Previous researchers have focused on the dual nature of Hong Kong/Chinese identity to describe the way many Hong Kong people view their identity (Wong, 1996; Lau, 1997, 2000; Fung, 2004). Ma and Fung (2007) identified a trend apparent from 1996 to 2006 whereby the discrete categories of 'Hongkonger' and 'Chinese' identities were giving way to the mixed identities of 'Hongkongers but also Chinese' and 'Chinese but also Hongkongers'. This 'hybridized' identity is important to understand since it has also been found in surveys involving students.

As part of the International Study of Civics and Citizenship Education (ICSS) (Schulz et al., 2010), the Hong Kong sample of students was administered a special set of questions relating to local citizenship issues (for a summary, see Lee, Kennedy and Law, 2011).[1] One question asked, "To what extent do you agree with the following statements in describing your identity?" There were four statements provided, each with four Likert response categories ranging from 'Strongly Agree' to 'Strongly Disagree'. Of the students (n = 4635), 86.5% either 'Agreed' or 'Strongly Agreed' with the statement 'I am Chinese' (with the weight of the response—49.2%—in the 'Agreed' category). Of the students, 83.3% either 'Agreed' or 'Strongly Agreed' that 'I am Chinese from Hong Kong' with responses distributed equally across the two categories. Of the students, 91.2% either 'Agreed' or 'Strongly Agreed' that 'I am Hong Kong people' with 47.6% in the 'Agreed' category; 86.0% either 'Agreed' or 'Strongly Agreed' that 'I am a global citizen' with the weight of the responses (48.2%) in the 'Agreed' category. Lee, Kennedy and Law (2011, p.3) commented in relation to these results that "this on the one hand reflects the unique position of Hong Kong being a part of China and an international city at the same time, and on the other hand the emergence of multiple citizenship identities in a globalized era". National identity, therefore, was not a single dimensional construct for the 14-year-olds surveyed. Perhaps the best way to describe it is an identity that is 'Chinese with Hong Kong and global characteristics'.

104 *Kerry J. Kennedy and Xiaoxue Kuang*

Another set of questions in the same survey presented students with a list of 17 local and national symbols and geographic features and they were asked, "Do you feel proud of the following?" The responses showed that in terms of symbols, 80.7% of students were proud of the Hong Kong Special Administrative Region (SAR) flag, while 79.8% were proud of China's flag. Of the students, 78.5% were proud of the national anthem. In terms of cultural icons, 91.9% of students were proud of the Great Wall of China and 88.5% were proud of China's territory, mountains and rivers. Of the students, 88.3% were proud of the night view of Victoria Harbour with 82.5% feeling proud of the Peak. China's achievements in the world—sporting, economic, science and technology influence—all attracted very strong endorsements from Hong Kong students with between 79% and 87.6% of students indicating they felt proud of these different achievements (sports topped the list, with 87.6% of students endorsing this item). Political aspects of China, such as the Communist Party and the People's Liberation Army (PLA), were less strongly endorsed (49.4% and 69.5%, respectively), while 87% endorsed the history and culture of China as something of which they were proud.

These responses appear to reflect students' national identity—they are proud of both Hong Kong and China. They are particularly proud of China's achievements but are not so keen to endorse more political aspects of the nation, although it should be noted that the PLA was endorsed positively with the Communist Party receiving a marginally negative endorsement. The relative rejection of the political is not unusual for young people, who always show a preference for the social, as was the case here in terms of geographic icons and culture aspects in general. What can be concluded from these responses is that Hong Kong students are firmly embedded in their local context, but they also recognize the value of the broader national context. They are not 'one-eyed' Hongkongers—they are aware of and proud of their nation and its social and cultural attributes. They may not be so embracing of the political context—but neither are young people anywhere (Kennedy, 2007). A further issue, however, is whether this 'two-way' national identity affects the patriotism of young Hong Kong people.

DOES NATIONAL IDENTITY INFLUENCE PATRIOTISM?

While patriotism as a curriculum objective was specifically raised in the recent debates about the proposed school subject of MNE (Kennedy, 2012), it was by no means the first time it had been discussed since Hong Kong's return to China (Yuen and Byam, 2007; Tse, 2007). While students are so often the focus of the discussion about patriotism, there has been very little attention paid to their views—given their 'two-way' identity, can they be considered patriotic? In the 2009 Hong Kong ICCS (Lee, Kennedy and Law, 2011) students were asked about each of the dimensions of patriotism as

National Identity and Patriotism in Hong Kong 105

defined by Fairbrother (2003, pp.75–78). These include emotional attachment to the nation, positive feelings about one's fellow citizens, a sense of duty towards the nation and the importance of national priorities' vis-à-vis individual and community interests. Student responses are reported below.

Emotional Attachment to the Nation

Of Hong Kong students, 80.3% indicated that they 'loved their country', 79.7% felt 'proud to be a Chinese' and 71.7% felt very proud of 'the changes China had made since the beginning of reform and openness'. Of the students, 77.7% indicated they were 'for the country, right or wrong', a somewhat controversial item as noted in the report.[2] Somewhat surprisingly, only 56.5% of students felt 'very happy (excited) when I hear China's national anthem at the Olympics'. Overall, however, the strong endorsements of the majority of these items suggest that Hong Kong students have an emotional attachment to China, a disposition often portrayed as a key element in patriotism (Kelman, 1996).

Attitudes to Fellow Citizens

What appears as students' relatively strong emotional attachment to China was not translated into automatic support for fellow citizens. While 72.5% of students felt 'Chinese people are more united than others in the world', only 42.7% felt the 'Chinese people are the finest in the world'. Of the students, 58.6% felt they 'have a favourable impression of the Chinese people', and 51.4% indicated that 'Chinese people are very altruistic'. At the same time, 73.8% of students felt that 'Chinese people are patriotic'. On the other hand, however, 68.9% agreed that they had 'respect for Chinese people'. These responses suggest that Hong Kong students have moderately positive attitudes towards their fellow citizens but they are not uncritical. When similar questions were used with a small sample of teachers, there were also negative responses from some of the respondents, leading to the conclusion that "emotional attachment, where the nation is defined in terms of its members, may or may not extend to positive feelings toward one's fellow nationals" (Yau, 2011, p.85). Hong Kong students are not really negative, but neither are their endorsements strong—they love the nation more than their fellow citizens.

Sense of Duty to the Nation

There are two types of responses to this issue. One the one hand, almost 80% of students felt that 'citizens have the duty to love China'; 74.2% indicated that 'it is my responsibility to help China develop'; 72.0% 'would personally like to help China attain its goals'; 67.3% said 'it is important for me to serve my country'; and 86.8% agreed that 'there are duties to fulfil for

106   *Kerry J. Kennedy and Xiaoxue Kuang*

the nation'. On the other hand, only 36.0% endorsed the idea that 'citizens should be willing to sacrifice their lives for their country', and 57.1% that 'the nation's needs have something to do with my own life goals'. The 2009 Hong Kong International Civics and Citizenship Education Study (Lee, Kennedy and Law, 2011) sought to explain these endorsements as somewhat typical of the views of 15-year-olds who tend to be more self-centred, even in collectivist cultures. Yet Fairbrother (2003 , p.88) noted even lower levels of endorsement for these two items with a first-year university sample of Hong Kong students (11.2% and 9.3%, respectively) although much higher levels of endorsements from a similar sample of Mainland Chinese students (59% and 88.1%). It seems for Hong Kong students, therefore, that individual concerns appear to outweigh national concerns even when overall students recognize a general duty to the nation.

Nation, Region or Individual?

65.8% of the students disagreed with the statement that 'the welfare of the individual is more important than the welfare of the nation', indicating that there was moderate support for regarding the nation as being more important than the individual. Similarly, 55.3% disagreed that 'I am first a citizen of my region and second a Chinese', suggesting again moderate support. These responses suggest that there is moderate support for the nation in relation to individuals and the region, but it is by no means unanimous. This tension between national and individual interests is maintained with only 53.8% of students agreeing that 'each of us can only make real progress when the nation as a whole makes progress' and with 84.2% of students agreeing that 'one cannot sacrifice one's own interests in order to satisfy the needs of the nation'. A similar tension is seen when it comes to regional and national commitments. While 50.5 % of students agree that 'my local region should make sacrifices to help a Chinese in need' and 66.2% that 'interests of the nation should come before local regional interests',69.3% of students indicated that 'I have a stronger connection to my own local region than to the nation'. Thus in comparative terms, the pre-eminence of the nation is not always put first (sometimes this set of questions is referred to as the 'Nation First Scale'). For many of these students, individual and local concerns and commitments are more important. The actual endorsements are in most cases equivocal with often just a small minority showing a positive response. It is perhaps the 'Hong Kong identity' of students that comes through when almost 70% of students see that they have a stronger connection to the region than to the nation.

Yet such results must be set against the strong emotional ties that many students indicated they have towards the nation (see response to 'Emotional Attachment to the Nation' items above). It seems that if students are asked to consider the nation on its own, they can identify this kind of emotional attachment, but when they are asked to balance individual and regional feelings against the larger national commitment, then they feel somewhat compromised. It may also be that individualism is stronger in Hong Kong because of long-term Western influences so that young people may be somewhat torn between their collectivist cultural heritage and their location in 'Asia's international city'.

It seems clear from the above analyses that the Hong Kong students have a developing national identity best characterized as 'Chinese with Hong Kong characteristics'—a kind of dual identity that reflects their local and national identifications. Yet this does not seem to stop them from developing patriotic feelings toward the nation to which they have a strong emotional attachment and sense of duty. They can be both Hong Kong residents and Chinese patriots—at age 14 these do not seem to be opposing pressures on students. The issue is what does the community expect of them and how can the school curriculum best accommodate these community expectations. These issues will be discussed in the following section.

NATIONAL IDENTITY, PATRIOTISM AND THE SCHOOL CURRICULUM

At the beginning of this chapter, reference was made to the problems encountered in attempting to introduce a new school subject concerned with national education. Yet it is important to stress that the development of national identity has been an overarching curriculum objective of Hong Kong's educational reforms since 2001 (Hughes and Stone, 1999; Kennedy, 2005). The very recent debates about national education in the Hong Kong community made it clear that even 15 years after the resumption Chinese sovereignty, there is not a consensus in the community about how national identity is best promoted amongst young people. The issue of how the school curriculum should handle issues of national identity and patriotism, therefore, becomes one of great sensitivity. The following sections will:

- Review the way national identity has been handled as a curriculum issue in Hong Kong.
- Identify the areas of sensitivity for implementing a national identity building curriculum.
- Suggest a way forward based on what has been shown in the previous sections about Hong Kong students' attitudes to national identity and patriotism.

National Identity as a Curriculum Issue in Hong Kong

From the initiation of Hong Kong's decade of curriculum reform, national identity was identified as a priority but pursued in what might be called a

108 Kerry J. Kennedy and Xiaoxue Kuang

'soft' manner. The broad objective was expressed by the Education Commission (EC) (2000, p.46) as a particular aspiration for students to:

> Have a deeper understanding of the history, culture, natural and human environments of China, strengthen their national identity, and will develop a social and humanistic perspective for making sound judgments about issues concerning the local community, the nation and the world.

This aspiration ended up as one of the seven learning goals for the new curriculum with the expectation that at the end of ten years of schooling students would (CDC, 2002b, p.4) "understand their national identity and be committed to contributing to the nation and society".

To achieve this goal there was no specific subject, no specific content, no examination. Rather national identity was meant to be promoted through civic and moral education, one of the four key tasks identified in the reform, and in a cross-curriculum manner through the key learning areas (KLAs). The recommendation to schools was "instead of imposing national sentiments on them (i.e. students), we must provide more opportunities for young people to develop a sense of belonging to China" (CDC, 2002a, p.3). This integrative approach to the development of national identity has been the main curriculum approach throughout the reform period.

The approach has been supplemented by a number of co-curricular activities of a more experiential nature. Mainland study and exchange activities have been supported by the Education Bureau with direct grants to schools. This provided the opportunity for Hong Kong students to have direct experience of China often through school exchanges and visits to areas thought to be of interest to students. The Hong Kong Federation of Workers developed the Mainland–Hong Kong eSister Program (http://www.jsit.net/sschool/sisBrochure5.pdf) with the aim of "fostering multi-cultural exchange, and facilitating the sharing and exchange of good teaching materials across cities". School subjects, such as the newly introduced Liberal Studies, also had access to resources to promote experiential learning through Mainland visit activities. There were also the government-promoted visits of China's Olympic team and astronauts that were designed to instil a sense of national pride in China's achievements. When the vice-premier, Li Keqiang, visited Hong Kong in 2012, he announced exchange opportunities for Hong Kong's university students as well as the relaxation of requirements for Hong Kong students wishing to enter Mainland universities.

For the most part this 'soft' approach to the development of national identity attracted little public attention. Flag-raising ceremonies in schools were encouraged but not enforced by the Education Bureau (EDB). When public concern was expressed about the development of a database by the EDB with the names of students who were involved in Mainland exchange activities, the database was disbanded. For a time, it seems, the official policy was to

National Identity and Patriotism in Hong Kong 109

move carefully on the issue of promoting national identity, ensuring that it had a role in the curriculum but avoiding any mandatory requirements. This all changed in October 2010 when the then chief executive, Donald Tsang, announced the government's intention to introduce a new school subject: MNE. This was to be mandatory at all levels of schooling. A soft approach to curriculum integration suddenly became hardened—in the following years 'national education' became a hot topic with the contested nature of the school curriculum becoming very public. What before had proceeded quietly attracting little attention was now very much in the public domain. The consequences will be discussed in the following section.

The Sensitivities of Developing a National Identity-Building Curriculum

It was not until September 2012 that the MNE school subject announced by Donald Tsang in 2012 was ready for implementation. By the time Tsang left office on 30 June 2012, he could well have thought that such a curriculum might have been counted as part of his legacy to Hong Kong's development. There had been the usual round of consultations on the draft documents prepared by the CDC commencing in May 2011, strong views had been expressed by groups such as the Hong Kong Professional Teachers' and EDB officials consulted with young people themselves. The texts of these official consultations have never been released, but the EDB has maintained that there was considerable support for the initiative. In response to the consultations, changes were made to the draft curriculum and different views were accommodated. On 1 July 2012, Leung Chun-ying succeeded Donald Tsang as the chief executive of the Hong Kong SAR. Implementation of the new school subject in all primary schools was set for September. But the intervening months proved that the issue of national identity and its expression in the *Moral and National Education Curriculum Guide* (CDC, 2012) was too explosive for a new government to manage and too much for a community that had become accustomed to the soft approaches to national identity formation that had characterized the period until 2010.

The trigger for the community disaffection was not so much the *Curriculum Guide* itself, which did represent some accommodation between the original proposal and the feedback from consultation. Rather, it was a set of resource materials popularly known as the 'China model', produced by the National Education Services Centre, that caused the major problem. The Chinese Communist Party was described in these materials as "progressive, altruistic and united" and multi-party systems were described as "malignant". This was enough to reignite a community debate about 'brainwashing' (a term that had been used much earlier in the debates around the new subject that was now revived). It led students to set up permanent protests outside government precincts and maintain them until the government relented and "shelved' the *Guidelines*, making them

110   Kerry J. Kennedy and Xiaoxue Kuang

optional and thus abandoning the September 2012 implementation. Curriculum issues relating to Hong Kong's proposed national education went to the fore in local and international media during the summer of 2012. Young protesters stood their ground supporting what they saw as Hong Kong's core values and rejecting attempts at what was portrayed in the China model materials as Mainland-style patriotic education. But what of the future? How will national identity be promoted in Hong Kong schools after this failed attempt to introduce a more focused national education? This issue will be discussed in the next section.

The Way Forward for National Identity Building in Hong Kong Schools

There is little doubt that national identity building as a curriculum goal will remain on the educational agenda in Hong Kong. It seems that the community, and as a result the government, has accepted that it needs to be done in a way that suits Hong Kong conditions, values and aspirations rather than through the imitation of the more explicit forms of patriotic education that characterize schools on the Mainland (Fairbrother, 2003). This may not be what was originally meant by "one country, two systems", but it needs to be recognized that Hong Kong's social system does have distinctive values and thus the school curriculum, as a reflection of society's values, needs to take account of these.

It also needs to be recognized, as shown in the first section of this chapter, that Hong Kong 14-year-olds already have a heightened sense of their identities and that part of this is their attachment to China. Thus it is not the case that schools have to promote national identity as some kind of new idea for students who will come to school already influenced by parents, peers, media and the community in general. The task of schools in national identity building is more to channel and develop feelings of national identity in positive and constructive ways. As has been shown in recent territorial disputes between different Asian nations (including China) it does not take long for patriotic feelings to become nationalistic, supporting one country's claim over another and thus asserting national superiority. National identity directed towards patriotism and love of country is one thing, but directed towards feelings of national superiority is quite another and something to be avoided. It is for this reason that philosophers such as Splitter (2011) have argued that any form of national education should be avoided because the line between patriotism and nationalism can too easily be crossed. Thus the need for well-directed national identity education remains important.

The issues now is what kind of curriculum can best achieve the goal of developing informed citizens with a sense of attachment to their fellow human beings, to their communities and to their nations? The 'soft'

National Identity and Patriotism in Hong Kong   111

approach described earlier in this chapter is one possible direction. This approach integrates key ideas about national identity into curriculum experiences for students. These experiences can be either in the classroom (for example, in History lessons), outside the classroom (for example, in school assemblies), in the community (for example, in service learning activities) or through direct experience by travelling to the Mainland and meeting with other students and seeing how fellow citizens experience life in a different geographic context.

The move towards a school subject for promoting national identity is the option that was defeated by community opposition in the summer of 2012. But exactly what was lost? Fairbrother and Kennedy (2011) showed that curriculum organization (integrated curriculum versus single subject curriculum) had no significant effect on civic learning. Students who had experienced a single subject did not do significantly better than those whose civics experiences were more of an integrated kind. Thus the integrated model of curriculum delivery appears to have the capacity to deliver important curriculum outcomes. This model utilizes classroom activities, such as mock parliaments and class forums; school activities, such as assemblies and service learning; and out of school activities, such as excursions and exchanges. School subjects are no guarantee of improved learning, although it is accepted that there is a certain status attached to subjects in terms of providing curriculum space and time. Hong Kong's national identity building, however, can continue to be pursued through the integrated processes that have been operating since 2001.

The real challenge for such an approach is political rather than educational. Authorities, both in Hong Kong and Beijing, need to be convinced that students in Hong Kong will continue to be engaged in national identity formation. In one sense, students cannot help but be engaged in such a process whether it is because of schools or whether it is just a natural development for young people as they mature and become active citizens. Hong Kong students, based on the results reported here, do not start out as resistors to national education or to the nation. Quite the contrary—they are emotionally attached to China and they have a sense of duty to their nation. At age 14, not a lot more can be expected and should not be expected. In a region such as Hong Kong with strong aspirations for democracy and with historical, social and cultural attachments to the nation, but also with a long history of colonialism, there are many issues to negotiate. Hong Kong can bring great benefits to the nation as a bridge to Western ideas, investments and institutions. A liberal and tolerant Hong Kong should be seen not so much as an exception to mainstream political ideas in China. Rather the city should be seen as an example of how citizens can be both patriotic and critical while not representing a threat to the nation. Young people in Hong Kong have a significant role to play in such a future and an integrated school curriculum promoting national identity can help them along the way.

CONCLUSION

Promoting national identity as a curriculum objective will always be contested, not only in Hong Kong but elsewhere as well. The social and political purposes of the school curriculum always attract great attention as communities struggle to ensure that young people have access to a curriculum that best serves community needs and aspirations. Different visions for any society will inevitably result in different views about the curriculum. For the current case, however, what is clear is that Hong Kong adolescents themselves have a voice in expressing what they think and believe about their own identities as citizens of China and residents of Hong Kong. Schools can facilitate the way they continue to think about their identities and can help them to channel their feelings and ideas in constructive ways. If out of national identity education comes active and concerned citizens willing to participate in the affairs of their city and their country, willing to contribute to debates and discussion, willing to make their voices heard on issues of importance, then schools and the curriculum will have done a good job. Developing citizens with the values and the sense of efficacy and knowledge to make an ongoing contribution to society may well be one of the enduring contributions schools can make in these uncertain times, and it should be a contribution encouraged by the community.

ACKNOWLEDGEMENT

The research reported in this chapter is part of a General Research Fund Project (HKIEd 842211), *Asian Students' Conceptions of Citizenship: Constructing Indigenous Views of Citizenship Education and the State*. It has been funded by the Hong Kong Research Grants Council. The views presented here are those of the authors and not the funding body.

NOTES

1. The survey involved more than 2,000 students in 71 randomly selected secondary schools. See the report cited above for details.
2. In Chinese this item was: 儘管祖國有優點有缺點，但我對祖國總是懷有好感, which is better understood to mean in English 'I have a positive feeling for my country, despite it having strengths and weaknesses'. This is considered to be an equivalent translation but with somewhat different connotations from the original English, 'I am for my country right or wrong' (p.87).

REFERENCES

Brewer, M. B. 1999, Multiple identities and identity transition: Implications for Hong Kong. *International Journal of Intercultural Relations, 23*, 187–197

National Identity and Patriotism in Hong Kong 113

Curriculum Development Council (2002a). *Basic curriculum guide: Booklet 3A.* Retrieved 3 April 2013, from http://cd1.edb.hkedcity.net/cd/EN/Content_2909/BE_Eng.pdf.

Curriculum Development Council (2002b). *Basic curriculum guide: Introduction.* Retrieved 3 April 2013, from http://cd1.edb.hkedcity.net/cd/EN/Content_2909/BE_Eng.pdf.

Curriculum Development Council (2012). *Moral and National Education curriculum guide (primary 1 to secondary 6).* Retrieved 16 February 2013, from http://www.edb.gov.hk/FileManager/EN/Content_2428/mne%20guide%20(eng)%20final.pdf.

Education Commission (2000). *Learning for life—learning through life: Reform proposals for the education system in Hong Kong.* Retrieved 3 April 2013, from http://www.e-c.edu.hk/eng/reform/index_e.html.

Fairbrother, G. (2003). *Toward critical patriotism: Student resistance to political education in Hong Kong and China. (* Hong Kong: Hong Kong University Press.

Fairbrother, G., & Kennedy, K. (2011). Civic education curriculum reform in Hong Kong: What should be the direction under Chinese sovereignty? *Cambridge Journal of Education, 41*(4), 425–443.

Fung, A. (2004). Postcolonial Hong Kong identity: Hybridising the local and the national. *Social Identities, 10*(3), 399–414.

Hughes, C., & Stone, R. (1999). Nation-building and curriculum reform in Hong Kong and Taiwan. *China Quarterly, 160,* 977–991.

Kelman, H. (1996). Nationalism, patriotism, and national identity: Social-psychological dimensions. In D. Bar-Tal & E. Staub (Eds.) *Patriotism in the lives of individuals and nations* (pp.165–189). Chicago: Nelson-Hall.

Kennedy, K. (2005). *Changing schools for changing times: New directions for the school curriculum in Hong Kong.* Hong Kong: Chinese University Press.

Kennedy, K. (2007). Student constructions of 'active citizenship': What does participation mean to students? *British Journal of Educational Studies, 55*(3), 304–324.

Kennedy, K. (2012). Patriotism Hong Kong style. *South China Morning Post,* 2 October, A11.

Lau, S.K. (1997). 'Hong Kong' or 'Chinese': The identity of Hong Kong Chinese 1985–1995. *Twenty-First Century, 41,* 43–58.

Lau, S.K. (2000). Hongkongese or Chinese: The problem of identity on the eve of resumption of Chinese sovereignty over Hong Kong. In S.K. Lau (Ed.) *Social development and political change in Hong Kong* (pp.255–283). Hong Kong: Chinese University Press.

Lee, F.L.F., & Chan, J.M. (2005). Political attitudes, political participation, and Hong Kong identities after 1997. *Issues & Studies, 41,* 2–35.

Lee, W.O., Kennedy. K., & Law, W.W. (2011). *International civic and citizenship education study 2009: A preliminary report on the study and the Hong Kong survey.* Retrieved 16 February 2013, from http://www.edb.gov.hk/FileManager/EN/Content_8319/iccs_2009_preliminary_report_e.pdf .

Ma, E., & Fung. A. (2007). Negotiating local and national identifications: Hong Kong identity surveys 1996–2006. *Asian Journal of Communication, 17*(2),172–185.

Ng, E. (2012). Transcript of *Newsline* interview by Michael Chugani. Retrieved 16 February 2013, from http://www.hkfew.org.hk/mned/article/2/20120826_210.html.

Schulz, W., Ainley, J., Fraillon, J., Kerr, D.,Losito,B. (2010). *ICCS 2009 International report: civic knowledge, attitude and engagement among lower-secondary school students in 38 countries.* Amsterdam: IEA

114 *Kerry J. Kennedy and Xiaoxue Kuang*

Splitter, L.J. (2011). Beyond citizenship? A critique of the 'citizenship industry'. *Journal of Social Science Education, 10*(1), 12–22.

Wong, T.W.P. (1996). *Ethnic identity and national identity of the people in Hong Kong. Occasional Paper, No. 50.* Hong Kong: Institute of Asia Pacific Studies, Chinese University of Hong Kong.

Tse, T.K.C. (2007). Remaking Chinese identity: Hegemonic struggles over national education in post-colonial Hong Kong. *International Studies in Sociology of Education, 17*(3), 231–248.

Yau, D.T.S. (2011). 'China Today' module , teachers' national attitude and their implementation of informal and nonformal education under 'One Country & Two Systems'. *New Horizons in Education, 59*(1), 79–94.

Yuen, T., & Byam, M. (2007). National identity, patriotism and studying politics in schools: A case study in Hong Kong. *Compare, 37*(1) 23–36.

Part III
Changing Classrooms

8 The Impact of the Learning Study Approach on Chinese Classrooms
The Hong Kong Experience

Po-Yuk Ko

INTRODUCTION

The Chinese Classroom—Revisiting the Stereotype

In much of the early Western literature, Chinese classrooms are described as conservative and dominated by drilling and rote learning (Cleverley, 1991). Teaching in Mainland China is most often delivered in a lecture and explanatory format. This has been described as the 'virtuoso' model, which is characterized by high-quality performance by teachers with direct, whole-group instruction and teacher talk (Paine, 1990). These conservative features are believed to have stemmed from two traditions: the Confucian pedagogical tradition that favours drilling and repetition skills in learning, and the Soviet mode of instruction that is basically textbook-based, teacher-centred and content overloaded (Leung, 1991). However, the fact that Chinese and other Asian students outperform their Western counterparts in international comparisons of student performance, such as the Trends in International Mathematics and Science Study (TIMSS) (http://timssandpirls.bc.edu) and the Programme for International Student Assessment (PISA) (HKPISA Centre, 2011), has led researchers to take a closer look at teaching in China and other parts of Asia influenced by the 'Confucian Heritage Culture' (CHC) (e.g., Lee, 1996; Watkins and Biggs, 2001). Such endeavours have resulted in a more pluralistic description of Chinese classrooms. For instance, researchers have noted that the lessons that they observed in several cities in China involved considerable student engagement and interaction with the teacher (Stevenson and Lee, 1997; Cortazzi, 1998). The lessons, although were very much teacher controlled, involved learners quite heavily and were "well-thought out, carefully timed, and broadly planned within the framework of interactive activities" (Cortazzi and Jin, 2001, pp.127). Similar research has revealed that Chinese teachers have a more profound understanding of subject matter, particularly in Mathematics, than their counterparts in Western countries, although the former have less formal education than the latter. The lessons taught by Chinese teachers look very traditional, but teaching is aimed toward achieving a conceptual understanding of Mathematics in the classroom (Ma, 1999).

118   *Po-Yuk Ko*

Researchers have also found that the particular teaching culture in China, which places great emphasis on lesson planning and classroom practice, contributes to the professional development of teachers and leads to outstanding student achievement. In China, a three-level nationwide teaching research network comprising a municipal-level Teaching Research Office (TRO), county-level TRO and school-level TRO has been established for more than 50 years. In the school-level TROs, teachers of the same subject at the same level meet frequently to study teaching materials and share ideas on teaching to foster a deeper understanding of subject matter through content research (Yang, 2009). The vision of education reform and policies is translated to users at the school level as 'content' and 'lessons' (Ko, 2012). The co-planning of lessons, peer observation and open lessons are common activities organized by school-level TROs. TRO activities involve 'learning-through-doing', whereby teachers gain grassroots professional development through their teaching practice (Paine and Fang, 2006).

Research on the TRO network revisits the stereotype of the Chinese classroom in the earlier literature. More importantly, it recognizes the limitation of labels such as 'traditional' and 'progressive' or dichotomous portrayals such as 'teacher-centred' and 'student-centred' commonly used in a Western context, which may not accurately reflect the pedagogical characteristics of the Chinese classroom (Mok and Ko, 2003). The apparent arrangement of student activities such as collaborative work or group-based activities should not be the sole means by which the effectiveness of teaching is judged. How the subject matter is actually handled by the teacher and experienced by the students may be more salient.

The Hong Kong Scenario

Hong Kong is a Chinese city, and the education system has been influenced by both CHC (Biggs, 1996) and the colonial administration (Morris and Marsh, 1992). The system has been criticized for being highly competitive and dominated by an examination-oriented culture (Pong and Chow, 2002). The school curriculum was traditionally characterized by a subject-dominated focus on remote and abstract knowledge (Morris, Kan and Morris, 2000). As the syllabus was content overloaded, students were driven to use rote learning to cope with it, which hindered the development of valuable capabilities such as creativity (Poon and Wong, 2008). Faced with such long-standing problems, the Hong Kong government launched a major education reform in the 2000s to improve the quality of teaching and equip students with high-order abilities to meet the challenges of a 'knowledge-based' society (Curriculum Development Council [CDC], 2000). The scope of the reform covered curricula, assessment mechanisms, admission systems, teacher professionalism and language policies. It was advocated that teaching should focus not just on subject matter but also on generic skills, such as problem solving, collaboration, communication and creativity (Education Commission [EC], 2000). Innovative teaching approaches,

The Impact of the Learning Study Approach on Chinese Classrooms 119

such as co-operative learning, using IT in education and project learning, were promoted. These reform measures placed new demands on teachers in terms of their professional responsibilities. To prepare teachers for the reform, the government emphasized the importance of teachers' continuous professional development (CPD) and encouraged teachers to participate in a wide range of CDP activities, such as school-based co-planning and the peer review of lessons, cross-school seminars and conferences. School-based action research was also highly recommended to help teachers to work collaboratively in reviewing and reflecting on their instructional problems for the improvement of teaching and learning (Au, 2004).

Traditionally, Hong Kong teachers have not had a culture of engaging in an enquiry approach to teaching and learning. Researchers have pointed out that the idea of action research has not been well received in Hong Kong because of constraints such as the legacy of the colonial administration, cultural factors and epistemological restrictions (Li et al., 1999). In the reform era, the concepts of lifelong learning, whole-person development and school-based action research have been gradually promoted with the aim of empowering teachers to improve student learning (CDC, 2000). Although Hong Kong teachers are not used to conducting action research, the demands of the reform have driven some schools to adopt this approach. With support from some government sections (such as the School-Based Curriculum Development [SBCD] Section) and university–school partnership schemes (such as the Catering for Individual Differences—Building on Variation project, which uses a collaborative model of research where a university team works closely with school teachers to improve pupils' learning), action research has begun to take root in some schools (Au, 2004).

Among the various kinds of school-based action research models, Learning Study, which was developed indigenously by a research team (most of the members of which came from a local teacher education institution) around 2000, was embraced by the education community in Hong Kong and has since been applied in more than 200 primary and secondary schools (more than one-fifth of the total number of local schools) (Lo, 2009b). Learning Study is a systematic process of enquiry into classroom teaching and learning that uses an action research methodology and has the improvement of classroom teaching and student learning as its core. The following section takes a closer look at the Learning Study approach to understand its development in Hong Kong, its implementation at the classroom level and its effect on classroom teaching.

THE LEARNING STUDY APPROACH TO
CLASSROOM REFORM IN HONG KONG

The development of Learning Study is related to Japanese lesson study, which is a professional teacher activity that has a long history in Japan (Ko, 2007; Watanabe, 2002). The lesson study model brings together groups of teachers

120   Po-Yuk Ko

to jointly plan a lesson, observe the lesson being taught in actual classrooms and then evaluate and reflect in a post-lesson meeting. The approach was made famous by Stigler and Hiebert (1999) in their book *The Teaching Gap*, which attributed the excellent performance of Japanese students to this culture. Lesson study has since spread rapidly throughout the United States (Puchner and Taylor, 2006) and other places such as Singapore and Indonesia (Lewis, 2002; Fernandez, 2002; Sarkar Arani and Matoba, 2005; Lim et al., 2011). Researchers suggest that lesson study is a possible model of teacher professional development activity that can be adopted worldwide for the ongoing improvement of instruction (Lewis, Perry and Hurd, 2004; Rock and Wilson, 2005; Lewis, Perry and Murata, 2006; Lieberman, 2009; Lim et al., 2011).

The Hong Kong research team agreed with the spirit of the lesson study approach, which emphasizes teachers working collaboratively on classroom instruction to improve lessons. However, they believed that the model could be enhanced with a learning theory to serve as a conceptual framework for planning and evaluating lessons. The team thus developed the lesson study approach by adding a theoretical framework based on Variation Theory developed by Ference Marton in Sweden (Marton and Booth, 1997). The research team called this kind of study 'Learning Study' to reflect the critical feature of the approach being informed by a particular learning theory.

The new approach was first tested in a three-year project funded by the Hong Kong government in 2000 (Lo, Pong and Chik, 2005). Through several university–school partnership projects supported by various sources of government funding, the research team has supported more than 200 local primary and secondary schools to conduct Learning Study, and has completed about 300 Learning Study cases in various subject areas (Lo, 2009b). The approach has had a considerable influence on both students and teachers' learning and on the school culture. For instance, a three-year project entitled Variation for Improvement of Teaching and Learning (VITAL) in which 120 schools participated in Learning Study between 2005 and 2008 showed that in more than half of the cases, classes taught in the final cycle showed the greatest improvement in the post-test, demonstrating that lesson plans had been refined and the teaching improved during the process. In many cases, students generally showed improvement after the research lessons, but the poorest performing group was able to catch up with the best performing group in the pre- and post-test comparison, indicating that the performance gap between the high and low achievers had been reduced (Lo, Pong and Chik, 2005; Lo, Hung and Chik, 2007). In many other cases conducted by the research team, it was similarly found that Learning Study helped teachers to make use of Variation Theory in their own teaching, strengthen their subject matter knowledge and pedagogical skills, improve the way in which they assessed learning and the effectiveness of their lessons, understand the importance of action research as a reflective process, stimulate their reflective ability and increase their sensitivity to students' learning difficulties and needs. Teachers also adopted the conceptual framework of Variation Theory as a basis for collaborative lesson planning after

The project had finished (Elliott and Yu, 2008, pp.171). Essentially, Learning Study promotes collaboration in schools and provides opportunities for teachers to learn in a community of practice to help students to learn better, which in turn supports teachers' professional development (Cheng, 2009; Cheng and Ko, 2012).

Theoretical Framework of Learning Study

Many initiatives promoted during the reform momentum in Hong Kong have emphasized the 'how' aspect, or the arrangement of classroom activities and teaching strategies (e.g., collaborative learning, Small Class Teaching [SCT]). The Learning Study approach, in contrast, premised as it is on Variation Theory, aims to help students to develop an in-depth understanding of the content being taught, and thus gives the 'what' aspect more serious consideration at the outset and throughout the process. The theory looks at learners' experience of the object of learning (i.e., what the learners are expected to learn) and the discernment of the critical features of the object of learning. The theory suggests that to discern the critical features of a particular object of learning, one must experience the variation among them (Marton and Booth, 1997). The theory also argues that teaching effectiveness is not directly related to the classroom setting (large or small classes, whole-class or small group learning) or the teaching strategies (direct teaching, co-operative learning), but is rather related to how the content is handled in the class and the 'pattern of variation' presented in the lessons. A 'pattern of variation' means varying certain critical aspects of the object of learning while keeping other aspects invariant to enable students to discern the critical aspects.

In terms of implementation, the Learning Study approach is very much in line with the spirit of the reform, which advocates teachers working in collaboration and taking an enquiry approach to teaching. Most Learning Study groups comprise teachers teaching the same subject at the same level, usually from the same participating school, and two or more other members (researchers or academics with expertise in the subject and the Learning Study methodology). Each Learning Study project is developed as a case study in its own right, and the process is designed as a tight 'procedural package' that includes planning, implementation, the refining of a research lesson and examination of the pre- and post-test results (Elliott and Yu, 2008). Each case study takes an average of about 10 to 12 meetings, usually held over a six-month period.

The approach emphasizes evidence-based student learning outcomes, and thus data such as the pre- and post-test results of students, videotaped research lessons, team meetings and students' sample interviews are carefully collected and analyzed to understand the results of the research lessons. The approach also values reflection, and all the participants (including teachers and researchers) reflect on all aspects of the process, from planning to implementation to assessment. The research team publicly reports the study through either seminars or booklets as a means of reflection and dissemination.

122   Po-Yuk Ko

CASE OF A LEARNING STUDY PROJECT

The following case illustrates how lessons and student learning were improved through a Learning Study project. Five teachers in the Chinese department of a secondary school worked with two researchers from a tertiary institute as a team to conduct the case.

The lesson was a secondary 1 (grade 7) Chinese Language lesson and the topic was 'writing the opening paragraph in expository writing'. The teachers chose this topic because they found that their students had difficulty in writing the opening paragraph in expository writing. After a literature search, the team identified a commonly used organizational pattern for an opening paragraph that comprises three main components: 'introduction', 'topic raising' and 'transition' (Wong, 1999). The 'introduction' provides the background to the main content, 'topic raising' directly relates to the title of the writing and 'transition' serves as the link to the paragraphs that follow. After several meetings, the team developed a plan for a one-hour lesson with the following sequence.

1. The teacher showed an article entitled 'The Fifty-Year History of Disneyland' with no opening paragraph and prompted the students to guess what message was missing (10 minutes).
2. The teacher explained the three-component organizational pattern ('introduction', 'topic raising', and 'transition') (10 minutes).
3. The students were asked to talk to their neighbours and complete the missing opening paragraph of the essay by choosing from some paragraphs written on paper strips prepared by the teacher and then to discuss their choices (15 minutes).
4. The teacher discussed the appropriateness of the different optional paragraphs with the whole class (15 minutes).
5. Group work: the students worked in a group of four to write an opening paragraph for an article on the topic 'The Thirty-Year History of Ocean Park' (15 minutes).
6. De-briefing: samples of the students' work were chosen to show on a projector for the whole class to comment on (10 minutes).

This plan was taught to five classes, with lesson observation, evaluation and refinement after each cycle of teaching.

The Intended and Enacted Pattern of Variation

Variation Theory was used as the guiding principle to develop the lesson plan and as a tool to evaluate and refine the research lessons. The lesson plan essentially incorporated the following three patterns of variation.

The Impact of the Learning Study Approach on Chinese Classrooms   123

1. To help students to become aware of the importance of the opening paragraph, an article with no opening paragraph (the variant) was shown to provide a contrast to a complete version of the same essay (the invariant).
2. To help students to become aware of the appropriateness of the different components of an opening paragraph, they were asked to choose the correct options for the 'topic raising' and 'transition' components and arrange them in order. The 'title' and 'introduction' components were invariant, and the options and combinations of the components 'topic raising' and 'transition' varied.
3. Different opening paragraphs (the variant) written by students for the same essay (the invariant) were compared and contrasted.

The five classes followed closely the plan in the classroom enactment. However, after the third cycle of teaching and the analysis of the results of the post-tests of three of the classes, the team found that the second intended pattern of variation had not been efficiently enacted, as reflected by the undesirable student response from classroom observation and the limited improvement in student performance in the post-tests (see Table 8.1). In the first three cycles, the students had to choose the optional paragraphs and discuss their appropriateness in the third and fourth activities. When the students selected the correct component, the teacher immediately removed the alternative without contrasting the different options. As the teachers in the first three cycles were concerned about time, the discussion focused only on the correct options. The 'incorrect' options were not mapped with the original text for the students to discuss their inappropriateness. The team found that without this contrast (the variation), the students did not have the opportunity to ponder the different combinations of options provided and hence did not experience sufficient variation.

Changes were subsequently made for the fourth cycle so that when the students made their choice, the teacher, rather than removing the alternative, posted it on the other side of the blackboard and asked the students to explain why the chosen option was better than the alternative. The same change was made when dealing with the third component. The following lesson episodes from the fourth cycle have been selected to illustrate the actual teaching enactment.

   T: Teacher S: Students

T: Now we have two options for each group, B1, B2 and C1, C2. Please choose the one from each group that you feel appropriate to form part of the first paragraph. I will give you five seconds to read them [*the whole class reads in silence*].
            B1: 'Let me introduce you to the best places in the park.'
            B2: 'Let us review the history of Disneyland.'
            C1: 'Disneyland already has a fifty-year history!'

124   *Po-Yuk Ko*

> C2: *'Disneyland is one of the top ten "must go" theme parks!'*

T: Please raise your hand if you choose B1 . . . how about B2? All of you choose B2. I will ask you later why you chose B2. Now look at part C . . . C1 and C2, which one will you choose? Those who choose C1, please raise your hand . . . and C2? It is 50–50, there is no consensus.

T: Let us look at part B first. Why did all of you choose B2? Peter?

S (Peter): I chose part B because it talks about Disney's history.

T: Right, it talks about history and it corresponds to what?

S (Peter): It corresponds to the first paragraph.

T: This [B2] actually is part of the first paragraph.

S (Peter): It corresponds to the topic.

T: Right, it [*pointing to B2*] corresponds to the topic. That is why all of you chose this answer . . . How about B1, why it is not appropriate . . . Jenny?

S (Jenny): It talks about the best places in the park . . . which is not about the history.

T: So . . .

S (Jenny): So it does not correspond to the topic.

T: Exactly! Good!

Although almost the whole class chose the B2 option, the teacher did not immediately take away B1 but instead prompted students to ponder why B1 was not an appropriate option. The students were led to contrast the correct and incorrect options. The teacher then led the class to discuss the choice of C1 and C2.

T: Then, part C . . . C1 and C2 . . . half and half . . . I want to first ask why you chose C2? Those who chose C2 . . . Lancy, what did you choose?

S (Lancy): C2.

T: Why did you choose C2?

S (Lancy): I chose C2 because it talked about Disneyland, which is very important.

T: In terms of the importance [of the part], why . . . what is mentioned in C1 that is not important?

S (whole class): This [the content of C1] has been mentioned previously.

T: Mm . . . this [the content of C1] has been mentioned previously. Let us do it this way—we will first use C1 to form a paragraph and then we will come back to C2.

T: Now we have A, B2 and C1, how should we arrange these three parts [to form a complete paragraph]? I will give you a worksheet that has the different parts printed on it so that you can read them carefully and then make your decision.

T: Fanny, in what order did you arrange the paragraphs?

The Impact of the Learning Study Approach on Chinese Classrooms 125

S *(Fanny):* A, then C1, then B2.

T: A, C1 and then B2 . . . Are there any other suggestions? Maybe we should read it out and see if the meaning is complete and the paragraph reads smoothly.

S: [*the whole class reads the paragraph aloud*]

      'Mickey Mouse, Peter Pan, the Little Mermaid, Donald Duck and Sleeping Beauty—can you guess where we can find all of these classical cartoon characters? Right, the answer is Disneyland—the wonderful dreamland.'

      'Disneyland already has a fifty-year history!' (C1)

      'Let us review the history of Disneyland.' (B2)

T: Okay, remember that half of the class chose the other option [C2] . . . Let us replace C1 with C2 and read it aloud.

      'Mickey Mouse, Peter Pan, the Little Mermaid, Donald Duck, and Sleeping Beauty—can you guess where we can find all of these classical cartoon characters? Right, the answer is Disneyland—the wonderful dreamland.'

      'Disneyland is one of the top ten "must go" theme parks!' (C2)

      'Let us review the history of Disneyland.' (B2)

T: So, we did not change the order of the three parts, but we replaced them with another option . . . What do you think?

S *(Fanny):* It does not read smoothly.

T: Why?

S *(Fanny):* It does not read smoothly because the whole article should introduce the history.

T: And the replacement of this makes it very odd, right?

S *(Lancy):* It does not seem consistent.

T: Which part is not consistent?

S: This [C2] is not about the history [of Disneyland].

T: That is why the answer should be C1. Let us give a round of applause to those who chose C1.

Rather than comparing the two options alone, the teacher asked the class to put one of the choices (the correct one, C1) together with the other two component parts to form a complete paragraph and then discussed the sequence of the three parts. After the students had decided upon the sequence, the teacher asked the class to replace C1 with C2 to see whether this option matched the other two parts to form a coherent paragraph. In this revised lesson, the class spent more time discussing the appropriateness of the different components and the correct sequence, which opened up the patterns of variation for them.

Before the lesson, the students sat a pre-test in which they were asked to write an opening paragraph on a given topic. The same test was then administered after the lessons to compare their performance. The pre- and post-test comparison indicated that the five classes that participated in the

126 *Po-Yuk Ko*

Table 8.1 Pre and Post-Test Comparison of the Number of Students Using the Three Components of 'Introduction', 'Topic Raising' and 'Transition' in the Opening Paragraph at the Same Time

	Pre-Test	*Post-Test*	*% Change*
1st cycle: 1D	4.9%	43.9%	39
2nd cycle: 1F	0%	25%	25
3rd cycle: 1B	15.8%	47%	31.2
4th cycle: 1E	0%	58.8%	58.8
5th cycle: 1A	14.3%	69%	54.7

project all showed an improvement in their ability to make use of all three components in writing the opening paragraph, as shown in Table 8.1. However, remarkable improvement was observed from the fourth cycle onward, which featured the revision and followed Variation Theory more closely.

DISCUSSION

The Learning Study approach was developed during the reform momentum in Hong Kong, when various innovative pedagogical approaches were being promoted. Distinct from most of the initiatives that emphasize the arrangement of classroom activities and teaching strategies, the Learning Study approach pays particular attention to the object of learning or the content that is intended to be learnt by students. Learning Study takes the object of learning as the point of departure and does not mandate any particular teaching strategy. However, the approach does not neglect the importance of teaching strategies. As illustrated by the foregoing case, appropriate teaching strategies (such as group work) can help bring about the intended pattern of variation to provide maximum opportunity for students to learn the content. The use of appropriate teaching arrangements to achieve the intended patterns of variation relies strongly on teachers' judgement, which is why the approach values teachers' collective effort and timely reflection on their teaching.

On the surface, the pedagogical features of classroom teaching in the case presented here seem not to meet the rhetorical characterizations of 'progressive' pedagogy that emphasize maximum student participation, as the research lesson contained many episodes of whole-class teaching and the teacher was very much in control of the classroom activities. However, nor do the characteristics of the research lesson fit the stereotyped portrayal of the conservative Chinese classroom dominated by didactic teaching and rote learning. The commonly used labels, such as 'teacher-centred' or 'student-centred', are insufficient to capture the characteristics of the research lesson, as the majority of whole-class teaching episodes consisted of teacher–pupil or pupil–pupil interactions. The students were highly active, but at the same time the lesson was well controlled. Task-based learning (TBL) and group work were used for about a third of the lesson. The lesson was not dictated by textbooks, as the materials were tailor-made by the teachers. The case illustrates features of a typical research lesson generated by the Learning Study approach, in that it was guided by Variation Theory and was well structured and choreographed but still provided plenty of opportunities for student participation. More importantly, by adopting a powerful learning theory, the students' focal awareness was directed to the intended object of learning, giving them the maximum opportunity to learn.

The case demonstrates that lessons can be gradually improved to give better students' performance when a sound theory is used as the guiding principle for designing and revising the lessons. The results of other Learning Study cases conducted by the research team also identified an immediate positive effect on students' learning, and in some cases a sustained positive effect on students' learning (Lo, 2009a). With numerous case studies and evidence-based results of student learning outcomes showing that the Learning Study approach obtains demonstrable results, the approach has become one of the most popular initiatives promoted by the reform. Learning Study as a kind of action research has also proved to be beneficial to teacher professional development. The teachers who participated in the case were particularly impressed to see that the change implemented from the fourth cycle onward, which was guided by Variation Theory, had a marked effect on the students' learning. They became convinced of the usefulness of the theory and acquired the conceptual lens of making use of a pattern of variation as a guiding principle of pedagogical design. In many other cases conducted by the research team, the teachers underwent permanent changes in mind-set or attitude after taking part in the Learning Study project, becoming more sensitive to students' learning difficulties and needs. The approach also stimulated their reflective ability and promoted a collaborative culture amongst the teachers in their schools (Elliott and Yu, 2008).

CONCLUSION

Education reforms that aim to foster large and systemic change in schools have become a prominent feature in many parts of the world in recent decades. The complex and comprehensive nature of education reform has not only changed the context in which teachers work but has also created a wider gap between central decision makers and front-line teachers. Translating the new ideas recommended in reform agenda into actual classroom practice is a huge challenge for educators. Hence, researchers argue that "if we want to improve teaching, the most effective place to do so is in the context of a classroom lesson" (Stigler and Hiebert, 1999, pp.111). The

128 *Po-Yuk Ko*

Learning Study approach is an initiative developed in the reform era in Hong Kong that has now been practiced for nearly a decade and has been embraced by the educational field, largely because of its focus on classroom practice and its positive effect on student learning, teacher learning and school culture (Lo, Pong and Chik, 2005; Ko, 2007; Lee, 2008; Gao and Ko, 2009; Cheng, 2009; Cheng and Ko, 2012). Hong Kong students, together with students in other Asian cities, have performed well in recent international assessment exercises, such as TIMMS and the PISA (HKPISA Centre, 2011). One of the main features of their outstanding academic performance is their emphasis on effort to achieve academic success, which originates from the Confucian tradition. However, the effect of some of the initiatives of the education reform in the past decade, and in particular those that have focused on classroom practice and teachers' professional development, may also have contributed to the improvement in the performance of Hong Kong students.

It is always challenging for educational initiatives to be applied at different scales and to endure. Whether teachers are able to continue to apply the new knowledge learned in the Learning Study approach or whether they regress to a traditional pedagogical routine will determine the ultimate success or failure of the initiative. The continued support of the government and the academic field is one of the keys to success, yet funding from government bodies often fluctuates because of changes in reform agenda item over time and the preference of policymakers for 'innovation' and new ideas. The Learning Study approach, which has now been practiced for more than a decade, is facing the challenge of its sustainability. Fortunately, the approach has already been incorporated into teaching education programmes in Hong Kong for nurturing both pre-service and in-service teachers (Ko, 2012). It has also attracted the attention of educators in Mainland China, and some schools in Beijing and Shenzhen are trying out the approach. It is hoped that the approach will be further disseminated and developed to make a sustained positive effect on classroom practice in Hong Kong and elsewhere.

REFERENCES

Au, Y.S. (2004). *Raising teachers' competence in action research*. Retrieved 25 August 2004, from http://content.edu.tw/primary/society/ks_ck/nine/n4.htm. (In Chinese)

Biggs, J.B. (1996). Western misperceptions of the Confucian-heritage learning culture. In D.A. Watkins & J.B. Biggs (Eds.) *The Chinese learner: Cultural, psychological and contextual influences* (pp.45–67). Hong Kong: Comparative Education Research Centre.

Cheng, C.K. (2009). Cultivating communities of practice via Learning Study for enhancing teacher learning. *KEDI Journal of Educational Policy, 6*(1), 81–104.

Cheng, C.K.E., & Ko, P.Y. (2012). Leadership strategies for creating a Learning Study community. *Journal of Educational Policy, 9*(1), 163–182.

The Impact of the Learning Study Approach on Chinese Classrooms 129

Cleverley, J. (1991). *The schooling of China*. North Sydney, NSW: Allen and Unwin.

Cortazzi, M. (1998). Learning from Asian lessons: Cultural experience and classroom talk. *Education 3 to 13, 26*(2), 42–49.

Cortazzi, M., & Jin, L. (2001). Large classes in China: 'Good' teachers and interaction. In D. A. Watkins & J.B. Biggs (Eds.) *Teaching the Chinese learner: Psychological and pedagogical perspectives* (pp.115–134). Hong Kong: Comparative Education Research Centre of the University of Hong Kong.

Curriculum Development Council (2000). *Learning to learn: The way forward in curriculum development: Consultation document*. Hong Kong: Curriculum Development Council.

Education Commission (2000). *Reform proposals for the education system in Hong Kong*. Hong Kong: Government Printer.

Elliott, J., & Yu, C. (2008). *Learning studies as an educational change strategy in Hong Kong. An independent evaluation of the 'Variation for the Improvement of Teaching and Learning' (VITAL) project*. Hong Kong: School Partnership and Field Experience Office, Hong Kong Institute of Education.

Fernandez, C. (2002). Learning from Japanese approaches to professional development: The case of Lesson Study. *Journal of Teacher Education, 53*(5), 393–405.

Gao, X., & Ko, P.Y. (2009). Learning study for primary school English teachers: A case story from Hong Kong. *Changing English, 16*(4), 397–404.

HKPISA Centre (2011). *The fourth HKPISA report PISA 2009 executive summary*. Hong Kong: HKPISA Centre, Chinese University of Hong Kong.

Ko, P.Y. (2007). Interpreting differences in learning in terms of differences in the pattern of variation and invariance in teaching: The Hong Kong Learning Study. *Journal of the Nagoya University, 3*, 1–15.

Ko, P.Y. (2012). Critical conditions for pre-service teachers' learning through inquiry—the Learning Study approach in Hong Kong. *International Journal for Lesson and Learning Studies, 1*(1), 49–64.

Lee, J.F.K. (2008). A Hong Kong case of lesson study—benefits and concerns. *Teaching and Teacher Education, 24*(5), 1115–1124.

Lee, W.O. (1996). The cultural context for Chinese learners: Conceptions of learning in the Confucian tradition. In D.A. Watkins & J.B. Biggs (Eds.) *The Chinese learner: Cultural, psychological and contextual influences* (pp.25–42). Hong Kong: Comparative Education Research Centre.

Leung, Y.M.J. (1991). Curriculum development in the People's Republic of China. In C. Marsh & P. Morris (Eds.) *Curriculum development in East Asia* (pp.61–81). Bristol: Falmer Press.

Lewis, C. (2002). Does lesson study have a future in the United States? *Nagoya Journal of Education and Human Development, 1*, 1–23.

Lewis, C., Perry, R., & Hurd, J. (2004). A deeper look at lesson study. *Educational Leadership, 61*(5), 18–23.

Lewis, C., Perry, R., & Murata, A. (2006). How should research contribute to instructional improvement? The case of lesson study. *Educational Researcher, 35*(3), 3–14.

Li, W.S., Yu, W.M., Lam, T.S., & Fok, P.K. (1999). The lack of action research: The case for Hong Kong. *Educational Action Research, 7*(1), 33–50.

Lieberman, J. (2009). Reinventing teacher professional norms and identities: The role of lesson study and learning communities. *Professional Development in Education, 35*(1), 83–99.

Lim, C., Lee, C., Saito, E., & Haron, S.S. (2011). Taking stock of lesson study as a platform for teacher development in Singapore. *Asia-Pacific Journal of Teacher Education, 39*(4), 353–365.

Lo, M.L. (2009a). The development of the Learning Study approach in classroom research in Hong Kong. *Educational Research Journal, 24*(1), 165–184.

130   *Po-Yuk Ko*

Lo, M.L. (2009b). The Learning Study—a framework for enhancing school-university collaboration that focuses upon individual lessons. In D. Boorer, J.S.H. Quintus Perera, K. Wood, S.P. Loo & S. Sithamparam (Eds.) Evolving Pedagogies: Meeting the Global Challenges of Diversity and Interdependence (pp.162–181). Brunei: Universiti Brunei Darussalam.

Lo, M.L., Hung, H.H.Y., & Chik, P.P.M. (2007). Improving teaching and learning through a Learning Study: Using patterns of variation to teach electro-chemical series in Hong Kong. *Curriculum Perspectives, 27*(3), 49–62.

Lo, M.L., Pong, W.Y., & Chik, P.P.M. (Eds.) (2005). *For each and everyone: Catering for individual differences through Learning Studies.* Hong Kong: Hong Kong University Press.

Ma, L. (1999). *Knowing and teaching elementary mathematics.* London: Lawrence Erlbaum.

Marton, F., & Booth, S. (1997). *Learning and awareness.* Mahwah, NJ: Lawrence Erlbaum.

Mok, A.C.I., & Ko, P.Y. (2003). Beyond labels: Teacher-centred and pupil-centred activities. In P.G. Stimpson, P. Morris, Y. Fung & R. Carr (Eds.) *Curriculum, learning and assessment: The Hong Kong experience* (pp.307–328). Hong Kong: Open University of Hong Kong.

Morris, P., Kan, F., & Morris, E. (2000). Education, civic participation and identity: Continuity and change in Hong Kong. *Cambridge Journal of Education, 30*(2), 243–262.

Morris, P., & Marsh, C. (1992). Curriculum patterns and issues in East Asia: A comparative survey of seven East Asian societies. *Journal of Education Policy, 7*(3), 252–266.

Paine, L.W. (1990). The teacher as virtuoso: A Chinese model for teaching. *Teachers College Record, 92*(1), 49–81.

Paine, L.W., & Fang, Y.P. (2006). Reform as a hybrid model of teaching and teacher development in China. *International Journal of Educational Research, 45,* 279–280.

Pong, W.Y., & Chow, J.C.S. (2002). On the pedagogy of examination in Hong Kong. *Teaching and Teacher Education, 18,* 139–149.

Poon, A.Y.K., & Wong, Y.C. (2008). Policy changes and impact of the education reform in Hong Kong. *Journal of National Taiwan Normal University: Education, 53*(3), 47–65. (In Chinese)

Puchner, L.D., & Taylor, A.R. (2006). Lesson study, collaboration and teacher efficacy: Stories from two school-based math lesson study groups. *Teaching and Teacher Education, 22*(7), 922–934.

Rock, T.C., & Wilson, C. (2005). Improving teaching through Lesson Study. *Teacher Education Quarterly, 32*(1), 77–92.

Sarkar Arani, M.R., & Matoba, M. (2005). Japanese approach to improving instruction through school-based in-service teacher training. *Comparative Education in Teacher Training, 3,* 59–63.

Stevenson, W., & Lee, S. (1997). The East Asian version of whole-class teaching. In W.K. Cumming & P.G. Altback (Eds.) *The challenge of Eastern Asian education* (pp.33–49). Albany: State University of New York Press.

Stigler, J., & Hiebert, J. (1999). *The teaching gap: Best ideas from the world's teachers for improving education in the classroom.* New York: Free Press.

Watanabe, T. (2000). Learning from Japanese lesson study. *Educational Leadership, 59*(6), 36–39.

Watkins, D.A., & Biggs, J.B. (2001). The paradox of the Chinese learner and beyond. In D.A. Watkins & J.B. Biggs (Eds.) *Teaching the Chinese learner: Psychological and pedagogical perspectives* (pp.3–23). Hong Kong: Comparative Education Research Centre.

Wong, X. (1999). *Examples of paragraphs and essays.* Beijing: Capital Normal University Press. (In Chinese)

Yang, Y. (2009). How a Chinese teacher improved classroom teaching in teaching research group: A case study on Pythagoras theorem teaching in Shanghai. *Mathematics Education, 41,* 279–296.

9 Small Class Teaching in Hong Kong
Seizing The Opportunities

Kwok-Chan Lai, Kam-Wing Chan and John Chi-Kin Lee

INTRODUCTION

Educators generally regard reduction of class sizes or Small Class Teaching (SCT) as a key factor in enhancing the quality of education. Nevertheless, policymakers are more often concerned with the financial affordability and cost-effectiveness of reducing class sizes. In this regard, class size reduction has often been a controversial issue in many countries (Blatchford and Lai, 2010). This controversy has been very noticeable in Hong Kong in the past decade in the context of a sharp decline in school enrolment and school closure. After years of hot debate, the government has decided to implement SCT in public sector primary schools with a standard class size of 25 pupils, starting from primary 1 in the 2009–2010 school year. Various types of teachers' professional development courses and school-based support projects, as well as learning circles within and across schools, have been organized to enhance the effectiveness of teaching and learning in small class environments. In addition, there have been an increasing number of professional exchanges with other cities in the greater China region which are implementing SCT. These developments have gradually led to a positive change in primary education, as well as professional growth of principals and teachers. In this chapter, we first review the contextual factors affecting the development of class size policies in Hong Kong, followed by an introduction of two case studies of schools which have made use of SCT as a facilitating condition to bring about school revival and improvement. The opportunities and challenges of implementing SCT are then discussed.

CLASS SIZE POLICIES IN HONG KONG 1950–2000

After World War II, the development of the education system in Hong Kong has undergone three main stages (Ip and Lai, 2004). The first stage was the expansion of basic education from the post-war period to the early 1980s. The second stage was between the early 1980s and 1997, during which the government began to pay more attention to the improvement of quality of education, including reduction of class size. The third stage started after the resumption of Chinese sovereignty in 1997, when the new Hong Kong Special Administrative Region (SAR) government begun to implement a large-scale reform of the education system. By coincidence, this third phase has witnessed an unprecedented and continual decline of student enrolment, which has led to heated debates in the society on whether SCT should be implemented.

First Stage: Expansion of Basic Education

From the 1950s to the 1970s, the government's primary concern was to provide enough school places to achieve universal education—the milestones being the implementation of free and compulsory education at the primary level in 1971 and at the junior secondary level in 1978, respectively. During this period of expansion, the government had adopted a low-cost and high-efficiency model in response to rapid population growth and limited government resources. For instance, the maximum class size in public sector schools was maintained at 45. Most of the primary schools were bi-sessional in order to accommodate more students.

The Second Stage: Improving the Quality of Education

Towards the end of 1970s, population growth had slowed down and the society had become better off. Under these circumstances, the government had shifted its focus from provision of school places to improving the quality of education. Hence the reduction of class size in public sector schools was on the policy agenda, which had gradually taken place in the 1980s and 1990s.

In 1981, a government white paper on *Primary Education and Pre-Primary Services* stated that "in view of the availability of adequate school places in the public sector, the time has come to reduce the maximum class size" (Hong Kong Government, 1981, para. 2.16). It was intended that, with effect from the primary 1 entry of 1983, the standard class size would be reduced by five pupils, that is, no class in the public sector should exceed 40. Furthermore, schools adopting the Activity Approach (AA) would be permitted to reduce their class size to 35. Nevertheless, the legal maximum class size of 45 would remain unchanged.

In 1982, the government commissioned an Organisation for Economic Co-operation and Development (OECD) panel to review the education system of Hong Kong. In its influential report, titled *A Perspective on Education in Hong Kong* (Llewellyn, 1982), the panel observed that "most of the schools we visited were spartan to say the least, with pupils filling the entire room—40 to 45 per class" (para. 3.4.16). It further cautioned that "class sizes [in Hong Kong] are extremely large by OECD standards and this

134   Kwok-Chan Lai, Kam-Wing Chan and John Chi-Kin Lee

inhibits any teaching style other than lecture or whole group tuition" (para. 3.4.5). The panel's criticisms had lent support to the recommendations of the white paper to reduce class sizes. Interestingly, it also emphasized that the benefits of class size reduction would only be maximized with changes in pedagogy, and teachers' professional development was essential.

> The experience of OECD nations regarding the benefits of expanding the number of teachers in order simply to reduce class size is instructive. While a strong case can be made for substantial reductions in pupil–teacher ratios, the large outlays involved in financing such a policy will only be worthwhile if teachers are willing and able to work differently with their fewer pupils. There is little to be gained by teaching 30 pupils in the same way as 40 might be taught. At present, teachers in Hong Kong have little opportunity to experiment with flexible small group techniques because their classrooms are packed and the physical facilities are not conducive. In order to capitalise on the potentially high-yield investment in class size reduction, resources must be allocated simultaneously to allow for in-service activities to help teachers adapt their teaching styles to this situation. (pp.87–88)

The government also accepted the panel's recommendation to set up a key advisory body, the Education Commission (EC). The EC had produced seven reports from 1984 to 1996, covering various policy issues, such as professionalization of teaching, medium of instruction (MOI), language teaching and assessment. In particular, the EC report no. 5 (ECR5) in 1992 recommended that, in view of the declining enrolment, the school environment should be improved by a substantial reduction of class size starting from September 1997:

> Having considered the opportunity provided by the reduction in enrolment, the possible constraints of accommodation and teacher supply, and the trend in other places with highly developed economies, we have concluded that a firm goal should now be set for achieving smaller standard class sizes. We therefore *recommend* a reduction in the standard class size of five places at each level from P1 to S5, to be achieved in phase with reductions in enrolment. (EC, 1992, p.32)

In 1992, the new governor, Chris Patten, unexpectedly announced in his first policy address that the ECR5 target would be advanced by five years, that is, the number of students would be progressively reduced, starting from primary 1 in 1993–1994 (Chan, 1994). In other words, the standard class size of all primary classes would be decreased from 40 to 35 for the traditional classes, and from 35 to 30 for the AA classes in the 1998–1999 school year. The reduction in Form 1–5 of secondary schools would follow, and the number of students would be reduced from 40 to 35 by the

2003–2004 school year. With the above policies, the average class size in conventional approach classes and AA classes in primary schools had dropped from to 36 and 32.1 in 1992–1993 to 34.5 and 30.2 in 1997–1998, respectively (Education and Manpower Bureau [EMB], 2002).

Class size reduction had widespread support of the education community. A research commissioned by the Board of Education (Board of Education, Sub-Committee on Review of School Education, 1997) reported that "both primary school teachers and secondary school teachers ranked 'reducing class size' as the top most effective measure (out of 33 given ones) to achieve the aims of 9–year compulsory education". The board also recognized "class size as an important factor in promoting effective learning", and commented that "improvements can be seen more readily if priority of class size reduction is given to schools with a high percentage of children with emotional and behavioural difficulties or pupils with weak academic performance" (para. 6.44).

The Third Stage: Large-Scale Education Reform

After the founding of the HKSAR in 1997, the first chief executive, Tung Chee-hwa, had given a high priority to education in his policy address. He requested the EC conduct a comprehensive review of the education system (Tung, 1997). The government also sped up the implementation of whole-day primary schooling, with a target to enable 60% of primary school students to study in whole-day schools by the 2002–2003 school year and all of them by 2007–2008. To cope with the financial burden of building new schools, the government decided to increase the standard class size in primary schools by two students, starting with primary 1 in the 1998/99 school year. The measures for class size reduction in secondary schools were also suspended.

Furthermore, the EC (2000) queried the effects of class size on the quality of education, which was a reversal of its stand taken eight years ago in ECR5:

> There was also a proposal to allocate resources to reduce class size and raise the teacher-to-student ratio so as to lighten teachers' workload and to enable them to raise the effectiveness of learning and teaching. . . . The general teacher-to-student ratios in Hong Kong are 1:22 and 1:19 for primary and secondary schools respectively. These ratios compare favourably with our neighbours . . . It is evident that we cannot simply equate the teacher-to-student ratio with the quality of education. Besides, the number of students in each class does not only depend on the number of teaching staff, but also the physical conditions of schools. A large number of school premises would have to be erected if we were to significantly reduce the number of students in each class. Such a proposition will face great practical difficulties under present circumstances in Hong Kong. (pp.146–147)

136 *Kwok-Chan Lai, Kam-Wing Chan and John Chi-Kin Lee*

The reform proposals of the EC (2000) stated that the priority of education in the 21st century should be to "enable our students to enjoy learning, enhance their effectiveness in communication and develop their creativity and sense of commitment" (p.4). In the following year, the curriculum reform document further elaborated that the overarching principle of curriculum development was "to help students learn how to learn" and a learner-focused approach should be adopted (CDC, 2001). Hence, the decision to increase class size was incompatible with the aims of the education reform which emphasized the importance of student-centred learning and the "no loser" principle.

THE CLASS SIZE DEBATE

Since 2000, Hong Kong has experienced a rapid decline in birth rates and a decrease in the number of school-age students in primary schools. For instance, the fertility rate of Hong Kong in 2002 was only 959 per 1,000, compared with 1,320 in Japan and 1,340 in Taiwan, which was one of the lowest in the world. The student intake at primary 1 had also dropped by nearly 40% from 78,365 in 2000 to 49,917 in 2009. As such, the issues of teacher redundancy and school closure had become very serious. Many educators regarded that the decrease in school-age population had allowed a "golden opportunity" for implementation of SCT to improve the quality of education. They perceived that, with the declining enrolment, the government could readily re-deploy the savings to SCT. The primary schools' councils also requested the government gradually revert the standard class size back to that of 1998–1999. In the Legislative Council, there were also debates on SCT, and many legislators commented positively on its value. The class size reduction policies in East Asia, notably Shanghai, which had pioneered the implementation of SCT in China since the early 1990s, were also frequently cited.

On the other hand, the EMB, now known as the Education Bureau (EDB), was very reluctant to reduce class sizes, which reflected not only a concern about financial viability but an overt scepticism of its effectiveness. In addition, local academics were also divided, with the opponents criticizing SCT as a "billion-dollar hoax" and accusing the teacher unions as really concerned about protecting teachers' jobs and not student learning. Amidst the heated debate, there was an extensive reference to the polarizing studies on class size effects by academics in Western countries. As the former secretary for education and manpower argued in a meeting of the Legislative Council (2002):

> "Class Size" is a highly controversial issue because of the inherent complex nature of the classroom as a place to construct knowledge. A lot of overseas educational research and experiences, which attempted to

establish a correlation between "Small Class Teaching" and enhancing the effectiveness of learning, have been inconclusive. Given the huge amount of resources involved, the cost-effectiveness of "Small Class Teaching" is also a point of contention . . . Some studies showed that teachers generally did not adjust their instructional methods to take advantage of the reduced class size. . . . From the perspective of cost-effectiveness, whether alternative measures (such as teachers' professional development, teaching assistants, and so on) could lead to similar benefits.

In this regard, SCT is probably the education policy in Hong Kong that has made most extensive reference to research literature. This intensive and politicized debate on SCT among the government, academics, the education community and the public had lasted for more than half a decade.

In what is widely perceived to be a delay tactic, the EMB decided to conduct its own research study on SCT with the purpose to "consider the issue thoroughly and rationally before making a decision on whether there is a need and, if so, how to implement 'Small Class Teaching'" (Legislative Council, 2002). In February 2004, it started to conduct a four-year experiment of SCT in 40 schools (37 schools finally joined), covering primary 1 and 2 students in the three school subjects of Chinese Language, English Language and Mathematics. Professor Maurice Galton of the University of Cambridge was commissioned to carry out the study.

Before the final report of the study was completed, the SCT policy had taken a U-turn in early 2007 during the election campaigns for the chief executive, with both candidates pledging their support for SCT in primary schools. The returning chief executive, Mr. Donald Tsang, finally announced the implementation of SCT in his 2007 policy address. The standard class size of primary schools would be reduced to 25 pupils by phases, starting from primary 1 in the 2009–2010 school year. More than 70% of the public sector primary schools have started to implement SCT.

SEIZING THE OPPORTUNITIES TO ENHANCE TEACHING AND LEARNING

While there were strong disagreements on the effects of SCT before its implementation in 2009–2010, there was a general agreement among the proponents and critics of SCT that teachers' professional development is crucial to its success. This had led to small-scale initiatives to support teachers' professional development, such as the forming of learning circles and partnerships on SCT, with the aim to make good use of the small class environment for enhancement of learning and teaching. For instance, the EMB had provided some professional support to the 37 schools joining its SCT Study. In addition, a few primary schools had experimented with SCT on a small scale in selected classes or school subjects, many with the support of the Centre for Development and Research in Small Class Teaching (CSCT) (now known as the Centre for Small Class Teaching) of the Hong Kong Institute of Education (HKIEd), which is the largest teacher education provider in Hong Kong (Lai and Ip, 2007). The CSCT also organized a wide range of professional development activities, including seminars and workshops as well as the annual Teachers' Development Days on SCT. It also initiated the building of collaborative partnerships among primary schools and fostered academic and professional exchange on SCT with cities in the greater China region. The topics of common interest included co-operative learning, catering for diversity and enhancing of school and classroom environments based on the principles of SCT. These early experiences have paved an important foundation for the more organized and government-resourced professional support activities after the implementation of SCT.

Following the implementation of SCT in 2009–2010, the EDB has been working in collaboration with tertiary institutions to organize teachers' professional development courses and building learning communities within and across schools, aiming to enhance the effectiveness of teaching and learning in small class environments. The SCT study has been influential, not so much in affecting the final policy decision but in steering EDB directives on teachers' professional development. In EDB's (2008) circular on SCT, it was remarked that:

> SCT should not simply involve a sheer reduction in class size. Schools should enhance the learning effectiveness of students by making good use of the classroom environment with a reduced class size. EDB will organize various professional development activities, including seminars, workshops, experience-sharing sessions, establishing partner schools on a district basis, and continuation of the school-based professional support services etc., so as to help teachers devise appropriate pedagogical strategies and apply different teaching modes in a small class teaching environment through theory learning, classroom practice and experience sharing etc.

In particular, the EDB has adopted the "six principles" recommended by Galton as a mandatory requirement for providers in designing and delivering of its commissioned courses:

> The professional development of teachers should be framed around six broad principles aimed at developing pupils' understanding, viz. (i) communicating learning goals to the class in terms of the learning process; (ii) providing more thinking time during questioning; (iii) boosting participation during class discussions; (iv) developing cooperation between pupils by pair/group work; (v) giving feedback which helps

Small Class Teaching in Hong Kong 139

pupils sort out their own mistakes; and (vi) using assessment to inform future instruction. (EDB, 2010)

According to Galton and Pell (2009), these six principles are underpinned by social constructivist theories of learning. They emphasized that it would be difficult for teachers to "implement pedagogic change of any kind" if they "do not have a grasp of the underlying theories which support the use of certain teaching approaches" (p.64). In professional support, teacher educators have taken the opportunity to relate SCT to the humanistic and constructivist theories of teaching and learning. The CSCT also selected school cases showing exemplary practices of SCT and published a compendium for distribution to schools (Ip et al., 2012).

If we view SCT as a platform or facilitating condition for enhancing learning and teaching, we may consider some basic issues for making SCT a success in schools. First, we need to enhance the school capacity, especially leadership in SCT. This refers to whether principals and teachers had firm beliefs about the values of SCT and whether they would work together to engage in curriculum and instructional improvement under the context of SCT. As the report of the SCT study revealed the school success factor (Legislative Council Panel on Education, 2010):

> While it was found that teachers felt more relaxed and enthusiastic when teaching a smaller class, it was worth noting that in schools with the most successful combined attitude and attainment profiles, principals were more experienced, held firmer beliefs in the value of SCT for improving pupil attainment and took a more active role in curriculum planning and teacher learning development. They also supported teachers by freeing them from lessons/duties for professional development. (p.4)

Another issue is how to make use of small class environment to tackle students' learning diversity, which becomes an acute challenge Hong Kong. As the above-mentioned compendium of teaching units in SCT reveals, many schools have attempted to cater for diversity through instructional design, fostering peer collaboration in pairs or groups, formative assessment and engaging teachers to reflect on their teaching strategies to cater for the needs of ethnic minorities (Ip et al., 2012).

In addition, the building of internal and external learning circles and collaborative partnerships are considered to be most important in the implementation of SCT:

> To facilitate teachers' paradigm shift in pedagogy, the approach of "Learning Circles" should be promoted for both inter-school sharing across subjects and intra-school sharing of pedagogical issues, which focuses at any one time on a specific aspects of pedagogy, allows

140 *Kwok-Chan Lai, Kam-Wing Chan and John Chi-Kin Lee*

teachers to observe and evaluate each other's classroom practice and thereby enhances the participants' professionalism. (EDB, 2010)

Two cases will be described below to illustrate how SCT can bring drastic changes to schools through the partnership of the HKIEd and the schools.

CASE 1

Lok Sin Tong Leung Wong Wai Fong Memorial School, established in 1983, is an aided primary school in the new town of Tuen Mun in northwest Hong Kong. Similar to many primary schools in the district, the school had suffered from under-enrolment since the 2000s because of the demographic decline in Hong Kong. In the 2008–2009 school year, the school was only able to admit seven students to primary 1, which was far below the minimum quota of 23 required by the EDB for a class to operate. As a temporary measure, the school had to inject its own funds to operate a primary 1 class. The situation was dire—if the school could not attract enough students to fulfil the minimum quota in the following school year, it would have to close down.

In September 2008, the school appointed Miss Ng, a former vice principal, to be the new principal. She was determined to revive the school by revisiting its mission and optimizing student learning through SCT. Three major strategies were adopted—establishing a caring school environment for the students, creating a classroom environment conducive to student learning and fostering teachers' development through institute–school partnership. After three years of strenuous efforts, the school's primary 1 intake has jumped to a total of 68 students, which were allocated to three classes. The achievement of the school has been recognized by external professional bodies, including the 2010 Inviting School Award presented by the International Alliance for Invitational Education. Its case has also been accepted to the Inventory of the Innovative Learning Environment Project conducted by the Centre for Educational Research and Innovation of the OECD (OECD, 2012).

Establishing a Caring School Environment for the Students

A majority of the school's students are under-privileged, being new immigrants from Mainland China or from single-parent families. They receive relatively less family care and are likely to drop out of school. In order to help these students continue their studies in the school, a number of programmes have been developed for the students during and after the school hours. These programmes include Reading Is Fun, tutorial classes and Caring Groups. Reading Is Fun is offered to students who need to come to school early as their parents have to work. Students can choose books of different interests to read before classes commence. In addition, at the end of a school day, a two-hour period is arranged for tutorial classes on academic and creative subjects. These activities give the students a family feel

Small Class Teaching in Hong Kong 141

and allow each of them work effectively to fulfil his or her potential in a happy and secure environment. To further develop a caring culture, more than 20 Caring Groups have also been set up. Each group consists of eight to ten mixed-age students and is led by a teacher. Different kinds of group activities are held once a month on Tuesday evenings. The group members can discuss the kind of activities they want to pursue with their friends and the teacher, for example, playing badminton, catching crabs at the beach and having a social gathering at a popular fast-food restaurant.

Creating a Classroom Environment Conducive to Student Learning

A number of targeted construction works for improving the school environment have been completed, including refurbishing the classrooms, building a distance learning classroom and a smart classroom, as well as establishing the Story Garden. The new and dynamic learning environment has nurtured the students' multi-faceted abilities in achieving a holistic development.

In order to provide an arena for catering learner diversity, each classroom is equipped with a mini performing stage and a reading corner. Students can perform on the stage or read books at the reading corner after they have finished their learning tasks. Old desks and chairs were replaced with new ones of different colours, which were grouped in fours to facilitate discussions in groups. To facilitate the use of technology to enhance teaching and learning, wireless Internet facilities are installed in the classrooms to provide the students with access to online learning. The well-equipped IT environment can also enable parents to observe lessons on the web and see how their children study in class. Furthermore, a distance learning classroom was built, which has enabled the students to observe classroom learning in other local schools and schools in Beijing, Shanghai and Guangzhou. These experiences have widened the exposure and the interest of students in learning. The teachers can also observe the lessons and share with their counterparts elsewhere.

The school is highly aware of the positive effects that plants and gardens have on the school environment and has strived to become a green garden school. With the help of the staff and parents, a garden was built. It has not only beautified the school environment but serves as an inviting place for students to create their writings, post them on adjacent walls and share them with their peers. The garden, named the Story Garden, has won the award for the best school garden in Hong Kong.

Institute–School Partnership

The revival and remarkable achievements of the school would not have been possible without the collaborative partnership between the school and the CSCT. The teachers of the school were empowered by participating in the SCT Leadership Project organized by CSCT. Besides helping the teachers to form an internal learning circle to share their experience in implementing SCT, the project also helps the school to form an external learning circle with principals and teachers from nine other participating schools.

The professional development programmes provided to the school mainly focused on catering for diversity through co-operative learning. Co-operative learning was adopted as research on co-operative learning across age groups, ability levels and cultural backgrounds suggests that it is effective in developing students' higher-order thinking skills, enhancing their motivation and improving interpersonal relations. The school was advised to restructure all classes in primary 1–6 and divided the students into small groups, each with three to four students. Each group was composed of more able and less able students. The heterogeneity of the grouping allowed students work together to maximize their own and each other's learning. Lesson observations conducted by the CSCT suggested a high quality of learning and teaching, in which teachers enjoyed their teaching and students showed a high level of engagement and motivation. The students also reported in interviews that they had a great improvement in their social skills and they respected each other and got help from each other.

CASE 2

Sir Robert Black College of Education Past Students' Association Lee Yat Ngok Memorial School (the school) was established in 1978 in Kwai Chung in southwest New Territories of Hong Kong. The school started to implement SCT in 2008–2009 under the leadership of a new principal, Mr. Lee, who was known for adopting the whole-school approach to integrated education in his former school. Unlike the school in Case 1, this school did not have any problem of under-enrolment. The implementation of SCT is aiming at better catering for learner diversity, supporting teachers' professional development and in meeting the long-term development needs of the school. Under the leadership of the new principal, the school has become popular with parents and attracted more students. Compared with three primary one classes in 2008/09, the school is now offering five primary 1 classes.

School-Based Policy of SCT

A special feature of the school is its formulation of a school-based policy on SCT. To facilitate the implementation of the policy, a central SCT working group was set up, composed of the principal, the vice principals, the Curriculum Leader (CL) and a designated SCT co-ordinator. The group first analyzed the factors facilitating and hindering the implementation of SCT. In addition, teachers were encouraged to form internal learning circles to share their good teaching practices.

A major objective of SCT in the school is to cater for students' learning differences. The principal and his teaching team believed that students have different learning styles, some learning better by listening, some by seeing, and others by doing. Apart from learning within the four walls of the classroom, opportunities are provided for the students to go out to the community for life-wide learning. In addition, various assessment modes are adopted to assess the different abilities of the students.

Similar to the school in Case 1, the school benefited from institute–school partnership, that is, participating in the SCT Leadership Project organized by the CSCT. With the support of experienced school development officers of the CSCT, the school has drawn up a multi-level framework to develop principal leadership, curriculum leadership, teacher leadership and student leadership.

Principal Leadership

The principal has brought change to the school by adopting a kind of distributed leadership. Instead of forcing the teachers to implement SCT, he distributed his power to the vice principals, the curriculum development leader and the SCT co-ordinator as well as every teacher. At the same time, the principal provides ample opportunities for the teachers to participate in SCT professional development programmes in order to well equip them with the knowledge and skills to implement SCT.

Curriculum Leadership

The CL of the school has played a pivotal role in co-ordinating the panel chairpersons of various subjects in adapting and implementing the curriculum in the SCT context. He also acts as a bridge between the principal and the teachers to enhance a smooth implementation of SCT.

Teacher Leadership

As mentioned above, teachers were encouraged to participate in various modes of professional development activities in SCT. In particular, they were invited to form internal learning circles and join external learning circles. Similar to the school in Case 1, co-operative learning has been adopted as a major strategy to enhance student learning in the small class environment. The outcomes have been highly positive.

Student Leadership

Student leadership is at the early stage of development. During classroom learning, students often work in co-operative groups, aiming to maximize one and each other's learning. The more able students are trained as 'little

144 Kwok-Chan Lai, Kam-Wing Chan and John Chi-Kin Lee

teachers' to help the less able students in their co-operative groups. They are encouraged to use explanation and informing feedback in their 'teaching' instead of just giving an answer to a question. They also learn how to use social skills to resolve conflicts among the group-mates.

Support and Development

An important success factor of the school is that the principal has the support of not only teachers and pupils but also the School Council and the parents. The School Council has trust in the principal and given unfailing support to its SCT reforms. Besides financial support for school renovation, it has provided moral support to boost up the morale of the principal and teachers.

To increase communication with parents, the school has set up an SCT area in the school playground, where parents gather together while waiting for their children after school. Display boards are set up in the area to demonstrate to the parents the advantages of SCT. In addition, parents are invited to observe how SCT is conducted in the classrooms. They can also see how their children are engaged in their learning and how the teachers cater for learner diversity.

At present, the school aims to excel in catering for learner diversity and become a 'system leader' of SCT in Hong Kong. On many occasions, the principal and the teaching team have shared their successful experiences in SCT with other schools and invited other teachers to participate in lesson observations and post-lesson discussions. The school has also received principals of SCT schools from Nanjing, China.

OPPORTUNITIES AND CHALLENGES

The experience of Hong Kong implementing SCT, with its focus on student-centred learning and catering for learner diversity, has given opportunities for improvement in teaching and learning. The successful experiences of the two case schools have further illustrated how implementation of SCT under strong principal leadership has brought positive changes to school improvement and student learning. They reinforce the international view that class size is a key facilitating condition, but a reduction in class size alone does not automatically bring benefits unless it is accompanied with teacher development and changes to learning and teaching (Blatchford and Lai, 2010).

A special feature of the Hong Kong experience is that professional discourse among teachers has been fostered by the wide variety of professional development activities, the building of learning circles and institute–school partnerships (Galton and Pell, 2009; Lai and Ip, 2007). The latter is especially valuable as past experiences of large-scale systemic curriculum initiatives in Hong Kong indicated the difficulty of translating top-down

Small Class Teaching in Hong Kong   145

change strategies into classroom practice (Carless, 1997). As Galton and Pell (2009) elaborate:

> Learning circles are important because they focus at any one time on a specific pedagogy, allow teachers to observe and evaluate each others classroom practice and thereby enhance the participants' sense of professionality. This allows teachers to move from a position where they looked to others to tell them what they should do to become an effective small class practitioner to a point where they are prepared to take responsibility for developing appropriate pedagogies. (p.x)

Lai (2010) contends that, compared with other educational initiatives, SCT has obtained the support of most teachers because it aligns with their core values in education. He observes that promising changes have taken place in primary schools. Nevertheless, to optimize the benefits of SCT, there is still a need of joint efforts at four levels:

1. System level: schools, under the support of government and tertiary institutions, will need to establish cross-school and cross-district learning communities in SCT to further promote exchange among schools. The government and school bodies should implement policies to create space to facilitate teachers' professional development.
2. School level: principal leadership is crucial to the successful implementation of SCT, as an effective leader does not only trigger change but also gives an organization a new direction (Grinyer, Mayes and McKiernan, 1988). To ensure success of SCT, the school leadership should establish a common vision based on student-centred principles and develop a school-based policy on SCT in articulation with the school's priorities. This planning process will allow the school better understand the needs of students, develop a professional development strategy for its teachers and improve the school and classroom environments.
3. Class level: to realize the vision, teacher leaders have to engage in curriculum and teaching innovations for enhancing student learning under a small class environment. After all, what takes place in classrooms is the core of SCT. Teachers need to set out clear educational objectives, tailor the curriculum, select appropriate teaching and assessment strategies that cater for learner differences.
4. Parents' level: The support by parents is also important. Parents were often educated by traditional methods and do not understand the principles behind SCT. As such, they often exert pressure on teachers—they expect standardized assessments, full coverage of textbook materials and a large amount of homework. The government and schools should explain the educational principles behind SCT to get their support.

During our review of class size policies in Hong Kong, we mentioned that the SCT policy in Hong Kong was introduced rather abruptly after years of contentious and politicized debates between the government and the education community. In this regard, there has not been sufficient buy-in by education officials and preparation by schools in general. Against this background, there is a noticeable lack of efforts to relate SCT to the relevant experiences acquired in past and current curriculum innovations in Hong Kong. The past reforms include the above-mentioned AA in primary schools from the early 1970s to early 1990s and the Target Oriented Curriculum (TOC) in the mid-1990s, both of which advocated student-centred learning. In addition, as mentioned earlier, the SCT policy is not officially linked to the education reforms that have taken place since 2000.

The AA was introduced to Hong Kong from the UK after the publication of the 1967 *Plowden Report* (Central Advisory Council for Education (England), 1967), which strongly advocated child-centred theories of Piaget over the traditional behaviourist theories. It advocated more diverse learning approaches, comprising whole-class teaching (initially 35 students), group work (six to seven students per group), self-choice learning and field observations. The standard size of an AA class was reduced by five students, which had allowed re-design of class layouts to facilitate sitting in groups, sitting in a base group close to the teacher, setting up of learning corners and display of student work on notice boards. In addition, informal assessment methods were promoted to reduce the over-reliance on standardized tests.

The TOC, on the other hand, was aimed at setting clear targets for teaching and learning, adopting a student-centred teaching strategy to cater for individual differences, putting equal emphasis on learning targets and processes, integrating assessment into teaching and learning, and strengthening feedback to help improve the quality of teaching and learning (Education Department [ED], 1999).

The current EDB guidelines of implementation of SCT are also drawn up exclusively based on the six principles elaborated in the Galton report without reference to past and current curriculum innovations. This unfortunate dissociation has led to confusion among many teachers, which is not conducive to optimizing the connection of valuable experiences in primary education. In this regard, further enquiries could be done in the following aspects: how could Galton's six principles be linked with the principles of TOC and AA and the current education reforms? What could we learn from successful school–university partnership experiences in Hong Kong (Lee, 2011), and how could these experiences be adapted in SCT-related projects and activities? Similarly, we believe it is important for all countries and regions to review and articulate the linkage between new education innovations, including SCT, with their past and current education initiatives.

Recently, with the declining enrolment in secondary schools, there has been a resurgence of debate on SCT in Hong Kong. The Education Bureau

Small Class Teaching in Hong Kong 147

(2012) insisted on adopting transitional measures to relieve "temporary student decline" and stated that "regarding the effectiveness of implementing SCT in secondary schools, conclusion is yet to be drawn from international studies". It has hitherto avoided using any good experiences of SCT in primary schools to inform the development of SCT at the secondary level. While some educators consider it important to consider the transition from students learning in small class environments in primary schools to the lower secondary level, this opportunity is not yet taken up.

ACKNOWLEDEGMENT

The authors would like to thank the principals and teachers of Lok Sin Tong Leung Wong Wai Fong Memorial School and Sir Robert Black College of Education Past Students' Association Lee Yat Ngok Memorial School for sharing their experiences of SCT and supporting the preparation of this chapter.

REFERENCES

Blatchford, P., & Lai, K.C. (2010). Class size—Arguments and evidence. In P. Peterson, E. Baker & B. McGaw (Eds.) *International encyclopedia of education, volume 6* (pp.200–206). Oxford: Elsevier.

Board of Education, Sub-Committee on Review of School Education (1997). *Report on review of 9-year compulsory education* (revised ed.). Hong Kong: Government Printer.

Carless, D.R. (1997). Managing systemic curriculum change: A critical analysis of Hong Kong's Target-Oriented Curriculum initiative. *International Review of Education, 43*(4), 349–366.

Central Advisory Council for Education (England) (1967). *Children and their primary schools : A report of the Central Advisory Council for Education (England)*. London: H.M.S.O.

Chan, F. M. (1994). *An analysis of changing official policies on class size in Hong Kong primary schools and their implications*. Unpublished M.Ed. dissertation. Hong Kong: University of Hong Kong.

Curriculum Development Council (2001). *Learning to learn*. Hong Kong: Government Printer.

Education and Manpower Bureau (2002). *Education statistics*. Hong Kong: Printing Department.

Education Bureau (2008). *Education Bureau circular No. 19/2008 "Small class teaching in public sector primary schools"*. Retrieved 7 October 2013, from http://www.edb.gov.hk/FileManager/EN/Content_4228/edbc08019e.pdf.

Education Bureau (2010). *Report of the study on small class teaching*. Hong Kong: Legislative Council Panel on Education. Retrieved 7 October 2013, from http://www.legco.gov.hk/yr09–10/english/panels/ed/papers/ed0513cb2–1484–6–e.pdf.

Education Bureau (2012). *LCQ4: Drop in S1 student population*. Hong Kong: Secretary for Education in the Legislative Council. Retrieved 7 October 2013, from http://www.info.gov.hk/gia/general/201210/17/P201210170472.htm.

Education Commission (1992). *Education Commission report no. 5 (ECR5)*. Hong Kong: Government Printer.

148 *Kwok-Chan Lai, Kam-Wing Chan and John Chi-Kin Lee*

Education Commission (2000). *Learning for life—learning through life: Reform proposals for the education system in Hong Kong.* Hong Kong: Government Printer.

Education Department (1999). *Target Oriented Curriculum.* Hong Kong: Legislative Council. Retrieved 7 October 2013, from http://www.legco.gov.hk/yr9899/english/panels/ed/papers/1063e03.pdf.

Galton, M., & Pell, T. (2009). *Study on small class teaching in primary schools in Hong Kong Final report.* Hong Kong: University of Cambridge and Education Bureau.

Grinyer, P.H., Mayes, D.G., & McKiernan, P. (1988). *Sharpbenders: The secrets of unleashing corporate potential.* Oxford: Basil Blackwell.

Tung, C.H. (1997). *Speech by the chief executive, the Honourable Mr. Tung Chee Hwa, at the ceremony to celebrate the establishment of the Hong Kong Special Administrative Region.* Hong Kong: Government Printer.

Hong Kong Government (1981). *Primary education and pre-primary services.* Retrieved 7 October 2013, from http://www.edb.gov.hk/FileManager/EN/Content_689/pried_e.pdf.

Ip, K.Y., & Lai, K.C. (2004). *Policy and effectiveness of small class teaching: The Hong Kong experience.* Presented at the Regional Symposium: Policy and Practice of Small Class Teaching in the East Asian Region, Hong Kong Institute of Education, February.

Ip, K.H., Liu, W.Y., Koo, H.C., & To, K.Y. (Eds.) (2012). *An illustration of teaching units design for small class teaching in primary schools in Hong Kong—Practice and experience sharing.* Hong Kong, China: Education Bureau.

Lai, K.C. (2010). Small class teaching still at beginning stage—avoid treating it as something routine. *Mingpao,* 5 February, A30. (In Chinese)

Lai, K.C., & Ip, K.Y. (2007). *Seeing large from small: Case studies of small class teaching.* Hong Kong: Step Forward Multi Media. (In Chinese)

Lee, J.C.K. (2011). School development, curriculum development and teacher development. In J.C.K. Lee & B. Caldwell (Eds.) *Changing schools in an era of globalization* (pp.123–141). New York: Routledge.

Legislative Council (2002). *Official record of proceedings, 13 November 2002.* Hong Kong: Legislative Council. Retrieved 7 October 2013, from http://www.legco.gov.hk/yr02–03/english/panels/ed/papers/ed0519cb2–2069–2e.pdf.

Legislative Council Panel on Education (2010). *Report of the study on small class teaching.* LC Paper No. CB(2)1484/09–10(06). Hong Kong: Legislative Council Panel on Education. Retrieved 7 October 2013, from http://www.edb.gov.hk/attachment/en/edu-system/primary-secondary/applicable-to-primary/small-class-teaching/ed0513cb2–1484–6–e.pdf.

Llewellyn, J. (1982). *A perspective on education in Hong Kong: A report by a visiting panel.* Hong Kong: Government Printer. Retrieved 7 October 2013, from http://www.edb.gov.hk/attachment/en/about-edb/publications-stat/major-reports/perspe_e.pdf.

Organisation for Economic Co-operation and Development [OECD] (2012). *OECD—innovative learning environment project.* Hong Kong: Hong Kong Lok Sin Tong Leung Wong Wai Fong Memorial School. Retrieved 7 October 2013, from http://www.oecd.org/edu/ceri/49751959.pdf.

Part IV
School Leadership

10 Transformational School Leadership
Principals' Strategic Vision and Teacher Development Practices

James Ko and Allan Walker

INTRODUCTION

Over the past decade, Hong Kong principals have been called upon to implement numerous far-reaching reforms. These reforms aimed to change school management and governance (e.g., External School Review [ESR] and School Self-Evaluation [SSE], school-based management [SBM]); teaching quality (e.g., language proficiency benchmarks for teachers, mandatory staff development); teaching practices (e.g., medium of instruction [MOI], inclusive education); and curriculum and student outcomes (e.g., IT in education, lifelong education, New Senior Secondary [NSS] education and higher education) (for details of these policies and their documents, see Cheng, 2009).

An important rationale for these reforms (as in other societies) is to increase teacher capacity by increasing motivation and commitment (Geijsel et al., 2003; Hallinger, 2003; Leithwood, Stenbach and Jantzi, 2002). Pathways to change include the vision that principals have for their schools (Chui, Sharpe and McCommick, 1996), the professional development of teachers (Youngs and King, 2002) and organizational learning (Lam, 2002). Transformational school leadership is often implicitly regarded in policy as a driving force in reforming school cultures from within (Leithwood and Jantzi, 1990).

After discussing the concept of transformational leadership, this chapter draws on evidence from a large-scale study of secondary school leadership in Hong Kong. We identify the key leadership practices associated with good student outcomes, construct a profile of 'strong' and 'weak' principal leadership and identify the school conditions associated with strong leadership. The findings from the study are used to illustrate that school leaders in Hong Kong display several characteristics associated with transformational leadership. Using a case study, the discussion then focuses on leadership actions in terms of principal vision and how this interacts with other leadership practices and school conditions. The case study explores practices around vision and teacher development as gleaned from interviews with key staff in a highly effective secondary school, Great Hope Secondary School,

152   *James Ko and Allan Walker*

and its principal, Principal Kay, who demonstrated exceptional overall leadership. Like the seminal works by Rosenholtz (1985, 1989), we trust that interpreting evidence found in effective schools will illuminate how leadership and teachers interact to make a difference in student learning.

TRANSFORMATIONAL LEADERSHIP AS A THEORY AND THE REALITY IN EDUCATION

Burns first introduced the concept of transformational leadership in 1978. Although built upon studies of leaders in non-education settings, the concept was soon applied to educational leaders (Leithwood, Tomlinson and Genge, 1996). In contrast to earlier leadership theories (e.g., trait theory, Stogdill, 1974; style theory, Blake and Mouton, 1964; contingency theory, Fiedler, Chemers and Mahar, 1976; Hersey and Blanchard, 1982), transformation leadership theory emphasizes the primacy of vision and mission, the empowerment of followers to 'live' the vision and the positive effects on productivity and outcomes. Transformational leadership differs from charismatic leadership in that it takes a broader, more organizationally grounded perspective (Bass, 1990; Bass and Bass, 2008). The word 'transformational' implies *change*, and particularly changes in people and outputs.

In essence, transformational leadership theory targets the improvement of organizational effectiveness by involving and developing people through delegation (Kuhnert, 1994), creating an effect 'at distance' (Yammarino, 1994) and promoting teamwork (Atwater and Bass, 1994). It emphasizes organizational decision making (Bass, 1994) and the adoption of strategies for change and improvement (Atwater and Atwater, 1994). When transformational leadership first came into vogue, it was called a 'new philosophy' and a 'new approach' to organizational change and human resource management (Kroeck, 1994). It was typically seen as an inclusive, all-encompassing theory of leadership.

Leithwood and Jantzi (2005) later conceptualized transformational leadership not as an exclusive theory but as one that could vary according to context and be enriched through juxtaposition with other leadership theories, such as transactional and instructional leadership, especially in educational contexts (Hallinger, 2003; Marks and Printy, 2003; Walker and Ko, 2011; Witziers, Bosker and Kruger, 2003).

In a recent review of the leadership literature, Hiller and colleagues (2011) examined the criteria selected by researchers to evaluate the effects of leadership. They grouped the criteria into four broad domains: (1) effectiveness (e.g., tangible outcomes, performance ratings); (2) attitude (e.g., attitudes such as identification, organizational commitment and satisfaction, motivations such as efficacy and empowerment, and emotions such as anxiety); (3) behaviour (e.g., group processes such as co-operation, organizational citizenship behaviour and self-reported behaviour such as turnover); and

Transformational School Leadership 153

(4) cognition (e.g., climate, perceived organizational support and perceived organizational structure). Hiller and colleagues (2011) found that research into transformational leadership approaches tended to focus more on attitudinal and motivational effects and organizational citizenship behaviour. These findings suggest that transformational leadership is mainly concerned with changes in subordinates' attitudes, motivations and behaviour.

Similar results were also obtained in Leithwood and Jantzi's (2005) review of transformational school leadership research between 1996 and 2005. Out of the 35 studies analyzed, most involved 'vision' (n = 27), 'intellectual stimulation' (n = 26) and 'individualized support' (n = 25), and much smaller proportions of the studies concerned 'building cultures' (n = 13), 'creating structures to foster collaboration' (n = 12), 'staffing management' (n = 3) or 'instructional support' (n = 4). Since Leithwood and Jantzi's review, numerous studies (e.g., Day et al., 2011; Heck and Hallinger, 2010; Hallinger and Heck, 2010; Walker and Ko, 2011) have contributed to the empirical knowledge of the effects of transformational leadership in an educational context.

To date, the published empirical work on transformational leadership in schools in Hong Kong is limited to the studies of Chui, Sharpe and McCormick (1996); Lam (2002); Yu, Leithwood and Jantzi (2002); and Walker and Ko (2011). Together, these studies have started to build an understanding of transformational leadership in Hong Kong. The study that is described in this chapter aims to further contribute to this understanding.

PRINCIPAL AND SCHOOL PROFILES IN
THE MISSING LINK PROJECT

The findings reported here are drawn from a larger study of the link between principal leadership and student outcomes in Hong Kong secondary schools (see Lee, Walker and Chui, 2012; Ko, Hallinger and Walker, 2012; Walker and Ko, 2011). The research investigated how the effect of school leadership on student outcomes is mediated by various school conditions. Three research questions guided the data collection.

1. What is/are the key strength(s) of local secondary school principals?
2. What school conditions do key staff see as important in schools with principals possessing strong leadership?
3. What are the characteristics of the strengths of principals with both strong leadership and successful academic student outcomes?

Answers to the first question provided a snapshot of principal leadership in Hong Kong secondary schools across seven leadership dimensions that were gleaned from data collected from key staff. Answers to question two allowed us to identify the school conditions that key staff perceived to be important in

154 *James Ko and Allan Walker*

schools with principals that they rated as 'strong'. Answers to the third question led us to explore the leadership characteristics and practices of principals who displayed strong leadership and whose schools had achieved relatively good academic student outcomes. The leadership of these principals had the most telling influence on student outcomes. We used the answers to these questions to identify a 'strong' principal who demonstrated characteristics of transformational leadership. We then drew on qualitative data collected from the key staff in this principal's school to construct a picture of a transformational school leader in Hong Kong. We will discuss our results with respect to their implications for principal and teachers' professional development for curriculum development and school improvement.

THE STUDY

Forty-eight principals offered access to their school achievement data after invitations to participate in the study were sent to all 498 public secondary schools in Hong Kong (for more information on the sampling, see Lee, Walker and Chui, 2012). The demographic information on the principals is summarized in Table 10.1.

The dominant category for each background item in Table 10.1 is shaded. The pattern of shading shows the typical profile of the principals in our sample: they are male, between 44 to 54 years old with a master's degree and have 12 years' or more experience as a principal, with three years' experience in their present school and little or no experience as a vice principal.

The participating schools were spread across different geographic areas and governed by a broad range of School Sponsoring Bodies (SSBs). Thus, although the sample is rather small, the schools included appear to be roughly representative of Hong Kong secondary schools. The key staff were chosen by their principals on the basis of their roles in improving student outcomes. They also had to have worked at the school for at least three years before the data collection, and were thus expected to understand school policies and their principals better than other teachers. To reduce the risk of potential bias favouring the principal, the questionnaires were completed anonymously and sent directly to the researchers. Demographic information on the key staff is shown in Table 10.2.

Two questionnaires collected the key staff's perceptions of their principals' leadership practices and the school conditions. Principal leadership practices were measured by a survey comprising 33 items in seven dimensions. The dimensions were designed to guide principal professional development across a range of courses and were later adopted as a framework for leadership professional development in Hong Kong (Walker and Dimmock, 2000). The leadership practice dimensions included *Strategic Direction and Policy Environment*; *Teaching, Learning and Curriculum*; *Leader and Teacher Growth and Development*; *Staff Management*;

Transformational School Leadership 155

Table 10.1 Descriptive Information on the Participating Principals

Aspects of Principal Profiles					Missing Value[a]
Gender		Male: 31 (75.6%) Female: 10 (24.4%)			0 (0%)
Age	25–34: 0 (0%)	35–44: 3 (7.3%)	45–54: 21 (51.2%)	55 or above: 16 (39%)	1 (2.4%)
Academic Qualification	Certificate: 0 (0%)	Bachelors: 1 (2.4%)	Masters: 29 (70.7%)	Doctoral: 10 (24.3%)	1 (2.4%)
Experience of Being Vice Principal	0–3 years: 19 (46.3%)	4–7 years: 8 (19.5%)	8–11 years: 6 (14.6%)	12 years or above: 5 (12.2%)	3 (7.3%)
Experience of Being Principal in Present School	3 years: 15 (36.6%)	4–7 years: 9 (22%)	8–11 years: 6 (14.6%)	12 years or above: 9 (21.9%)	2 (4.9%)
Experience of Being Principal in Total	0–3 years: 11 (26.8%)	4–7 years: 4 (9.8%)	8–11 years: 8 (19.5%)	12 years or above: 17 (41.4%)	1 (2.4%)

a   The missing values are based on the number of returned questionnaires (n = 41) rather than the number of participating schools.

Resource Management; *Quality Assurance and Accountability*; and *External Communication and Connection*.[1] The respondents were asked to rate the extent to which the statements in the questionnaire characterized their schools on a six-point forced-choice Likert scale indicating their agreement or disagreement (i.e., 'slightly', 'moderately', and 'strongly'). For example, three of the items measuring the leadership dimension *Strategic Direction and Policy Environment* were (1) 'help clarify the reasons for our school's improvement initiatives'; (2) 'give staff a sense of the overall purpose of the school'; and (3) 'provide assistance to staff in setting goals for teaching and learning'. The validity and reliability of the instrument were informed by similar projects in other settings, the relevant literature and the contextual considerations of school leadership in Hong Kong.

The instrument measuring key staff perceptions of school conditions was adapted from Leithwood and Jantzi's (2000a, 2000b) *Organizational Conditions and School Leadership Survey*. Thirty-two items were selected to cover seven school conditions: *Trust*; *Communication*; *Professional Learning*; *Alignment, Coherence and Structure*; *Resource Capacity*; *Workload of Teachers*; and *Support for Students*. Respondents were expected to rate the extent to which the statements characterized their school on a six-point forced-choice Likert scale, indicating the magnitude of their agreement or disagreement (i.e., 'slightly', 'moderately', and 'strongly'). For example, one

156 *James Ko and Allan Walker*

Table 10.2 Demographics of the Key Staff

					Missing Value
Gender	Male: 107 (59.8%) Female: 70 (39.1%)				2 (1.1%)
Age	25–34: 17 (9.5%)	35–44: 77 (43%)	45–54: 71 (39.7%)	55 or above: 13 (7.3%)	1 (0.6%)
Academic Qualification	Certificate: 3 (1.7%)	Bachelor degree: 63 (35.2%)	Master's degree: 107 (59.8%)	Doctoral: 3 (1.7%)	3 (1.7%)
Current Roles	Vice Principals: 56 (31.3%); Panel Chairs: 96 (53.6%); Senior Teachers: 46 (25.7%)				
Experience of Teaching in Present School	0–3 years: 2 (1.1%)	4–7 years: 15 (8.4%)	8–11 years: 18 (10.1%)	12 years or above: 132 (73.7%)	12 (6.7%)
Experience of Teaching in All Schools	0–3 years: 0 (0%)	4–7 years: 7 (3.9%)	8–11 years: 9 (5%)	12 years or above: 159 (88.8%)	4 (2.2%)
Experience in Current Role in Present School	0–3 years: 46 (25.7%)	4–7 years: 46 (25.7%)	8–11 years: 34 (19%)	12 years or above: 50 (28%)	3 (1.7%)
Experience in Current Role in All Schools	0–3 years: 44 (24.6%)	4–7 years: 38 (21.2%)	8–11 years: 29 (16.2%)	12 years or above: 55 (30.7%)	13 (7.3%)

Note: The figures are shown as count (N = 179) followed by the percentage in brackets.

item measuring *Alignment, Coherence and Structure*, was 'our strategies are formulated around our school purposes', and an item measuring *Support for Students* was 'our school provides after school academic support activities for students'.

Key 'Strengths' of Hong Kong Secondary School Principals

Table 10.3 shows the maximum, minimum and mean scores of the sample for the seven specific leadership practices. The highest scoring dimension was *Strategic Direction and Policy Environment*. This was thus regarded as the *key strength* of the principals in our study. Interestingly, in Chui, Sharpe and McCormick's (1996) study, vision was regarded as the most important attribute of effective transformation school leaders. In the

Table 10.3 Maximum, Minimum and Mean Overall and Specific Leadership Practice Scores in the Missing Link Project

N = 48	Overall Leadership	Strategic Direction and Policy Environment	Leader and Teacher Growth and Development	Staff Management	External Communication and Connection	Resource Management	Quality Assurance and Accountability	Teaching, Learning and Curriculum
Highest	5.19	5.50	5.23	5.30	5.45	5.42	5.46	5.56
Lowest	3.31	4.00	3.33	3.20	2.25	3.33	3.00	2.83
Mean	4.55	4.77	4.47	4.48	4.57	4.66	4.35	4.58
SD	0.32	0.40	0.47	0.46	0.61	0.46	0.53	0.51

158   James Ko and Allan Walker

literature, leadership practices associated with principals' vision for their schools and teachers account for the largest proportion of leadership effects (Leithwood and Day, 2007).

Relationships between the Key Leadership Strength and Other Leadership Practices

The fact that *Resource Management* was the second ranked strength of principals suggests the importance of transactional leadership functions in Hong Kong secondary schools, and also that much of a principal's work involves allocating resources sensibly, including those crucial to their strategic vision.

In contrast, the principals seemed to perform less well in *Quality Assurance and Accountability*. We doubt that this is a major issue for secondary school principals, because instructional leadership is more difficult to achieve with the many technical subjects that are taught in secondary schools. However, it is somewhat worrying that the principals were also weaker in terms of human resource management and development. The mean scores for *Leader and Teacher Growth and Development* and *Staff Management* were below the mean overall leadership score. These results suggest that principals may be able to inspire vision at a cognitive level, but are less likely to be able to motivate and empower their teachers to implement sustainable change.

Relationships between Leadership Practices and School Conditions

As discussed above, transformation implies change, particularly change in people and in output through work alignment. We further explored the associations among the specific leadership aspects to see whether *Strategic Direction and Policy Environment* was strongly correlated with *Leader and Teacher Growth and Development* and the school condition factor that measured alignment of work, coherence and structure in the school. The results are summarized in Table 10.4.

The results indicate that *Strategic Direction and Policy Environment* was indeed most strongly correlated with *Leader and Teacher Growth and Development*, followed by *Teaching, Learning and Curriculum* and then *Resource Management*. The close connections of these leadership practices with *Strategic Direction and Policy Environment* suggest that principals may have to work on other leadership practices to fulfil their visions. The impact of vision in a school may not endure without the corresponding leadership and professional development among teachers and improvements in teaching, learning and curriculum or resource reallocation. Strategically, human resource development may be most crucial in the longer term.

In Hong Kong, principals can formally support teacher development by assigning teachers to relevant programmes organized by local tertiary

Table 10.4 Correlations of Specific Leadership Practices and the School Condition Alignment, Coherence and Structure

	Strategic Direction and Policy Environment	Leader and Teacher Growth and Development	Staff Management	External Communication and Connection	Resource Management	Quality Assurance and Accountability	Teaching, Learning and Curriculum	Alignment, Coherence and structure
Strategic Direction and Policy Environment	1							
Leader and Teacher Growth and Development	.776**	1						
Staff Management	.728**	.779**	1					
External Communication and Connection	.681**	.734**	.744**	1				
Resource Management	.744**	.783**	.756**	.729**	1			
Quality Assurance and Accountability	.682**	.694**	.724**	.643**	.690**	1		
Teaching, Learning and Curriculum	.748**	.759**	.751**	.710**	.712**	.806**	1	
Alignment, Coherence and Structure	.472**	.503**	.456**	.448**	.449**	.375**	.422**	1

160 *James Ko and Allan Walker*

institutes but mostly funded by the government (Ng, 2003). However, moral support from the principal often plays out informally, favouring teachers who show caring attitudes to students and commitment to the school (Ng, 2003). A transformational principal may also find that it is "necessary to develop a 'critical mass' of teachers before any significant organisational change may take place" (Ng, 2003, p.665), because bringing about change in teaching, learning and curriculum requires collaboration among colleagues.

Communicating vision to teachers is also important but may be superficial if there is no corresponding action. We tested this assumption by multiple regression analysis using *Strategic Direction and Policy Environment* as the dependent variable and the other three leadership practices as the predictors or independent variables. The results confirmed our assumption: *Leader and Teacher Growth and Development, Teaching, Learning and Curriculum* and *Resource Management* were the only significant predictors of *Strategic Direction and Policy Environment*, respectively explaining 10.26%, 10.14% and 7.07% of the variance.

Table 10.4 also shows that the condition *Alignment, Coherence and Structure* was most strongly correlated with *Leader and Teacher Growth and Development* and *Strategic Direction and Policy Environment*. In our previous work (Walker and Ko, 2011), we showed that *Alignment, Coherence and Structure* were explained by *Strategic Direction and Policy Environment* until *Leader and Teacher Growth and Development* was also included as a predictor, which then became the only statistically significant predictor. In other words, alignment of work in a school may be initially promoted through a shared vision, but eventually relies on the successful development of teachers who both receive the principal's personal endorsement and also take up leadership roles and collaborate with other colleagues on school improvement projects.

We explored the relationship between leadership practices and school conditions by comparing the conditions in schools with strong and weak leadership in the sample. Figure 10.1 summarizes these comparisons. Four interesting findings emerge.

First, as expected, teacher workload in schools with stronger leadership seemed to be 'heavier' than in schools with weaker leadership. Second, *Resource Capacity* was perceived somewhat negatively by key staff, regardless of the strength of principal leadership. Moreover, resource capacity was lower in schools with *stronger* leadership than in schools with *weaker* leadership. This may be associated with workload differences in these schools. Fourth, *Trust, Communication* and *Professional Learning* seemed less likely to be affected by strength of principal leadership. This suggests that these ratings may better reflect conditions at the teacher level.

The relative gap between schools with the strongest and weakest leadership seemed to be larger for *Alignment, Coherence and Structure* and *Support for Students*. This finding suggests that stronger leadership is required to create the consistency and cohesion that leads to better support for students.

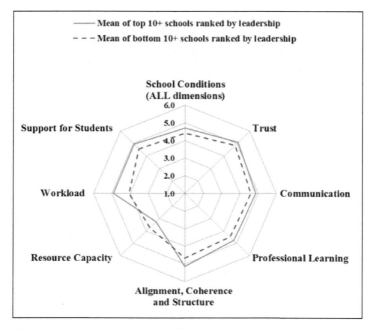

Figure 10.1 Comparison of the conditions of schools with the highest and lowest leadership scores.

A Brief Profile of an Effective School and Its Principal

We selected Great Hope Secondary School for in-depth analysis because of its outstanding academic achievement and highly rated leadership. Although located in one of the lowest socio-economic catchment areas, the school has managed to achieve positive value-added (VA) stanines from 2006 to 2008 in the three core subjects and in students' Best 6 subjects. Its VA stanines were the second highest (i.e., 8, the top 21%) in 2006 and the highest (i.e., 9, the top 4%) in 2007 and 2008, indicating its exceptional achievement in school improvement. Thirteen out of 18 subjects had a positive VA stanine in 2006, but the figure had jumped to 17 by 2008, the highest in our sample. Great Hope was one of six schools that showed a trend of consistent positive value-added stanines in most subjects over three years.

Table 10.5 shows that Principal Kay was highly rated by the key staff. She emerged as an exemplar of transformational leaders in the key staff survey and interviews. Her overall leadership score ranked the highest of all principals in the study, distinctly outperforming the average in every dimension. She scored highest in *Resource Management* and second highest in *External Communication and Connection*, indicating that these are her key strengths in leadership. She maintained above average scores in *Teaching, Learning and Curriculum* and *Quality Assurance and Accountability*, but did not excel notably in these areas.

Table 10.5 Overall and Specific Leadership Practice Scores of Principal Kay and Their Ranks in the Missing Link Project

N = 48	Overall Leadership	Strategic Direction and Policy Environment	Leader and Teacher Growth and Development	Staff Management	External Communication and Connection	Resource Management	Quality Assurance and Accountability	Teaching, Learning and Curriculum
Principal Kay	5.19	5.40	5.10	5.08	5.45	5.40	4.73	5.15
Her Rank out of 48	1	3	7	6	1	3	11	8

Table 10.6 Overall and Specific School Condition Scores of Great Hope Secondary School Compared with the Scores of All Schools in the Missing Link Project

N = 48	Overall School Condition	Trust	Communication	Professional Learning	Alignment, Coherence and Structure	Resource Capacity	Workload	Support for Students
Highest	5.32	5.81	5.88	5.55	5.70	5.10	5.58	5.63
Lowest	3.15	2.25	3.90	2.50	3.00	2.00	2.78	2.50
Mean	4.55	4.91	4.67	4.61	4.83	3.55	4.52	4.77
SD	0.34	0.54	0.44	0.49	0.48	0.68	0.50	0.51
Great Hope	4.96	5.35	5.25	5.00	5.48	3.60	4.87	5.20
Its Rank	7	7	5.5	9.5	3.5	23.5	14.5	9

164   *James Ko and Allan Walker*

Table 10.6 compares the averages scores of Great Hope Secondary School with the maximum, minimum and mean scores of the sample for overall school condition and the seven specific school conditions. Among the various school conditions, *Alignment, Coherence and Structure* was most highly regarded by the key staff, confirming their collective efficacy. Although ranked slightly lower within the top ten range, the levels of communication and trust among the teachers also matched their level of work alignment. The school was above average across all school conditions except for *Resource Capacity*, in which it ranked average. The school seems to be a typical example of schools in our sample, with strong leadership but a moderately high teachers' workload and a low *Resource Capacity*. The school has been fighting against the odds in a challenging context in which students receive little support in their learning and on average one-third of the families receive (relatively) comprehensive welfare benefits. The workload of teachers is moderately high because their support for students often extends beyond academic matters. Both professional learning and support for students were just within the top ten rankings, but this may be limited by the level of workload and resource capacity of the school.

Four Characteristics of Principal Vision

Our survey data confirmed that *Strategic Direction and Policy Environment*, the 'vital attribute' of transformational leadership, was the dominant strength shared by the principals in the sample. However, the significance of this strength cannot be understood in isolation, but must be related back to its meaning, purpose and impact for teachers and students. In an in-depth interview with the key staff of Great Hope Secondary School, we identified four features that characterize the vision of transformational school leaders.

Extending the Time Frame of a Vision

First, the key staff acknowledged that creating a vision was the principal's key strength but emphasized the qualitative difference between her vision and theirs. Her vision tended to be far-reaching and to look to the future in a time frame longer than that of most of the teachers. The key staff unanimously pointed out that the greatness of a vision is dependent on its relevance to the future.

> *Principal Kay has really proved that her point of view is correct in the past few years. Principal Kay has a vision for future development. We are certain in that respect. Sometimes, we regard three years or five years as a very long period, but the principal views it as a short period. The principal even thinks that it is awesome for them to see the result within three to five years. From the principal's point of view, we need at least five years to see the result. Again, the principal always has a greater vision than us.*

Transformational School Leadership 165

In a separate analysis (Ko, Hallinger and Walker, 2014), we show that school improvements in the sample may take three years or more to come into effect.

Contextualizing a Vision with Meanings That Are Significant to People

The key vision that Principal Kay set for Great Hope Secondary School when she took the post as principal in 2005 has proven to be 'correct': *to become a school that uses English as the MOI* (i.e., an EMI school). This vision conveys a value that is *contextually distinctive and meaningful*, because all of the surrounding schools had to use Chinese for instruction under the government's new MOI policy in 1998. To become an EMI school was considered an 'impossible dream' by most teachers because they could not see that the government would compromise on the issue. Principal Kay did not just articulate her vision but put in place arrangements to make it happen. She had to be flexible and tactful in resource management. Transformational leadership practice must be supported with corresponding transactional leadership practice.

> *The principal is good at distributing resources. In the last few years, it has been obvious that the English subject has been given more resources. I have experienced that. However, the principal has made it clear that the resources will be reallocated to the other subjects later on. The English subject needs to be prepared to receive fewer resources than before.*

To achieve her vision, Principal Kay exempted all English subject teachers from the administrative and functional duties that were previously shared equally among the teachers, but she made them accountable for the students' English proficiency. Rather than distributing resources equally, her strategy was to put more resources into one area. She had to change daily practices, organizational structures and roles and responsibilities to achieve her vision. The contextual meaning of Principal Kay's endeavour would have been lost had it been viewed merely as a restructuring task. Restructuring is often a risky business when people cannot agree on its contextual relevance. Pumping resources in to enhance students' English outcomes seemed a risky move and required exceptional courage to implement. It was actually a high-performance expectation that the teachers and students *of Great Hope Secondary School* shared, but did not have enough confidence to set formally. What Principal Kay did was to reaffirm their collective efficacy by reallocating the necessary concrete resources and setting a more realistic time frame.

> *Our principal is very courageous. She not only planned the future school policy but most importantly was brave enough to put it into practice. The principal has been here for five years. We all feel that the*

166   *James Ko and Allan Walker*

> *principal has done a lot for future school policy. I can certainly say that the principal has helped the school.*

Charging a Vision with Emotional Appeal and Impact

The key staff all admired Principal Kay's courage in articulating her vision for the school, which was finally realized in 2010 when the government granted it EMI status. This meant that the school had convinced the education authority that the teachers were ready to teach in English and that the majority of students had the ability to learn in English for all subjects except Chinese. The new status was emotionally meaningful to teachers and students because this meant that Great Hope Secondary School was recognized not just as a good school but as a great school in terms of teaching and learning. It acquired a status beyond people's expectations of a typical CMI school in a challenging context in Hong Kong. Under the new MOI policy, CMI schools are often regarded as inferior to EMI schools, as all EMI schools are also Band 1 schools. To instil high expectations in teachers and students, transformational leaders depend on emotions. Principal Kay's courage 'to be great' was seen as an inner strength that moved her staff. Her vision was communicated and shared emotionally and became a collective commitment.

> *I have a deeper feeling. When the principal works, you can definitely feel the enthusiasm within.*

Aligning Actions with the Ultimate Purpose

As a transformational leader, Principal Kay affected her teachers through her passion. They could not help but know the *ultimate purpose* of her unusual resource management. Everything she did aimed to meet high learning goals and high learning needs. The moral imperative of schools lies in teaching and learning. All visions for schools should have a purpose that is ultimately related to enhancing teaching and learning outcomes, a core value that is shared across educational settings.

> *You can sense the enthusiasm in the changing of classroom practice and the fight for teaching media and changes. We can see that the principal is always striving for progression. The principal always has a strong hope, which pushes the school to higher levels. The attitude of the principal positively affects our teachers, which is good.*

The key staff told us that there was always construction going on in the school because they had to continuously change the learning environment to meet new and diverse learning needs. There was no debate at Great Hope Secondary School about whether Small Class Teaching (SCT) was more

Transformational School Leadership 167

beneficial, because the teachers believed that class size should not be the factor that defines a conducive learning environment.

> *The principal wants to reconstruct some rooms, and hopes that larger classes will have more interactive elements. We wish to accomplish this with larger class learning. If classes have the same lesson and the content is the same, then we can teach the lesson in a larger class.*

> *Structurally, we have to divide [the form] into three or four small classes, but the class size is quite flexible. We flexibly change these things to fit the learning environment. The principal has been aware of the needs of general education in high schools for a long time.*

> *In establishing a good learning environment, the principal is really bold and creative. There are many things that she has been bold enough to put it into practice. The principal rebuilt the classrooms so that the students can see them from outside, which creates peer observation among students.*

The foregoing analysis illustrates that the strategic direction of transformational leaders can be understood in terms of four characteristics: (1) relevance to the mid- or long-term future, (2) contextual meanings and changes, (3) emotional origin and impact and (4) an ultimate purpose of outstanding teaching and learning.

The Four Signs of Teacher Growth

Although "central to the ways in which successful leaders integrate the functional and the personal" (Leithwood, Harris and Hopkins, 2008, p.6), transformational leaders often prioritize teachers' individual and collective growth and development. Developing people cannot rely merely on professional training programmes that focus on knowledge and skills, or the know-how aspect of personal growth and organizational capacity. In our interviews with the key staff, we identified four features of teacher growth that characterize the leadership of transformational leaders.

Fuelling Teacher Growth with Exceptional Team Spirit

Transformational leaders are often not only architects of a vision. They are also engineers of group souls. Principal Kay fuelled teacher growth with team spirit.

> *One of the principal's strengths is to encourage teachers. The principal thinks highly of teamwork. The principal stresses team spirit all day long and always tells us that as a school, we are one and a team. The principal is the leader who guides us to carry out school reform.*

168   James Ko and Allan Walker

Human growth is spiritual and collective and unites people to share the same spirit, have the same dream and march in the same direction.

> *In sum, the principal acts as a navigator to lead us forward in the same direction. We are comfortable following the principal. The principal always says that no matter what your post is, you need to have a dream. Only if you have a dream can you build a better learning environment.*

Changing Formal Structures and the Power Hierarchy for Closer Teacher Collaboration

Leaders exist in teams, and teams nurture leadership. Researchers argue that teacher leadership beyond the classroom leads to the improvement of teacher morale and the quality of work lives in school through increased engagement and collaboration (Frost and Harris, 2003). Teacher leadership promotes collegiality, such that the collective capacity of teachers is enhanced for change and school improvement (Muijs and Harris, 2003). A lack of formal and informal channels for wider decision making among teachers is the reality in Hong Kong (Dimmock and Walker, 1998) and Balkanization among departments is common in schools (Ng, 2011). These form two major obstacles that impede teacher leadership, collaborative culture and the successful implementation of reform in local schools. Thus, teacher leadership is more likely to be realized by decentralizing decision-making processes to break the power hierarchy in schools, and by building communication and co-operation channels between teachers and between departments.

Principal Kay's key staff introduced themselves to us during the interviews with multiple designations, such as school development co-ordinator or teacher representative of home–school co-operation. These posts are cross-departmental by nature, revealing the demands of new duties and responsibilities around the new structures introduced by the principal. The key staff did not hold traditional key posts such as vice principal, head of academic affairs or discipline master. Principal Kay's designations indicate an extension of the traditional boundaries of 'key staff' in Hong Kong schools. The multiple posts not only reflect her empowerment of teachers, whose primary roles are traditionally lower in the power hierarchy in the school, but also promote dialogue and collaboration between and beyond existing departments.

> *You can feel that the principal has a lot of new ideas. For example, the principal has introduced a collaborative culture between colleagues and departments and encourages more communication between departments. Because of that, we have got to know each other and different departments better. We now co-operate better.*

Transformational School Leadership 169

Extending the Perspectives of Teachers beyond Their School

Distributed leadership is vital for teacher leaders' job satisfaction and organizational commitment (Hulpia, Devos and Rosseel, 2009). Whether the distribution of leadership at Great Hope has been extended beyond the key staff that were interviewed is unclear, but Principal Kay has prepared her teachers to grow by widening their opportunities and perspectives beyond their school.

> *The principal actually sees more than we do. The principal encourages colleagues to go out and see the world. The principal asked us to travel to different places to find out what is worth learning from others. Almost everyone here has gone out, am I right?*

Principal Kay systematically sent different groups of teachers and students on external school visits. These exchanges were exercises to develop their mental flexibility in problem solving, and were critical in nurturing democratic and strategic leadership.

Rewarding Teachers with Recognition and Satisfaction

The last sign of teacher growth in the school is the exceptionally high level of teacher satisfaction. The key staff explained to us that they were satisfied because of the principal's bottom-up management. They contrasted the top-down and bottom-up approaches of Principal Kay and previous principals in dealing with challenges and responsibilities.

> *This principal is very different from the last one. Before, if the former principal encountered any difficulties, he would call for help immediately even if we were teaching in class. However, the new principal doesn't do that.*

> *This principal is willing to take responsibility, and takes the job personally.*

Teachers care about small gestures of recognition from top management.

> *The principal knows how to encourage everyone. If teachers perform well, then the principal gives out small gifts. Sometimes, the principal may even order a roasted pig for us to share. It simply makes everyone happy.*

Teachers also expect the principal to show trust in their work and to recognize their autonomy.

> *The principal values trust, which means that she trusts the teachers very much. When work is given to a teacher, the principal does not*

170   *James Ko and Allan Walker*

> *have to worry whether the work will be done. The principal guides us but does not check on us all the time.*

The teachers also found their jobs very rewarding because they had gained the recognition of the local community.

> *Sometimes when we chat with people in the neighbourhood, we hear that they like our students very much. The neighbourhood has commented that our students are very disciplined and polite. To tell you the truth, we as teachers are really proud to hear others praise our students.*

The teachers appeared satisfied that they could identify with the school mission and culture in promoting the long-term achievements of students.

> *I totally agree with the school culture and tradition. Our school encourages students to go out, explore and widen their horizons. We wish to establish a culture that helps students to cultivate their own vision. We have a student leadership development programme. We hope that our students will be leaders in future society. This is the characteristic of the people at Great Hope.*

Thus, teachers experience their growth through enhanced teacher efficacy, which is linked to commitment to organizational values (Ross and Gray, 2006).

In sum, teacher leaders in the school demonstrate a high level of teacher growth in four aspects: (1) team spirit, (2) collaborations between and beyond existing school structures, (3) extended perspectives and (4) job satisfaction rewarded from multiple sources.

CONCLUSION

The leadership practices identified in the case above match at least four of the seven vital characteristics of effective leadership summarized by Leithwood, Harris and Hopkins (2008, pp.27–28).

1. The ways in which leaders apply basic leadership practices—not the practices themselves—demonstrate responsiveness to, rather than dictation by, the contexts in which they work.
2. School leaders improve teaching and learning indirectly and most powerfully through their influence on staff motivation, commitment and working conditions.
3. School leadership has a greater influence on schools and students when it is widely distributed.
4. Some patterns of distribution are more effective than others.

Principal Kay appears to be an effective transformational leader, as demonstrated by the four 'characteristics' of her vision and the four aspects of teacher growth identified and understood by the key staff.

Several interesting points emerged from our analysis have implications for the professional development of aspiring school leaders and principals. First, as Shamir (2011) recently noted, leadership takes time. This means that the effects of leadership may not easily fit the traditional short observation time frame common in much leadership research. Although many policymakers, practitioners and researchers acknowledge that school improvement takes time, it appears rare for time frames over three years to be recognized. Under Hong Kong's school management regulations, school administrators are required to set annual and mid-term plans (Dimmock and Walker, 1997, 1998). Second, although much of the effect of transformational leadership seems to rest upon teachers' emotional responses, principal professional development programmes too often fail to address this because they over-emphasize effectiveness and the behavioural and cognitive aspects of leadership effects. Gu and Day (2007) found that teachers' resilience is crucial for maintaining their commitment and effectiveness in through their successful management of the situational demands in work and life. Thus, training school leaders to deal with the emotional needs of teachers to promote teacher efficacy and resilience deserves more attention in professional development programmes. Third, researchers may recognize the dilemmas that principals face in implementing new education policies, such as conflicting values, contrasting paradigms of educational goals and challenging contexts (Dimmock, 1999; Harris et al., 2006; Levin, 2006; Walker and Dimmock, 2000; Walker and Walker, 1998), yet such dilemmas are rarely viewed as a constructive element in the realization of a school's defining vision. It may be that the process of courageously coping with multiple dilemmas is a necessary part of the process of change and achieving a vision. For example, Tjosvold and Sun (2003) found that open discussion and communication that promotes interpersonal warmth to be a useful conflict-management skills among Chinese teams. Finally, while leadership practices associated with visions and strategic directions were found to be strong among the principals of our sample, they were not often matched with similar strengths in terms of their leadership practices around curriculum management and quality assurance (QA) of instruction. This may suggest that a stronger emphasis on developing principals' instructional leadership practice is desirable for their future professional development. Such an emphasis may be critical for the successful implementation of the New Academic Structure and Curriculum Reform in schools.

ACKNOWLEDGEMENT

The authors acknowledge the Research Grants Council of Hong Kong for its support through the General Research Fund (GRF 451407).

NOTE

1. Details of the validation of the instruments are reported in our unpublished report (Ko and Walker, 2010).

172   *James Ko and Allan Walker*

REFERENCES

Atwater, L.E., & Atwater, D.C. (1994). Organizational transformation: Strategies for change and improvement. In B.M. Bass & B.J. Avolio (Eds.) *Improving organizational effectiveness through transformational leadership* (pp.146–171). Thousand Oaks, CA: Sage Publications.

Atwater, D., & Bass, B.M. (1994). Transformational leadership in teams. In B.M. Bass & B.J. Avolio (Eds.) *Improving organizational effectiveness through transformational leadership* (pp.48–77). Thousand Oaks, CA: Sage Publications.

Bass, B.M. (1990). From transactional to transformational leadership: Learning to share the vision. *Organizational Dynamics, 18*(3), 19–31.

Bass, B.M. (1994). Transformational leadership and team and organizational decision making. In B.M. Bass & B.J. Avolio (Eds.) *Organizational effectiveness through transformational leadership* (pp.104–120). Thousand Oaks, CA: Sage Publications.

Bass, B.M., & Bass, R. (2008). *The Bass handbook of leadership: Theory, research, and managerial applications.* New York: Free Press.

Blake, R.R., & Mouton, J.S. (1964). *The managerial grid.* Houston, TX: Gulf.

Burns, J.M. (1978). *Leadership.* New York: Harper and Row.

Cheng, Y.C. (2009). Hong Kong educational reforms in the last decade: Reform syndrome and new developments. *International Journal of Educational Management, 23*(1), 65–86.

Chui, H.S., Sharpe, F.G., & McCormick, J. (1996). Vision and leadership of principals in Hong Kong. *Journal of Educational Administration, 34*(3), 30–48.

Day, C., Sammons, P., Hopkins, D., Harris, A., Leithwood, K., Gu, Q., Brown, E., Ahtaridou, E., & Kingston, A. (2011). *Successful school leadership: Linking learning and achievement.* Berkshire, Open University Press.

Dimmock, C. (1999). Principals and school restructuring: Conceptualising challenges as dilemmas. *Journal of Educational Administration, 37*(5), 441–462.

Dimmock, C., & Walker, A. (1997). Hong Kong's change of sovereignty: School leader perceptions of the effects on educational policy and school administration. *Comparative Education, 33*(2), 277–302.

Dimmock, C., & Walker, A. (1998). Transforming Hong Kong's schools: Trends and emerging issues. *Journal of Educational Administration, 36*(5), 476–491.

Fiedler, F.E., Chemers, M.M., & Mahar, L. (1976). *Improving leadership effectiveness: The leader match concept.* New York: Wiley.

Frost, D., & Harris, A. (2003). Teacher leadership: Towards a research agenda. *Cambridge Journal of Education, 33*(3), 479–498.

Geijsel, F., Sleegers, P., Leithwood, K., & Jantzi, D. (2003). Transformational leadership effects on teachers' commitment and effort toward school reform. *Journal of Educational Administration, 41*(3), 228–256.

Gu, Q., & Day, C. (2007). Teachers' resilience: A necessary condition for effectiveness. *Teaching and Teacher Education, 23*(8), 1302–1316.

Hallinger, P. (2003). Leading educational change: Reflections on the practice of instructional and transformational leadership. *Cambridge Journal of Education, 33*(3), 329–352.

Hallinger, P., & Heck, R.H. (2010). Leadership for learning: Does collaborative leadership make a difference? *Educational Management Administration and Leadership, 38*(6), 654–678.

Harris, A., Chapman, C., Muijs, D., Russ, J., & Stoll, L. (2006). Improving schools in challenging contexts: Exploring the possible. *School Effectiveness and School Improvement, 17*(4), 409–424.

Heck, R.H., & Hallinger, P. (2010). Testing a longitudinal model of distributed leadership effects on school improvement. *Leadership Quarterly, 21*, 867–885.

Transformational School Leadership 173

Hersey, P., & Blanchard, K.H. (1982). *Management of organizational behavior: Utilizing human resources* (4th ed.). Englewood Cliffs, NJ: Prentice Hall.

Hiller, N.J., DeChurch, L.A., Murase, T., & Doty, D. (2011). Searching for outcomes of leadership: A 25-year review. *Journal of Management, 37*(4), 1137–1177.

Hulpia, H., Devos, G., & Rosseel, Y. (2009). The relationship between the perception of distributed leadership in secondary schools and teachers' and teacher leaders' job satisfaction and organizational commitment. *School Effectiveness and School Improvement, 20*(3), 291–317.

Ko, J., Hallinger, P., & Walker, A. (2012). Exploring school improvement in Hong Kong secondary schools. *Peabody Journal of Education, 87*(2), 216–234.

Ko, J., Hallinger, P., & Walker, A. (2014). Exploring whole school versus subject department improvement in Hong Kong secondary schools. *School Effectiveness and School Improvement*, DOI: 10.1080/09243453.2014.882848. Retrieved on March 3, 2014.

Ko, J., & Walker, A. (2010). *The validation of instruments in the Missing Link Project.* Unpublished Interim Report, APCLC, Hong Kong Institute of Education.

Kroeck, K.G. (1994). Corporate reorganization and transformations in human resource management. In B.M. Bass & B.J. Avolio (Eds.) *Improving organizational effectiveness through transformational leadership* (pp.173–201). Thousand Oaks, CA: Sage Publications.

Kuhnert, K.W. (1994). Transforming leadership: Developing people through delegation. In B.M. Bass & B.J. Avolio (Eds.) *Improving organizational effectiveness through transformational leadership* (pp.26–47). Thousand Oaks, CA: Sage Publications.

Lam, Y.L.J. (2002). Defining the effects of transformational leadership on organisational learning: A cross-cultural comparison. *School Leadership & Management, 22*(4), 439–452.

Lee, M., Walker, A., & Chui, Y.L. (2012). Contrasting effects of instructional leadership practices on student learning in a high accountability context. *Journal of Educational Administration, 50*(5), 586–611.

Leithwood, K., & Day, C. (Eds.) (2007). *Successful school leadership in times of change.* Toronto: Springer.

Leithwood, K., Harris, A., & Hopkins, D. (2008). Seven strong claims about successful school leadership. *School Leadership & Management, 28*(1), 27–42.

Leithwood, K., & Jantzi, D. (1990). Transformational leadership: How principals can help reform school cultures. *School Effectiveness and School Improvement, 1*(4), 249–280.

Leithwood, K., & Jantzi, D. (2000a). The effects of transformational leadership on organizational conditions and student engagement with school. *Journal of Educational Administration, 38*(2), 112–129.

Leithwood, K., & Jantzi, D. (2000b). Principal and teacher leadership effects: A replication. *School Leadership & Management, 20*(4), 415–434.

Leithwood, K., & Jantzi, D. (2005). A review of transformational school leadership research 1996–2005. *Leadership and Policy in Schools, 4*(3), 177–199.

Leithwood, K., Steinbach, R., & Jantzi, D. (2002). School leadership and teachers' motivation to implement accountability policies. *Educational Administration Quarterly, 38*(1), 94–119.

Leithwood, K., Tomlinson, D., & Genge, M. (1996). Transformational school leadership. In K. Leithwood (Ed.) *International handbook of educational leadership and administration* (pp.785–840). Dordrecht: Kluwer Academic Publishers.

Levin, B. (2006). Schools in challenging circumstances: A reflection on what we know and what we need to know. *School Effectiveness and School Improvement, 17*(4), 399–407.

174   *James Ko and Allan Walker*

Marks, H.M., & Printy, S.M. (2003). Principal leadership and school performance: An integration of transformational and instructional leadership. *Educational Administration Quarterly, 39*(3), 370–397.

Muijs, D., & Harris, A. (2003). Teacher leadership—improvement through empowerment? An overview of the literature. *Educational Management Administration & Leadership, 31*(4), 437–448.

Ng, H. M. (2003). An analysis of continuous teacher development in Hong Kong. *Journal of Education Policy, 18*(6), 657–672.

Ng, S. W. (2011). Managing teacher balkanization in times of implementing change. *International Journal of Educational Management, 25*(7), 654–670.

Rosenholtz, S. (1985). Effective schools: Interpreting the evidence. *American Journal of Education, 93*(3), 352–388.

Rosenholtz, S. (1989). *Teachers' workplace: The social organization of schools.* New York: Longman.

Ross, J.A., & Gray, P. (2006). Transformational leadership and teacher commitment to organizational values: The mediating effects of collective teacher efficacy. *School Effectiveness and School Improvement, 17*(2), 179–199.

Shamir, B. (2011). Leadership takes time: Some implications of (not) taking time seriously in leadership research. *Leadership Quarterly, 22*(2), 307–315.

Stogdill, R.M. (1974). *Handbook of leadership: A survey of theory and research.* New York: Free Press.

Tjosvold, D., & Sun, H.F. (2003). Openness among Chinese in conflict: Effects of direct discussion and warmth on integrative decision making. *Journal of Applied Social Psychology, 33*(9), 1878–1897.

Walker, A., & Dimmock, C. (2000). Leadership dilemmas of Hong Kong principals: Sources, perceptions and outcomes. *Australian Journal of Education, 44*(1), 5–25.

Walker, A., & Ko, J. (2011). Principal leadership in an era of accountability: A perspective from the Hong Kong context. *School Leadership & Management, 31*(4), 369–392.

Walker, A., & Walker, J. (1998). Challenging the boundaries of sameness: Leadership through valuing difference. *Journal of Educational Administration, 36*(1), 8–28.

Witziers, B., Bosker, R., & Kruger, M. (2003). Educational leadership and student achievement: The elusive search for an association. *Educational Administration Quarterly, 34*(3), 398–425.

Yammarino, F.J. (1994). Indirect leadership: Transformational leadership at a distance. In B.M. Bass & B.J. Avolio (Eds.) *Improving organizational effectiveness through transformational leadership* (pp.26–47). Thousand Oaks, CA: Sage Publications.

Youngs, P., & King, M.B. (2002). Principal leadership for professional development to build school capacity. *Educational Administration Quarterly, 38*(5), 643–670.

Yu, H., Leithwood, K., & Jantzi, D. (2002). The effects of transformational leadership on teachers' commitment to change in Hong Kong. *Journal of Educational Administration, 38*(29), 112–129.

11 Curriculum Leadership Developments
Lessons Learned and Achievements Made

Kwok-Tung Tsui

INTRODUCTION

Driven by globalization and economic development, curriculum reform has become a development priority in education for most Asian societies (Kennedy and Lee, 2008, p.89), and they have set similar goals to pursue through curriculum reform and initiatives (Lee, 2001). The most decisive underlying principle commonly adopted by the Asian societies in this wave of curriculum reform is the paradigm shift from the tradition of centralized curriculum decision making to the advocacy of decentralization of curriculum decision making. Thus, teachers and school leaders are required to participate actively in school-based curriculum development (SBCD) initiatives and practices (Kennedy and Lee, 2008; Tsui, 2010). Policymakers and researchers are aware of the limitations of traditional school leadership in leading schools and front-line teachers to implement the new curriculum reform effectively. This initiative sets high expectations on the student learning process, outcomes and all-round development. Researchers and school professionals are urging a new kind of leadership for curriculum leaders (CLs) in assuming responsibilities specifically related to curriculum decision making and development and implementation for enhancing student learning at the school sites (Tsui, 2010).

The quest for curriculum leadership has special importance and meaning to Hong Kong schools and teachers when the government announced the large-scale launching of the "Learning to Learn" education reform in 2000. The reform required schools to develop and implement a more flexible school-based curriculum as a strategy to realize the new aims of education for the 21st century (Curriculum Development Council [CDC], 2001). This move had become a great challenge to all schools in Hong Kong, in particular primary schools that have fewer resources as compared with secondary schools in staff provisions (number of teachers and senior teachers, teacher qualifications) and infrastructure (school building and facilities). Hence, a genuine need arose to bring in additional staff who could take up the role of CLs to support primary schools in the implementation of curriculum reform and SBCD at schools.

176   Kwok-Tung Tsui

ENGINE OF SCHOOL-BASED CURRICULUM DEVELOPMENT—INSTALLATION OF CURRICULUM LEADERS IN HONG KONG PRIMARY SCHOOLS

Hong Kong, like many other developed countries, spent huge resources and efforts in the implementation of major school reforms and curriculum initiatives in the 1980s and 1990s. However, the results were disappointing. Two major problems were identified from these unsuccessful reforms and initiatives. One is the lack of teacher support and involvement (Carless, 1997; Tsui and Cheng, 2000), and the other one is the failure to empower teachers adequately with required professional knowledge, skills and the time to assume new responsibilities and to participate actively in SBCD processes (Tsui, 2010). Learning from these unsuccessful experiences, the Hong Kong government realized that the key to successful curriculum reform is the development of curriculum leadership among educators at all levels in the school sites and, in particular, the primary school sector (Chan, 2008). Against this background, Mr. Tung, the chief executive of the Hong Kong Special Administrative Region (SAR), announced in his 2001 policy address, "To complement curriculum reform, Curriculum Officer posts [CLs] will be created in stages to lead internal [school-based] curriculum development [in primary schools]" (Tung, 2001, paras. 37–38). On 10 April 2002, the Hong Kong government released details of the measure (*scheme*) announced by the chief executive. This scheme was the provision of an additional teacher post (for leading curriculum development in primary schools) to primary schools in formulating curriculum development strategies and implementing curriculum reforms. The scheme would be introduced by phases of three years starting from the 2002–2003 school year, and it was expected to reach its final phase in 2004–2005 (Information Services Department, 2002). This scheme was considered a very forward but costly initiative, which was unique in the Chinese societies and most developed countries (Tsui, 2010). This move clearly demonstrated the determination of the government to curriculum reform in terms of policy orientations and investment of resources (Law, Galton and Wan, 2007).

In the original plan of the government was meant to be a five-year time-limited provision of an additional teacher carrying the post of Primary School Curriculum Leader (PSCL). The first batch, comprising 232 PSCLs, was appointed for five years in 2002–2003. Until the end of 2004–2005, 610 posts of PSCLs had been created, which indicated that almost all primary schools in Hong Kong had been provided with one PSCL under this scheme (Tsui, 2008). Dramatically, approaching the end of the scheme on 27 February 2006, the former Secretary for Education and Manpower Bureau (EMB) (which is now renamed as Education Bureau [EDB]) announced that, together with a series of long-term support measures for teachers, the five-year time-limited PSCL posts would be turned into permanent posts effective from school year 2007–2008. Although this move can be seen to be a compromise that the EDB had come to terms with the political pressures from teachers and politicians triggered by the education reform, the EDB endorsed the achievement of this scheme, which is its positive impact on student learning, teacher development and collaboration in primary schools (Chan, 2008; Tsui, 2008).

CONCEPTUALIZING CURRICULUM LEADERSHIP

The literature review indicates that a loosely defined conception of curriculum leadership was introduced initially as an aspect of principal leadership by assuming it as one of the responsibilities of school principals. School principals are proclaimed to be the undisputed educational leaders of their schools (Pajak and McAfee, 1992, p.21), or in some cases this responsibility is delegated to a deputy principal or designated teachers (Cardno, 2006). The term 'curriculum leadership' has been used interchangeably with educational leadership, instructional leadership and instructional management (Blase and Blase, 2004; Bossert et al., 1982; Glatthorn, 1987; Lee and Dimmock, 1999; Murphy, 1990). The rise of teacher leadership and the advocacy of teachers as keys for successful curriculum reform resulted in a distributed nature of curriculum leadership (Elliott et al., 2005). From this perspective, curriculum leadership does not necessarily rest exclusively with the principal (Hopkins, 2003), thus, the CL could refer to anyone who is actively engaged in the functions of curriculum leadership (Gross, 1998). A growing body of literature emphasizes the professional aspects of curriculum leadership that focus on effective student learning, curriculum development and curriculum implementation. More authors argue that teachers should be empowered to be CLs because teachers are front-line workers who implement curriculum programmes and who have direct linkage to students (MacPherson and Brooker, 2000). Along this line of thinking, Glickman (1989) argues that "a principal should be the leader of teachers as curriculum leaders, rather than as the sole curriculum leader" (as cited in Lee and Dimmock, 1999, p.458). This concept would greatly impact on curriculum development and implementation at school levels through distributed instructional leadership (Hallinger and Lee, 2012). Tsui (2010) concludes that the concept of curriculum leadership is different and unique from other educational leadership that can be understood from three perspectives. Firstly, curriculum leadership is defined more by function than organizational position. Secondly, curriculum leadership is about the behaviours performed or actions taken by a CL resulting in effective teaching and learning at schools. Thirdly, curriculum leadership is a process. CLs are engaged in activities for improving the quality of the curriculum or the learning programme in school.

178 *Kwok-Tung Tsui*

ROLE AND DUTIES OF THE PRIMARY SCHOOL CURRICULUM LEADER

The PSCL post was a newly created position to provide support to primary schools in formulating SBCD strategies and implementing curriculum reform. The first priorities on the agenda of the EDB were to conceptualize the meaning of curriculum leadership and to define the specific role and duties of PSCL as a CL in the primary school setting. Needless to say, the decision of the EDB had great impact on the preparation and work of the CLs, which in turn would contribute to the success of the "Learning to Learn" education reform. Tsui (2010) concludes that seven core components of the curriculum leadership of the principal could be drawn from the literature:

1. Goal setting and defining the purpose of the school
2. Establishing the curriculum development structure and procedures
3. Directing, coaching and monitoring the curriculum planning and design activities
4. Culture building for SBCD
5. Developing capability of teachers for engaging in curriculum development processes
6. Implementing curriculum evaluation and quality assurance (QA) to ensure quality of student learning
7. Consolidating and allocating resources to support curriculum development

However, relatively few studies on curriculum leadership for teacher leaders and subject teachers from local researchers could hardly inform the EDB officials of the best practices in the field at the time they started to plan for the implementation of the PSCL scheme. Against this background, the EDB had to take a more pragmatic approach to conceptualize curriculum leadership based on the needs of the PSCLs in achieving the stated aims of the scheme. Largely, PSCLs are expected to assist the school head in formulating SBCD strategies and implementing curriculum reform. Thus, core components of curriculum leadership for PSCLs could model on the seven core components of curriculum leadership of principal as suggested by Tsui (2010). Although school heads and PSCLs are expected to work as CLs at different levels, the former group is expected to focus more on the 'abstract' aspects, such as higher-level decision and policy making, while the latter is deemed to concentrate more on the 'concrete' aspects, such as working with and through teachers. This assumption, to a large extent, is reflected in the roles and duties of PSCLs specified by the EDB in its circulars to announce the arrangements of the scheme. Below is the description extracted from the latest circular in 2007 (Tsui, 2010, p.87):

Role: The Primary School Curriculum Leader will serve as the leader to help the school in reforming the curriculum in accordance with the educational aims to promote whole-person development and lifelong learning.

Duties:

1. To assist the school head to lead whole-school curriculum planning and facilitate implementation of the plans;
2. To support the school head in planning and coordinating assessment policy and assessment practices;
3. To lead teachers/specialist staff in improving learning and teaching strategies;
4. To promote a professional exchange culture; and
5. To take up a reasonable teaching load (about 50% of the average teaching load of a teacher in the school) for trying out or piloting different strategies for further curriculum development.

The descriptions show that PSCLs have very clear and specific roles in helping their schools implement curriculum reform to achieve the aims of the "Learning to Learn" education reform launched in 2000. Specifically, PSCLs are required to assist their school heads in five broad school activities, which are whole-school curriculum planning, assessment policy and assessment practices, improving learning and teaching strategies, professional culture, and piloting different strategies for further curriculum development. All five broad school activities are geared to the major strategies advocated by the government in implementing the curriculum reform under the big picture of the "Learning to Learn" education reform. Although the EDB has not explicitly spelled out its own definition of curriculum leadership, in practice the PSCLs are required to exercise a new type of leadership. This leadership, which largely matches the three major perspectives of curriculum leadership discussed in the earlier section of this chapter, includes (1) *executing specific functions*—assisting/supporting the school heads in leading internal curriculum development; (2) *performing specific tasks and taking actions related to curriculum development*—lead, co-ordinate, plan, promote and facilitate; and (3) *being actively engaged in curriculum development processes*—piloting different strategies for further curriculum development.

Kennedy and Hui (2006) assert the key to the success of the whole scheme is to determine the most effective preparation for newly appointed PSCLs. Unlike the usual practice to provide newly promoted senior teachers with short training courses, the EDB considered the complexity of the role and duties assigned to newly appointed PSCLs. Thus, the EDB adopted a unique and tailor-made professional development model to empower and develop PSCLs into new types of leaders to spearhead SBCD in primary schools. Under this model, all newly appointed PSCLs are required to complete the professional development programmes on curriculum leadership on or before the first year of their appointment (Tsui, 2008).

180 Kwok-Tung Tsui

INNOVATIVE PROFESSIONAL MODEL
FOR DEVELOPING SUCCESSFUL PSCLS

To empower the newly appointed PSCLs, this innovative professional model comprises two components through (1) change of formal school organizational structure and (2) tailor-made professional development programmes. These components are two sides of the same coin. The PSCLs could not discharge their duties successfully without either one of these two components. To 'legitimize' the role and authority of the PSCLs in leading internal curriculum reform in schools, the EDB made a very decisive and bold decision to change the existing primary school organizational structure by creating a new senior teacher post in every primary school. In the new primary school structure, the appointed PSCL is a senior teacher with the rank just under the school head (also under the deputy school head when this new post was installed in 2008).

The rank carried by PSCL represents a status associated with legitimate power (Dambe and Moorad, 2008), which was regarded by most teachers in Hong Kong and the Chinese societies as the foremost identity of a leader at workplace because of the influence of traditional Chinese or Confucian culture. As pointed out by several experienced and successful PSCLs, their official title (rank) is one of their most important and necessary assets that enables them to discharge their roles and duties effectively in school. Once they obtain the title, their colleagues respect them and accept their advice and request for co-operation. According to Confucian Analects *míng zhèng yán shun* (名正言順), their words carry weight because they are with the right title (Tsui, 2008). However, the EDB understood clearly that without solid expertise and professional knowledge in curriculum development, the PSCL would be a CL in title only, and incapable of supporting the school and leading internal curriculum reform and development in real practice. Thus, the second side of the same coin is to empower the PSCLs with expert power (Dambe and Moorad, 2008) through tailor-made professional development programmes. When the scheme was launched in school year 2002–2003, the EDB developed and delivered an intensive in-service professional development programme for the first cohort of newly appointed PSCLs. Since then, the EDB continues to run the same programme every year, with some modifications in the training content and duration. Below are examples that show the major milestones in the development of the programme.

Example 1—Components of Professional Development Programme for Newly Appointed PSCL 2002–2003(First Cohort) (136 Hours)

- A. Seminars on 'Curriculum Reforms in Hong Kong' (27 hours) (delivered by the EDB)
- B. Web-based course on curriculum reform and leadership and management (20 hours)
- C1. Course on 'Curriculum Planning and Design, Learning Theories, Learning and Teaching Strategies' (20 hours)

C2. Course on 'Action Research, Professional Development, and Organizational Learning' (30 hours)
C3. Workshop on 'Change Agents in Curriculum Reform' (6 hours)
C4. 'Building a Learning Community: Reflective Action in School-Based Curriculum Development' (12 hours)
D. Course on 'Assessment for Learning' (9 hours)
E. Course on 'Learner Diversity—Catering for Individual Differences' (9 hours)
F. Winding session (3 hours)

Example 2—Components of Professional Development Programme for Newly Appointed PSCL 2006–2007(Fourth Cohort) (101 Hours)

A. Seminar on 'The CDC Basic Education Curriculum Guide and the Role and Duties of the Primary School Curriculum Leader' (3 hours) (delivered by the EDB)
B. A series of seminars on 'Introduction to Curriculum Leadership for Primary School Curriculum Leaders' (18 hours) (delivered by the EDB)
C1. Course on 'Curriculum Planning and Design, Curriculum Change, Curriculum Leadership and Management, Learning Theories, Leaning and Their Application in Designing Curriculum and Developing Learning and Teaching Strategies, and Curriculum-Based Assessment' (50 hours)
C2. Course on 'Action Research, Professional Development, and Organizational Learning' (30 hours)

Example 3—Component of Professional Development Programme for Newly Appointed PSCL 2008–2009 (101 Hours)

A. Introduction of Curriculum Leadership and Management Series (21 hours) (delivered by the EDB)
B1. Course on 'Curriculum Planning, Design and Implementation, Curriculum Change, Curriculum Leadership, Curriculum Management, Learning Theories and Their Applications in Design of Curriculum Units and Development of Learning and Teaching Strategies, Curriculum-Based Assessment and Professional Development and Organizational Learning' (60 hours)
B2. Course on 'Action Research, Action Research Project, and Reflective Practices' (20 hours)

Example 4—Components of Professional Development Programme for Newly Appointed PSCL 2012/2013 (110 Hours)

A. Introduction of Curriculum Leadership and Management Series (30 hours) (delivered by the EDB)

182   *Kwok-Tung Tsui*

B1. Course on 'Curriculum Planning, Design, and Implementation, Curriculum Change, Curriculum Leadership, Curriculum Management, Learning Theories and Their Applications in Design of Curriculum Units and Development of Learning and Teaching Strategies, Curriculum-Based Assessment and Professional Development and Organizational Learning' (60 hours)

B2. Course on 'Action Research, Action Research Project and Reflective Practices' (20 hours)

The above descriptions show that the professional development programme has undergone continuing modifications and consolidation since its inception to meet the changing needs of the PSCLs and to align with the progress (phases) of curriculum reform implementation based on the feedback collected from the PSCLs during programme evaluations. The major changes or modifications made to the programme can be summarized in three aspects: *mode of delivery*, *content* and *duration*. From the four examples shown above, we interestingly find that a 20-hour web-based course on curriculum reform emerged only in example 1 despite noting that this web-based course had once been promoted as the signature feature of this professional development programme (Information Services Department, 2002). This situation probably occurred because based on the adverse feedback and criticisms received from the first three cohorts of PSCLs after completion of the programme (Tsui and Lo, 2004), the EDB decided to withdraw this web-based course from the programme starting from the fourth cohort in year 2006–2007. This change has significant implications on the design of the training programme from the pedagogical and financing perspectives. First, the literature on adult learning and teacher development indicates that "adults [teachers] prefer a learning structure that emphasizes flexibility of time and pacing" and enables individualized learning (Glatthorn and Fox, 1996, p.8). Along this line of thinking, web-based learning should be a flexible and efficient learning mode preferred by teachers, particularly for pursuing continuous professional development and in-service training. Second, from the financial perspective, a web-based course should be a more cost-effective means of delivering standardized courses to different cohorts over a period of time. Thus, why did the EDB bother to make the change? The following quote from an interview of a participant in this programme may provide a clue:

> For the [web-based] course . . . yes, adult education should have a lot of freedom . . . I wonder how many colleagues had got into the Web platform for discussion . . . I also doubt the effects of this Web talk . . . Personally, I prefer to read a book or have a case to analyze . . . This is more practical . . . In the end, we just had to hand in an ordinary assignment. I really don't know how much leadership we have learnt. (A003) (Tsui and Lo, 2004)

Curriculum Leadership Developments   183

This comment clearly shows that PSCLs, while acknowledging the flexibility of web-based learning, criticized that this self-learning mode could neither suit the nature of the course content nor provide them with useful consultation support for completing the course assignments. Given that the programme was supposed to help the PSCLs develop their leadership and management skills for implementing curriculum reform, they wanted to interact with instructors and share experiences with and learn from other co-workers. Thus, they preferred face-to-face discussions and a hands-on type of learning that can help them process their experience through reflection, analysis and critical examination (Glatthorn and Fox, 1996). The aforementioned web-based course evidently failed to satisfy the fundamental needs and expectations of PSCLs, which explains why starting from the fourth cohort, all courses in this programme have been delivered in face-to-face mode, that is, in the form of seminars or group teaching (about 30 participants), although this face-to-face training mode is significantly more expensive from a financial perspective. As shown in examples 1 to 4, the content of this programme can be grouped into seven major areas/themes directly related to the work of PSCLs: teaching and learning strategies, curriculum development and implementation, student assessment, curriculum leadership and management, action research, professional development and organizational learning, and curriculum reform policies and documents. The programme is organized and delivered under different components. As shown in the examples, the programme had undergone a series of developments and consolidations, such that a concise programme structure gradually emerged. Since 2008–2009 and onwards, the programme has had a two-stage structure: stage one is called component A, whereas stage two is called component B (comprising B1 and B2). Component A is a compulsory component that the PSCLs are required to complete before they can move on to the second stage of the programme. This component is designed and delivered in the format of a series of seminars aimed at helping newly appointed PSCLs become familiar with curriculum reform policies, mandates, initiatives, guidelines, reports and requirements, as well as resources and support provided by the EDB for implementing curriculum reform. The time allocated to this component varies from 21 hours to 30 hours on a need basis. This component is organized and conducted by EDB officials and can be seen as the EDB's strategy to control the platform to 'orient' newly appointed PSCLs to the new job and develop a 'favourable attitude' toward and 'proper understanding' of curriculum reform policies, mandates and requirements. The PSCLs are then expected to disseminate further this set of 'EDB-endorsed' attitudes and understanding to their colleagues through internal staff development and participation in the actual SBCD processes.

On the other hand, component B aims to empower the PSCLs with a solid foundation of theory and practice of curriculum leadership so that they can discharge their responsibilities effectively and efficiently. Notably,

184   *Kwok-Tung Tsui*

component B comprises two parts: B1 and B2, which account for 60 and 20 hours, respectively. Component B1 is a 60-hour course covering a wide range of theories, strategies and skills mainly aimed at enhancing PSCLs' competencies in leading SBCD and implementation under the overarching curriculum reform framework. Component B2 is a 20-hour course dedicated to the development of PSCLs' ability to conduct action research and to serve as a catalyst for developing schools into learning communities by engaging teachers in collaborative action research and reflective enquiry, thus enabling teachers to initiate SBCD and reflective practices in teaching and learning. In studying this course, each participant is required to undertake an action research project in SBCD or teacher professional development under the guidance of a supervisor. It is hoped that the PSCL can become the leader to create a collaborative environment in school and encourage teachers to conduct subject-based or school-based action research and try out practices to improve learning and teaching. The importance of the action research element in preparing teachers and teacher leaders to perform their responsibilities well in a 21st century classroom and school is acknowledged by the Organisation for Economic Co-operation and Development (OECD) in its background report for the International Summit on the Teaching Profession—*Preparing Teachers and Developing School Leaders for the 21st Century: Lessons from around the World* (Schleicher, 2012). For example, Finland is well known for its students' achievement in the Programme for International Student Assessment (PISA) studies. It is noted in the report that 'research-based' is one of the distinguishing qualities of teacher education in Finland:

> Teacher candidates are not only expected to become familiar with the knowledge base in education and human development [. . .] Upper grade teachers typically pick a topic in their subject area; primary grade teachers typically study some aspect of pedagogy. The rationale for requiring a research-based dissertation is that teachers are expected to engage in disciplined inquiry in the classroom throughout their teacher career. (p.39)

In the other part of the world, Japan makes all teachers participate in regular lesson studies in their schools, which provides one of the most effective mechanisms for continuous improvement of teachers' teaching competencies. The report further highlights:

> This school-by-school lesson study often culminates in large public research lessons. For example, when a new subject is added to the national curriculum, groups of teachers and researchers review research and curriculum materials and refine their ideas in pilot classrooms over a year before holding a public research lesson, which can be viewed electronically by hundreds of teachers, researchers and policymakers. (p.48)

Curriculum Leadership Developments 185

In addition, in Shanghai:

> teachers are trained to be action researchers in effective practice, with the best teachers going on to support new teachers and helping to improve lesson quality [. ..] The authorities in the Shanghai province of China emphasize giving prospective teachers the skills they will need for action research, and their method for improving their education system over time relies on research performed by teachers. (p.48)

In Hong Kong, the instrumental role played by action research in supporting curriculum reform is best illustrated by the CDC (2002), which claims that "collaboration action research is recommended as a strategy in teacher professional development and school-based curriculum development [. . . such that] the main purpose of action research is to improve practices and to generate knowledge based evidence through teachers working together" (p.13). Hui (2010) echoes this view and argues that CLs are meant to ensure that curriculum reform works and to bring in action research determinably for curriculum development. This condition can be attributed to the fact that the government had adopted a gradual approach (ten-year plan) to implement this "Learning to Learn" education and curriculum reform, with 2001–2002 to 2005–2006 as the short-term phase, 2006–2007 to 2010–2011 as the medium-term phase, and 2011–2012 and beyond as the long-term phase. According to this schedule, the schools should achieve specific goals in different phases. In the short-term phase, based on their individual strengths and contexts, schools are expected to strengthen students' learning capabilities and change the school curriculum at their own pace with the understanding that the short-term phase is meant to enable schools to lay a good foundation for implementing more fundamental changes in the medium-term and long-term phases. In the medium-term phase, schools are expected to conduct collaborative action research as a strategy to improve plans and action based on a review of their achievements and progress in 2006. In the long-term phase, based on the experience gained in early stages of curriculum reform, schools are expected to have the capacity to achieve the long-term goals of curriculum reform: "make good use of effective learning and teaching strategies to help students attain all-round development and life-long learning [and] develop school-based curricula that suit the needs of their students, on the basis of central curriculum framework" (CDC, 2001, pp.iii–iv).

In summary, this action research element adds value to role of PSCLs and the related professional development programme, thus making the PSCL scheme a unique model for supporting the implementation of "Learning to Learn" curriculum reform. The EDB apparently needs to draw from the expertise of academics and curriculum development experts. As such, component B is usually commissioned to tertiary institutions for course design and delivery. This arrangement demonstrates how the scheme and the

186 Kwok-Tung Tsui

PSCLs can benefit from the collaboration between the technocrats (EDB) and the academics (tertiary institutions), which has significant implications on the success of this scheme.

Notably, Singapore, a keen competitor of Hong Kong, also employs action research as a powerful tool to drive school curriculum reform. Both Hong Kong and Singapore have been highly praised by international organizations for their excellent performance in various international student comparison studies. The recent 2010 McKinsey & Company report classifies both jurisdictions as one of the very few "sustained improvers" (the best category) in the world for their continuing achievements in improving their school systems over the last two decades (Mourshed, Chijioke and Barber, 2010). To further support the schools in implementing the "Teach Less, Learn More" initiative launched in 2004, the Singapore Ministry of Education provides each school with one teacher receiving specialized training in research under the Research Activist Attachment Scheme since 2006 as a strategy to support teachers in undertaking practice-oriented action research and to develop schools into professional learning communities (PLCs) (Hogan, Teh and Dimmock, 2011). To a large extent, Singapore's Research Activist Attachment Scheme and Hong Kong's PSCL scheme share a very similar rationale, that is, to promote action research as a tool to drive curriculum reform and SBCD.

CONCLUSION

As previously discussed, the PSCL scheme and the professional development model used to prepare these newly appointed CLs are expensive and demanding in terms of resource input and the commitment of the trainers and trainees. The government, researchers, school personnel and the public are keen to know whether this professional development model is effective and capable of meeting the needs of the PSCLs. Kennedy and Hui (2006, p.119) argue that the success of this professional development model (training programme) can be judged by "the extent to which it led to growth in capacity of the newly appoint curriculum leader" and "their potential to undertake the kind of job for which they were employed". The latter is even more important as it directly points to the relevancy to the PSCLs' jobs or duties. They also assert that the capacity to be developed should include a set of skills that can empower the PSCLs to function as effective teacher leaders to support the wide-ranging curriculum reform at school sites, that is, being a good teacher as well as a mentor, a colleague, a strategic thinker and a planner. Furthermore, they proposed that teacher self-efficacy was a robust construct that could be adopted as an outcome measure for evaluating the success of the training programme, in other words, its impact on the growth of the CLs. They adopted a one-group pre-test–post-test design and surveyed 228 newly appointed PSCLs who had undertaken the training programme. The results of their study indicate a positive relationship between professional development and growth of self-efficacy in the PSCLs. The training programme encouraged PSCLs to believe in their capacity to perform well in SBCD. In a more straightforward approach to understanding how successful the training programme was in preparing newly appointed PSCLs to perform their duties, EDB conducted surveys on the effectiveness of the training programme in three consecutive years from 2003 to 2005. Upon completion of the training programme in the end of the first year of service, the PSCLs were asked to evaluate their own overall performance in a five-category scale (excellent, good, satisfactory, fair and unsatisfactory). In parallel their school heads were also surveyed to evaluate the performance of the PSCLs using the same scale independently. The results are shown in Table 11.1.

Two conclusions can be drawn from the survey results. First, approximately 40% of the PSCLs and 60% of their school heads rated the performance of the PSCLs as good or excellent. On the other hand, only a very small number of the PSCLs' performance (approximately 3%) was rated unsatisfactorily by themselves or their school heads. Second, both sets of ratings given by the PSCLs themselves and the school heads were consistent and skewed toward the high side (good and excellent). Notably, the school heads' ratings were significantly higher than the PSCLs' ratings, particularly

Table 11.1 Performance Evaluation of PSCLs after Completion of the Professional Development Programme

	First Cohort	*Second Cohort*	*Third Cohort*
PSCL's Self-Ratings			
Excellent	3.5%	2.7%	1.5%
Good	39.4%	35.6%	39.3%
Satisfactory	39.0%	40.9%	36.9%
Moderate	16.0%	16.9%	18.0%
Unsatisfactory	0.9%	3.1%	2.9%
(No Response)	(1.2%)	(0.8%)	(1.4%)
School Heads' Ratings			
Excellent	32.0%	28.4%	18.0%
Good	46.8%	49.3%	49.3%
Satisfactory	13.4%	13.8%	21.0%
Moderate	4.3%	4.4%	8.8%
Unsatisfactory	0.9%	3.1%	2.4%
(No Response)	(2.6%)	(1.0%)	(0.5%)

Source: Adapted from Tsui (2008).

188 *Kwok-Tung Tsui*

in the excellent category. Results suggest that the training programme was generally successful in developing newly appointed PSCLs into competent CLs in both the eyes of the PSCLs themselves and their school heads.

Notably, promising ratings were given by the school heads in comparison with the PSCLs themselves. In Chinese culture societies such as Hong Kong, people tend to be 'humble' in rating their performance, unlike their counterparts in Western societies. Also, this condition might be attributed to the fact that the PSCL post was newly created in primary schools, such that these newly appointed PSCLs did not have any good reference or benchmark by which to judge their own performances in this new context. Therefore, they tended to be conservative in giving the ratings. By contrast, school heads were the most qualified to rate the performance of PSCLs from their supervisors' and co-workers' eyes because the major duties of PSCLs are to assist their school heads in leading whole-school curriculum development. Thus, their ratings were useful to triangulate the PSCLs' self-ratings and to provide a more valid judgement on the growth these CLs gained from undertaking this tailor-made training programme. Based on school heads' ratings, the newly appointed PSCLs generally demonstrated good performance in performing their duties as CLs although these PSCLs underestimated their own capacity or performance. In a similar vein, Tsui (2008) conducted a series of surveys of four cohorts of newly appointed PSCLs upon completion of the component B training programme in the period from 2005 to 2008. They were asked to use a five-point scale (1 is very unsatisfactory and 5 is very satisfactory) to rate their own performance in discharging the four major duties (excluding the fifth one on teaching) prescribed by the EDB. In addition, they were also asked to rate their overall performance in a five-point scale. Results show that the PSCLs were satisfied with their overall performance (mean scores of the four cohorts ranged from 3.13 to 3.40). As regards their four major duties, PSCLs were more satisfied with their performance in "to assist the school head to lead whole-school curriculum planning and facilitate implementation of the plans" (mean scores ranged from 3.37 to 3.57) and moderately satisfied with their performance in "to promote a professional exchange culture" (mean score ranged from 3.00 to 3.17). The findings of the above studies provide useful and consistent evidence showing that this innovative professional development model adopted by the EDB is successful in developing competent CLs in local primary schools. To conclude, based on the report presented by Chan (2008, pp.3–4) at the 2008 International Education Leaders' Dialogue, the major achievements and effectiveness of this PSCL scheme can be summarized as follows:

1. The PSCL scheme started in the 2002–2003 school year. The scheme provides additional resources for each school to appoint an experienced teacher to be a CL to assist the school head in leading whole-school curriculum development.
2. The majority of schools have set up a curriculum development team, headed by the CL, to co-ordinate the curriculum development of all

Curriculum Leadership Developments 189

key learning areas (KLAs) and cross-curriculum elements. Around the same period, the professional development of the CL together with their school heads, panel chairpersons and teachers brought about a cascading effect on SBCD.

2. As evident from the evaluation study administered in consecutive years, the scheme was instrumental in laying a good foundation for reform in secondary schools. The scheme has had a positive impact on student learning, teacher development and collaboration in schools.

4. All CLs are provided with a tailor-made programme in the first year of their appointment to enhance curriculum leadership in areas such as whole-school curriculum planning, pedagogy, assessment policy and catering for diversity, as well as moral and civic education.

5 .Enrichment programmes are also provided in the following years for continuous development. The participants are also formed into a network of learning communities that meet regularly to support professional sharing and growth. This initiative further empowers CLs as change agents in promoting SBCD.

REFERENCES

Blase, J., & Blase, J. (2004). *Handbook of instructional leadership: How successful principals promote teaching and learning* (2nd ed.). Thousand Oaks, CA: Corwin Press.

Bossert, S.T., Dwyer, D.C., Rowan, B., & Lee, G.V. (1982). The instructional management role of the principal. *Educational Administration Quarterly, 18*(3), 34–64.

Cardno, C. (2006). Leading change from within: Action research to strengthen curriculum leadership in a primary school. *School Leadership & Management, 26*(5), 453–471.

Carless, D. (1997). Managing systemic curriculum change: A critical analysis of Hong Kong's target-oriented curriculum initiative. *International Review of Education/Internationale Zeitschrift fuer Erziehungswissenschaft/Revue Internationale de l'Education, 43*(4), 349–366.

Chan, C.K.K. (2008). *The Hong Kong case study report—supporting reform for 'whole-person development and life-long learning'.* Paper presented at the 2008 International Education Leaders' Dialogue, Melbourne, Australia, 1–3 December.

Curriculum Development Council (2001). *Learning to learn—The way forward in curriculum.* Hong Kong: Printing Department. Retrieved 23 September 2013, from http://www.edb.gov.hk/index.aspx?nodeID=2877&langno=1.

Curriculum Development Council (2002). *Basic education curriculum guide: Building on strengths (primary 1—secondary 3).* Hong Kong: Curriculum Development Council.

Dambe, M., & Moorad, F. (2008). From power to empowerment: A paradigm shift in leadership. *South African Journal of Higher Education, 22*(3), 575–587.

Elliott, B., Macpherson, I., Mikel, E., Joseph, P.B., Crosswel, L., & Aspland, T. (2005). Defining a conversational space for curriculum leadership. *Journal of Curriculum & Pedagogy, 2*(2), 119–138.

Glatthorn, A.A. (1987). *Curriculum leadership.* Glenview, IL: HarperCollins.

190   Kwok-Tung Tsui

Glatthorn, A.A., & Fox, L.E. (1996). *Quality teaching through professional development*. Thousand Oaks, CA: Corwin Press.

Gross, S.J. (1998). *Staying centered: Curriculum leadership in a turbulent era*. Alexandria, VA: Association for Supervision and Curriculum Development.

Hallinger, P., & Lee, M. (2012). A global study of the practice and impact of distributed instructional leadership in International Baccalaureate (IB) schools. *Leadership and Policy in Schools, 11*(4), 477–495.

Hogan, D., Teh, L., & Dimmock, C. (2011). *Educational knowledge mobilization and utilization in Singapore*. Paper prepared for the 2011 Conference of the International Alliance of Leading Educational Institutes, OSIE, University of Toronto, Canada. 3 March, 2011. Retrieved, 23 September 2013 from http://www.oise.utoronto.ca/oise/UserFiles/File/Singapore.pdf.

Hopkins, D. (2003). Instructional leadership and school improvement. In A. Harris, C. Day, M. Hadfield, D. Hopkins, A. Hargreaves & C. Chapman (Eds.) *Effective leadership for school improvement* (pp.55–71). London: RoutledgeFalmer.

Hui, S.K.F. (2010). Validation of curriculum leaders' attitudes toward research scale. *Asia-Pacific Education Researcher, 19*(2), 301–310.

Information Services Department (2002). *Additional teachers for curriculum development. (Press Release of Hong Kong SAR Government)*. Retrieved 23 September 2013, from http://www.info.gov.hk/gia/general/200204/10/0410236.htm.

Kennedy, K.J., & Hui, S.K.F. (2006). Developing teacher leaders to facilitate Hong Kong's curriculum reforms: Self-efficacy as a measure of teacher growth. *International Journal of Educational Reform, 15*(1), 114–128.

Kennedy, K.J. & Lee, J.C.-k. (2008). *The changing role of schools in Asian societies: Schools for the knowledge society*. New York: Routledge.

Law, E.H.-F., Galton, M., & Wan, S.W.-Y. (2007). Developing curriculum leadership in schools: Hong Kong perspectives. *Asia—Pacific Journal of Teacher Education, 35*(2), 143–159.

Lee, J.C.-K., & Dimmock, C. (1999). Curriculum leadership and management in secondary schools: A Hong Kong case study. *School Leadership & Management, 19*(4), 455–481.

Lee, W.O. (2001). Trends in educational reform and new demands on teacher quality. *Journal of Quality School Education, 1*, 11–19. (In Chinese)

MacPherson, I., & Brooker, R. (2000). Positioning stakeholders in curriculum leadership: How can teacher educators work with teachers to discover and create their place? *Asia-Pacific Journal of Teacher Education, 28*(1), 69–85.

Mourshed, M., Chijioke, C., & Barber, M. (2010). *How the world's most improved school systems keep getting better*. New York, NY: McKinsey & Company. Retrieved 23 September 2013, from http://mckinseyonsociety.com/how-the-worlds-most-improved-school-systems-keep-getting-better/.

Murphy, J. (1990). Instructional leadership: focus on curriculum responsibilities. *NASSP Bulletin, 74*(525), 1–4.

Pajak, E., & McAfee, L. (1992). The principal as school leader, curriculum leader. *NASSP Bulletin, 76*(547), 21–30.

Schleicher, A. (Ed.) (2012). *Preparing teachers and developing school leaders for the 21st century: Lessons from around the world*. Paris, France: OECD Publishing. http://dx.doi.org/10.1787/9789264174559-en. Retrieved 23 September 2013, from http://www.oecd-ilibrary.org/education/preparing-teachers-and-developing-school-leaders-for-the-21st-century_9789264174559-en

Tsui, K.-T. (2008). *Curriculum leadership in Hong Kong primary schools: Creating teacher leaders*. Paper presented at the APERA Conference 2008, NIE, Singapore, 26–28 November.

Tsui, K.-T. (2010). Curriculum leadership and school development: Review and prospects. *New Horizons in Education, 58*(2), 83–92. (In Chinese)

Tsui, K.-T., & Cheng, Y.C. (2000). Multi-dimensional teacher performance in the new century: Implications for school management. *Asia-Pacific Educational Researcher, 9*(2), 184–208.

Tsui, K.-T., & Lo, Y.-C. (2004). *Transforming primary teachers into curriculum leaders.* Paper presented at the International Council on Education for Teaching (ICET) World Assembly, Hong Kong, 13–17 July.

Tung, C.H. (2001). *Policy Address 2001.* Retrieved 23 September 2013, from http://www.policyaddress.gov.hk/pa01/e37.htm.

Part V

Curriculum Change and Implementation

12 Initiating Change and Innovations

Edmond Hau-Fai Law

BACKGROUND

Hong Kong's educational system is considered one of the few educational systems in the world that demonstrate a range of features which characterize efficient organizations. A 2010 study highlighted six factors that account for the success of an educational system. This chapter concentrates on the processes and the organizational features which "perpetuate innovative practices" at the school level (Law, 2014; Law et al., 2014). This chapter bases its report on a series of design-based studies conducted and led by the author in the last ten years in his attempt to uncover the key organizational features which are likely to enhance opportunities that generate new and innovative ideas in pedagogical change at the school and at the classroom level (Law and Wan, 2006; Law, Galton and Wan, 2007; 2010; Law et al., 2010; Law, 2011; Law et al., 2013). My studies also have a background on key policy change in engineering a new pedagogical role and identity for teachers in the last 30 years in Hong Kong.

Policy changes often consider the possibility that putting policies into practice while faithfully adhering to their intentions is unlikely. This situation occurred specifically in educational reforms in the 1960s when large-scale educational reforms were initiated and designed by central curriculum agencies. However, these policies encountered resistance from schoolteachers. Reflections on strategies led to the belief that change is a highly contextualized and situated social phenomenon brought about by a network of agencies within the social context in which change is initiated, developed and institutionalized.

In 1982, the Llewellyn Report marked a new era in educational change in Hong Kong. A panel of foreign educational experts led by Llewellyn recommended that teachers' roles and identities needed to be changed to bring about changes and innovations to the traditional classroom practices of using a transmission model as a major pedagogical strategy (Llewellyn, 1982). Teachers must assume new responsibilities as professionals in making decisions about what the key learning objectives should be and how objectives can be achieved in practice. Teacher participation in curriculum

196   Edmond Hau-Fai Law

decision making and design has been increasing (Yeung et al., 2012). Moreover, schools are expected to play a major role in introducing changes to their traditional culture of being a teaching community, rather than a community of practices, which has the capacity of generating changes and innovations. Both institutions and individuals are expected to play a role in change processes and their mutual support. In case of non-alignment, their internal exclusiveness and conflicts are key variables in the successful implementation of changes and innovations.

One key research issue in this study is identifying the conditions and processes that engage teachers in professional activities which provide room for new ideas and for proposals to be developed, and determining which processes are being put into practice. What can the teachers learn and how can teacher leadership develop in the process of engaging in professional activities at the school-based level? These issues serve as the basis for discussion in the following sections.

DEVELOPING TEACHER CURRICULUM LEADERSHIP

Two major development projects with similar organizational and educational principles were conducted over two periods (2004–2006 and 2007–2008) in two Hong Kong primary schools. These two projects were funded by the Quality Education Fund (QEF), which was established by the government in 1998 to support development initiatives and school-based innovations. The projects were designed according to the following contemporary educational principles in human learning.

- The development activities should be school-based and problem-oriented, focusing on pedagogical change and improvement.
- Teacher participants should be collaborative, and the model of power hierarchy typical of Asian culture should be mediated to an extent that social interactions allow active participation and individual contributions to the completion of the tasks.
- Interactions within teams should be open and reflective.
- Development activities should be organized in phases, beginning with planning and initially reviewing the current curriculum practice in classroom, to the design and application in classrooms, and to the final phase in which actions and practices are evaluated.
- The development activities should be organized in ways which sustain the motivation and the momentum of change, and should be spirally and cyclically arranged to engineer and sustain a culture of change and lifelong learning.

The projects were called 'Accelerating School-Based Curriculum Development' and aimed to develop teacher leadership skills in curriculum planning, designing and implementing innovations at the classroom level. Three curriculum development teams in each school were subject-based and formed, including the three key school subjects in Hong Kong, namely, Chinese, English and Mathematics. Each team had around five to six teachers of different grades and experiences. Each team followed a similar pattern of procedures and steps which was modelled and modified after key components in the action research and Engeström's (2008) cycles of expansive learning. A simplified model is listed in the following.

Stage One: Planning and Reviewing

The team sat together and identified a key topic or an issue which the team generally found difficult to teach children. The members shared their common practices and traditional pedagogical strategies in organizing and managing learning activities on the topic. Then the team adopted an approach or strategy that was different from the traditional one. The purpose was to engage each in a new or innovative alternative, which influenced the teachers to reconsider their own approaches and accept risk-taking actions to implement change.

Stage Two: Implementation and Trial

The team designed appropriate strategies and developed a lesson plan for the tryout. The team prepared the teaching materials and the learning activities that supported the achievements of the learning objectives in the lesson. In Hong Kong, each level has three to four classes of 30 students, and each member in the team was able to teach a class with the use of the same lesson plan. However, the project purposely arranged for each member to take turns in teaching a class. A time gap was set between the first, second and third classes. The gap allowed the members to observe the lessons and reflect on the approach used during each lesson, and thus revise the lesson plan to suit the students' needs which each member had in mind.

Stage Three: Reflection

The team recorded all trial lessons and conducted a reflection meeting on the basis of the evidence from the observations and video-recorded lessons. The purpose was to engage the team in a collectively reflective dialogue. This dialogue allowed the team to express diverse views on the basis of the commonly shared evidence among the team members.

This method is considered essential if the cycle of planning, implementing and reflecting is repeated with each team in another semester on another topic in the subject curriculum. This being so, the team would develop self-regulatory patterns of planning, implementing and reflecting

198 *Edmond Hau-Fai Law*

components, and the established procedure and steps are assumed to generate innovative changes to the traditional patterns of teaching and learning at the classroom level.

METHODS OF DATA COLLECTION

Data collection methods are multi-targeted and aimed at different types of data for triangulation and crystallization. The methods are considered cost-effective if the project could generate more international publications. Therefore, our design followed a comprehensive approach to cover as many useful data throughout the project as possible. The following is an outline of the key methods at each stage of the procedure.

Stage One: Planning and Reviewing

1. Documenting the planning meetings by using a video recorder
2. Collecting lesson plans
3. Interviewing each member
4. Collecting written feedback from members
5. Collecting email communications and feedback from external consultants

Stage Two: Implementation and Trial

1. Recording all lessons by using a video recorder
2. Collecting all discussion notes
3. Interviewing each member
4. Interviewing groups of students
5. Collecting peer observation notes

Stage Three: Reflection

1. Collecting self-evaluation notes and checklists
2. Documenting the reflection meeting by using a video recorder
3. Interviewing both teachers who conducted the trial lessons and the members who conducted the observations

Although the project engaged 13 to 15 teachers in each of the two schools, the project ultimately aimed to disseminate innovative ideas and practices among teachers of the two schools. Therefore, seminars were organized and presentations of findings were regularly arranged in staff meetings. Feedback was collected from the school community, as well. This method sought to enhance the professional commitment of the teachers as well as the professional capacity of the school community as a whole.

FINDINGS

The data obtained from the projects are varied and numerous. In addition, we believe the data serve multiple purposes. At various stages of the project development, the researchers employed different theoretical perspectives in understanding and reading the data. For example, the interview data were analyzed from a grounded perspective, whereas the interactional data from meetings were analyzed by using a discourse approach with additional theoretical perspectives from socio-cultural traditions. The following list of findings did not adhere to a particular dimension in the study. However, the findings have a broad range and focus on the development of distributed leadership among teachers in curriculum development. Neither all data nor their meanings and implications have been exhausted.

Leadership Styles and Expanding Spaces for Teacher Learning

The teams in the two schools exhibited different types of interactions as a result of their leadership styles. The impact of leadership styles was significant in the projects because a claim of the effectiveness of a school-based approach to innovations is one of the positive effects on teacher development and learning. In this study, the two leadership styles do not necessarily have negative connotations from the perspective of the author.

Two types of leadership styles have impacts on the interactional patterns of the meetings and in the interview data. These impacts led to a qualitatively different distribution of participation among members in the meetings and discussions. Further details on this matter will be discussed later in the chapter.

The first type of leadership style is the authoritarian and directive leadership style which is considered typical of Asian societies. The panel chair of the Chinese Language team was assertive and reiterated his right to have access to the teaching materials of the other teachers. He gave clear instructions on what to do and how things should be done during the meetings. His language was directive. On the contrary, the panel chair of the Mathematics team demonstrated a non-directive style without appearing to be power-coercive. She often adopted a tentative tone in her language and allowed the members more leeway during the discussions. These two contrasting leadership styles were triangulated with the patterns of interactions in the meetings, and, in particular, the distribution of communicative acts among members of the team with different positional powers in the social hierarchy of the school. For example, the number of communications was counted against the positional powers of the members. In the authoritarian leadership style, those who were in a higher positional power had more communicative acts, had more time to speak and made more assertions than those in the lower hierarchy. In the open and non-directive

200 *Edmond Hau-Fai Law*

Table 12.1 Characteristics of Leadership Styles and Their Impacts on Team Interactions

	Subject Team Chinese	*Subject Team Maths*
Leadership Style	Dominated	Distributed
Mediating Factors	Assertive panel head	Less assertive panel head
	Didactic consultant	Facilitating consultant
Effects	Less team spirit	Stronger team spirit
	Resentment within team	Collaboration within team
Discourse Style	Closed and informative	Open and exploratory
	Less interactive	More interactive
Participation Style	Dominated by positional leadership	Multidirectional interactions
Teacher Learning	Modeling and subservient	Engagement and decision making

leadership style, the number of communicative acts was more evenly distributed among members, and people participated more actively regardless of their ranks and status.

The interactions among team members were also analyzed to show the nature of the contributions and participations. For example, the number of initiations and responses among members were the essential elements in our analyses. Under a more assertive leadership style, initiations were restricted to a few members of the team who had more positional power and higher status. The non-directive style allowed more interactions among members, and initiations were more evenly distributed among all members regardless of rank and status.

The impacts of the two contrasting leadership styles on the distribution and the nature of participations in the interactions are significant to our argument about the effectiveness of using a school-based curriculum development (SBCD) as an instrument for engineering changes in teacher professionalism. Constraints were identified in the interactions under the assertive and authoritarian leadership style. Participations were restricted, and initiations were limited to a few members. Meanwhile, the non-directive leadership style provided more opportunities for members to participate. This leadership style encouraged members to take part in negotiations and to shape the final decisions. It also allowed members to be in charge of the discourse and to guide it to their preferred direction. In sum, the first type of participation is more quantitative, whereas the second type of participation is more qualitative.

The directive and authoritarian leadership style is close to the Asian model of social hierarchy, whereas the non-directive and participatory model is close to the traditional concept of a SBCD model (Skilbeck, 1984).

Initiating Change and Innovations   201

This study does not aim to identify which model is more effective in terms of achieving pedagogical changes in schools. However, the latter model provides teachers more space for decision making than the former one.

Developing Teacher Curriculum Development Skills

School-based models of improving teacher skills in curriculum development have been proposed for some time. According to a portion of the 1982 Llewellyn Report in Hong Kong, teacher participation in curriculum development would enhance teacher professionalism in general. This idea was recommended against the background of a strong central curriculum agency which provided detailed guidelines for the school curriculum. Such guidelines leave little room for school and teacher autonomy, and that prevents them from making decisions regarding curriculum adjustments and pedagogy to benefit individual students. Uniform learning outcomes and learning progression were expected. However, Hong Kong schools offer mixed-ability classes, and Hong Kong has implemented inclusive policies. Therefore, different needs and learning outcomes among students of diverse backgrounds cannot be accommodated by traditional curriculum models.

In our projects, we perceived the various skills that teachers could have acquired while making curriculum decisions at various stages of our model. In the observations and in the interview data, we identified quite a number of situational and generic skills that were essential to being a leader in curriculum decision making. We argued that making curriculum decisions should be an essential skill of all teachers, particularly when their students have diverse abilities and backgrounds. This topic is in line with Hong Kong educational policy and matches the common understanding of the general professional teacher capacity. The following list of skills was identified in our projects in two schools in Hong Kong, although the items may not be different from those used in another system, whereas curriculum skills were greatly diffused among teachers of all grades and status in schools.

1. Teachers experiment with alternative approaches in planning and designing a learning unit. This risk-taking experience is likely to introduce new approaches to the traditional style, which is characterized by stability, in schools.
2. Teachers make decisions regarding new learning objectives aligned with educational reforms on lesson contents and alternative assessment methods. These objectives become part of the teachers' responsibilities and their daily classroom skills.
3. In the traditional curriculum models, all curriculum materials and progressions are standardized, with uniformity being the norm. During the projects, teachers were encouraged to adopt an alternative approach in designing and selecting curriculum contents to suit

202 Edmond Hau-Fai Law

students' needs. The task was not easy, and it required substantial experience from the team.

4. Adjusting curriculum experiences according to the needs of the students is a tremendous responsibility for teachers of a class with more than 30 students. Unlike class sizes of around 20 or 25, which are common in other countries, a large class size prevents teachers from developing a more interactive teaching style.

5. Teachers adopt a more systematic model which involves planning and reviewing, designing and implementing, and reflecting on practical experiences in the projects. Generating new ideas and alternatives and testing innovations are not innate to every teacher. This self-regulatory procedure of generating innovations and reflecting on actions enhances teacher professionalism in general.

Situational and Deep Learning

One argument for school-based models for developing teacher professionalism is the practical and situational nature of the changes and innovations that are planned, reviewed, designed and implemented directly by the teachers with a pragmatic orientation in teams. The developmental nature of the experiences challenges and raises issues with the traditional practices and beliefs that are deeply rooted in actions and current practices. Traditional beliefs and practices do not necessarily have a negative effect on current reforms nor do they deserve to be ignored by practitioners. However, this study is mainly concerned with introducing new ideas and innovative practices to classrooms, institutionalizing new ideas and practices within the current school infrastructure and establishing a mechanism for generating innovative ideas within the school boundaries.

One of the basic underlying principles of our projects is to establish cycles of learning and models of planning, implementing and reflecting on changes and innovations in teams. Thus, teachers are engaged in a series of developmental but professional activities that result in changes and a new curriculum. The processes are meant to be creative, and the teachers are no longer curriculum users or consumers of the ready-made or teacher-proof curriculum materials. The processes gave participants the opportunity to negotiate a new learning unit which was the outcome of the efforts and collaboration of the teams. The new experiences were exploratory and have become part of the real-life experiences of the teachers in the team. According to interviews with the teachers, they learned a great deal from the project, and their beliefs were challenged. New ideas that came about through actions and practices were incorporated with their beliefs which guided participant actions. Reflective statements from the teachers in the interviews, such as "but now we adapted, revised, discussed, I think good, teach lively and not blindly" and "teachers should abandon our traditional perspectives", prove that their new experiences were in contrast to their traditional practices and beliefs. However, we have no further evidence that these new practices had long-term significance and impact on the future professional actions of these teachers.

Furthermore, the learning experience was exploratory and was at times a personal and professional experience in which the participating teachers discovered something new. Discovery is essential because it may pave the way for new learning and allow teachers to cultivate a new professional identity and responsibility. In a traditional curriculum, uniformity in terms of learning objectives, progressions and outcomes is expected and embedded. Teachers rarely adjust their educational strategies to suit diverse student needs. However, in a curriculum which emphasizes learning generic skills and competencies rather than focusing on the amount of knowledge, teachers instantly adjust their educational strategies to suit the social or psychological needs of students. Teachers' statements during the interviews, such as "our classes used different methods and we thought it was impossible and would waste our time . . . however, we found that we could do different things in different ability classes", show that the introduction of new teaching styles has significant impacts on student learning. Teachers thought that the experience of seeing, feeling and learning how professional alternatives or decisions were put into practice, as well as their effects on student learning, was exciting. The experience was a reward for their attempts to revitalize classroom learning.

DISCUSSIONS AND FUTURE RESEARCH

SBCD, as a major change strategy conceptualized in Western literature, particularly in Anglo-Saxon traditions, has its experiential basis in practice and in the cultural milieu of the school context in the 1970s. SBCD was conceptualized as a cluster of school-based initiatives led either by the teachers or by the school institutions, and it is embedded in democratic beliefs and the powerful function of the active participation of the practitioners in making curriculum decisions relevant to the enhancement of student learning. Skilbeck's SBCD model was based on a pragmatic approach to adopting a problem-oriented strategy in teacher participation, which presumably enables participants to focus on tasks relevant to student learning. His theoretical approach and practical SBCD model were modelled on an action research approach. The model consisted of the following key steps: identifying key problems; designing solutions; testing feasibility and viability; and, finally, conducting a series of reflections for improvements in the next cycle of development work. The model was a basic one, even though it was a breakthrough in the conceptualization of how a school-based model can work in its early stage of development and dissemination when teachers and schools were still very much accustomed to the curriculum guidelines mostly initiated and developed by the central curriculum agencies in the

204 Edmond Hau-Fai Law

1960s. The adoption of SBCD in many Asian countries, such as Mainland China, Taiwan, South Korea, Singapore and Hong Kong, as a major change initiative in the late 1990s has not deviated much from its original conception and its practical model generated by Skilbeck (1984). The problems involved in implementing a practical model were derived from a basically participatory democratic tradition in Asian countries, which have a culture that respects seniority and hierarchy, and have raised fundamental issues about social theories of change and how innovations could be initiated, generated, developed, accepted and institutionalized in countries with very different cultural milieu (Kennedy, 2011). Various studies attempted to bring new information and experiences into our understanding of the nature of these issues and sought to establish several grounds in further developing a theoretical framework and a practical model in key East Asian countries with several common cultural traditions amidst obvious diversity in language, population and geographical locations (Lee, 2009). The following are key elements to the establishment and development of such a common understanding on a culturally viable model of SBCD in generating, developing, designing and implementing innovations and changes at the school level.

Leadership is a key consideration in curriculum development teams. Based on the research data and experiences in our design-based projects, a rotational leadership, from positional leaders to teacher leaders as a form of distributed leadership, should be viable in Asian countries given practical experience and administrative abilities of the leaders in the hierarchy. However, this form of leadership should be considered the initial step in fostering team spirit and a preliminary step in developing a culture of generating changes. Much relies heavily on the second and the third steps to sustain the change momentum. The first step is to develop an infrastructure and a pattern of procedures which facilitate discussions and allow new ideas to be tested. This task is an important step in establishing the basic understanding of the framework of practice that is to be led by another participant, presumably by an experienced teacher without positional power. With a less dominant leadership style, this step facilitates more open discourse and communication network. People are encouraged to participate actively because of blurred leadership, and distribution of participation in discussions and in decision making will be made possible. Therefore, a distributed form of leadership will emerge. The participant's initiatives will occupy the discussions, and the adoption of a particular line of thought would be based on a rational model rather than a positional model if a clear positional leader is taking the parole of the team. Then the third step of moving the leadership role to an inexperienced teacher in the team is the most essential because through rounds of planning, generating new ideas, designing unit plans and lesson plans, application in classes and conducting evaluations and reflection meetings have been completed. The inexperienced teacher will be familiar with the basic structure and organization

Initiating Change and Innovations   205

of the innovation as well as the requirements and qualities of a leader who will facilitate discussions and allow the active participation of all members in the processes involved in developing a new student curriculum. The completion of the cycle and its report to the whole school community to cultivate a sense of change are essential and should be carefully planned and organized with the support of the school administration. The cycle repetition with the same procedures and requirements can establish an infrastructure of change and innovation in the school community. Moreover, each teacher should be expected to participate in the whole process at least twice in a year.

The second component is the partnership with university faculties. Our research experience and data show that university faculties stimulate thinking and provide current ideas as well as issues in the educational world in terms of their theoretical basis and global nature. School communities focus on practices, and in many cases, attention to development activities is neglected in favour of good examination results in response to parental pressures and public accountability to external reviews imposed as a quality assurance (QA) mechanism in many countries. Constant new inputs from various information sources and new ideas should become a sustainable feature of development action plans within the school infrastructure. These new ideas and inputs should be part of the planning and reviewing stage of each cycle of the curriculum development actions. The goal is to ensure that innovation plans are closely aligned with the best current practices supported by sound educational principles available in the best literature in education and curriculum.

The third component is the institutionalization of good practices and an infrastructure and organization that works well with the school in generating pedagogical innovations with clear evidence of achievements in student learning and teacher learning. This component is the most essential step in completing the cycle of transforming the school culture into one which can generate new ideas and new practices by itself. Institutionalization means adopting new practices as a permanent and sustainable component of the organic whole of the school community. This component is not an easy task, and it requires school leadership with insights and persistence to change and to the achievements of a new culture that generates innovations, designs actions to implement innovations, and evaluates and reflects on evidence of innovative achievements.

CONCLUSION

This chapter tried to outline the key features of a series of design-based research studies in our attempt to uncover the key issues in adopting a school-based approach in developing innovative practices in schools in Hong Kong. The original model was based on a participatory democratic

206 Edmond Hau-Fai Law

tradition which values the rights of every teacher in making decisions. However, such a model encountered resistance during its implementation in East Asian countries which value teacher seniority and status. Based on research studies, this chapter provided evidence that a form of rotational leadership in which positional leaders and potential teacher leaders take part in a series of cyclical actions of planning and reviewing the current practices, designing and applying innovations, and finally evaluating and reflecting on the effectiveness of the innovations is preferable to a leadership model based either on Western democratic traditions or on Eastern hierarchical traditions. Our research experience shows that a combination of both is likely to bring about changes to the school community, and the proposed rotational leadership and infrastructure of a cyclical model can provide schools and their communities with a model of sustainable change.

REFERENCES

Engeström, Y. (2008). *From teams to knots: Activity-theoretical studies of collaboration and learning at work*. Cambridge: Cambridge University Press.

Kennedy, K. (2011). Transformational issues in curriculum reform: Perspectives from Hong Kong. *Journal of Textbook Research, 4*(1), 87–113.

Law, E.H.F. (2014). In search of a diverse curriculum: Toward the making of a post-modern Hong Kong in the 21st century. In W. Pinar (Ed.) *International Handbook of Curriculum Research* (2nd ed.) (pp.217–226). New York: Routledge.

Law, E.H.F., Lee, J.C.K., Wan, S., Ko, J., & Hiruma, F. (2014). Influence of leadership styles on teacher communication networks: A Hong Kong case study. *International Journal of Leadership in Education: Theory and Practice17* (1), 40–61.

Law, E.H.F., Galton, M.,& Wan, S. (2010). Distributed curriculum leadership: a Hong Kong case study. *Education Management Administration & Leadership. 38*(3),286–303.

Law, E.H.F. (2011). Exploring the role of leadership in facilitating teacher learning in Hong Kong. *School Leadership & Management, 31*(4), 393–410.

Law, E.H.F., & Wan, W.Y.S. (2006). Developing curriculum leadership in a primary school: A Hong Kong case study. *Curriculum and Teaching, 21*(2), 61–90.

Law, E.H.F, Galton, M., & Wan, W.W.S. (2007). Developing curriculum leadership in schools: Hong Kong Perspectives. *Asia-Pacific Journal of Teacher Education, 35*(2), 143–159.

Law, E.H.F. ., Wan, W.W.S., Galton, M., & Lee, J.C.K. (2010). Managing school-based curriculum innovations: A Hong Kong case study. *Curriculum Journal, 21*(3), 313–332.

Lee, J.C.K. (2009). The landscape of curriculum studies in Hong Kong from 1980–2008: A review. *Educational Research Journal, 24*(1), 95–133.

Llewellyn, J. (1982). *A perspective on education in Hong Kong*. Hong Kong: Government Printer.

Skilbeck, M. (1984). *School-based curriculum development*. London: Harper and Row.

Yeung, S.S.Y., Lam, J.T.S., Leung, A.W.L., & Lo, Y.C. (2012). *Curriculum change and innovation*. Hong Kong: Hong Kong University Press.

13 Curriculum Reform Implementation at the Classroom Level
Impacts and Challenges

*Jacqueline Kin-Sang Chan
and Ping-Kwan Fok*

INTRODUCTION

Curriculum change and implementation in Hong Kong before 1997 were rather piecemeal, and the outcome "was a reliance on symbolic policies" which demonstrated a scenario of "the government introducing a policy intention but not taking action to ensure its implementation" (Morris and Adamson, 2010, p.183). Since 1997, the Hong Kong government has adopted a different approach towards the large-scale curriculum reform which is intended to bring about short-term and long-term impacts to schooling in Hong Kong. The reform has been supported by various levels of government implementation strategies and eventually brought significant impacts to local school contexts, especially on teachers and classroom teaching (Chan, Kennedy and Fok, 2008). This chapter aims to address the issues of curriculum implementation in Hong Kong, in particular how teachers perceive curriculum changes, their responsive actions in light of the reform and the impact that have on classrooms.

CURRICULUM REFORMS IN HONG KONG AFTER 1997

As mentioned in earlier chapters, the curriculum reform in Hong Kong is a large-scale one with an intention to bring about changes from K–12 to tertiary education. It has taken place from 2001–2002 to 2005–2006 as the short-term phase, from 2006–2007 to 2010–2011 as the medium-term phase, and beyond 2011 as the long-term phase. The nature of the change cannot be understated as it denotes a kind of radical shift, which sometimes may be referred to as a paradigm shift in terms of knowledge organization and enquiry. To realize the change, the picture of reform consists of two major aspects. Traditional subjects integrate with others into generic or skill-based subjects, which are to be delivered through a diverse mode of teaching and learning. Assessment reform that emphasizes the theme of assessment on learning is presumed to be better aligned with the intended curriculum change. The reform is also said to be a vital move in the history of Hong Kong education, which has currently been pursuing a vision of empowering students to achieve all-around development and lifelong education. However, the reform has encountered various challenges from time to time as the implementation is carried out.

As pointed out by scholars, the rationale behind the large-scale reform is economic rather than political (Kennedy, 2005; Morris and Adamson, 2010). No doubt the curriculum reform was considered as one of the major tasks in the post-1997 Hong Kong government policy. Based on the analysis of the interview data of the central policymakers, Kennedy, Fok and Chan (2006) contended that the curriculum agenda was instrumental in nature. Although the post-1997 reform agenda was driven by the government, an entirely different implementation strategy was adopted by the Hong Kong government at that time. The post-handover Hong Kong government has learned several lessons from past experiences of reform, with failures pinpointed by scholars as: a lack of clarity of the innovations, schools' and teachers' lack of resources and support from the central government agencies, leadership problems, a top-down model of change, the stress of public examinations in relation to university admission policies and so on (Koo, 1996; Tang, 1995).

Combating the previous insufficiencies, government officials have recognized the necessity of establishing leadership in schools and the significance "for teachers to take up the reform proposals". Policymakers believed that "while the road ahead was still a difficult one, there was some confidence that the reform agenda was achievable" (Kennedy, Fok and Chan, 2006, p.118). Accordingly, the Hong Kong government started to adopt implementation strategies which inclined towards a 'soft' policy approach aiming at progression of schools and teachers in local contexts through a range of resource allocation. In operational terms, 'soft' policy denotes the use of non-binding instruments such as guidelines, informational devices or voluntary agreements and there are no enforcement or compliance mechanisms (Cini, 2001; Torenvlied and Akkerman, 2004). The 'soft' policy has been adopted by the Hong Kong government in the implementation of the large-scale curriculum reform since 2001, with a view to enhance schools' and teachers' development, and co-ordinate policies across different units situated at multiple layers.

THE IMPLEMENTATION STRATEGIES

To achieve a smooth implementation of the curriculum reform initiatives in school and classroom contexts, the government has adopted a set of strategies highlighting the development of teachers' professionalism and differing from the pre-handover policy.

The strategy selected in the curriculum implementation mainly included providing resources and support to schools in various stages of development, as shown in Table 13.1.

Curriculum Reform Implementation at the Classroom Level 209

Table 13.1 The Development Strategies Adopted by the Government at Different Stages of Implementation

Short-Term (2001–2002 to 2005–2006)	Render support to schools by providing curriculum guides, teacher and principal development programmes, on-site school-based support, etc.
	Work in partnerships with schools and tertiary institutions to conduct "seed" projects to generate and disseminate successful experiences as references for other schools.
	Conduct a review by the end of the short-term phase to take stock of the overall progress and to consolidate successful experiences.
Medium-Term (2006–2007 to 2010–2011)	Consolidate and disseminate systematically the experiences accumulated during the short-term phase to help develop school-based curricula and improve learning and teaching strategies.
	Continue with the tasks undertaken in the short-term and improve plans and actions based on the review in 2005–2006.
Long-Term (beyond 2011)	Continue to update and improve the curriculum framework according to the needs of society and students.
	Continue to work in partnership with schools and various concerned parties to generate and accumulate successful experiences with a view to further improve the quality of education.

Source: Adapted from CDC (2001).

According to Kennedy, Chan and Fok (2011), these strategies can be classified as 'soft' policy that is non-binding and voluntary in nature. The main purpose of the policy is to encourage active school participation in the implementation of the reform deemed desirable by the government. In essence, 'soft' policy instruments, including both contents and methods, are optional policy recommendations, guidelines, informational devices or voluntary agreements (Torenvlied and Akkerman, 2004). In relation to curriculum, examples of 'soft' policy instruments include broad policy guidelines, professional development opportunities, school evaluations and performance indicators (PIs), best practice dissemination and other voluntary agreements (those without legally binding commitments, sanctioning mechanisms and other enforcement procedures).

Based on Ahonen's typology as shown in Table 13.2, Kennedy, Chan and Fok (2011) analyzed the 'soft' methods used by the Hong Kong government in the curriculum reform. Accordingly, the 'soft' methods are classified as regulative, redistributive and allocative and which are operated in various strengths. The regulative soft methods are those "affect normatively the addressees of information or declare normative agreements reached between given actors". The redistributive soft methods are those that affect the distribution of information, the perspectives that the users

210 *Jacqueline Kin-Sang Chan and Ping-Kwan Fok*

Table 13.2 'Soft' Methods Used in the "Learning to Learn" Reform

'Soft' Methods	Examples	Structural / One-Way/ Two-Way	Stronger	Intermediate	Weaker
Redistributive	Curriculum guides	Structural	√		
	Authentic exemplars of curriculum	One-Way		√	
	Textbooks	Structural	√		
	Develop learning and teaching materials	One-Way		√	
Allocative	All concerned parties will collaborate with tertiary institutions to disseminate good practices	Two-Way		√	
	Seed projects	One-Way			√
	Professional development programmes	Two-Way			√
	Examples of strategies to support library development	One-Way			√
	On-site advice for school-based curriculum development	Two-Way			√
	Resources provided for creating time and space for teachers,	One-Way			√
	Dissemination and networking	Two-Way			√
	Inviting experts to deliver advice.	One-Way		√	

Source: Adapted from Kennedy, Chan and Fok (2011).

of information may apply and the cohesion of the users as to their provision with information. The allocative soft methods relate to "increase the quantity or quality of information available to users" (Ahonen, 2001, p.5). The expected strength of each soft method is expressed as stronger, intermediate or weaker. Stronger in strength means those measures that help the policy to be institutionalized; intermediate in strength refers to sets of frameworks, guidelines and some benchmarks in place; and weaker in strength includes information and recommendations provided in the policy.

There are substantive incentives for schools to carry out school-based development with regard to the priorities of government reforms. In particular, the provision of government funds to progress schools and

Curriculum Reform Implementation at the Classroom Level 211

teachers included the following items (Curriculum Development Council [CDC], 2001):

- Curriculum resources and support materials
- Collaborative research and development (RD), "seed projects"
- Teacher and principal development programmes
- Library development
- School-based support for curriculum development
- Creating time and space for teachers and learners
- Dissemination strategies and networks
- Involvement of experts

Using a 'soft' policy, in some sense, is welcomed by schools institutionally but not by teachers administratively. In a study concerning the use of 'soft' measures at school level, it shows that schools are receptive to "redistributive soft methods" and "allocative soft methods" (see Table 13.2). The 'soft' measures—including accreditation and incentives to practise the new initiatives, dissemination of materials through government guidelines, textbooks, exemplars, seminars and workshops and so on—are powerful tools in co-ordinating schools' implementation, which are closely in line with the government intentions, leading to the successful facilitation of reform particulars outlined in the official curriculum documents (Chan, 2012). However, the implementation strategy is supplemented by methods that are regulatory in nature, such as the government's use of strict measures like the Territory-Wide System Assessment (TSA) and External School Reviews (ESRs). In these policies, school performances are evaluated by preset indicators or statistical comparisons among schools. These regulatory measures have exerted pressure on schools with low student enrolments.

ISSUES AND CHALLENGES TO TEACHERS AND THEIR IMPLEMENTATION IN CLASSROOMS

It is easy to understand that schools would welcome more resources for putting the reforms into practice. However, the substantial workloads that accompany these resources have burdened and pressured teachers.

On one hand, Hong Kong students' performances are so competitive that Hong Kong has been rated in the top ten of the Organisation for Economic Co-operation and Development (OECD) participating countries during the past ten years (OECD, 2005, 2009, 2010) with the TSA results revealing a satisfactory level of competency in the key subjects of English, Mathematics and Chinese achieved by students. On the other hand, teachers' professional development was found to be hindered by the tight working schedule induced by government policies on quality education and assessment (Chan, 2010). Teachers' stress has become more serious as they are now working in a far

212 *Jacqueline Kin-Sang Chan and Ping-Kwan Fok*

more complex system subject to changes that demand a high level of teacher performance and student output. For example, teachers are expected to play the following new roles according to the government policy (CDC, 2002, p.2):

> Specific roles of teachers in helping to create a climate conducive to educational and social development:
> - To strengthen the development of generic skills, in particular, critical thinking, creativity and communication skills through the learning and teaching of Key Learning Areas (KLAs).
> - To use appropriate teaching and assessment strategies to motivate students in learning.
> - To listen to students and help them to improve their learning by making use of appropriate learning and teaching resources in support of the curriculum change.
> - To develop a personal plan of professional development and life-long learning in order to keep abreast of the latest developments and changes.
> - To collaborate with fellow teachers or external supporting agents in lesson preparation and in the exercise of strategies which impose a positive impact upon learning.
> - To collaborate with community workers to bring about life-wide learning amongst students.
> - To be reflective in daily practices and ready to discuss issues, knowledge and experiences with other teachers.
> - To communicate with parents in order to explain the curriculum and learning policy and seek their support and assistance in learning enhancement.
> - To help parents understand the purposes of assessment and the strengths and weaknesses of their children and to help them to see that marks and ranking in class do not necessarily reveal much about the learning progress of their children.

These roles assigned to teachers are considered idealistic and irrelevant to their working conditions. In fact, it is not facile for teachers to shift their roles radically given the divergence in education systems and teachers' roles between the colonial and post-1997 period (Chan, Kennedy and Fok, 2008).

First, Hong Kong teachers are trained to be subject-oriented experts who do not possess the adequate knowledge to take up a leading role in promoting integrated learning and cross-disciplinary teaching. The case of a new subject, Liberal Studies, which was created in the New Senior Secondary (NSS) School Curriculum in 2009 illustrates the difficulties in the implementation as below:

> Unwillingness among teachers arose because of their lack of confidence and the level of workload involved. Lack of confidence arose from the

Curriculum Reform Implementation at the Classroom Level 213

breadth of topics within the LS curriculum and the issue-based enquiry teaching strategy that was new to most of them. (Lam and Chan, 2011, p.27)

Second, the resources supplied in the reform fail to sharpen teachers' professionalism effectively. In most cases, the teachers are expected to execute the initiatives right after the workshops and with little practical support. Teachers have also found the short-term professional development programmes unhelpful, especially those externally run workshops and seminars, which are usually superficial and without in-depth discussion on critical reform issues. Furthermore, the curriculum reform should be readjusted owing to the impediments caused by the mixed use of 'soft' and 'hard' policies, for instance, the simultaneous application of provision of resources (soft policy) and the assessment system (hard policy). It is inconsistent to practise contradictory policies together at the same time, such as evaluating schools with the TSA results when teachers are busy dealing with curriculum reforms. The following is extracted from the findings of a case study report (Chan, 2010, p.104):

> The results of the study revealed that teachers in the study have been working under great pressure. Many of them have been anxious about their work, particularly the TSA results achieved by their students each year and the inspection of the quality assurance team.

Third, easy access is limited to only a small range of resources, while the majority of them remained untouched. Taking the Quality Education Fund (QEF) as an example, the multitudinous documentation and administrative work has prevented certain schools from applying. For smoothly operated schools with well-managed school administration and professional staff, fewer resources would not impact them momentously. However, for small schools with less funding, extra resources would mean a great deal to them. As a result, the disparities in school development and capacity building in schools require further consideration for funding support allocated by the government, as contended by Chan (2012, p.385):

> At the school level, capacity building varied from school to school and this variation will continue if the same level of resources and supports are provided to each school, regardless of need. It is appropriate for the government to consider the level of support provided to schools and the balancing point of the support and regulatory measures.

Finally, teachers who have continuously been burdened by packed schedules and work might not find their professionalism remarkably improved. In the face of the uncertainties, overwhelming resources and the urge for implementation, teachers might be left with no choice but to be asked to take

214   Jacqueline Kin-Sang Chan and Ping-Kwan Fok

on immense changes to ensure school efficiency. Negative feelings among teachers could be therefore generated and eventually lower the morale and harm the working environment in schools.

THE CASE OF PROJECT LEARNING

The situation of Hong Kong curriculum reform implementation at the classroom level can be effectively reflected by the enforcement of project learning. "Learning to Learn" advocated reading to learn, moral and civic education, project learning and information technology for interactive learning as four key tasks (CDC, 2001, p.83). Project learning aims to develop students' independent learning capabilities through and across key learning areas (KLAs). "Learning to Learn" recommended schools to use project learning because of its efficiency in promoting independent learning and accomplishing the specified learning targets (CDC, 2001, p.83). Since the introduction of project learning, several articles have discussed the theoretical foundations and disseminated practical experiences of project learning (Lee, 2004; Lo, 2004).

Implementation of Project Learning

Hong Kong government officials have made concerted efforts to influence schools and teachers to implement project learning. Again, these efforts can be described in terms of 'soft' and 'hard' policy instruments (Fok, Kennedy and Chan, 2010, p.5). Speaking of 'soft' policy instruments, schools might implement project learning in a flexible way. Schools could utilize an adaptive mode, which fits varying contexts and complements the additional resources and practical exemplars provided by the central support units. First, the government has used extensive curriculum guidelines (e.g., CDC, 2001, 2002) to recommend project learning to schools and teachers (Chan, Kennedy and Fok, 2008). Second, the QEF is employed as another 'soft' policy instrument to trigger the implementation of project learning. QEF (1998) promotes and disseminates good practices distilled from projects. After the release of major reform documents in 2001, the QEF has approved proposals in line with the curriculum reform and funded 27 proposals directly related to project learning (QEF, 2004), and this demonstrates the influence of reform agenda on QEF priorities. Third, the 'seed project scheme' promoted project learning. Align with curriculum reform, the Curriculum Development Institute (CDI) initiated a series of collaborative research and developmental projects (seed projects) in schools (Chan, 2004). Fourth, the CDI supplied numerous project learning exemplars to schools. Among them, one sample set is uploaded to the CDI official website. The content of this website includes the guiding steps over project learning stages, curriculum modes, tools for project learning and four

Curriculum Reform Implementation at the Classroom Level 215

models: 'Understanding Wong Tai Sin'; 'Interdisciplinary Project Learning Scheme'; 'Healthy Super Kids'; and 'Understanding Our Food'. These resources have helped schools and teachers to construct their project learning programmes.

Besides using 'soft' policy instruments, the government also utilized 'hard' policy instrumental measures to conduct project learning. These measures cover the implementation of quality assurance inspection (QAI), School Self-Evaluation (SSE) and ESR, which are under the umbrella of school development and accountability (SDA) (Fok, Kennedy and Chan, 2010, p.7).

From the government officials' point of view, the initiation of project learning and other curriculum policies are perceived as 'soft' instruments. However, schools and teachers associate these curriculum policies with 'hard' policies and perceive all measures as 'hard' policy instruments. Thus, schools treated all recommendations and suggestions in curriculum guides (CDC, 2001) as compulsory measures.

Positive Achievements of Project Learning Implementation

The results of using 'soft' and 'hard' policy instruments to implement project learning have, to a certain extent, been successful. First, in terms of quantity, the implementation was regarded as excellent in past years. Project learning, as a teaching strategy, has been used in the classroom but was not popular before the 2001 curriculum reform (Chan, 2003). After initiating project learning in the recent curriculum reform, nearly all schools have executed the four key tasks. In 2003, the Division of Social Studies, City University of Hong Kong, was commissioned by the CDI, in the Education and Manpower Bureau (EMB), to conduct a survey on 148 primary schools and 101 secondary schools. Among these schools, 98.4% of primary schools and 96.5% of secondary schools responded as having implemented project learning as a teaching approach (Education Bureau [EDB], 2004; Fok, Kennedy and Chan, 2010).

Second, as supported by several examples from research articles, it is suggested that teachers and students held positive attitudes toward project learning and most students found the strategy beneficial to the learning. Ko (2004) found that both teachers and students identify their initiative as constructive. Though finding it difficult and boring, students accentuate the value of project learning in their study. Siu (2004) also confirmed teachers' enthusiasm towards project learning for it could improve classroom teaching. She explained that students have developed all generic skills, gained knowledge, better expressed their talents, grew in learning interest and gained confidence when conducting projects. Leung (2008, p.87) learnt that teachers and students both benefit from the process of project learning. Students have profited from a more dynamic learning atmosphere and enhancement of their relationship with parents, while teachers have

216　*Jacqueline Kin-Sang Chan and Ping-Kwan Fok*

benefited from the improved knowledge of students and better catering to student needs.

Third, ESR report 2009–2010 (EDB, 2011, pp.12–13) reveals that the review of most schools and the promotion of project learning are either led by the General Studies panel or conducted through cross-subject collaboration. The emphasis of project learning is placed on authentic student experiences. The review team found that students' generic skills have been fostered by project learning. Moreover, one inspection report (QAD, 2004, p.7) praises a secondary school for its learning and teaching strategies centring on project learning:

> Individual subject departments engaged actively in cross-curricular collaboration in promoting project learning and some others implemented curriculum innovations, both leading to quality learning outcomes.

In addition, Leung (2008) discovered that teachers in three of the schools perceived the fact that both teachers and students could benefit from the implementation of project learning. This result echoed the goals of curriculum reform, such as "Learning to Learn", nurturing generic skills and all-round development of students.

In a general sense, the push-pull effects of both 'hard' and 'soft' policy instruments accounted for the widespread practice of project learning. To attain government objectives, policymakers have used various policy instruments in a logical and avowedly supportive way (Fok, Kennedy and Chan, 2010, p.9).

Problems Arising from Project Learning Implementation

Although 'soft' and 'hard' policy instruments have brought positive results to project learning implementation, it was found that teachers considered these instruments as threatening and coercive yet have complied with the directions of reform policy (Fok, Kennedy and Chan, 2010, p.9). In discussion of the management of change process, Brady and Kennedy (2007) proposed the need for school collaborative cultures, which could encourage opportunities to learn, improve teacher effectiveness, applicably respond to change, foster continuous school improvement, reduce workload and create professional confidence.

In fact, the development of curriculum resources in project learning has consequently become critical and essential for schools in Hong Kong. Leung (2003, 2004, 2006) has argued that teachers may use a project approach to help students to widen their horizons globally. To accomplish the development of such goals, teaching competence, advancement in professionalism, enhancement of teachers' capability in curriculum planning and the collegial teamwork in schools are inevitable.

Curriculum Reform Implementation at the Classroom Level   217

On the other hand, the huge amount of workload elicited from the practice of curriculum changes would burden and pressure teachers even if additional resources are provided. Teachers have struggled with the new roles which they are expected to take on when implementing project learning.

First, teachers, trained to be subject experts, face challenges in the realization of project learning of a cross-disciplinary nature. According to the ESR report in 2009–2010 (EDB, 2011, pp.12–13), many schools conducted project learning through cross-subject collaboration. Though in some schools the initiative was led by the General Studies panel, the panel also sought support from various disciplines. Actually, most teachers expressed a negative stance towards curriculum integration in project learning. Teachers found the interdisciplinary project implemented in a school appropriate, but they did not consider it as a systematic way towards curriculum integration (Ko, 2004). This is still a dilemma for those teachers who focus on subject-based curriculum.

Second, there is a debate whether teachers' professionalism facilitates the curriculum change or not. According to a study on primary school teacher professional development, the reform is conducted by teachers with proper training in implementing project learning and with three years' experiences. However, from views of education planners and school heads, teachers do not fully comprehend the purpose and method of the implementation (Siu, 2004). Teachers in three primary schools encountered challenges in instructing project learning. One of the main concerns was the lack of professional training (Leung, 2008, p.86). Moreover, the essentials of teacher professional development are still subject to debate. Based on the interviews with pre-service secondary schoolteachers, a study shows that project learning tutors echo the recurrent themes of survival and discovery in the early stage of teacher development. However, the researcher argues that teachers' experience and self-realization should be the foundation for further pursuit of knowledge and skills advancement (Yeung, 2008, p.41). Taking the above pieces of research into account, teacher professional development is complicated especially when it is related to personal development based on self-understanding and possible change of belief. Though the EDB has provided plenty of professional development programmes since the implementation of curriculum reform in 2001, the quest for a review of professional development programmes, concerning both quality and quantity, has not been unusual in recent years (Fok, 2005; Leung, 2008, p.86).

Third, the lack of teaching resources in realizing project learning is one of the most common problems of the schools in teaching project learning. Although the EDB has provided much support for teaching resources since curriculum reform in 2001, the resources distributed are by no means sufficient and the situation should be continuously monitored. Indeed, teachers regard special time arrangement and resources allocation for the execution of project learning the major concerns (Leung, 2008, p.89).

218 *Jacqueline Kin-Sang Chan and Ping-Kwan Fok*

Fourth, implementing a project learning approach has brought a heavy workload to teachers. In research enquiring into project learning implementation in primary schools, many teachers consider its time-consuming nature and heavy workload as major drawbacks. The results conclude that as students are not accustomed to self-learning, they are not able to acquire necessary social skills and need additional time to learn new things, thus teachers have to spend extra time on assisting students in learning (Chan, 2003). Moreover, project learning emphasizes the process of learning and the learning product is identified as another problem because considerable efforts are demanded from teachers (Siu, 2004). While teachers are aware of the favourable effect project learning has upon student learning, they are concerned about personal commitment, scheduling and time factors in their practice (Leung, 2008, p.89).

CONCLUSION

This chapter analyzes the Hong Kong curriculum reform via exemplifying project learning. 'Soft' and 'hard' policy instruments have provided incentives for effective implementation but have exerted pressure on teachers. Understanding of 'Soft' and 'hard' policy instruments opens to the possibility of composing an effective assessment scheme to evaluate the implementation of policy and the pressure on teachers (Fok, Kennedy and Chan, 2010). In the end, it is worthwhile emphasizing the role of policymakers:

> Policymakers need to take into consideration the professionalism of teachers and the social and political contexts that regulate schools and schooling. Failure to do so leads to the kind of results reported here— results that can be attributed to poor policy decision making rather than poor teachers. (Fok, Kennedy and Chan, 2010, p.10)

For large-scale curriculum reforms implemented in Hong Kong, 'soft' and 'hard' policies have demonstrated the powerful effects that they have on school and teacher development. Although it is not yet known how strongly each 'soft' method has impacted schools, the government should consider various factors affecting implementation in the local context and constantly examine various challenges that schools and teachers are facing so as to provide relevant support to schools and teachers in a timely manner.

REFERENCES

Ahonen, P. (2001). *Soft governance, agile union: Analysis of the extensions of open coordination in 2000*. Maastricht: EIPA.
Brady, L., & Kennedy, K. (2007). *Curriculum construction* (3rd ed.). Frenchs Forest, N.S.W.: Pearson

Curriculum Reform Implementation at the Classroom Level 219

Chan, J.K.S. (2010). Teachers' responses to curriculum policy implementation: Colonial constraints for curriculum reform. *Educational Research for Policy and Practice, 9*(2), 93–106.

Chan, J.K.S. (2012). Curriculum policy implementation: How schools respond to government's 'soft' policy in the curriculum reform. *Curriculum Journal, 23*(3), 371–386.

Chan, J.K.S., Kennedy, K.J., & Fok, P.K. (2008). 'Hard' and 'soft' policy for the school curriculum: The changing role of teachers in the 'Learning to Learn' reform. In J. Lee, L. Lo & L.P. Shiu (Eds.) *Developing teachers and developing schools in changing contexts* (pp.135–153). Hong Kong: Chinese University Press.

Chan, K. K. (2004). Collaborative Research and Development ("Seed") Projects for 2004–2005 (Education & Manpower Bureau Circular Memorandum No.71/2004) (EMB(CD)/ADM/150/1/129(1)). Retrieved 23 July 2013, from http://cd.emb.gov.hk/seed/circular/CM71_2004_E.pdf.

Chan, K.W. (2003). Investigating the success and failure of project learning: Teacher and student factors. *New Horizons in Education, 48*, 51–55.

Cini, M. (2001). The soft law approach: Commission rule-making in the EU's state aid regime. *Journal of European Public Policy, 8*(2), 192–207.

Curriculum Development Council (2001). *Learning to learn: The way forward in curriculum.* Hong Kong: Printing Department.

Curriculum Development Council (2002). *Basic education curriculum guide: Building on strengths (primary 1—secondary 3).* Hong Kong: Printing Department.

Education Bureau (2004) *Report of survey on the school curriculum reform and implementation of key learning area curricula in schools 2003.* Hong Kong: Education Bureau.

Education Bureau (2011). *Quality assurance inspection annual report 2009–2010.* Hong Kong: Education Bureau.

Fok, P.K. (2005). Professional development of curriculum masters in Hong Kong: Design catering for needs. *New Horizons in Education, 52*, 22–38. (In Chinese)

Fok, P.K., Kennedy, K.J., & Chan, J.K.S. (2010). Teachers, policymakers and project learning: The questionable use of 'hard' and 'soft' policy instruments to influence the implementation of curriculum reform in Hong Kong. *International Journal of Education Policy and Leadership, 5*(6). Retrieved 23 July 2013, from http://www.ijepl.org.

Kennedy, K.J. (2005). *Changing schools for changing times: New directions for the school curriculum in Hong Kong.* Hong Kong: Chinese University Press.

Kennedy, K.J., Chan, J.K.S., & Fok, P.K. (2011). Holding policy makers to account: Exploring 'soft' and 'hard' policy and the implications for curriculum reform. *London Review of Education, 9*(1), 41–54.

Kennedy, K.J., Fok, P.K., & Chan, J.K.S. (2006). Reforming the curriculum in a post-colonial society: The case of Hong Kong. *Planning and Changing, 37*(1–2), 111–130.

Ko, S.Y. (2004). *Project-based learning in a Hong Kong secondary school.* Unpublished master's thesis, University of Hong Kong.

Koo, C.N.A. (1996). *The implementation of design and technology in the sixth form curriculum.* Unpublished M.Phil. thesis, Chinese University of Hong Kong.

Lam, C.C., & Chan, J.K.S. (2011). How schools cope with a new integrated subject for senior secondary students: An example from Hong Kong. *Curriculum Perspectives, 31*(3), 23–32.

Lee, J.C.K. (2004). Project learning: In search of theoretical foundation for curriculum reform. *Hong Kong Teachers' Centre Journal, 2*, 93–104. (In Chinese)

Leung, W.L.A. (2003). Integrating primary school curriculum in Hong Kong Special Administrative Region of China. *Asia-Pacific Education Researcher, 12*(2), 177–203.

220 *Jacqueline Kin-Sang Chan and Ping-Kwan Fok*

Leung, W.L.A. (2004). Integrating the school curriculum into lifelong learning. *Education Today, 54*(1), 11–17.

Leung, W.L.A. (2006). Teaching integrated curriculum: Teachers' challenges. *Pacific-Asian Education Journal, 18*(1), 88–102.

Leung, W.L.A. (2008). Teacher concerns about curriculum reform: The case of project learning. *Asia-Pacific Education Researcher, 17*(1), 75–97.

Lo, S.Y. (2004). Implementing social project learning in the key learning area of personal, social and humanities. *Hong Kong Teachers' Centre Journal, 2*, 105–108.

Morris, P., & Adamson, B. (2010). *Curriculum, schooling and society in Hong Kong.* Hong Kong: Hong Kong University Press.

Organisation for Economic Co-operation and Development (2005). *PISA 2003 technical report.* Paris: OECD.

Organisation for Economic Co-operation and Development (2009). *PISA 2006 technical report.* Paris: OECD.

Organisation for Economic Co-operation and Development (2010). *PISA 2009: What students know and can do: Student performance in Reading, Mathematics and Science.* Paris: OECD.

Quality Assurance Division (2004). *External School Review report: Ho Fung College (sponsored by Sik Sik Yuen).* Hong Kong: Education and Manpower Bureau.

Quality Education Fund (1998). *QEF general information.* Retrieved 24 November 2005, from http://qef.org.hk/eng/main.htm?plan/plan02.htm.

Quality Education Fund (2004). *Effective learning: Project learning.* Retrieved 13 February 2008, from http://qcrc.qef.org.hk/qef/result.phtml?nature_id=6&subnature_id=63&subcat_id=6303&app_no=-1&benef=-1&mode=browse.

Siu, S.M. (2004). *Primary school teachers' perceptions of project learning.* Unpublished master's thesis, University of Hong Kong.

Tang, Y.N. (1995). *The implementation of a new sixth-form integrated subject: The case study of Liberal Studies.* Unpublished M.Phil. thesis, Chinese University of Hong Kong. (In Chinese)

Torenvlied, R., & Akkerman, A. (2004). Theory of 'soft' policy implementation in multilevel systems with an application to social partnership in the Netherlands. *Acta Politica, 39*, 31–58.

Yeung, A.S.C. (2008). Implementation of project learning in Hong Kong: Experiences of pre-service teachers. *Hong Kong Teachers' Centre Journal, 7*, 41–51. (In Chinese)

14 Changes in English-Language Education
Ideology and Reform Strategies

Alice W.K. Chow

INTRODUCTION

Curriculum change is a complex enterprise, and its success depends on a number of factors. The most important factor is a strategic approach to managing change at key stages of the endeavour, taking into consideration the contextual environments in which the change is situated. This chapter charts the journey that Hong Kong has embarked on reforming its policies and practices in English-language education. It describes the context of the reforms and the strategies committed to getting the proposed precepts by reform architects and policymakers formalized into the central curriculum frameworks and transformed into classroom practices. The aim is to illustrate the change strategies engineered during key stages of the reform implementation spectrum to maintain the momentum of the reform initiatives as they trickle the system, gain the requisite support of various stakeholders and bring about pedagogical change in line with the original reform rhetoric. The nature of the change tactics applied to orchestrate a whole system reform will be outlined and the associated challenges discussed.

CURRICULUM INNOVATION AND CHANGE STRATEGIES

The status of English in Hong Kong has always been high. Its importance is attributed not only to its British colonial history of 150 years but also to Hong Kong's unrelenting attempt at internationalization in an increasingly globalized world. English is widely considered the language of international business, trade and professional communication, and therefore proficiency in English is perceived as essential for helping Hong Kong to maintain its current status and further strengthen its competitiveness as a leading finance, banking and business centre in the world. The recent reform agenda proposed since the late 1990s by the Curriculum Development Council (CDC), the central educational agency, emphasized the role of English in empowering learners with the capabilities necessary for lifelong learning, innovation, problem solving and adapting to the rapid

222 Alice W.K. Chow

changes and demands of society, and opening up the world of leisure and entertainment for learners (CDC, 1999, 2002a). This conception represents 'a modern growth theory' perspective which stresses aligning curriculum reforms for maintaining Hong Kong's competitiveness in the new economy (Kennedy, 2005). In essence, it is believed that the mastery of English is vital to learners in Hong Kong as it opens up new possibilities in intellectual and social development, educational attainment, career advancement, personal fulfilment and cultural understanding. Given the long-standing importance attached to English for societal and personal development, understandably, English-language education has always been given top priority in the government agenda for sharpening Hong Kong's competitive edge against the challenges and competition from neighbouring cities and emerging economic powers, such as Singapore and Shanghai. In fact, efforts to improve English-language education were started by the Hong Kong Education Bureau (EDB) as early as in the 1980s alongside curriculum reforms in other areas at system level.

The employment of different approaches to change at different times in the change process involves short-term, medium-term and long-term strategies. The three approaches to change strategies discussed by Bennis, Benne and Chin (1989), Kennedy (1987), Lamie (2005) and Nation and MaCalister (2010) are particularly relevant to an analysis of reform efforts in English-language education in Hong Kong. The three approaches are power-coercive, rational-empirical and normative–re-educative strategies. The power-coercive approach is typical of 'a centre–periphery model' (Nation and MaCalister, 2010, p.177), in which the authority imposes a change by legislating it. This approach is often adopted when the change may not be supported by the people most affected by it. By mandating the change, the authority wishes to eliminate resistance. However, in view of the unidirectional nature of imposition, such an approach may at best lead to superficial compliance rather than fundamental change in teachers' beliefs or practices. The second approach referred to as rational-empirical is typical of 'a research, development and diffusion model' (Nation and MaCalister, 2010, p.177), where influence is exercised through the 'power of knowledge' (Bennis, Benne and Chin, 1989, p.39) and the change is achieved through rationalization and persuasions (Lamie, 2005). It is assumed that by presenting to the public the benefits brought by the change, teachers would be persuaded to embed it in their practices. However, both Kennedy (1987) and Nation and MaCalister (2010) contended that just by informing the stakeholders about the benefits may not lead to effectual change unless they are already sympathetic towards it. The third approach, normative–re-educative, is typical of 'a problem-solving model' (Nation and MaCalister, 2010, p.177) in which bottom-up initiatives become the driving force. It is believed that fundamental change involves changes to entrenched practices, and that 'a collaborative, problem-solving approach' involving all stakeholders in the decisions making process is likely to make

Changes in English-Language Education 223

the change acceptable. Nation and MaCalister (2010) argued that there can be an eclectic combination of the three approaches because reforms or innovations are likely to succeed if people see that they have 'the support of authority . . . (power-coercive); if they see that there are good reasons for the change (rational-empirical); and if they feel that they 'own' the change (normative–re-educative)' (p.177).

Tracing the many reforms in English-language education that have taken place in Hong Kong in the last 30 years, one can see that a centre–periphery approach was the main approach employed in the initiations of reforms, supported by corresponding policy-led research undertaken outside the classroom to determine the directions and blueprint of the reforms. A rational-empirical approach was used to put forward the reasons and the need for change to stakeholders, such as schools, teachers, parents and students, to rally their support for the reforms. To enhance the sustainability of reform efforts by front-line practitioners, a normative–re-educative approach was adopted to bring about pedagogical change in the classroom through collaborative problem-solving projects undertaken by schools and teachers with the assistance from academic consultants from higher education institutes or the central curriculum development institute.

This chapter describes the commitment of the Hong Kong government to reform its English-language curriculum, and the efforts it has made to realize the changes through a mix of change strategies. It also outlines the challenges involved in taking the reforms to the next level of success and the way ahead for continuous capacity building and collaborative partnership.

The following paragraphs outline the changes in the conceptualization and design of the English-language curriculum that took place in Hong Kong in the past 30 years. Such changes were responses to the major changes in ideology and values systems that emerged in the global context of education, as well as the social, political and economic conditions of Hong Kong. A brief summary of English-language teaching (ELT) methodology adopted prior to the reforms introduced in the 1990s will be presented first to provide a backdrop against which the recent reforms were situated.

ENGLISH-LANGUAGE EDUCATION REFORMS AND IDEOLOGY

A Classical Humanist Approach to English-Language Education during the Post-War Period

During the British colonial rule of 150 years until 1997, the educative processes of ELT in Hong Kong had been shaped to support an English-speaking elite for government and commerce (Postiglione, 1992; Sweeting, 1992). ELT methodology in the post-war era reflected the characterizing features of classical humanist thought (Skilbeck, 1982), which emphasized an elitist, educational goal of developing broad intellectual capacities

224   *Alice W.K. Chow*

that include memorization and the ability to analyze and reconstruct the elements of knowledge. Such an approach to education when applied in the context of English-language education in Hong Kong gave rise to the grammar translation approach, which emphasized conscious awareness of rules and patterns. The English-language content taught and learnt was expressed in terms of the phonology, grammar and vocabulary that make up a language. To develop students' intellectual capacities, students were expected to understand and memorize the rules behind the elements, analyze sentences into constituent parts, apply the rules in sentence constructions and re-synthesize their grammatical knowledge in translation and essay work. There were no curriculum guides on curriculum aims or teaching methodologies until the 1970s. Instead, an examination blueprint, outlining the generic contents of examination papers, was used as a guide for instructional planning (Walker, 1999). Norm-referencing assessment was adopted to select an appropriate number of students for the next stage of education and to place them in homogeneous groups so that students progressed in their studies at the same pace. Reflecting an elitist philosophy of education, only 5% of secondary school graduates were provided with the opportunity to pursue university education in the two local universities (the University of Hong Kong and the Chinese University of Hong Kong). Most students at that time left school after six years of free primary education introduced in 1971. The majority (53%) worked in secondary industries, such as textiles, manufacturing and small businesses (Morris, 1995).

Following the development of ELT approaches in the West, the oral-structural approach, closely resembling the audiolingual method (Richards and Rogers, 1986), became the dominant method practiced in the early 1970s. A provisional syllabus for English (Forms 1–V) published in 1975 and intended as a guide to the teaching of English as a second or foreign language advocated the adoption of the 'oral-structural' approach to modern language learning (CDC, 1975). Yet this approach still featured a strong focus on repetitive practice of the structural patterns of the language so that linguistic habits were formed through the manipulation of the forms (CDC, 1983). It was considered limiting in enhancing students' abilities to use the language for communicative purposes (Tsui, 1993; Harris, 1993; Pang and Wong, 1999). The rise of communicative language teaching (CLT) in the West, regarded partly as reactions to the audiolingual method, also influenced the ELT approach promoted by the ED in Hong Kong in the 1980s. The emphasis in the CLT approach shifted from enabling students to master the formal structure of the language to preparing students to develop functional competences so that learners could use the language as a medium of communication.

A Reconstructionist Approach to Reconfiguring a Selective School System for Universal Education in the 1980s

The advent of CLT in the West also coincided with the demographic and economic changes in the mid-1970s in Hong Kong. The influx of refugees

Changes in English-Language Education 225

from the People's Republic of China (PRC) and the emergence of a middle class in view of Hong Kong's success in entrepôt trade resulted in public demand for basic education, social mobility and greater equality of opportunity within its education system. These were the spurs behind the increase in government spending on public education. To meet the public demand, nine-year free education (for children aged 6 to 15) was introduced in 1978. It signified the move from elite education to free basic education for all, reflecting a reconstructionist view of education (Skilbeck, 1982), which is concerned with effecting social change through (1) education characterized by comprehensive schooling with mixed ability classes; (2) the equal valuing of all citizens; and (3) achieving social goals important to a nation through well-planned means (Clark, 1985). The 1980s was the period during which government interventions focused on configuring the foundations of the school system with a substantial increase in public spending on education by doubling the expenditure from more than HK\$3.4 million in 1980 to HK\$7.7 million in 1984 (Education Commission [EC], 1984, p.82). The reconfiguration involved the introduction of nine-year free education and expansion of post-Form 3 educational opportunities (for children aged 15).

In view of the shift to mass education, corresponding changes were required to cope with the challenges involved in opening up educational opportunities to those who would have been screened out and eliminated from the elitist school system in the pre-1978 era. One of these challenges was the perceived decline in the standard of English.

> It has been suggested that there has been a significant decline in the ability of tertiary students to communicate effectively either in Chinese or in English . . . arising from the extension of the period of free and compulsory education to nine years in 1978. Certainly the broadening of the education base by the introduction of nine years' free and compulsory education has lowered the average standard in English of Secondary 3 students. (EC, 1988, pp.21–22)

To avert any consequential drop in the standard of English attributable to reduced exposure, various measures were introduced to strengthen the teaching of English. They included the strengthening of preparation for teachers of English through the employment of expatriate lecturers of English for the teacher training colleges; establishment of an Institute of Language in Education (ILE) to raise the quality of language teaching in schools; an increase in native English speakers and fluent speakers of English in schools as English teachers, representing a reversal of the 'localization of staffing policy'; extra teachers in secondary schools for remedial teaching; revisions of English-language syllabuses; installation of wire-free induction loop system; additional resources given to schools which adopted Chinese as the medium of instruction (MOI); and the introduction of reforms in the curriculum and teaching methods in schools, in particular in the sixth forms.

226   *Alice W.K. Chow*

A Progressivist Approach to Transforming English-Language Education in the 1990s

In response to the rapid growth in knowledge and advances in information technology in the 1990s, education systems both local and worldwide underwent major changes which entailed a significant move away from a focus on the transmission of immutable truths or knowledge to one that sees the learner as a whole person having intellectual, social and emotional needs. This represents a progressivist approach to education that attempts to promote the development of the learner through the provision of learning experiences from which learners can learn by their own efforts. Learning is seen as a continuum which can be broken into several key stages, and the goal of education is to develop in the learner a capacity for lifelong learning. Education is no longer seen as a process for the transmission of a set of fixed facts, but a creative problem-solving process (Clark, 1985). The changes in curriculum aims of the English-language syllabuses from 1975 to 1999 and 2002 (based on the 1999 syllabus) are outlined in Appendix 14.1.

Echoing the international trend in educational renewals embracing a progressivist and constructivist philosophy to education planning and processes, a Targets and Target Related Assessment (TTRA) framework emerged in 1992 in Hong Kong. It first appeared in the EC's *Report 4* (1990) and was later replaced by a Target Oriented Curriculum (TOC) framework. Both sets of framework placed emphasis on the process of purposeful and contextualized learning and the alignment between teaching, and learning with assessment. Effective learning is viewed as *holistic, purposeful, contextualized, interactive* and *task-centred*, involving active construction and extension of knowledge (Clark, Scarino and Brownwell, 1994). Learning targets are significant in the TTRA and TOC frameworks for setting the directions for learning and for ensuring consistency of purpose, both long and short term at all levels of the curriculum. For instance, learning targets are set for the curriculum as a whole, for each curriculum area, for each subject, for dimensions of each subject and within dimensions. Students' learning from primary 1 to secondary 5 is described through a progressive series of stages from key stage 1 covering learning from primary 1 to 3, key stage 2 from primary 4 to primary 6, key stage 3 from secondary 1 to secondary 3, and key stage 4 from secondary 4 to secondary 5. The notion of learning target for the subject of English at each key stage is further expanded in the *Syllabuses for Primary Schools English Language Primary 1–6* (CDC, 1997), , and the *Syllabus for Secondary Schools English Language Secondary 1–5* (CDC, 1999). Appendices 14.2 and 14.3 outline the organization of the English-language curriculum.

Another important feature of the TOC framework and the central tenet of the earlier TTRA initiative was the shift away from the use of norm-referenced assessment principles to the use of criteria and standards-referenced assessment to monitor "the learning progress of all students against

Changes in English-Language Education 227

progressive standards and using the results to inform the teaching/learning process" (Clark, Scarino and Brownell, 1994, p.52).

Based primarily on the principles explicated in the Clark, Scarino and Brownell's (1994) document, subsequent curriculum guides and syllabuses for English language published in 1997 and 1999 (on which the 2002 syllabus is based) accentuated the central role of integrated tasks and task-based learning (TBL) in English-language education. It is consistent with the TTRA and TOC frameworks, which advocated the student-centred approach to learning and stressed the all-round development of every child in various domains, including cognitive, interpersonal and experiential dimensions. It is apparent that the latest curriculum reform initiative, as compared against the post-war foreign language teaching approach, no longer treats English "as a finite set of items or functions", but as "a medium of thinking, studying, and expressing one's own experiences" (Pang and Wong, 1999, p.206). Appendix 14.4 illustrates the methodological principles underpinning the different CDC English-language syllabi developed over the last 40 years.

The 1990s was a period which witnessed a further increase in public spending on education in the tertiary sector with the expansion of first-year, first-degree places from about 7% of the appropriate age group in 1988 to 18% by 1994. The increase was meant to meet the demand for better educated manpower in the face of continuing shift from manufacturing into knowledge intensive service industries (EC, 1990).

A "Learning to Learn" Approach to Consolidating and Sustaining Momentum of Reforms in a Techno-Globalized Age

Undoubtedly we are living in an era of knowledge explosion and changing technologies, in which the world's knowledge and information is increasing at exponential rates because of advances in communications technologies (Tyler, 2008). For instance, it has been estimated that the number of text messages sent and received every day exceeds the total population of the planet. There are more than 2.7 billion searches performed on Google each month and 3,000 new books published every single day. Under the impact of the new technologies we live increasingly in a borderless world, with information and global cultural flows transgress the boundaries of time, space, nations and localities. Because changes in technologies and increase in information are exponential, it seems impossible to determine with certainty what students need from schools, and therefore the capacity for creating and choosing has become more important than following existing knowledge. School curriculum needs to be designed in ways that strengthen as well as stretch the students' capacity for information management, self-organization and adaptability. These considerations provide the context for the Hong Kong educational reform agenda in the 2000s, which aims to consolidate the fundamental transformations forged in the

228   Alice W.K. Chow

past decades. The main thrust of the consolidation efforts seeks to sustain and expand the fundamental alterations in the role of teachers and students and pedagogical practices with the goal of making students self-conscious participants in the process of knowledge construction. This is necessary considering that manufacturing and labour-intensive jobs are no longer the driving force behind Hong Kong's economy, and the goal of education is no longer targeted at making students 'workplace ready' but equipping students with generic skills for participation in a globalized community. To achieve this, a holistic review of the school curriculum started in 1999 aiming to prepare the younger generation for the following challenges in the 21st century (CDC, 2001, p.6):

- A knowledge-based society
- Globalization
- The impact of information technology
- The transience of things
- The rising need for moral considerations
- Increasing public participation in government affairs
- The interdependent but competitive world

In 2001, a new curriculum framework embodying the key concept of "Learning to Learn" was announced. It aims to help students learn how to learn through the cultivation of positive values, attitudes and a commitment to lifelong learning and development of generic skills to acquire, construct and communicate knowledge. Nine types of generic skills identified as fundamental for helping students to learn better are collaboration skills, communication skills, creativity, critical thinking skills, information technology skills, numeracy skills, problem-solving skills, self-management skills and study skills. Among the four key tasks promoted as tools to develop independent learning capabilities is the emphasis on 'reading to learn', which aims to develop a reading culture and students' competence in and love for reading, and is considered essential for lifelong learning. It is also one of the seven learning goals of the school curriculum to be achieved by 2014 (CDC, 2002a). 'Learning to read' is no longer considered sufficient for a knowledge-based society and for lifelong learning. Possession of the skills of 'reading to learn' is believed to improve students' language proficiency and their capabilities for communication and for academic and intellectual pursuits; to develop students' thinking skills; to enable students to achieve a better quality of life through reading for diverse purposes; and to cultivate an open mind and deepen and broaden their understanding of life in order to face its challenges (CDC, 2001). Corresponding strategies in support of the 'reading to learn' initiative will be outlined in a later section.

To tackle the decline in average standards resulting from the transformation of a relatively selective school system to one that provides mass education, it was considered necessary to revise and update the common core curriculum to bring it in line with community needs and to put in much more effort in curriculum development, support services and teacher education. Since 2007, Hong Kong secondary schools have been going through yet another change. This time the change is a structural one, which brought the Hong Kong secondary school structure in alignment with that adopted in the PRC, symbolizing a final separation from Britain, the former colonial sovereign. In the former school system of 3+2+2+3, all secondary school students underwent a three-year junior secondary education (for students aged 12–15), followed by a two-year senior secondary education for the majority of students and a two-year advanced-level education for one-third of the students of whom 18% would be selected for three-year university education. This structure was changed to a 3+3+4 model starting in 2007 in which a three-year junior secondary, three-year senior secondary and four-year university education system is adopted. This structural change is intended to allow every secondary school student to have one more year of secondary education. Because of this change, a New Senior Secondary (NSS) curriculum has been drawn up. The broad curriculum aims of the English-language curriculum at the senior secondary level are more or less the same as those outlined in the 1999 syllabus. The main difference lies in a new component, known as an Elective Part, which provides a range of modules intended to add variety to the English-language curriculum, broaden students' learning experience and cater for their diverse needs and interests.

With the newly introduced elective component, there will be more time and opportunities for developing and applying language skills in a variety of contexts. It is also hoped that in addition to developing learners' language skills, the elective modules will enhance the further development of generic skills, such as communication, critical thinking, creativity and collaboration. Appendix 14.5 shows the characteristics of the NSS English-language curriculum as compared with the pre-1999 and existing English-language curriculum. What is worthy of attention with regard to the change is the emphasis on 'language arts' as an important area in the Elective Part. Language arts have always been one of the curriculum components in the English-language syllabus since 1983, but they have never occupied such importance as in the NSS in which the amount of class time that could be spent on them is specified, They have also been included in Hong Kong Diploma of Secondary Education (HKDSE) examination, which is a high-stakes public examination that all secondary school students sit at the end of their six-year secondary education. This new addition would certainly broaden students' experience and exposure to English, beyond contexts that involve academic studies, in the ways that English is used in the real world for specific purposes, such as using English in the workplace, debates and discussions about social issues, as well as for sports communication, entertainment and leisure.

Another major reform in English-language education is the incorporation of school-based assessment (SBA) in the public examination that students sit

230   Alice W.K. Chow

at the end of their secondary education. It was introduced in 2007, and aims to "to assess learners' achievement in areas that cannot be easily assessed in public examinations whilst also enhancing the capacity for student self-evaluation and life-long learning" (Hong Kong Examinations and Assessment Authority, 2005, p.4). Accounting for 15% of the English paper, the SBA component is administered in schools with the flexibility for teachers and students to select and adapt a range of assessment tasks, so that students are given the opportunity to perform to the best of their abilities. Formative teacher feedback, peer evaluation and self-evaluation performed by students are emphasized in the assessment process. The SBA initiative is a clear attempt in Hong Kong to promote a culture of Assessment for Learning (AfL) in which even high-stakes summative assessment can be planned and used for formative purposes, and such formative assessments become the foundation for better learning and teaching (Wiliam, 2001; Black et al., 2003). The success of any reforms is dependent on a combination of change strategies. The following sections outline the change strategies adopted in the process of English-language curriculum renewals in Hong Kong since the 1990s.

CHANGE STRATEGIES

From Centre–Periphery Initiation to Rational-Empirical Persuasion

Throughout the history of educational reforms in Hong Kong, important education policy and curriculum decisions have been formulated and implemented through different central agencies, such as the EC, the CDC and the Curriculum Development Institute (CDI). As a non-statutory body, the EC was established in 1984, performing the functions of an adviser to the government on the long-term strategic development of major education initiatives in Hong Kong. Before the handover, it was appointed by the British colonial government and comprised members who were experts and educationists. After thorough research and consultations, the EC put forward recommendations to the EDB (formerly known as the ED) for endorsement and implementation. The EC played a very active role during the 1990s in making recommendations to the Hong Kong government on major reforms. Between 1984 and 1996, it published six biannual reports, which cover different areas of school education, including teacher quality, private sector school improvements, curriculum development, school conditions, special education and language teaching and learning (which appeared in almost all the reports).

In the efforts to win public support for the reforms, consistent themes adopted in the reports have been (1) societal change and (2) concentration on student learning. The importance of education has always been highlighted in the reports as the key to the prosperity of Hong Kong society. For instance, in EC *Report 1* (1984):

Changes in English-Language Education   231

From the outset, we have been keenly aware of the fact that human resources have been, and will remain, a principal asset of Hong Kong, and that education is the key to their development. (p.4)

In fact, its importance was considered to have priority over individual aspirations. For instance, in the same report:

Within the resources available, the needs of the community must first be considered, though in a free society, the wishes of the individual should, within this constraint, be accommodated as far as possible. (p.11)

The broad rationale for the TTRA initiative (proposed by EC, 1990) was framed in such a way that it highlighted the initiative being the answer to the challenges facing Hong Kong in the wider context of socio-economic changes.

The Education Commission's Report No. 4 published in November 1990 . . . recommended that a Framework of Targets and Target-Related Assessment would serve to further improve the quality of learning for all individual students from Primary 1 to Secondary 5, which was later approved by the Governor-in-council. . . . TTRA initiative emerges from the context of Hong Kong society and the need for education to meet the requirements of that society and individuals within it. (ED, 1992, pp.3–4)

Hong Kong's economy is progressively moving away from dependence on labour-intensive manufacturing towards an ever-increasing dependence on finance, commerce and other service industries. These are knowledge-intensive and demand a highly educated workforce. . . . In order to maintain a place with other advanced economies, the education system in Hong Kong must promote effective thinking, and communication among all students . . . develop further their capability to learn how to learn, to think for themselves, to develop and use knowledge, to solve problems, to access information and process it effectively, and to communicate with others so that they can meet the challenges that confront them now and in the future . . . a strong foundation for long-life learning. (ED, 1992, pp.4–5)

It emphasized teacher and school role in advancing the reform, in that:

the most significant feature of the educational context of Hong Kong is that it is moving towards a phase of development in which teachers and schools are given greater responsibility in exercising their professional judgment to make decisions at the local level. (p.6)

232   Alice W.K. Chow

One interesting phenomenon about the strategies adopted in government-initiated reforms in language education in Hong Kong, as in the case of TTRA and TOC, was that related research and development activities were sponsored by a bank, that is, the Hong Kong and Shanghai Banking Corporation through the Hong Kong Bank Foundation and its Language Development Fund. The Hong Kong Bank Foundation is a charitable trust funded by the endowment and ongoing contributions from the Hong Kong and Shanghai Banking Corporation. It was established in 1981 to co-ordinate its extensive community support programmes in Hong Kong and Mainland China, and has since its establishment contributed more than HK$1 billion to charitable causes. Its principal interests are in the areas of education, community welfare, environmental protection and charitable projects enhancing links between Hong Kong and the Mainland. The Language Development Fund provided funding for the publications of Brownell and Scarino (1993) and Clark, Scarino and Brownell (1994) on the theoretical bases of the TOC framework, which later became the blueprint for the development of a task-based curriculum for the subject of English language.

Despite the fact that TTRA was a top-down initiative, a soft approach was adopted as a change strategy (Kennedy, Chan and Fok, 2011). When TTRA met with significant criticisms on the issues of complexity, impracticality and insufficient teacher training (Carless, 1997), the government repackaged and re-titled it as TOC in 1994. In the repackaged version, the notion of target-related assessment intended to be administered internally and regularly by teachers as school-based assessment was dropped. Instead, the focus was placed on designing teaching and learning activities around identified targets to be attained at progressive stages of learning. Again, in promoting the TOC reform, the rationale for an overhaul of education practices within a changing environment put forward by the TTRA research and development team remained. It emphasized:

> the nature of the knowledge based society and requirements for its maintenance and growth are fundamental ideas for the design of the target-oriented curriculum framework. . . . Educational programmes . . . should emphasize learning how to learn. (Brownell and Scarino, 1993, p.18, p.21)

The replacement of TTRA with TOC within two years reflects the government sensitivity and swift response to teachers' negative sentiment and resistance towards the assessment aspect of the TTRA initiative, which was meant to be administered by teachers as part of the teaching, learning and assessment cycle. The TTRA reform created immense demands on the professional knowledge and competence of teachers in relation to the conceptualization, development and administration of learning-oriented assessments. Instead of hastily dumbing down an assessment framework on

Changes in English-Language Education 233

teachers, the official tactics in the TOC framework were to emphasize the teaching and learning aspects of the initiative, focusing on aligning teaching and learning focus with progressive targets and the holistic development of students. The conceptualization of the TOC initiative remained at the rhetorical level unaccompanied by any evaluative mechanism to ascertain its enactment at the classroom level.

Nonetheless, the criterion-referenced assessment framework in the original TTRA initiative, which measures student performance at key stages of learning against targets and standards, did not go away completely. Instead, it emerged in 2004 as the Territory-Wide System Assessment (TSA), which was a pen-and-paper assessment within the Basic Competency Assessments (BCAs) in Chinese Language, English Language and Mathematics, set out in the EC's report entitled *Learning for Life—Learning through Life* (Education Commission, 2000). The main purposes of TSA, as stated in official documents, are to provide the government and school management with information on school standards in key learning areas (KLAs) for the purposes of school improvement. It is believed that the TSA data will inform government of provision of support to those schools in need of assistance, and will enable participating teachers to understand the key process involved in making sense of the TSA results to inform learning and teaching.

From a Laissez-Faire Approach to a Fine-Tuned Policy on Language in Education

Another example of a soft approach to change introduction concerns the policy on language in education. Despite the concern over the quality of language teaching in the classroom (EC, 1984) and the popular belief that, all things being equal, teaching and learning would be generally more effective if the MOI were the mother-tongue, the colonial government maintained a laissez-faire policy on the issue of MOI in secondary schools for many years prior to the changeover of sovereignty in 1997. During the colonial era, individual school authorities could themselves decide whether the MOI should be English or Chinese. Although there are strong academic arguments for mother-tongue education, it seems plausible that the reasons behind the British colonial government's reluctance to mandate mother-tongue education could have been motivated by economical and political considerations. For instance, the government argued "there was general agreement among the public that the emphasis on English in schools could not be reduced if Hong Kong were to retain its position as a leading industrial, commercial and financial centre" (EC, 1984, p.33). Imposing mother-tongue education could have been seen as a move that would deprive students of the opportunities for quality English-language education, thus affecting their chances for education and career advancement and for upward mobility. Instead, the colonial government adopted a positive discrimination policy in which schools opting for Chinese as the MOI would be provided with more

234 Alice W.K. Chow

resources. Furthermore, it removed the largely defunct distinction between Anglo-Chinese and Chinese middle schools, hoping to eliminate the perceived disadvantage that children studying in schools where Chinese was used as the MOI might encounter. Similarly, the language medium indicator in the Hong Kong Certificate of Education was removed in 1986. These moves indicate the colonial government's aversion to adopting a hard-line approach to mandating a top-down policy on MOI, and its tactics in soft-selling mother-tongue education through positive incentives, masking the problem by enhancing resources provisions and removing labels that stigmatized the distinctions between schools adopting a different MOI policy.

The government's laissez-faire policy underwent a drastic change in 1998. Despite extensive objections from schools, students and parents who perceived mother-tongue education as undermining students' chances for university and career prospect, a 'Firm Guidance' was issued to schools, mandating the adoption of Chinese as the MOI in junior secondary classes unless schools could demonstrate that their students had sufficient language abilities in order to benefit from English as the MOI. As a result of this top-down imposition, which was likely to have been motivated by political reasons in view of the change of sovereign power in 1997, the percentage of English-language medium schools dropped from 90% in the 1980s to 25% in 1998, thus reversing "the 40-year-long English dominant era in the history of Hong Kong secondary school education" (Lai, 1999, p.191). This top-down MOI policy had been in place for more than 11 years until 2009, when the EDB put forward a fine-tuned framework which provided flexibility for schools to decide on their MOI arrangements. There are two major items in the 'fine-tuning' policy under which schools can run classes where English is used as the MOI: if 85% of the students in a class meet government criteria for English as the MOI, and if up to 25% of lesson time in 'Chinese as the MOI' classes can be in English. Since the English subject, by itself, can take up to 25% of lesson time, it would mean that in 'Chinese as the MOI' classes, 50% of the lesson time can be in English. As a result of the fine-tuned MOI policy, schools would no longer be classified according to the language adopted as MOI. The change was triggered by extensive criticism over the perceived declining standard of English among students who learn through the medium of the Chinese language arising from the mandated mother-tongue education, adverse labelling effect on schools which adopted Chinese as the MOI and reduced chances of students from such schools for university education (Tsang, 2008). This also illustrates the Hong Kong government's willingness to relax and adjust its education policy in light of diminishing political pressure to institutionalize mother-tongue education because of the change of sovereign power, but mounting social pressure from parents and students for wider and more inclusive access to opportunities in which students are educated through the medium of the English language, and from the business sector for a repositioning of Hong Kong in the globalized economy.

A Normative–Re-Educative Approach to Sustaining Reforms

Instead of adopting a linear and segmented pattern, 'a holistic approach that considers sustainable changes achieved through learning by individuals, singly and collectively' (Stoll, 2009, p.123) is practiced by the Hong Kong government in promoting its various educational reforms. This is inspired by the belief that individual actions within any system have 'rippling effects on their environment' (p.123), and therefore sustainable changes depend on systemic changes taking place in an aligned, coherent and consistent manner.

For the success of educational renewals which require a paradigm shift from a teacher-centred methodology to a student-centred pedagogy, such as the TOC, TBL and NSS reforms, corresponding changes in the epistemological orientations, educational practices such as homogeneous and teacher-directed teaching, and uniform and centralized assessment practices are of paramount importance. It also entails an awareness that further development requires not only the remedying of perceived shortcomings but also the tackling of more fundamental issues to ensure education catches up with society. Since the 1990s, various initiatives targeting enhancement of teacher professional competence for enacting innovations in the classroom have been introduced. The 1990s was a period which saw the professionalization of teachers, with special provisions to enable 80% of graduate teachers to be professionally trained by 1994, with the capacity rising further to achieve 90% in the long run. The ILE was formed in the late 1980s upon the recommendation of the EC to provide professional training for language teachers on innovative reforms, such as the TTRA and TOC. In fact, teacher educators from the ILE were seconded to the TTRA and TOC units to be engaged in research and development projects on the initiatives. Since the mid-1990s, the government has commissioned a large number of professional development programmes offered by higher education institutions on the TBL, SBA and NSS reforms.

In addition to centrally administered efforts to raise the academic and professional education for language teachers, vast amounts of funding were allocated to schools for school-based curriculum and professional development initiatives to support innovations engineered at the school and classroom levels. Such school-based projects are often supported by academic consultants from higher education institutions, such as the Chinese University of Hong Kong through its government-funded accelerated schools projects or the Hong Kong Institute of Education through its government-funded Lesson and Learning Study projects.

A key initiative that represents a normative–re-educative approach is the establishment of the Quality Education Fund (QEF) in 1998 to finance projects for the promotion of quality education in Hong Kong. Its establishment is one of the major recommendations of the EC's report *Enhancing Language Proficiency* (1996). With $5 billion start-up funding, the QEF

236   Alice W.K. Chow

Table 14.1   Focus of QEF Projects on Improvement of English Language Learning

Project focus	Number of projects
Innovative methods	66
Creating rich language environment beyond the classroom	31
Language across the curriculum	4
Profession development for language teachers	2
Language studies	1
Total no.	104

provides a channel for worthwhile projects from the school sector to be funded. It caters for initiatives within the ambit of basic education, including pre-primary, primary, secondary and special education. Since 1998, it has funded more than 8,000 projects totalling more than HK$3.890 billion. Between 1999 and 2010, more than HK$90 million was spent on 104 projects that aimed to improve English-language learning. Table 14.1 shows the focus of the projects.

For instance, in the year 2010, HK$3 million was allocated to English-language development projects on a range of topics, for example, raising English-language proficiency through campus TV, analysis of primary school students pronunciation errors, drama teaching for improving English reading and speaking skills, bridging the MOI gap between primary and secondary schools, dialogic reading and creative books, learning English through understanding social issues, and teaching and learning of English across the curriculum.

In view of the importance that the Hong Kong government attaches to language education, a special committee, the Standing Committee on Language Education and Research (SCOLAR), was established in 1996. It is responsible for policy formulation and implementation of measures that address language learning and teaching in Hong Kong. Its main function on advising the government on policy on language education led to the setting of language attainment targets and identification and co-ordination of research and development projects for the enhancement of language proficiency. One of its recommendations includes the introduction of subject knowledge and subject teaching competence requirements for language teachers. Starting from the 2004–2005 school year, new Chinese- and English-language teachers in primary and secondary schools should hold at least a Bachelor of Education degree in the relevant language subject, or both a first/higher degree in the relevant language subject and a recognized teacher training qualification in the relevant language subject. Teachers without such qualifications are allowed three to five years to undertake professional training and/or formal assessment in order to meet the requirements. SCOLAR also provides advice on the operation of the Language Fund, which between 1994

Changes in English-Language Education 237

and 2003 provided more than HK$181 million to support more than 100 projects that aimed to enhance English-language proficiency among students and the general public. Examples of the projects funded included organization of English-language camps for school students, immersion programmes for English-language teachers, language improvement projects, self-access learning materials, English for the workplace projects, recruitments of native speakers of English as ELT assistants in local schools and so on.

SCOLAR also recommended the setting up of a task force, within the CDI, of teaching consultants to provide Chinese-language (including Putonghua) and English-language support services to all primary and secondary schools in 2004, which symbolizes a dedicated effort of the government to focus specifically on the enhancement of the professional capacity of Chinese and English panel heads and teachers to implement the curriculum reform. On-site support is provided to schools to help build the expertise of teachers in designing curriculum plans, exploring different learning and teaching strategies and using assessment to improve learning and teaching. Teachers and schools interested in pursuing further development in particular curricular areas, for example, grammar in context, speaking, literacy and NSS, come together and form networks through which they share teaching ideas and resources.

Corresponding strategies to implement the 'reading to learn' initiative include the allocation of additional library resources; appointment of teacher librarians in primary schools; professional enhancement of teachers in areas of reading instruction; promoting reading across the curriculum; collaborative research and development projects on reading to learn and provision of teaching and learning packages for teachers and school librarians; and introducing a basic competency assessment to help schools to see whether their students have achieved the appropriate competency level.

The deployment of native-speaking English teachers (NETs) to assist in the reading-focused Primary Literacy Programme (PLP-R) in primary schools also serves as a support strategy for the reading to learn initiative. The NET scheme was originally intended as a measure to address the problems of perceived declining English-language proficiency identified in EC (1996). Its modified version started in 1997 in secondary schools, which was then extended to primary schools in 2002. Its objectives are three-fold:

1. Enrich the English-language learning environment in schools.
2. Enhance the learning and teaching of English with linguistically and culturally authentic materials and resources.
3. Strengthen teaching capacity through school-based professional development and collaboration between NETs and English panel members.

The NETs play an important role in supporting the development and implementation of the reading-focused PLP-R in primary schools, which started

238   Alice W.K. Chow

in 2004 in response to the recommendation of the CDC (2004) that a Reading Workshop component should make up 40% of the English lesson time in the school-based English-language curriculum. Advisory teachers from the advisory teaching teams formed under the CDI's NET section, comprising a mix of NETs and local English teachers, made frequent visits to the PLP-R participating schools to provide support through centralized and school-based professional development workshops, classroom observations and provision of feedback for the teachers involved in the programme. The research results of a three-year evaluation of the primary NET scheme (Griffin et al., 2007) indicated positive trends in PLP-R students' reading and writing proficiency and changes in classroom practices in participating schools. The programme was later revised, adopting a holistic approach incorporating the four language skills maintaining an emphasis on reading and writing. To date, 1,910 primary teachers have been trained and the programme has involved a total of 40,267 students. The PLP-R initiative can be viewed as a capacity-enhancing endeavour to improve the quality and practice of reading instruction in primary schools, alongside the funding provided by the government to appoint teacher librarians in primary schools to promote 'reading to learn'.

Another key capacity-enhancing strategy in support of the current education reforms is the provision of continuing profession development (CPD) opportunities for serving teachers through the Collaborative Research and Development ("Seed") Projects introduced in 2001. In these projects, teachers, with the support provided by the curriculum development consultants from CDI, engage in development and research activities in curriculum planning, implementation and evaluation. Some of these projects also involve secondment of teachers to CDI and the provision of teaching relief so that seconded teachers have the space for professional enhancement in the areas targeted for innovations. Seminars and workshops are organized for the dissemination of innovation practices among front-line educators and curriculum developers that helps the building up of a professional community striving for improvement and professional enhancement. Since its inception in 2001, close to 300 projects spanning across all levels of pre-primary to secondary sectors have been conducted.

In addition to the above initiatives, financial resources were provided to support school-based renewal projects for the common purpose of ELT and learning enhancement in conjunction with the implementation of the government's policy on MOI. Such resources include the introduction of the English enhancement scheme in 2006, the English-language primary enhancement grant in 2009 and the refined English-language enhancement scheme in 2010. They signify efforts of the government to encourage bottom-up school and teacher initiatives. Under the English enhancement scheme, each school which adopts Chinese as MOI is provided with HK$500,000 a year over six years to build up school and teacher capacity for curriculum and pedagogical renewals in ELT. Each school which adopts English as MOI was granted a total of HK$500,000 for the same purpose.

The English enhancement grant scheme for primary schools began in 2009 to provide a time-limited grant of HK$500,000 to each primary school for adopting school-based English enhancement measures. These additional resources were meant to build up school capacity for raising students' English proficiency and to achieve sustainable effects after the completion of the scheme. A further HK$1 million was provided to each secondary school for the implementation of the fine-tuned MOI policy starting from the 2010–2011 school year. The funding was intended for enhancing teachers' capability to teach in English. More than HK$1.4 billion has been set aside for funding the three English enhancement schemes. As expected, a recent survey conducted in three secondary schools (Poon, 2012) showed the majority of students surveyed (70%) felt that English medium instruction helped enhance their English proficiency. The gains in second language proficiency has always been perceived as the goals of language immersion programmes in which students' second language is the medium of classroom instruction in school subjects other than English. The main purpose of this method is to foster bilingualism, in other words, to develop students' communicative competence in their second language.

The above professional development and capacity enhancement provisions reflect the government's attempts to support and sustain bottom-up initiatives at the school and classroom levels to bring about pedagogical changes in line with the reform precepts accentuated in the central curriculum reform documents.

CONTINUING CHALLENGE AND FUTURE DIRECTIONS

The need to reform the examination system remains one of the challenges connected with a learner-centred philosophy of education in the context of Hong Kong, which has a strong tradition of didactic pedagogy in which classroom teaching is mostly expository and sharply focused on preparation for external examinations that are highly competitive and exert excessive pressure on teachers and students (Morris, 1992). In addition to HKDSE, a large-scale public examination at the end of secondary schooling, there are the TSA at the levels of primary 3, 6 and secondary 3 (at the age of 8, 11 and 15, respectively) and numerous and frequent internal school examinations and tests, sometimes held even weekly. In general, the modes of teaching and learning in senior secondary language classrooms (referred to as 'examination classes' by local teachers) will remain similar as those before the reform, featuring an exam-oriented pedagogy dominating most if not all NSS classes in which the teaching syllabus is replaced by the exam syllabus and contents of lessons feature predominately mechanical drills and practice for the public exams. Despite the emphasis the CDI places on AfL, it was envisaged that there would be little change in assessment pedagogy, as HKDSE is still seen as performing a gate-keeping function. Teachers still shape their pedagogy based on requirements of public exams and their firm

240   *Alice W.K. Chow*

belief that 'practice makes perfect'. It is likely that teachers will continue to carefully study the HKDSE exemplars published by the HKEAA and plan lesson contents accordingly.

To encapsulate the true spirit of AfL that embraces a learning- and learner-focused orientation, alternative assessments in the form of portfolio assessment should be given the strongest impetus by the government to emphasize the language learning process as an active demonstration of knowledge, competence and development. School-based portfolio assessment will be particularly relevant to the Elective Part of the English-language paper of HKDSE, which aims to broaden student learning experiences, promote development and application of language skills in a variety of contexts and cater for diverse needs and interests. It embodies a task-based and process-based approach to learning, teaching and assessment, and it encourages students' involvement in their assessments. It emphasizes assessing individual student growth rather than competition with other students, which is particularly important as a strategy to address the issue of learner diversity resulting from the NSS reform. Portfolios have three main purposes, one of which is for assessing progress, achievement, developmental strengths and areas for continued work. The teacher can use the materials included in an evaluative portfolio to complete both formative and summative evaluation of progress. Another purpose is for self-assessment and reflection, where students can chart their progress and take ownership of their learning. Furthermore, portfolios can be used as a means for reporting progress and achievement, as in showcase portfolio used as a means to share accomplishments with parents, prospective employers or for admission to higher education institutions. Students can also be encouraged to develop an archival portfolio which shows a history of student work that follows from class to class, and which can pass along information about the student from one teacher to another as well as allow a student to look back at his or her own progress over time. Portfolio assessment is in fact not a completely new concept as it has already been adopted in other school subjects, such as Visual Arts, Music and Literature in English. It is envisaged that in the early phase of introduction, there might be initial resistance from teachers similar to the level and nature of teacher criticism during the first launching of SBA in 2005. When implementation issues such as grading moderation and standardization have been resolved, it is likely teachers will gradually appreciate the pedagogical value of portfolio assessment in developing independent, self-directed learners, bolstering learner confidence and celebrating individual achievements against defined assessment criteria rather than comparing students' performances against one another's.

The NSS reform has intensified the issues of learner diversity in the English-language classroom which now comprises students who are not academically oriented and who, prior to the NSS reform, would have been channelled to other pursuits, as earlier as at the end of their nine-year compulsory education. The greatest challenge faced by teachers in implementing the current NSS reforms is devising ways to address the issues of student diversity

Changes in English-Language Education 241

arising from an increase in the number of non-academically-oriented students remaining in the school system until the end of their 12-year education, while at the same time helping these low-proficiency students to cope with the demand of the HKDSE examination which they would not have to attempt prior to the NSS reform. The Elective Part of the NSS curriculum is intended as a 'space' in the curriculum to provide differentiation and to cater for learner diversity apart from adding variety to the curriculum. In the earlier years of implementation of NSS, most schools based their decisions on the offering of elective modules on 'convenience' for teachers rather than as a strategy to suit students' interests or abilities. This needs to be changed so that students will be provided with the choice of selecting three elective modules out of a range of options that suit their needs and interests.

The issue of MOI has been a cause for concern in the past decades both before and after 1997 (Chow and Mok, 2004). A number of measures have been introduced by the government to address the problems caused by students having to struggle to learn a foreign language while their English proficiency is below the necessary threshold level (EC, 1990). In fact, despite outstanding students' reading performance in international tests, such as the Progress in International Reading Literacy Study (PIRLS), reflecting some success of the 'reading to learn' initiative in bolstering student reading literacy in Chinese, a recent study (Tse et al., 2010) shows that less than 10% of the primary school students tested in the study were reading at a level at which they would be able to cope without difficulty with a curriculum delivered in English in the secondary school. Tse et al.'s study suggests that the majority of primary school students are better equipped linguistically to learn subjects taught in Chinese, their mother-tongue. The recent 'fine-tuned' MOI policy of the government has been hailed as a right move in the eyes of the general public because of the flexibility it allows schools to make decisions on MOI arrangements, yet it is questionable whether both teachers and students are well equipped and proficient enough in using a foreign language in the teaching and learning of academic subjects that involve cognitively demanding tasks and purposes. To ensure that students will genuinely benefit from the fine-tuned MOI policy, and their command of subject knowledge will not be compromised because of a lack of sufficient competence in a foreign/second language which is used as the instructional medium of content subjects in schools which aspire to operate English MOI classes in subjects other than languages, there needs to be a comprehensive language education policy which puts Language across the Curriculum (LAC) into practice. LAC as a concept acknowledges the fact that language education in school takes place in every subject (including both content and language subjects) across the whole school curriculum (Vollmer, 2006). It focuses on the role of language in subject-specific learning and teaching, and it aims to help students to master new domains of language use and discourse types and extend and transform their existing language proficiency into a higher and deeper level of cognitive-academic use. Schools which aim to offer English MOI classes could also consider adopting content-based instruction (Brinton, Snow and

242 *Alice W.K. Chow*

Wesche, 1989) for the integration of language and content. LAC and content-based instruction require both language teachers and content subject teachers to rethink their roles in enhancing student learning. In view of the special language needs of students in English MOI classes, where they have to study content subjects through English, the role of the English-language curriculum in supporting their academic studies will need to be carefully reconsidered, the corresponding subject target of English be re-defined and its contents re-structured. Both LAC and content-based instruction involve interdisciplinary collaboration. For successful LAC and content-based instruction implementation, Chow, Tse-tso and Li (2005) and Chow (2006) argued for transformations in academic culture and practices featuring the following characteristics:

- School administrators fully support both conceptually and financially the development of content-based instruction through interdisciplinary collaboration.
- Language and content disciplines should be recognized as equal in importance, their interdependence valued. Shared responsibility among language and discipline specialists should be fostered and underscored.
- Systematic and highly co-ordinated planning of content-based instruction based on students' current proficiency levels and subject content objectives and needs should be organized and supported.
- Intensive and ongoing staff development opportunities and professional dialogues among language and discipline specialists should be provided and encouraged.

The above conditions require fundamental changes in language teachers' and content subject specialists' perceptions of their roles in the academic growth and language development of their students. Not only do they need to recognize their shared responsibilities in enhancing students' learning of English and through English; they also need to operationalize a 'new' mode of partnership and collaboration in curriculum design, instruction and evaluation (Stewart, Sagliano and Sagliano 2000)

CONCLUSION

The success factor of any innovations and change is a combination of centralized design, school-based implementation and professional support (Mourshed, Chijioke and Barber, 2010). To garner support from the general public for and to build legitimacy of educational reforms, the Hong Kong government demonstrated ambitious goals for education to meet both the socio-economic targets of the community and the aspirations of its individual members. To manage public perception regarding the need for change, the central policy agencies put forward a strong rationale for a

Changes in English-Language Education 243

fundamental change in society that requires new ways of looking at human learning and to meet individual aspirations through the TOC, TBL, SBA and NSS reforms orchestrated in English-language education. The reform challenges the very basics of student learning and how such learning can best be achieved. Sustained emphasis on education for social and economic advancements in the face of international competition from neighbouring cities, such as Singapore and Shanghai, attracts the attention of the entire society and their support for mobilizing community resources for educational development. For instance, in his policy address delivered in October 2009, the chief executive of Hong Kong announced the development of six industries where Hong Kong enjoys clear advantages, one of which included education services.

Another effective strategy employed is the use of a long lead time. Learnt from the TTRA lesson, which was scrapped in a year or two, the central education agencies set short-, medium- and long-term goals and plans (2001–2002 to 2005–2006, 2006–2007 to 2010–2011 and beyond 2011, respectively) to ease schools into the changes, to develop schools' ownership of the reforms and to minimize unnecessary resistance during the long reform process. The positive non-intervention approach adopted means that government intervention should be minimal, and one of the pieces of evidence includes the government's reluctance to rank schools or to insist on uniform implementation of TOC or TBL. Schools are allowed to develop their own mechanisms of collective decision making on measures and directions for school improvement with generous financial support from the government through various language funds, enhancement schemes and school support services, hence the evolution of schools into more autonomous entities.

The centrally initiated reforms provide schools with a platform for change and innovations, supported by resources and corresponding changes in the public examination as well as university admissions, and yet leaving the process of reforms to schools. The reform pushes schools and teachers to exercise professional autonomy and adapt the changes to best fit their respective student bodies. Nevertheless, there is still the need for more drastic changes in public examination formats, for instance, through the introduction of portfolio assessment to address the issues of learner diversity and to actualize a process-oriented and learner-centred approach to learning. The fine-tuned MOI policy provides schools with the flexibility of making school-based decisions on their MOI arrangements. The success of this policy in schools which plan to operate and increase the number of English MOI classes will depend on a comprehensive and well-thought-out language education policy, realized through carefully co-ordinated LAC and content-based instruction programmes. Transformation in academic cultures and practices involving partnership and interdisciplinary collaboration at all levels of curriculum design, instruction and evaluation, and continuous professional development for both content subject and language teachers are among the key requisites for a successful LAC policy.

244 *Alice W.K. Chow*

Appendix 14.1   English-Language Curriculum Aims in the 1975, 1983, 1999 and 2002 Syllabuses

1975	"The general aim of the Secondary Syllabus is to enable pupils to consolidate and extend the English already learnt by them in the primary school. This means that at whatever stage of the Syllabus they have arrived, they should be capable of speaking, reading, writing and understanding English within the range of structural patterns prescribed up to that point, using with a reasonable degree of confidence and accuracy the basic vocabulary of the Suggested Syllabuses for Primary Schools (English), extended by controlled exposure to spoken and written English" (CDC, 1975, p.6).
1983	"The principal objective of the English language curriculum in the schools of Hong Kong is to provide every pupil with the opportunity to develop the maximum degree of functional competence in English of which he or she is capable given the constraints inherent in the situation, in particular competence in those domains of use which are specially appropriate to the Hong Kong situation" (CDC, 1983, p.8).

"This syllabus ... is a continuation of Stages One and Two which cover the first five or six years of English language teaching. Like the first two stages, it reflects a more communicative, purposive type of approach rather than a structural one" (CDC, 1983, p.5).

1999 and 2002	"The overall aims of the English Language Education curriculum are as follows

a) to offer every student the right to a second language which provides further opportunities for extending their knowledge and experience of the cultures of other people, including opportunities for further studies, pleasure, and work in the English medium; and
b) to enable every student living into the twenty-first century to be prepared for the changing socio-economic demands resulting from advancement in information technology; , including the interpretation, use and production of materials for pleasure, study and work in the English medium.

The Subject Target for English Language is therefore for learners to develop an ever-improving capability to use English
- to think and communicate;
- to acquire, develop and apply knowledge;
- to respond and give expression to experience;

and within these contexts, to develop and apply an every-increasing understanding of how language is organized, used and learned"

(CDC, 1999, p.2; 2002b, p.17).

Appendix 14.2 An Overview of the Hierarchy of Learning Targets and Objectives for the Subject of English Language

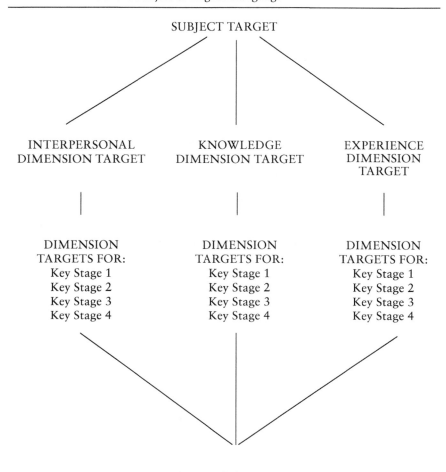

Source: CDC (1999, p.7).

246　*Alice W.K. Chow*

Appendix 14.3　Subject and Dimension Targets for the Subject of English Language

---

Subject Target

To develop an ever-improving capability to use English:

- to think and communicate
- to acquire, develop and apply knowledge
- to respond and give expression to experience

and with these contexts, to develop and apply an ever-increasing understanding of how language is organized, used and learned.

Interpersonal Dimension (KD)

To develop an ever-improving capability to use English:

- to establish and maintain relationships
- to exchange ideas and information
- to get things done

Interpersonal Knowledge Dimension (ID)

To develop an ever-improving capability to use English:

- to provide or find out, interpret and use information
- to explore, express and apply ideas
- to solve problems

Experience Dimension (ED)

To develop an ever-improving capability to use English:

- to respond and give expression to real and imaginative experience

Source: Adapted from CDC (1999, p.8)

Changes in English-Language Education 247

Appendix 14.4 Comparison of Teacher Roles and Skills

Syllabus	1975	1983	1999
Methodology	Oral structural	Oral structural with "communicative" elements	Communicative and task-based
Language Focus	Structural knowledge and accuracy emphasized in speech before writing	Accurate and fluent language use emphasized in both speech and writing	Fluency, accuracy, appropriacy and creative language use emphasized
Teacher's Role	• Knowledge transmission and academic knowledge • Director of classroom language learning	• Organizer and manager of class activities • Resource person • Material developer	• Organiser and manager of class activities • Resource person • Material and curriculum developer • Participant in negotiated activities • Participant in "English scene" and in larger educational scene
Knowledge/ Skills Required	• Discrete language skills, with ability to speak accurately foremost • Ability to give detailed grammatical and lexical explanations and feedback	• More discoursal (i.e., situationally appropriate) language skills • Ability to integrate skills in class • Materials adaptation	• High level of all skills at all discoursal levels • Ability to contextualize skills in class • Materials development • School-based and systemic curriculum development • Information technology knowledge and skills • Ability to support individual students' active learning • Negotiating and collaborative skills • Creativity

Source: Walker, Tong and Mok (1999, p.285).

Appendix 14.5   Characteristics of the Secondary English-Language Curriculum (New versus Old and Existing)

	Old (Pre-1999)	*Existing (1999 Syllabus + 2002 Curriculum Guide)*	*New Senior Secondary (including 2007 CE English Language)*
Aims	Focuses largely on helping students to develop functional competence in English	A broader focus aiming at: (1) Developing students' capability to use English for: • Interpersonal communication • Development and application of knowledge • Responding and giving expression to experience (2) Developing students' generic skills as well as positive attitudes and values for lifelong learning	Builds on the aims of the existing curriculum to enhance students': • language proficiency for further studies, vocational training and work • capacity for lifelong learning as well as cultural understanding and global competitiveness
Design	A single, coherent curriculum for all school levels from primary 1 to sixth form, with emphasis on English as a formal, linguistic system and a medium of communication	A stronger student-centred orientation, emphasizing development of language knowledge and skills, as well as application through meaningful contexts for purposeful communication	Builds on the existing curriculum and consists of a Compulsory Part (forming essential learning content including the four skills, grammar, communicative functions, vocabulary and text types) and an Elective Part (comprising a variety of modules to extend students' learning experience, and to allow them to use the language they have learnt in a broad range of contexts)
Learning and Teaching Approach	Focuses largely on the four language skills as essential components of communication	A broader focus aimed at: (1) The learning and teaching of the four language skills through use of meaningful tasks and activities (2) The promotion of learner autonomy and creativity through self-access learning and the teaching of language arts, respectively	Continuation of current practice, with emphasis on the development of learning communities between teachers and students, and between students themselves, to cater for learner diversity and to facilitate effective learning, teaching and school-based curriculum development

Assessment	Emphasis on Assessment of Learning	While acknowledging the importance of Assessment of Learning, considerable emphasis is placed on Assessment for Learning through encouraging the use of both formative and summative assessment as well as appropriate use of feedback	Continuation of current practice and further emphasis on assessment for learning, through the: • Adoption of Standards-Referenced Assessment (SRA) to recognize what each learner can do against a set of performance standards at the end of the three-year senior secondary education; and • Adoption of school-based assessment (SBA) to assess students' achievement in areas of learning not easily assessable in public examinations
Contents of Textbooks and Learning & Teaching Materials	Emphasis on practicing: • Grammatical items and structures • The communicative functions and uses of English Text types largely informational or transactional in nature	Emphasis on providing opportunities to: • Learn grammar in context • Develop and apply language as well as generic skills through meaningful tasks or activities for purposeful communication A broader range of text types, including language arts texts	Continuation of current emphasis with greater exposure to a variety of text types and more opportunities to apply the language learnt in a broad range of contexts

Source: Adapted from Professional Development Course (2013)

250   Alice W.K. Chow

REFERENCES

Bennis, W.G., Benne, K.D. & Chin, R. (1989). *The Planning of Change.* Fort Worth: Harcourt Brace Jovanovich, Inc.

Black, P., Harrison, C. Lee, C., Marshall, B., & Wiliam, D. (2003). *Assessment for learning.* New York: Open University Press.

Brinton, D.M., Snow, M.A, & Wesche, M.B. (1989). *Content-based second language instruction.* Boston: Heinle and Heinle.

Brownell, J.A., & Scarino, A. (1993). *The theoretical bases of the proposed target-oriented curriculum framework for Hong Kong.* Hong Kong: Institute of Language in Education.

Carless, D. (1997). Managing systemic curriculum change: A critical analysis of Hong Kong's target-oriented curriculum initiative. *International Review of Education, 43*(4), 349–366.

Chow, A. (2006). Enhancing subject learning through English: Insights for content based instruction. *South-East Asia: A Multidisciplinary Journal, 6*(1), 51–70.

Chow, A., & Mok, Cheung A. (2004). English language teaching in Hong Kong SAR: Tradition, transition and transformation. In W.K. Ho & R. Wong (Eds.) *English language teaching in East Asia today: Changing policies and practices* (pp.150–177). Singapore: Eastern Universities Press.

Chow, A., Tse-tso, Y.W., & Li, B. (2005). Learning English or learning through English: Evaluating an English enrichment programme in post-colonial Hong Kong. In S. May, M. Franken & R. Barnard (Eds.) *LED2003: Refereed conference proceedings of the 1st International Conference on Language, Education and Diversity.* CD-ROM. Hamilton: Wilf Malcolm Institute of Educational Research, University of Waikato.

Clark, J.L. (1985). *Curriculum renewals in school foreign language learning.* Oxford: Oxford University Press.

Clark, J.L., Scarino, A., & Brownell, J.A. (1994). *Improving the quality of learning; A framework for Target Oriented Curriculum renewal in Hong Kong.* Hong Kong: Hong Kong Bank Language Development Fund and ILE.

Curriculum Development Council (1975). *Syllabuses for secondary schools. Provisional syllabus for English (Forms I–V).* Hong Kong: Government Printer.

Curriculum Development Council (1983). *Syllabuses for secondary schools. Syllabus for English (Forms I–V).* Hong Kong: Government Printer.

Curriculum Development Council (1997). *Syllabuses for primary schools. English Language (Primary 1–6).* Hong Kong: Government Printer.

Curriculum Development Council (1999). *Syllabuses for secondary schools. English Language (Secondary 1–5).* Hong Kong: Government Printer.

Curriculum Development Council (2001). *Learning to Learn: The way forward in curriculum development.* Hong Kong: Government Printer.

Curriculum Development Council (2002a). *Basic education curriculum guide.* Hong Kong: Government Printer.

Curriculum Development Council (2002b). *English language curriculum guide (primary 1–secondary 3).* Hong Kong: Government Printer.

Curriculum Development Council (2004). *English language education key learning area English language curriculum guide (primary 1–6).* Hong Kong: Government Printer.

Education Commission (1984). *Report 1.* Hong Kong: Government Printer.

Education Commission (1988). *Report 3.* Hong Kong: Government Printer.

Education Commission (1990). *Report 4.* Hong Kong: Government Printer.

Education Commission (1996). *Report 6. Enhancing language proficiency: A comprehensive strategy.* Hong Kong: Government Printer.

Education Commission (1997). *Report 6. Quality school education.* Hong Kong: Government Printer.

Changes in English-Language Education 251

Education Commission (2000). *Learning for Life- Learning through Life. Reform Proposals for the Education System in Hong Kong.* Hong Kong: Government Printer.

Education Department (1992). *General introduction to targets and target-related assessment. TTRA.* Hong Kong: Government Printer.

Griffin, P., Woods, K., Storey, P., Wong, E.K.P., & Fung, W.Y.W. (2007). *Evaluation of the native-speaking English teacher scheme for primary schools in Hong Kong.* Melbourne: University of Melbourne.

Harris, J. (1993). Teaching grammar in a communicative context in the primary EFL classroom. In Education Department, English Section, Advisory Inspectorate (Eds.) *Teaching grammar and spoken English: A handbook for Hong Kong schools* (pp.31–42). Hong Kong: Government Printer.

Hong Kong Examinations and Assessment Authority (2005). *2007 HKCE English language examination. Introduction to the school-based assessment component.* Hong Kong: Hong Kong Examinations and Assessment Authority.

Kennedy, C. (1987). Innovating for a change. *ELT Journal, 41*(3), 163–170.

Kennedy, C., Chan, J.K.S., & Fok, P.K. (2011). Holding policy-makers to account: Exploring 'soft' and 'hard' policy and the implications for curriculum reform. *London Review of Education, 9*(1), 41–54.

Kennedy, K. (2005). *Changing schools for changing times: New directions for the school curriculum in Hong Kong.* Hong Kong: Chinese University Press.

Lai, M.L. (1999). Hong Kong: Language and education in the post-colonial era. *Language, Culture and Curriculum, 12*(3), 191–195.

Lamie, J.M. (2005). *Evaluating change in English language teaching.* New York: Palgrave Macmillan.

Morris, P. (1992). Preparing pupils as citizens of the Special Administrative Region of Hong Kong: An analysis of curriculum change and control during the transition period. In G. Postiglione (Ed.) *Education and society in Hong Kong: Towards one country and two systems* (pp.117–145). Hong Kong: Hong Kong University Press.

Morris, P. (1995). *The Hong Kong school curriculum.* Hong Kong: Hong Kong University Press.

Mourshed, M., Chijioke, C., & Barber, M. (2010). *How the world's most improved schools keep getting better.* New York: McKinsey & Company. Retrieved 10 May 2012, from http://mckinseyonsociety.com/how-the-worlds-most-improved-school-systems-keep-getting-better/.

Nation, I.S.P., & Macalister, J. (2010). *Language curriculum design.* New York: Routledge.

Pang, M.Y.M., & Wong, W.S.Y. (1999). Reviewing the primary English language syllabi (1976–1997). Implications for curriculum study. In Y.C. Cheng, K.W. Chow & K.T. Tsui (Eds.) *School curriculum change and development in Hong Kong* (pp.201–226). Hong Kong: Hong Kong Institute of Education.

Poon, A.Y.K. (2012). Language use, language policy and planning in Hong Kong. *Current Issues in Language Planning, 11*(1), 1–66.

Postiglione, G.A. (1992). *Education and society in Hong Kong. Toward one country and two systems.* Hong Kong: Hong Kong University Press.

Professional Development Course (2013). *Understanding and Interpreting the New Senior Secondary (NSS) English Language Curriculum for English Teachers.* Hong Kong: The Hong Kong Institute of Education.

Richards, J.C., & Rodgers, T.S. (1986). *Approaches and methods in language teaching.* Hong Kong: Cambridge University Press.

Skilbeck, M. (1982). *Culture, ideology and knowledge.* London: Open University Press.

Stewart, T., Sagliano, M., & Sagliano, J., (2000). An alternative team teaching model for content-based instruction. *APJTED, 3*(1), 211–241.

252 Alice W.K. Chow

Stoll, L. (2009). Capacity building for school improvement or creating capacity for learning? A changing landscape. *Journal of Educational Change, 10*(1–2), 115–127.

Sweeting, A.E. (1992). Hong Kong education within historical processes. In G.A. Postiglione (Ed.) *Education and society in Hong Kong. Toward one country and two systems* (pp.39–82). Hong Kong: Hong Kong University Press.

Tsang, W.K. (2008). *The effect of medium-instruction policy on educational advancement.* Hong Kong: Chinese University of Hong Kong.

Tse, S.K., Loh, K.Y.E., Lam, Y.H.R., & Lam, W.I. (2010). A comparison of English and Chinese reading proficiency of primary school Chinese students. *Journal of Multilingual and Multicultural Development, 31*(2), 181–199.

Tsui, A.B.M. (1993). *Report to the Hong Kong Language Campaign.* Hong Kong: Hong Kong Language Campaign.

Tyler, R. (2008). The knowledge explosions: Implications for secondary education. *Educational Forum, 29*(2), 145–153.

Vollmer, H.J. (2006). *Language across the curriculum.* Language Policy Division, Council of Europe, Strasbourg. Retrieved 25 May 2013, from http://www.coe.int/t/dg4/linguistic/Source/Vollmer_LAC_EN.doc

Walker, E. (1999). An analysis of changes in the aims and objectives of the secondary English syllabi (1975–1999). In Y.C. Cheng, K.W. Chow & K.T. Tsui (Eds.) *School curriculum change and development in Hong Kong* (pp.227–257). Hong Kong: Hong Kong Institute of Education.

Walker, E., Tong, A., & Mok, A. (1999). Changes in secondary school English teaching methodologies and content (1975–1999). In Y.C. Cheng, K.W. Chow & K.T. Tsui (Eds.) *School curriculum change and development in Hong Kong* (pp.259–293). Hong Kong: Hong Kong Institute of Education.

Wiliam, D. (2001). An overview of the relationship between assessment and the curriculum. In D. Scott (Ed.) *Curriculum and assessment* (pp.165–181). Westport, CT: Ablex Publishing.

Part VI

Assessment

15 Assessment for Learning in Hong Kong
Conceptions, Issues and Implications

Rita Berry

INTRODUCTION

Hong Kong has a long history of using formal, high-stakes summative tests as the sole assessment method to make decisions on individuals' educational upward movements, employment opportunities and social mobility. Standardized tests and examinations are set at different stages in the education system as the screening device. To survive this exam-oriented system, a common practice is to teach and learn to the tests. Many teachers review past examination papers, make educated guesses on the questions for the examinations, provide students with model answers and make them memorize the answers by heart. This kind of rote learning suppresses thinking and minimizes creativity. Being aware of these problems, the Hong Kong Special Administrative Region (SAR) government has taken bold initiatives to make a change. These include the large-scale attempt in reforming learning and assessment practice using the Target Oriented Curriculum (TOC) and its linked Target Oriented Assessment (TOA) in the 20th century and the Assessment for Learning (AfL) movements in the education reform in the 21st century. The focus of these two main initiatives has been to make assessment work for learning, as reflected in the concepts of AfL (used interchangeably with formative assessment) (Berry, 2011b).

The fundamental principle of AfL is making a strong connection between assessment and learning. Being an integral part of the curriculum, pedagogy and assessment cycle, assessment is used to induce, promote and advance learning. It helps teachers to monitor student learning, identify the learning needs of the students during their learning progression and, when the needs have been identified, provide direction or feedback to the students in the steps to be taken to enhance learning. Students' involvement in the assessment activities is taken seriously, as they are the main players of learning. The information gathered from assessment is interpreted and with the new understanding of student learning, decisions can be made on different educational levels including adjustment of teaching content and activities, modification of curriculum plans and amendment of policies.

256 Rita Berry

THE ASSESSMENT FOR LEARNING LANDSCAPE IN HONG KONG

In the last two decades, the call in education worldwide for a change of assessment culture has been echoed by some AfL advocates in Hong Kong. These advocates criticized that the then prevailing curricula in Hong Kong schools were primarily academic, teacher- and textbook-centred and driven by high-stakes, norm-referenced examinations. Biggs (1996), for example, criticized that, for years, educators had based their assessment practices on assumptions inappropriately adopted from psychology and from the testing establishment. He drew people's attention to the education function of assessment—using assessment as the means to support learning. The SAR government responded positively to the AfL movements. In the 1990s, the government introduced the TOA in its large-scale curriculum reform. The TOA was the assessment component of the TOC. Based on the TOC Assessment Guidelines (Education Department [ED], 1998), Morris et al. (1999) elaborate the purposes and characteristics of TOA, as follows:

Purposes of target-oriented assessment:

Target-oriented assessment is an integral part of the Target Oriented Curriculum. Its fundamental purpose is to promote learning. TOA involves:
- making considered judgement of learner performance, based on explicitly stated criteria;
- recognizing learners' strengths and areas for improvement in learning; and
- assisting learners to make further progress and charting the changes in their learning.

TOA allows for continuity in assessment of learner progress which can be monitored and supported over time, within and across stages.

Characteristics of target-oriented assessment:

Target-oriented assessment
- is based on criterion-referencing principles;
- is valid and reliable;
- covers a comprehensive range of purposeful and contextualized assessment activities and reporting strategies;
- requires teachers to include a range of well-planned assessment activities and recording/reporting formats in the teaching/learning plan; and
- acknowledges that the complexity of learner performance cannot be described by a single test score.

These characteristics highlight the integration of teaching, learning & assessment and holistic learning in TOC. (p.3)

This government-led TOC was a large-scale attempt to link assessment with learning. It was a form of outcome-based education in which students progressed towards specific learning targets through carrying out learning tasks (Morris and Adamson, 2010). TOA required teachers to record students' learning outcomes in a highly detailed fashion, which teachers generally found very tedious, difficult and too time-consuming to conduct. The formative assessment initiatives of TOC were unfortunately not well received despite their good intentions. Though perceived as unsuccessful, the AfL concepts embedded in the TOC were regarded as theoretically sound and were promoted heavily in the education reform conducted in the 21st century.

Since 2000, the SAR government has embarked on a new round of education reform, which highlights assessment as key for learning. In its document *Learning for Life—Learning through Life* (Education Commission [EC], 2000), the government points out the inadequacies of the existing education system, saying that the learning effectiveness of students remains not very promising and that learning is still examination-oriented and scant attention has been paid to "Learning to Learn". The Curriculum Development Council (CDC, 2002) advises that all schools should review their current assessment practices and put more emphasis on *AfL* and that teachers should seek to identify and diagnose student learning problems and provide quality feedback for students on how to improve their work. The council, in its most recent published assessment guidelines (CDC, 2009), stresses the strong linkage between curriculum, pedagogy and assessment. The guidelines point out that assessment involves collecting evidence about student learning and interpreting information and making judgements about students' performance with a view to providing feedback to students, teachers, schools, parents, other stakeholders and to the education system.

Two new initiatives were included in this new round of assessment reform, including the implementation of Basic Competency Assessment (BCA) for primary and junior secondary education and school-based assessment (SBA) solely for secondary education. Both of them are used as vehicles to drive AfL forward (Berry, 2011c). BCA covers three subjects, namely, English Language, Chinese Language and Mathematics. It consists of two components—Student Assessment (SA) and the Territory-Wide System Assessment (TSA). SA is a resource bank provided through the internet for the purpose of assisting teachers to identify the learning strengths and weaknesses of their students. With the information obtained, teachers could then organize or reorganize their teaching to enhance learning in students. TSA is conducted by the government, collecting information from students at the end of their primary 3, primary 6 and secondary 3 schooling. This kind of assessment takes the paper-and-pencil mode except for the oral assessment component of English Language and Chinese Language. Only a random sample of students is involved in these assessments. The aim of these assessments is to help the government review policies and provide

258 Rita Berry

focused support to schools. The government stresses that BCA is low stakes in nature, aiming at using assessment to enhance teaching and learning (Hong Kong Examinations and Assessment Authority [HKEAA], n.d.[a]). However, school personnel see this differently, criticizing that these are the strategies the government uses to close down schools which perform poorly in the TSA. To help students achieve better results in the TSA, many teachers use the assessment items in the SA resource bank to 'drill' their students instead of using them to support learning.

SBA, formative in nature, is an assessment conducted by the teachers at secondary schools. SBA is a salient feature of the Hong Kong Diploma of Secondary Education (HKDSE) examination, first administered in 2012. HKDSE is a high-stakes public examination which students take at the end of their six-year secondary schooling (new 3+3+4 education structure—six years of secondary and four years of tertiary). In the HKDSE, all the 24 subjects include an SBA component (Berry, 2008, pp.34–36, table 2.4). In this new curriculum and assessment structure, SBA is treated as a part of the public examination system. Marks are collected from students by various types of assessment methods over a period of time in their secondary school and will count towards the total marks of the certification system in Hong Kong. The contribution to the summative measurement varies from subject to subject, from 15% to 50% (HKEAA, n.d.[b]). The government sees the potential of SBA in enhancing teaching and learning, reducing examination pressure and improving the validity and reliability of assessment, as well as creating a positive backwash effect on teaching. The government expects that there will be a de-emphasizing of the summative tests, in favour of the practice of formative assessment, which emphasizes the provision of quality feedback from teachers as well as the active involvement of students in the assessment process.

Despite all these efforts, Hong Kong has been struggling with bringing AfL into fruition. In its early days of implementation, in 2003, a government-commissioned report was released (IBM, 2003) asserting that assessment had not been widely used as a means to improve learning. Kennedy et al. (2008) point out that in Hong Kong, even though there has been considerable support for making assessment a vehicle for learning, the high-stakes social function of assessment gives it a role and function that can trivialize these plans. The investigation conducted by Berry (2010) found that many teachers still adopted a competitive and selective approach for assessing their students internally, rather than assessing through formative and supportive means. The assessments the teachers used were largely paper-and-pencil tests and the main purpose of assessment was oriented towards surface knowledge acquisition through rote memory retention and not conceptual understanding. In a further study, Berry and Adamson (2012) found that teachers were rather limited in their understanding of the concepts and practices of AfL, had contradictory views about the purposes and values of assessment and were not ready to alter their power dynamics

Assessment for Learning in Hong Kong 259

within the classroom. There are a number of other issues that impact on the successful implementation of current assessment reform (Berry, 2008, pp.32–37). For example, there are concerns about the reliability, validity and trustworthiness of SBA results and how the results of TSA are used by the government. As mentioned previously, there is a widespread speculation that TSA is a means to close down some schools. One of the most noted issues is the readiness of teachers for AfL. On the whole, teachers are generally underprepared for the new assessment initiatives. Teachers are one important agent of educational change. To make this assessment reform a success, teachers do need more detailed and substantial ideas to help them implement AfL in their classroom teaching. Many teachers are in fact very enthusiastic about AfL; however, they lack the knowledge and skills in translating AfL conceptions into classroom practices (Berry, 2011a).

THE STUDY

The study was conducted to respond to the needs of the teachers mentioned previously. Current initiatives of the SAR government seek to reduce the focus on tests and results, attempting to make assessment serve learning purposes. This is a substantial challenge for a culture in which parents, pupils and teachers are oriented towards tests and improving results (Carless, 2011). The rationale for this research was that, while acknowledging this pull, it provided intensive support and encouragement to help teachers explore other emphases in classroom assessment. An AfL implementation framework (Berry, 2007, p.13; 2008, pp.14–18), supported by ten AfL guiding principles (see Figure 15.1) and their linked 50 AfL indicators (see Table 15.1), was set out to empower teachers with AfL knowledge and skills for teaching and student learning. In this study, the framework was incorporated into a teacher professional development programme. Sixteen schools, including, in the first year, eight primary and, in the second year, four primary and four secondary, took part in this Hong Kong project. A total of 52 teachers from these schools participated in the project. Three teachers of English Language, Chinese Language and Mathematics from each participating school were recruited. Two classes of similar academic abilities in each school were involved in the study (primary 4 and secondary 1). The research aimed to investigate the impact of the foresaid Assessment for Learning Professional Development Programme (AfL PDP) on teaching and learning. The results reported below were based on the analysis of the data collected in the first year of implementation, during which 24 teachers from eight primary schools in Hong Kong and a number of their senior school personnel were interviewed. Other research methods included pre- and post-tests, sample group student interviews and researchers' observations, as well as comments from the project external examiner. The AfL PDP is presented in Figure 15.1.

260 *Rita Berry*

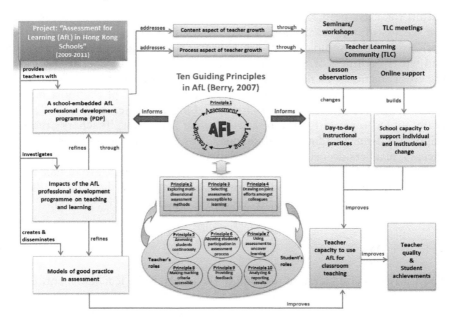

Figure 15.1 The AfL PDP.

There were two key elements in the professional development programme. The first element was the provision of an AfL implementation framework mentioned previously, as the *content* or knowledge dimension, to allow teachers to link AfL theory to classroom practice. AfL is a holistic concept that is not easily understood unless it is further deconstructed in concrete terms. The framework was used as the basic structure for increasing teachers' understanding of AfL in their professional development. It is worth noting that the ten principles should not be viewed as separate entities; instead, they should be seen as complementing each other in supporting learning. In the framework, the ten AfL guiding principles are grouped into three tiers with the first one 'Aligning Assessment to Teaching and Learning' (Principle 1) being located at the top, highlighting the contention that assessment should be seen as an interconnected part of teaching and learning and that assessment should be consistent with the objectives of the course or the curriculum. The second tier emphasizes the teacher's role in using assessment for the purpose of supporting student learning. As assessment can vary in form, depth or breath, teachers can 'Explore the Use of Multi-Dimensional Assessment Methods' (Principle 2) and 'Select those Assessment Methods which Are Susceptible to Learning' (Principle 3). Teachers may want to 'Consider Drawing on Joint Efforts among Colleagues' (Principle 4) to brainstorm, plan, implement and evaluate their AfL practices. The third tier, Principles 5 to 10, focuses on the interaction

Table 15.1 AfL Indicators

Principle 1 Aligning Assessment to Teaching and Learning	1. The teacher aligns the assessment and teaching objectives with one another, as reflected through the curriculum.
	2. The teacher uses assessment strategies/methods that match the teaching focuses of the curriculum.
	3. The teacher uses assessment tasks that are related to the teaching content.
	4. The teacher uses the information gathered from assessment to understand students' learning progress.
	5. The teacher adjusts his/her curriculum and teaching after understanding about students' performances.
Principle 2 Exploring Multi-Dimensional Assessment Methods	6. The teacher uses different kinds of strategies/methods to assess students, for example, standardized paper-and-pencil tests and alternative assessment, for example, portfolio assessment, project assessment, worksheets and observations.
	7. The teacher uses various kinds of assessment strategies/methods to help student achieve different learning outcomes.
	8. The teacher uses various kinds of assessment strategies/methods to cater for different learning needs.
	9. The teacher uses different kinds of assessment strategies/methods to arouse students' interests in learning.
Principle 3 Selecting Assessments Susceptible to Learning	10. The teacher is aware of a variety of assessment strategies/methods.
	11. The teacher is aware of the differing functions of various types of assessment strategies/methods.
	12. The teacher is able to use various types of assessment strategies/methods for teaching.
	13. The teacher's selection of assessment strategies/methods provides students with a wealth of opportunities to learning.
	14. The teacher's selection of assessment strategies/methods provides students with multi-faceted learning.

(continued)

Table 15.1 (continued)

Principle 4 Drawing on Joint Efforts amongst Colleagues	15. The teacher is involved in assessment planning activities. 16. The teacher discusses and mutually establishes assessment common standards with colleagues. 17. The teacher develops assessment activities collaboratively with colleagues. 18. The teacher regularly reviews with colleagues on the development and implementation of assessment activities in the school.
Principle 5 Assessing Students Continuously	19. The teacher gives students formative assessment (e.g., small assessment tasks to enable s tudents learn progressively, periodical tests and examinations). 20. The teacher conducts observations to analyze the performance of their students during teaching. 21. After understanding students' learning progress, the teacher offers encouragements and guidance and provides students with constructive feedback. 22. The teacher gives students appropriate number of assessment activities.
Principle 6 Allowing Student's Participation in Assessment Process	23. The assignments the teacher designs help develop student learning. 24. The teacher communicates with his/her student what is to be learnt and why they have to learn it. 25. The teacher facilitates students to work collaboratively (e.g., in small groups or in pairs) for the purpose of helping them learn. 26. The teacher lets students check the assignments and lets them record the progress of their own learning. 27. The teacher allows students to reflect on and to discuss their own learning with others. 28. The teacher allows students to self-assess and provide feedback to their peers. 29. The teacher helps students understand what they have accomplished. 30. The teacher helps students see/understand the intended learning outcomes and gets students to be involved in the assessment activities that support them to achieve these outcomes. 31. The teacher allows students to engage in discussing and establishing new learning goals.

Principle 7 Using Assessment to Uncover Learning	32. The teacher thinks that assessment can provide information which reflects what students have learnt and what is yet to be learnt. 33. The teacher is able to assess a broad range of learning outcomes. 34. The teacher uses formative assessment to provide continuous feedback as well as to plan future teaching and learning activities. 35. The teacher uses summative assessment to compare and report results, deliberate inter-class or inter-level curriculum plans.
Principle 8 Making Marking Criteria Accessible	36. The teacher clearly explains assessment tasks to his/her students. 37. The teacher helps students understand assessment criteria. 38. The teachers provides students with past students' work as examples, to demonstrate what is required of them in their courses. 39. The teacher asks students to present their work and take this as an opportunity to inform/show students the required standards.
Principle 9 Providing Feedback	40. The teacher offers compliments when students have achieved satisfying results. 41. The teacher offers specific comments on students' achievements. 42. The teacher explains why the answers are right or wrong. 43. When dealing with unsatisfactory work, the teacher gives concrete suggestions for improvement. 44. The teacher informs students of the best and of alternative methods to carry out assignments. 45. The teacher provides students with timely feedback to aid their learning.
Principle 10 Analyzing and Reporting Results	46. The teacher analyzes quantitative data collected from the students. 47. The teacher analyzes qualitative data collected from the students. 48. The teacher determines which areas of the curriculum need modifications based on the results of the analysis. 49. The teacher uses quantitative reports to report on student performance. 50. The teacher uses narrative reports to report on student performance.

264 Rita Berry

between teachers and students. Teachers are encouraged to allow 'Students to Take Part in the Assessment Process' (Principle 6). Classroom activities should be designed to allow students to self- and peer-assess their work. 'Making Marking Criteria Accessible for Students' is designed to facilitate self- and peer-assessment (Principle 8). Teachers can 'Use Different kinds of Assessment Strategies to Uncover Students' Learning' (Principle 7) and use them to 'Assess Students Continuously throughout the Learning Processes' (Principle 5). Then, it is suggested that they 'Analyze and Report on Their Students to Understand How Students Learn' (Principle 10). The report is used as a means to 'Provide Feedback to Students to Facilitate Learning' (Principle 9). To support learning, feedback needs to be constructive and timely. With marking criteria provided and explained to them, students are informed about the expected standards of their work. To teachers, marking criteria can also be used as a basis for giving feedback and communicating results to different parties. To help teachers further consolidate their understanding of the ten guiding principles, 50 AfL indicators were developed (see Table 15.1).

A total of eight one-day seminar/workshop sessions were held periodically in the first phase of the project (first year). All the seminars and workshops aimed to provide teachers with a basic understanding of the fundamentals of AfL and strategies/methods. Real classroom examples such as questioning skills, self-assessment and peer assessment and giving quality feedback were given to the teachers at the seminars and workshops to help teachers link AfL theory to classroom practice. Activities of the AfL PDP also included a number of executive meetings for school representatives for planning, communication and project evaluation purposes.

The second element was a heightening of teachers' agency in relation to AfL practices, as the *process* dimension. The *process* by which the project sought to effect these changes was via school-embedded teacher learning communities (TLCs), which were perceived to have the potential to provide teachers with the information and support they needed to develop their practice in deep and lasting ways. They were allowed to choose one or multiple aspect(s) of AfL they would want to try out for their teaching. Hargreaves et al. (2013) suggest that choice, initiation by the participants and relevance to their own situations are important ingredients for the effectiveness of the development process. Each training event included a TLC session to allow teachers opportunities to share their experience in implementing AfL with their project counterparts and to draw on feedback from their peers and researchers. To help teachers internalize their understanding in AfL, the researchers paid four visits to each school in the first year of AfL implementation. Each visit included peer lesson observations of the three participant teachers at a project school and a post-lesson school-based teaching learning community meeting (SB-TLC). SB-TLCs, while sharing similar vision as TLCs, had a specific mission—to create a learning community in individual schools. The intention was that these budding school-based learning communities could

Assessment for Learning in Hong Kong 265

grow in capacity over time, benefiting the project teachers initially and, in the long run, the educational site they worked at. The teachers were encouraged to conduct informal peer observations and meet as regularly as they could during the term time. The ten AfL guiding principles and their linked 50 AfL indicators were used as the basis for discussing teachers' AfL practices at the TLC and SB-TLC meetings. To further this, teachers were encouraged to keep a portfolio so that they could keep track of their professional growth over the project period.

THE IMPACT OF THE AFL PDP ON LEARNING

Pre- and Post-Tests

The two-group control group design was used as one research method to investigate the impact of AfL PDP on learning. Pre–and post–AfL PDP intervention tests were used to provide some measure of impact as a result of the intervention. Shuttleworth (2009) stresses that this kind of research method is, by far, the simplest and most common of the pre- and post-test designs and is a useful way of ensuring strong level of internal validity. Cohen, Manion and Morrison (2003), however, point out some potential threats to internal validity of this research method. They say that, frequently in educational research, events other than the experimental treatments occur during the time between pre- and post-test observations. Such events produce effects that can mistakenly be attributed to differences in treatments. Also, it is very difficult, if not impossible, to judge whether the process of pre-testing actually influenced the results even if a reasonable time gap is given between the two administrations of the same test. There is no guarantee on external validity, either. For example, it is both unethical and impossible to isolate the two groups of students and also their teachers in the same school during the whole investigative period. Therefore, it is reasonable to assume that these students, and also their teachers, mix outside lessons and share ideas, potentially contaminating the results. But, if students are drawn from different schools to prevent this, the chance of selection bias arises. All in all, Shuttleworth (2009) contends that, as long as its limitations are fully understood, the two-group control group design is a very useful research method to study impact of treatment.

With the support of the BCA team at the Education Bureau (EDB), the test items were adapted from TSA past papers used in 2008 for students at the end of their primary 3 (Key Stage One). The paper assessed the basic competencies of the students in the different dimensions of three subjects (i.e., English Language, Chinese Language and Mathematics). There were four sub-domains in English Language and Chinese Language (i.e., reading, listening, writing and speaking), each of which was tested separately. There were four sub-domains in Mathematics (i.e., arithmetic

266 Rita Berry

operations, fractions, parallel and perpendicular lines, and quadrilaterals), which were combined into one paper. The pre-test was administered at the beginning of the AfL PDP and the post-test was administered at the end of the programme (one academic year time gap). Test questions were the same at both points of time. Two target groups of similar academic abilities studying in primary four were identified in each school, one to act as a control group and the other to act as an experimental group. In the first cohort, a total of 523 students in eight primary schools completed the pre- and post-tests. Only six students from each class (sample group of 96 students), representing high, medium and low academic abilities, took speaking tests of the English and Chinese languages. Comparison of the effect size of the experimental and control groups showed that the AfL PDP had positive impacts on student learning. There were clear improvements between the pre- and post-tests in the different subject areas in all schools for the experimental group students (effect size: English Language 0.3998, Chinese Language 0.4036 and Mathematics 0.2855). Given the limitations of pre- and post-tests, as mentioned previously, additional qualitative data were collected to help validate the findings revealed by the pre- and post-tests.

Interviews

Interviews were conducted with senior school personnel, participating teachers, the external examiner and a sample group of students. Interviews from different sources converged on the same conclusion that students in the experimental group had become more engaged in their learning. Summary of the interviews are displayed below.

From the senior school personnel:

> *Students had many opportunities to participate in the assessment activities. They enjoyed the learning that came with them. Students were very engaged in learning.*

From the project teachers:

> *Students became more active and were more engaged in the lessons. They were more aware of their strengths and weaknesses and would think about how they could improve their learning.*

From the external examiner of the project:

> *Hong Kong students are usually very passive in learning. But the students of the lessons observed were very engaged in all learning activities.*

Assessment for Learning in Hong Kong 267

From the students themselves:

> *We were feeling happy in the lessons. We learnt more when we felt happy. We learnt better in the new teaching mode.*

THE IMPACT OF THE AFL PDP ON TEACHING

A number of research methods were used to collect data to investigate the impacts of the AfL PDP on teaching. Below are some of the comments directly made by the teachers:

> *Whenever we come across the word 'assessment' or 'internal assessment', we automatically associate it with the tests and exams in our school. Grades and marks are our concern. In fact, assessment can be used to support learning. We could pay more attention to setting criteria and understanding how students learn and monitor student learning.*

> *I think my understanding of assessment has changed a lot since I participated in the AfL PDP programme. First of all I come to understand that assessment is not just about giving students a grade or grouping them into different levels.*

> *The function of assessment also includes facilitating teaching and enhancing learning. Assessment can help us examine how effective our teaching and learning is.*

> *After joining this PDP, when I plan my lessons, I would deliberate 'What' and 'How' I should assess my students.*

> *We've benefited from the AfL PDP. From the workshops and seminars, we got to understand and learn the skills and theories of AfL. We learnt the ten AfL guiding principles and how to integrate them for use in preparing our lessons. With the support from the professors, we felt that we have made a lot of progress in teaching.*

> *Being able to self-reflect is very important to teachers' professional development. Throughout the process, we continuously reflect on our assessment practices and make necessary changes to teaching so that students can learn better.*

> *And the TLC meeting . . . different subjects of TLC meetings, for me is Mathematics TLC meeting . . . the presentations and discussions of the TLC meetings enabled us to learn more. And lesson observation*

268   Rita Berry

> . . . we observe lessons of three different subjects and learn from our other colleagues.

> The students can understand more about their own learning and be more able to judge what they needed. These would give teachers some directions in designing their lessons.

> On the right-hand side is a picture that shows our interpretation of how assessment is linked with teaching and learning in the curriculum. Having clear assessment criteria is important as it lets us know what sorts of standards we are aiming at. Teachers can choose the kind of assessment strategy to match the important areas to assess.

In summary, the *interviews with teachers* revealed that the teachers were satisfied with the programme and they acknowledged the changes in them. They said that when compared with the past, they were more aware of the criteria of assessment and how assessment should be related to their lesson activities. In the past they seldom considered what abilities or what aspects of the students they would need to assess. After their experience in the AfL PDP, they had enhanced their knowledge in what and how to conduct assessment and feedback. They became more aware of the importance of providing effective assessment and of putting theories into practice. They perceived themselves incorporating AfL into lesson and curriculum planning in the future.

Data analysis of the interviews of *senior school personnel* revealed that the senior personnel were very happy with their teachers' deeper understanding of AfL. They all said they witnessed an improved teaching quality amongst their teachers involved in this project. They commented that the participating teachers had become more attentive to the needs of students and the progress of student learning and that the teachers were more able to integrate assessment activities into teaching. Below are some of the comments directly made by the senior personnel.

> Previously, teachers did not know that assessment could support learning. Certainly, they did not use assessment to uncover student learning.

> Now teachers are more aware of the usefulness of assessment for teaching and learning.

> At the beginning of the project, teachers were not able to link assessment with teaching and learning. Some time into the project, they were more familiar with AfL concepts. Integrating assessment activities into teaching thus became easier to them.

> It was obvious that teachers paid more attention to students' needs now.

They wanted to know whether their students understood what had been taught to them.

The project is helpful for the teachers.

Taken together, the AfL PDP provided evidence that implementing effective formative assessment in Hong Kong schools was a powerful mechanism for improving student achievement and closing the achievement gap. There was evidence to show that the programme had raised the teachers' awareness of the importance of AfL in teaching and learning. All project teachers made an effort, though of differing intensities, in connecting assessment with teaching. They incorporated assessment elements of their choice in their teaching plans. Some teachers displayed a stronger understanding of AfL and used the newly acquired knowledge and skills better than their counterparts. As observed, the students of these teachers were particularly engaged in learning. Highlights of the outcomes and challenges of the programme are given below.

Outcomes

- Project teachers had changed their attitudes from doubtful to convinced about AfL, after experiencing the benefits of using AfL techniques in their classrooms.
- Teachers' practices had changed in the classroom, as they discovered that they could reinterpret assessment in other ways.
- Project teachers generally paid more attention to assessment activities in lesson planning.
- Teachers became more aware of the learning processes of students than they had been before. Some adjustments to their subsequent lesson planning were evident.
- Student actively participated in the lessons.
- The teachers actively discussed with and sought feedback from the researchers and peer teachers in TLC and SB-TLC meetings for their next round of action planning.
- Participants expressed a desire to continue to use these new approaches in the future, thus ensuring a measure of sustainability in the pilot schools.

Challenges

- Although the project teachers exhibited a deeper understanding of AfL, their conceptual understanding of AfL was still fresh and their skills in linking AfL concepts with classroom practice were still in the developmental stage. The intention of TLCs and SB-TLCs was to help teachers take control of their AfL development over time. With

270 Rita Berry

the support of the researchers, both types of teaching and learning communities made a good start. However, without an overarching policy from the government, these new found AfL dialogues in the inter- and intra-school teaching and learning communities may not be sustained. Understandably, with the annual budget given by the government, schools have their own priorities in resource allocations and these vary from year to year.

- During the project period, it was noted that individual schools had different resource allocation plans; consequently, not all participant teachers received the amount of time and space that they would need. A comment was heard that some teachers used a lot of their personal time in planning and conducting assessment activities during the project period.
- Teachers' participation in the training sessions was generally high. However, there were cases that teachers missed a session or a TLC meeting on a training day. The AfL PDP was designed in a way that high attendance was required for teachers' continual development in understanding of AfL concepts and how the concepts can be translated into classroom practice.
- The senior management of the project schools, in particular, saw the AfL PDP and the researchers as an advisory body. The long tradition embedded within the Chinese culture of 'looking up to the senior and the experts for solutions' had made it hard to facilitate teacher agency in AfL (the *process* element of the project).

CONCLUSION AND IMPLICATIONS

The current Hong Kong classroom context presents a number of challenges to the success of AfL implementation. Several features make implementing AfL in the Hong Kong context difficult, as highlighted below.

- There was a lack of deep understanding amongst the teaching force about the relationship between assessment and learning.
- Although guidelines and directories were provided to schools and teachers, there were very few concrete ideas available in helping teachers translate AfL concepts into classroom practice. As said previously, AfL is a holistic concept that is not easily understood unless it is further deconstructed in concrete terms.
- There was a lack of time and space for teachers to engage with changing their practice to embrace AfL when other pressing concerns have greater priority.
- The dominance of examinations in the education system and the perception that assessment principles enshrined in AfL would be, to some extent, in conflict with traditional forms of assessment.

Assessment for Learning in Hong Kong 271

The above-mentioned challenges may have posed some threats to the successful implementation of the AfL movements in Hong Kong. The brighter side of the movements is that the society is getting more aware of the learning function of assessment. Thirteen years into the current education reform, school personnel are currently more susceptible to the ideas of AfL. Many teachers are basically very enthusiastic about using assessment to promote learning. Exploration into teachers' readiness for changing conceptions of formative assessment, however, has indicated that teachers were generally not ready for the new assessment policy and this explains why there has not been much change in their assessment practices in the classroom. The SAR government in fact has put a lot of effort into promoting AfL for teaching and learning. To facilitate the change of teachers' assessment practice, the government has offered teachers professional development through numerous seminars and workshops. However, these single, isolated professional training events which aim at meeting the immediate needs of teachers are inadequate to help teachers sustain their newly learnt AfL practices. It is postulated that, to accomplish the paradigmatic shift of assessment in the classroom, a large-scale professional development programme is needed. The programme will have to be a comprehensively planned professional upgrading training which addresses the *content* side and the *process* side of teacher development. Borrowing the terms from modern technology, the content side is the hardware and the process side is the software for teacher development. The hardware is best to contain some catalysts such as models, frameworks, guidelines, advice and other guidance to help teachers achieve a thorough understanding of the concepts. These catalysts would provide systematic, well-delineated ways of describing and explaining how concepts and practice could bring about teaching and learning improvements. The software will be the empowerment of teacher agency. Professional development that is considered helpful usually belongs to the category which treats improving classroom practice as a collaborative and negotiated activity, rather than a 'top-down' initiative. The AfL PDP developed for the investigation reported in this chapter was designed based on the above-mentioned concepts. It provided, on the content side (the hardware), an AfL implementation framework aiming at empowering teachers with AfL knowledge and skills for their everyday teaching. The framework comprised ten baseline AfL concepts (ten AfL guiding principles), which were further deconstructed to 50 AfL indicators with a purpose to provide teachers with concrete ideas in bridging the gap between theory and practice. The process side (the software) was the intensive support and encouragement to teachers, aiming at helping them to take control of using assessment to support learning. Jointly, the two, as revealed by the findings of the study reported in this chapter, made positive impacts on teaching and learning. Exciting as the results seemed, a professional development programme of this kind of scale and intensity has resource implications. There is only so much that a project can do to help, no matter how substantial the funding is. It is because once the project ends, the

272   *Rita Berry*

support from the researchers will be lifted. Then it will be very much down to the commitment of individual schools as to how much they would be willing to allocate of the school's resources towards consolidating their teachers' newly acquired AfL knowledge and skills. Until now, the SAR government has been very committed to helping the teachers, and one would imagine quite a sizeable amount of government budget has already been spent on increasing teachers' understanding of AfL. This has been quite successful in arousing teachers' awareness of AfL; however, it has not been as successful in changing teachers' assessment practices in the classroom. It is perhaps time to think forward to what the next step should be at this point of time in the assessment reform—what can be done to deepen teachers' understandings of AfL, how to turn their understandings in AfL into real practice and how to sustain their AfL practice for teaching and learning in the long run. A long-term well-resourced professional development programme which addresses the content and process sides in AfL could be the way to go.

ACKNOWLEDGEMENTS

The author would like to thank the Quality Education Fund (QEF) and the BCA team of the EDB of the SAR government, the Hong Kong Institute of Education, the Institute of Education, University of London, the school personnel and the students involved in the project, the researchers and research assistants for their support of the project.

REFERENCES

Berry, R. (2007). Assessment to support learning. In P.W. Leung & R. Berry (Eds.) *Learning-oriented assessment: Useful practices* (pp.7–19). Hong Kong: Hong Kong University Press. (In Chinese)

Berry, R. (2008). *Assessment for Learning.* Hong Kong: Hong Kong University Press.

Berry, R. (2010). Teachers' orientations towards selecting assessment strategies. *New Horizons in Education, 58*(1), 96–107.

Berry, R. (2011a). Assessment reforms around the world. In R. Berry & B. Adamson (Eds.) *Assessment reform in education: Policy and practice* (pp.89–102). Dordrecht: Springer.

Berry, R. (2011b). Assessment trends in Hong Kong: Seeking to establish formative assessment in an examination culture. *Assessment in Education: Principles, Policy & Practice, 18*(2), 199–211.

Berry, R. (2011c). Educational assessment in Mainland China, Hong Kong and Taiwan. In R. Berry & B. Adamson (Eds.) *Assessment reform in education: Policy and practice* (pp.89–102). Dordrecht: Springer.

Berry, R., & Adamson, B. (2012). Assessment reform in Hong Kong Schools. *SAeDUC Journal, 9*(1). Retrieved 6 March 2014, from http://www.nwu.ac.za/webfm_send/57763.

Biggs, J. (1996). *Testing: To educate or to select?* Hong Kong: Hong Kong Educational Publishing.

Assessment for Learning in Hong Kong 273

Carless, D. (2011). *From testing to productive student learning*. New York: Routledge.

Cohen, L., Manion, L., & Morrison, K. (2003). *Research methods in education* (5th ed.). New York: RoutledgeFalmer.

Curriculum Development Council (2002). *Basic education curriculum guide: Building on strengths (primary 1—secondary 3)*. Hong Kong: Curriculum Development Council.

Curriculum Development Council (2009). *Senior secondary curriculum guide (secondary 4—6)*. Hong Kong: Curriculum Development Council.

Education Commission (2000). *Learning for life—learning through life: Reform proposals for the education system in Hong Kong*. Retrieved 8 September 2013, from http://www.e-c.edu.hk/eng/reform/annex/Edu-reform-eng.pdf.

Education Department (1998). *Target Oriented Curriculum assessment guidelines for English language*. Hong Kong: Education Department.

Hargreaves, E., Berry, R., Lai, Y.C., Leung, P., Scott, D., & Stobart, G. (2013). Teachers' experiences of autonomy in continuing professional development: Teacher learning communities in London and Hong Kong. *Teacher Development, 17*(1), 19–34.

Hong Kong Examinations and Assessment Authority (n.d.[a]). *Basic competence assessment*. Retrieved 8 September 2013, from http://www.hkeaa.edu.hk/en/bca_tsa/.

Hong Kong Examinations and Assessment Authority (n.d.[b]). *School-based assessment*. Retrieved 8 September 2013, from http://www.hkeaa.edu.hk/en/sba/sba_hkdse/.

IBM (2003). *Strategic review of Hong Kong Examinations and Assessment Authority: Final consultancy report*. Hong Kong: IBM.

Kennedy, K.J., Chan, J.K.S., Fok, P.K., & Yu, W.M. (2008). Forms of assessment and their potential for enhancing learning: Conceptual and cultural issues. *Educational Research for Policy and Practice, 7*(3), 197–207.

Morris, P., & Adamson, B. (2010). *Curriculum, schooling and society in Hong Kong*. Hong Kong: Hong Kong University Press.

Morris, P., Adamson, B., Chan, K.K, Che, M.W., Chik, P.M., Fung-Lo, M.L., Ko, P.Y., Kwan, Y.L., Mok, A.C., Ng, F.P., & Tong, S.Y. (1999). *Target Oriented Curriculum: Feedback and assessment in Hong Kong primary schools (final report)*. Hong Kong: Faculty of Education, the University of Hong Kong and Curriculum Development Institute, Education Department.

Shuttleworth, M. (2009). *Pretest-posttest designs*. Retrieved 8 September 2013, from http://explorable.com/pretest-posttest-designs.

16 School-Based Assessment in Secondary Schools

Zi Yan

RATIONALE OF SCHOOL-BASED ASSESSMENT

The purpose of assessment is conventionally classified into two types, namely, 'formative assessment' and 'summative assessment'. Formative assessment is defined as "encompassing all those activities undertaken by teachers, and/or by their students, which provide information to be used as feedback to modify the teaching and learning activities in which they are engaged" (Black and Wiliam, 1998, p.7). It emphasizes the learning process and is usually conducted on a daily basis. On the other hand, summative assessment is the practice of collecting information that summarizes how much learning has taken place. It focuses on the learning product and usually takes place at the end of a period of instruction. School-based assessment (SBA), administered in schools and marked by the students' own teachers, is expected to provide students with learning tasks for formative assessment purposes in a low-stakes context, but, at the same time, it could provide evidence of students' learning outcomes and serve as the summative assessment purpose. SBA attempts to provide better alignment between assessment and curriculum and to enhance students' ability of self-evaluation and lifelong learning (Davison, 2007). The promotion of SBA occurs under the context of global educational reform, which is trying to lessen the negative impact and consequences of summative educational assessments by placing more emphasis on formative assessment to enhance teaching and learning (Brown et al., 2011).

Despite the often-heard claim that the pressure in schools to improve students' achievement in external high-stakes examinations precludes the use of formative assessment (Wiliam et al., 2004), there is a worldwide movement to integrate formative and summative assessment in order to promote students' learning, and educational bureaucracies are trying to develop assessment structures for the high-stakes accountability based on the principles of formative assessment (Hay, 2006). In SBA, the formative and summative assessments are no longer seen as distinctly different, and teachers are required to exercise both functions in assessment practice (Davison, 2007). The evidence collected through SBA has to meet the requirements for summative reporting, at the same time enhancing learning

School-Based Assessment in Secondary Schools 275

and teaching in a formative manner. Harlen (2004) argues that the evidence collected initially by teachers for formative purposes can also be used for summative purposes if appropriate procedures are available to assure quality. A good example is the senior secondary courses in Queensland, Australia, where an SBA is utilized to serve both formative functions with respect to learning and summative functions with respect to summarizing students' learning outcomes (Queensland Studies Authority, 2010).

IMPLEMENTATION OF SBA IN HONG KONG

SBA is, in fact, not a recent innovation in the Hong Kong education system. Back in 1978, SBA, which was then called Teacher Assessment Scheme (TAS), was firstly incorporated into the Hong Kong Advanced Level Examination (HKALE) for the Chemistry subject. TAS in the Chemistry subject focused on students' practical skills, and teachers were required to conduct continuous assessment on their own students over the whole period of the course. The weighting of SBA was 20% of the final grade of the subject. Subsequently, SBA was extended to various HKALE subjects during the following few decades. The Hong Kong Certificate of Education Examination (HKCEE) also started SBA for two subjects (i.e., Design and Technology and Electronics and Electricity) in 1980 and has extended it to 14 subjects since then. SBA for HKALE and HKCEE is normally conducted in the form of practical work, project and portfolio so as to cover learning areas that are difficult to be assessed by public examinations and reduce the dependence on a 'one-shot' external examination.

A significant educational reform was carried out in 2009 in Hong Kong where the 5+2 year secondary curriculum was replaced by a 3+3 year system (New Senior Secondary [NSS]). The two public examinations, i.e. HKCEE and HKALE, were replaced by the Hong Kong Diploma of Secondary Education (HKDSE) examination. An SBA component that accounts for a certain percentage of the final grade is introduced into the public assessment across most NSS subjects, with three exceptions, including Mathematics, Business, Accounting and Financial Studies, and Physical Education. Part of the high-stakes assessment responsibilities are shifted from external examinations to classroom teachers, and teachers' marks have direct influence on students' opportunities of further education or employment. The reasons for introducing SBA into the NSS public assessment include: (1) to enhance the validity of overall assessment; (2) to provide a more holistic assessment which covers areas that are difficult to be assessed by public examinations; (3) to provide a more reliable indication of the actual abilities of students by assessing them over an extended period; and (4) to promote a positive 'backwash effect' on students and teachers.

The weighting of SBA in the final grade and the implementation timetable in various NSS subjects are presented in Table 16.1.

276 *Zi Yan*

Table 16.1 Weighting and Implementation Timetable for SBA in HKDSE

Subject	Weighting	Implementation Time	Subject	Weighting	Implementation Time
Core Subject			**Elective Subject**		
Chinese Language	20%	2012	Chemistry	20%	2014
English Language	15%	2012	Physics	20%	2014
Liberal Studies	20%	2012	Literature in English	20%	2019
Mathematics	--	--	Chinese Literature	35%	2019
Elective Subject			Economics	15%	2019
History	20%	2012	Ethics and Religious Studies	20%	2019
Chinese History	20%	2012	Geography	15%	2019
Information and Communication Technology	20%	2012	Health Management and Social Care	30%	2019
Visual Arts	50%	2012	Music	20%	2019
Design and Applied Technology	40%	2012	Technology and Living	30%	2019
Science: Combined Science	30%	2014	Tourism and Hospitality Studies	30%	2019
Science: Integrated Science	20%	2014	Business, Accounting and Financial Studies	--	--
Biology	20%	2014	Physical Education	--	--

Source: HKEAA (retrieved 28 July 2013, from http://www.hkeaa.edu.hk/en/SBA/sba_hkdse/SBA_timetable.html).

CHALLENGES ASSOCIATED WITH SBA

The incorporation of SBA into HKDSE is by no means a small change to Hong Kong's education system. It is a major assessment reform that embraces significant change in school culture and structures as well as in teachers' role and instruction (Davison, 2007). Although the sound principles of SBA were generally acknowledged by teachers, major problems have occurred during the implementation process (Reyneke, Meyer and Nel, 2010). A number of studies have been done to explore Hong Kong teachers' views, mainly their concerns about SBA in subjects such as English (Davison, 2007); Biology (Cheung and Yip, 2004; Yip and Cheung, 2005); Chemistry (Cheung and Yip, 2004); and Mathematics (Lam and Chan, 2010). For instance, Yip and Cheung (2005) reported that the major concerns of Hong Kong teachers related to TAS include lack of resource materials, lack of training, the heavy workload, the undesirable impact of the assessment scheme on student learning and the possible unfairness caused by the assessment. Davison (2007) classified Hong Kong teachers' concerns related to SBA of HKCEE into three types, namely, *socio-cultural*, *technical* and *practical*. Such concerns and inadequacies hinder the successful implementation of SBA, which, in turn, may result in the public questioning of the usefulness and effectiveness of SBA.

Socio-cultural concerns refer to doubts about fairness and equity principles in SBA practices. Important issues include maintaining the consistency of teacher judgement about student performance within a school and ensuring the comparability of teacher judgement across schools. SBA has the potential to enhance the validity of assessment by examining a wide range of areas, which are difficult to assess by public examinations, over an extended period. At the same time, however, SBA may increase the risk of introducing unfairness into assessment since student performances are rated by different teachers from different schools. Although handbooks and guidelines are available, there is no guarantee that all schools will adopt SBA practices in an even way and each teacher within the same school will have the same level of leniency. Given that the SBA scores will constitute a certain, substantial for some subjects, percentage of the final grade and that the target for most Hong Kong schools is to help students achieve higher scores in high-stake examinations, it is not surprising that teachers have motivation to give their students high grades in SBA. Even within the same school, teachers may interpret the guidelines or specifications of criteria in an inconsistent way, which results in unfairness across classes.

Technical concerns are about the question of ensuring high reliability and validity of SBA. Harlen (2004) emphasizes the importance of ensuring the construct validity and reliability of teacher assessment when it serves summative purposes. However, psychometric understanding of validity and reliability associated with conventional assessment is different from that of SBA, which is a highly contextualized and dynamic practice (Davison, 2007). As pointed out by Willingham, Pollack and Lewis (2002), while SBA is used to improve test validity, it is not fully trusted as an accurate measure of educational outcomes. Since teachers have motivation to overrate students' performance in SBA to compensate their poor results on the central examination, the validity also becomes questionable (Luyten and Dolkar, 2010). In other words, the validity challenge for SBA is

278 *Zi Yan*

that teachers' ratings could only serve as an indicator of students' relative position among their peers in the same school but fail to reflect their real academic abilities.

Practical concerns are mainly related to difficulties in resources or manpower which schools are facing during preparation and implementation of SBA. For example, teachers have concerns about a lack of resource materials for SBA, such as sampled assessment tasks and clear and practical specifications of criteria. Lack of professional training is also an often-mentioned challenge for teachers. It is impossible for teachers to conduct SBA if they are not equipped with the necessary skills and knowledge. The time and workload associated with SBA are other important issues that need serious consideration. Many teachers perceived SBA to be an added burden rather than an integrated part of regular instruction, and such perceptions result in great resistance to SBA.

Furthermore, cultural factors and local contexts should never be ignored in investigation of major educational reforms such as SBA. Previous experience indicated that it is necessary to consider local cultures and institutional discourses before incorporating assessment theories from the international research literature into public policy (Adamson and Davison, 2003). Therefore, assessment is not simply a technical issue but should be interpreted in broad social contexts (Brown et al., 2009). In a traditional exam-dominated culture such as Hong Kong, where the results of public assessment are heavily related to students' future lives, how do teachers view the shift of high-stakes assessment responsibilities from external examination to themselves? Are they ready for or confident about this shift? How do they demarcate the roles of teacher and assessor? The real cases depicted in the following sections will help to seek information to address such important issues.

CASES IN HONG KONG

This section describes SBA practices in two Hong Kong secondary schools. The stories of what happened in these schools will, as examples, shed light on some important issues related to SBA, such as how the schools plan, prepare and implement SBA; how teachers perceive SBA in terms of benefits and challenges; and how, in their opinions, the current situation could be improved.

Case 1: SBA in Chinese Language and Liberal Studies

Chinese Language is one of the core subjects in the NSS curriculum leading to the HKDSE. The public assessment for Chinese Language comprises two components: the public examination (80%) and SBA (20%).The areas assessed by SBA include a Compulsory (8%) and Elective Part (12%). The Compulsory Part comprises reading activities, daily assignments and other Chinese learning activities. The Elective Part includes daily learning performance and final performance at the end of the selected two units (HKEAA, 2012a). The first SBA of NSS Chinese Language was implemented in 2012.

Liberal Studies is another core subject in the NSS curriculum. Similar to Chinese Language, the public assessment for Liberal Studies consists of the public examination (80%) and SBA (20%). SBA in Liberal Studies adopts Independent Enquiry Study (IES) as the mode of assessment. IES aims to develop students to be independent and self-directed learners through the enquiry process. The assessment is conducted in two stages, that is, the project proposal stage and the product stage. During each stage, students will be assessed on two components, namely, process (20%) and task (25% for the project proposal stage and 55% for the product stage) (HKEAA, 2012b). The first SBA of NSS Liberal Studies was also implemented in 2012.

School A is a relatively small-scale school with less than 300 students. There are two classes for each year level of the senior secondary and around 140 students are enrolled. Teacher X is one of the four teachers in the school teaching NSS Chinese Language and teacher Y is on the panel of Liberal Studies that is co-ordinating and teaching NSS Liberal Studies. As stated by teacher X, the Compulsory Part of SBA in Chinese Language for HKDSE is somewhat similar to that for HKCEE but an Elective Part is added into the SBA for HKDSE and the total weighting increases from 15% to 20%. Basically, the SBA in Chinese Language is undertaken in accordance with its original design. That means the assessment tasks are integrated into the regular teaching and students are assessed based on their daily performances. It seems that not much extra burden in terms of teaching and assessment has been introduced. An observable 'backwash' effect is that students are more motivated to engage in daily assignments since their performances on those assignments might constitute one part of the final SBA grade (in this school, the highest score on daily assignment for a student will be submitted). The greatest burden associated with SBA is the administrative work, such as photocopying, scanning and submitting the sample scripts to HKEAA. This workload is perceived by teacher X as completely unnecessary. The school can keep all the records ready for external checking and teachers should be released from such tedious work.

It is a more challenging task to conduct SBA in Liberal Studies than in Chinese Language. Since the launch of SBA, as reported by teacher Y, the guidelines for SBA in Liberal Studies have had two major revisions to reach their current form. This results in a high level of uncertainty among teachers. The challenges are especially salient for low-banding schools since most of the students in those schools are incapable of doing IES even with teachers' support. In school A, a segregated mode rather than an integrated mode is adopted to conduct the IES in Liberal Studies. In this mode, an extra lesson in addition to the regular lessons is scheduled for Liberal Studies each week. This lesson is provided to students particularly for conducting IES under teachers' supervision. Furthermore, besides three Liberal Studies

280 *Zi Yan*

teachers, three teachers from other subjects have been invited to supervise students' IES projects, resulting in each teacher supervising seven to ten students. Obviously such SBA practices become an added burden for teachers as well as the school. Although teacher Y admitted that this mode of SBA is inconsistent with the spirit of Assessment for Learning (AfL)—that assessment should be an integrated part of teaching—in reality the IES will be an impossible mission for most of the students without additional lessons and specific support. In spite of such inadequacies, teachers recognize that IES provides a good opportunity for students to gain learning experiences other than those obtained in the classroom. The abilities essential to independent and self-directed learners, such as goal setting, planning, problem solving and critical thinking, have been developed during the enquiry process.

Despite the differences in conducting SBA in Chinese Language and Liberal Studies, teachers X and Y shared some common opinions. One of these is that SBA grades are not as important as they are expected to be. Since all SBA grades will be moderated with reference to the public examination scores of the same group of students, the public examination will still play the dominant role and, in fact, determine students' SBA scores. In other words, even though students from two groups performed at exactly the same level in SBA, the group with higher public examination scores will have higher SBA scores and the group with lower public examination scores will have lower SBA scores because of the central moderation. In this sense, SBA grades can rank students within the school but are incapable of changing students' final grades substantially.

As for teacher training, which concerns many stakeholders regarding implementation of SBA, teachers from school A reported that the government had provided plenty of training opportunities for teachers, including workshops, seminars and sharing sessions. This is different from the findings of previous studies (e.g., Cheung and Yip, 2004; Davison, 2007; Yip and Cheung, 2005) which investigated teachers' opinions about SBA in HKALE or HKCEE. These studies reported that lack of teacher training is a common concern shared by teachers. It seems that the government has taken teachers' feedback into consideration and purposefully enhanced teacher training during implementing SBA in HKDSE. The effectiveness of the training, however, is still questionable because most of the training only focused on the theories, guidelines and general principles of SBA. Successful cases were available in some occasions but the implications of those cases were limited because of the diversity of school backgrounds.

Case 2: SBA in Physical Education

Physical Education is one of the elective subjects (PE elective hereafter) in the NSS curriculum. Similar to the core subjects such as Chinese Language and Liberal Studies, the original design of public assessment for PE elective comprises two parts, that is, the public examination (70%) and SBA (30%). The areas assessed by SBA include students' attainment in two physical activities (10% each), physical fitness test and performance in planning, and implementation and evaluation of an individualized physical fitness enhancement programme (10%) (HKEAA, 2009). However, the government recently announced that, after a comprehensive review on the NSS and taking into account the practical concerns of schools and front-line teachers, the SBA component in the public assessment for PE elective will be replaced by centrally administered practical examinations in order to "address the total workload of teachers and students on SBA in both quantitative and qualitative terms" (Education Bureau [EDB], 2013, p.42). Nevertheless, it does not mean that PE SBA is at a dead end since the policy will be subject to regular review. The case described below, which is a trial SBA programme, could be useful to shed light on the future development of PE SBA by identifying the major challenges and corresponding potential solutions.

School B is a subsidized secondary school located in northeast Hong Kong. This school has a student population of around 1,000. Four PE teachers are responsible for the regular PE lessons (one double lesson per week) and two of them, including teacher Z, are teaching the PE elective for which there are seven double lessons per week. There are 20 form 4, 20 form 5 and seven form 6 students enrolled in the PE elective subject.

Teacher Z reported that they place different teaching focuses in forms 4–6 to cater for different areas assessed by SBA. To enhance students' attainment in two physical activities (10% each), intensive training programmes have been developed for students in form 6 based on students' selection from each of the two categories, including: (1) badminton, basketball, football, table tennis and volleyball and (2) athletics, gymnastics and swimming. The teaching focus for form 4 and form 5 is on another area assessed by SBA, that is, physical fitness and performance in planning, implementation and evaluation of an individualized physical fitness enhancement programme (10%). Students are required to take part in six rounds of physical fitness testing each year and individualized feedback and training programmes are provided to students. In addition to the formative form of physical fitness assessment, the school designed a school-based PE programme which extends for the whole semester and embeds assessment tasks serving for both formative and summative purposes. This programme is embedded into the Standard Chartered Hong Kong Marathon, which is held in Hong Kong once a year. Students are required to participate in this event under teachers' supervision and PE instruction and assessment are integrated in the whole process of preparation and participation. Students are encouraged, with teachers' support and guidance, to enhance their fitness levels as well as the understanding of relevant knowledge through different activities, such as designing a training plan for themselves, implementing and monitoring

282   *Zi Yan*

the progresses of the plan, analyzing the psychomotor movement and psychological skills needed during the marathon, studying the history and social impact of the event, and observing the way to organize such a large-scale event. The programme enhanced students' physical fitness and covered almost all the nine theoretical learning domains which will be examined in the public examination.

Although this PE programme is not really an SBA task that will produce assessment scores to be submitted as a part of the final grade, the teachers believe that this is the right direction in which the SBA in PE should be developed. Such assessment not only makes it possible for students' performance in SBA areas (attainment in physical fitness test and performance in planning, implementation and evaluation of an individualized physical fitness enhancement programme) to be assessed by their own teachers over an extended period but also promotes a positive 'backwash effect' on students. Students are motivated to engage in the learning activities and learn in a more self-directed approach. Such assessment practices provide students with learning tasks for formative assessment purposes while, at the same time, providing evidence of students' learning outcomes and serving summative assessment purposes.

Some problems, however, remain unresolved from teachers' perspectives. The foremost concern of PE teachers in this school comes from practical aspects. A dilemma is that if student performance is to be judged based on only one single SBA task, there is no big difference from centralized practical examination except shifting responsibility from central authority to schoolteachers. If, however, students are allowed to participate in several rounds of SBA and the aggregate grades are to be reported, it will be a heavy burden for teachers' workloads. It is also believed to be the main reason for the suspension of PE SBA.

Another practical hurdle for PE SBA in Hong Kong schools is that some options of physical activities, even if they are on the list for selection, are practically unavailable because of the restricted campus or facilities of most schools. For example, gymnastics, which is one of the optional physical activities, is actually rarely selected by students. This is not because students have no interest or talent in gymnastics, but there are no facilities for students to practice. Some games in athletics (e.g., javelin and discus) face the same situation. Furthermore, the optional list itself is a problem. The first physical activity has to be selected among five games, namely, badminton, basketball, football, table tennis and volleyball. What if a student has a strong interest and good potential in squash or martial arts? The limit set by this relatively narrow scope contradicts with the educational goal which embraces students' individualized potential and promotes diverse achievements. Fairness issues also concern teachers. Since the SBA items in PE, unlike those in other subjects, are fixed, it is unlikely for PE teachers to overrate their students' performance by setting relatively easy assessment

School-Based Assessment in Secondary Schools 283

items. However, the difference existing in teachers' interpretations of assessment criteria and expertise in the selected physical activities certainly have influences on their ratings.

IMPORTANT ISSUES

The cases reviewed in the above sections uncover that the core concerns about SBA still regard fairness issues, particularly the impact of moderation, and practical restrictions, such as teachers' workloads and professional training. It seems that much more effort needs to be made for successful implementation of SBA in Hong Kong schools. Particularly, the following three issues deserve special attention: external moderation, common assessment criteria and standards, and teacher training and support.

Moderation

'Moderation' refers to processes after the implementation of SBA within schools to ensure consistency of grades and comparability of teacher judgement across schools. For the sake of fairness of assessment and maintaining the validity and credibility of SBA, moderation of SBA ratings is necessary given that: (1) teachers from different schools may have varied levels of leniency in their judgements even though they are using the same assessment criteria; (2) teachers are not necessarily familiar with the standards set across all schools; and (3) schools and teachers have motivation and pressure to overrate student achievement levels (Luyten and Dolkar, 2010). The HKEAA has adopted two moderation methods: the statistical approach and expert judgement approach to accommodate different subjects in HKDSE. The statistical approach is used for subjects in which the SBA and the public examination share a substantial portion of common (e.g., Mathematics), while the expert judgement approach is adopted for subjects with a small candidature or which involve different outcomes assessed by the SBA and the public examination (e.g., Design and Applied Technology). The general principle of the moderation is to adjust the average and the spread of SBA scores of students in a given school with reference to their public examination scores (for statistical approach) or to expert judgements of samples of students' work (for expert judgement approach). Students' SBA grades may be modified after the moderation, but the rank order of students within the school will remain unchanged. The adaptation of the statistical moderation intends to ensure the comparability of SBA marks across schools by building a common framework based on the public examination scores. Such attempts, however, render SBA into a position subordinate to the public examination. Imagine two students A and B having similar performances on both SBA and the public examination. Student A studies in a high-banding school and B in a

284   *Zi Yan*

low-banding school. These two students may have quite different moderated SBA scores since A's SBA score might be increased because s/he is in a school with higher public examination score, but B's SBA score might be reduced because s/he is in a school with lower public examination score. Students get different marks not because of their performances but because of the school they belong to! Alternatively, the expert judgement moderation seems to echo the rationale of SBA—to provide a more holistic assessment which covers areas that are difficult to be assessed by public examinations—and makes it an independent part of the public assessment.

In addition to moderation which is conducted after SBA, some proactive procedures occurring midway through the process of SBA could be considered to ensure the comparability of SBA marks. For example, the central examination authority could monitor the practice and process of SBA across schools and give advice to schools to make sure that the same framework and standards are shared by all schools.

Common Assessment Criteria and Standards within Schools

Since each individual school is taken as a moderation unit in the central moderation of SBA marks conducted by HKEAA, standardization must be achieved in order to make sure that the same assessment criteria and standard are applied to all students if there is more than one subject teacher teaching and assessing the same cohort of students in the school. First of all, a common assessment criteria and performance standards must be established and shared by all involved. Second, a shared understanding of the specification of criteria among all involved teachers must be maintained. Some monitoring mechanisms to ensure the consistency among teachers within schools seem necessary. HKEAA provides some suggestions to maintain the within-school standardization in SBA (e.g., HKEAA, 2012a, 2012b). Such maintenance of a common assessment criteria and performance is also a necessity to ensure the validity and reliability of SBA. Detailed instructions and guidance, standardization of the assessment process, descriptors of levels of performance, standard assessment tasks and samples, regular teacher training, within-school standardization meetings, and professional discussions could be helpful to achieve compliance to the common criteria and standards.

Teacher Training and Support

Successful implementation of SBA used in high-stakes examination systems requires huge investments in teacher training and assessment resources (Luyten and Dolkar, 2010). Teachers need extensive training in order to be familiar with the rationale and principles of SBA as well as to be equipped with sufficient skills to plan, design and administer SBA tasks with reference to the school context. Although, as stated by teacher X and Y from school A, plenty of training opportunities related to SBA are available for Hong Kong teachers, more in-depth discussions and tailor-made strategies are still needed. In addition to one-off training seminars, continuous support during the process of SBA is necessary and professional advice should be provided to assist and reassure teachers in the decision-making process. Such a 'monitoring' process is helpful to enhance the comparability of SBA scores across schools. Teacher support for SBA also includes the resources allocated to facilitate SBA in schools. Some resources should be provided by the central examination authority, such as detailed guidelines and handbooks, standard assessment criteria and sample assessment tasks. The others could be provided within the school, such as special administrative arrangement, manpower support and so on. Regular discussions and consultations are essential during the process of implementation of SBA to collect feedback from front-line teachers and refine the support measures to facilitate the implementation of SBA in schools.

CONCLUSION

It is a fact that, although SBA is not a recent innovation in the Hong Kong education system, the challenges have never ceased since its first launch. It was expected that SBA could provide authentic assessment with higher validity; however, its fairness became a big concern among stakeholders. It was also expected that SBA would form an integral part of the learning and teaching process although its modes may vary across subjects. But the practices in schools sometimes fail to achieve this goal. There is a long way ahead to find the appropriate mode of SBA in various subjects and enact the advantages of SBA in high-stakes assessments. Before making a conclusion about the effectiveness of SBA in Hong Kong, some key issues need to be addressed with stronger empirical evidence. For example, what are the conceptions and intentions regarding SBA of different stakeholders, especially teachers who carry out SBA? How can we understand and better address the validity and reliability issues in SBA? Do current moderation mechanisms ensure a fair assessment? How can we reconcile the formative and summative purposes of SBA? What forms of teaching training and support can maximize the advantages of SBA? These questions come even more to the fore when teachers have to cater for the SBA requirements under the ongoing curriculum reform in Hong Kong.

ACKNOWLEDGEMENTS

The author would like to express his gratitude to Mr. Tam Chi Chun, Mr. Poon Kai Cheung, Ms. Cheung Yin Yee and Mr. Wong Shing Yuen for providing their valuable opinions regarding SBA practices in their schools.

286   *Zi Yan*

REFERENCES

Adamson, B., & Davison, C. (2003). Innovation in English language teaching in Hong Kong primary schools: One step forwards, two steps sideways. *Prospect, 18*, 27–41.

Black, P., & Wiliam, D. (1998). Assessment and classroom learning. *Assessment in Education: Principles, Policy & Practice, 5*(1), 7–74.

Brown, G.T.L., Hui, S.K.F., Yu, F.W.M., & Kennedy, K.J. (2011). Teachers' conceptions of assessment in Chinese contexts: A tripartite model of accountability, improvement, and irrelevance. *International Journal of Educational Research, 50*, 307–320.

Brown, G.T.L., Kennedy, K.J., Fok, P.K., Chan, J.K.S., & Yu, F.W.M. (2009). Assessment for student improvement: Understanding Hong Kong teachers' conceptions and practices of assessment. *Assessment in Education: Principles, Policy & Practice, 16*(3), 347–363.

Cheung, D., & Yip, D.Y. (2004). How science teachers' concerns about school-based assessment of practical work vary with time: The Hong Kong experience. *Research in Science & Technological Education, 22*(2), 153–169.

Davison, C. (2007). Views from the chalkface: English language school-based assessment in Hong Kong. *Language Assessment Quarterly, 4*(1), 37–68.

Education Bureau (2013). *The New Senior Secondary learning journey—moving forward to excel.* Retrieved 18 December 2013, from http://334.edb.hkedcity.net/doc/eng/FullReport.pdf.

Harlen, W. (2004). *A systematic review of the evidence of reliability and validity of assessment by teachers used for summative purposes.* Retrieved 16 December 2013, from http://eppi.ioe.ac.uk/cms/LinkClick.aspx?fileticket=6_1H03rsumM%3D&tabid=117&mid=923.

Hay, P.J. (2006). Assessment for Learning in Physical Education. In D. Kirk, D. Macdonald & M. O'Sullivan (Eds.) *The handbook of Physical Education* (pp.312–325). London: Sage Publications.

Hong Kong Examinations and Assessment Authority (2009). *HKDSE examination: School-based assessment teachers' handbook (Physical Education).* Hong Kong: Hong Kong Examinations and Assessment Authority.

Hong Kong Examinations and Assessment Authority (2012a). *HKDSE examination: School-based assessment teachers' handbook (Chinese Language).* Hong Kong: Hong Kong Examinations and Assessment Authority.

Hong Kong Examinations and Assessment Authority (2012b). *HKDSE examination: School-based assessment teachers' handbook (Liberal Studies).* Hong Kong: Hong Kong Examinations and Assessment Authority.

Lam, C.C., & Chan, K.S. (2010). *The interface between the new secondary school curriculum and the tertiary education.* Unpublished research report, Hong Kong Institute of Education.

Luyten, H., & Dolkar, D. (2010). School-based assessments in high-stakes examinations in Bhutan: A question of trust? Exploring inconsistencies between external exam scores, school-based assessments, detailed teacher ratings, and student self-ratings. *Educational Research and Evaluation, 16*(5), 421–435.

Queensland Studies Authority (2010). *School-based assessment: The Queensland system.* Retrieved 18 December 2013, from http://www.qsa.qld.edu.au/downloads/approach/school-based_assess_qld_sys.pdf.

Reyneke, M., Meyer, L., & Nel, C. (2010). School-based assessment: The leash needed to keep the poetic 'unruly pack of hounds' effectively in the hunt for learning outcomes. *South African Journal of Education, 30*, 277–292.

Wiliam, D., Lee, C., Harrison, C., & Black, P.J. (2004). Teachers developing Assessment for Learning: Impact on student achievement. *Assessment in Education: Principles, Policy & Practice, 11*(1), 49–65.

Willingham, W.W., Pollack, J.M., & Lewis, C. (2002). Grades and test scores: Accounting for observed differences. *Journal of Educational Measurement, 39*, 1–37.

Yip, D.Y., & Cheung, D. (2005). Teachers' concerns on school-based assessment of practical work. *Journal of Biological Education, 39*(4), 156–162.

17 Accountability and Improvement
Lessons from Studying Hong Kong Teachers' Conceptions of Assessment

Sammy King-Fai Hui

INTRODUCTION

Assessment reform has become an important part of the reform agenda for the education system in Hong Kong, as it reaffirms the main aim of assessment: to support student learning, otherwise known as Assessment *for* Learning (AfL). In contrast to assessment *of* learning, which is summative and "intended to certify learning and report to parents and students about students' progress in school, usually by signalling students' relative position compared to other students" (Earl, 2003, p.22), AfL offers an alternative perspective to traditional assessment in schools. AfL is a process of seeking and interpreting evidence for use by learners and teachers, in order to decide where the learners are in their learning, where they need to go and how best to get there (Assessment Reform Group, 2002). The idea of AfL has its roots in the research conducted by Black and Wiliam (1998), which reviewed more than 250 assessment studies to present strong evidence of how formative assessment, or AfL, could improve student learning and development. The AfL movement reached its full potential with the identification of ten principles (Assessment Reform Group, 2002) for teachers to determine the crucial elements of effective classroom assessment practices and to understand why it is important to use AfL. This trend was echoed in Hong Kong and the government document *Basic Education Curriculum Guide* (Curriculum Development Council [CDC], 2002) which stated:

> All schools should review their current assessment practices and put more emphasis on assessment for learning. The latter is a process in which teachers seek to identify and diagnose student learning problems, and provide quality feedback for students on how to improve their work. Different modes of assessment are to be used whenever appropriate for a more comprehensive understanding of student learning in various aspects. (p.1)

It is recommended that schools evaluate their own assessment policies and practices. Teachers should find out what students have learned and why

Accountability and Improvement 289

they have difficulty in learning, give feedback to students on their strengths and weaknesses, and employ different assessment strategies to help students improve their performance. These strategies could range from teachers' verbally questioning and observing student behaviour to students' completing authentic and formative tasks (Black et al., 2003). The idea of reform follows closely with the global agenda of emphasizing the quality of school education (Kennedy and Lee, 2008; Ross and Jürgens-Genevois, 2006). This is because assessment not only measures the ability of the assessed but also influences student development; for example, as Stobart (2008) argued, assessment could help students manage their own learning and develop the necessary skills for future work and life situations.

Based on the shift in emphasis from assessment *of* learning to AfL— from judging to supporting student learning—Earl (2003) highlighted the role of students as critical connectors to the assessment-learning process, an assessment *as* learning approach. Students as active and engaged and critical assessors are the link between assessment and learning because they "can make sense of information, relate it to prior knowledge, and master the skills involved" (p.25). Assessment *as* learning then refers to the process when students "personally monitor what they are learning and use the feedback from this monitoring to make adjustments, adaptations, and even major changes in what they understand" (p.25). Table 17.1 gives a summary of the key features of these three assessment approaches.

Assessment reform, as one of the major reform initiatives of the post-1997 education reform in Hong Kong, challenged the age-old practice of assessment *of* learning and proposed a paradigm shift to AfL and assessment *as* learning at different levels of schools. As the Hong Kong Special Administrative Region (SAR) government's Education Bureau's (EDB's) (2010a) official website explains:

> The concept of assessment for learning is not new. It is underpinned by the confidence and belief that every student is unique and possess the ability to learn, and that we should develop their multiple intelligences and potentials. To promote better learning, assessment is conducted as an integral part of the curriculum, learning and teaching, and feedback cycle. [. . .] Fundamental changes in school assessment practices to bring a better balance across assessment for learning and assessment of learning need to be planned, discussed, shared, negotiated and agreed by all teachers in each school.

Government bodies and different higher education institutes have offered various types of support to teachers to help them better implement assessment reform policy in Hong Kong, including (1) the *Assessment for Learning Resource Bank* and its extensive professional development seminars and training workshops of the EDB (2010b); (2) public lectures and development projects of the Assessment Research Centre of the Hong Kong Institute of

290 Sammy King-Fai Hui

Table 17.1 Features of Assessment *of, for* and *as* Learning

Approach	Purpose	Reference Points	Key Assessor
Assessment of learning	Judgments about placement, promotion, credentials, etc.	Other students	Teacher
Assessment for learning	Information for teachers' instructional decisions	External standards or expectations	Teacher
Assessment as learning	Self-monitoring and self-correction or adjustment	Personal goals and external standards	Student

Source: Adapted from Earl (2003, p.26).

Education (HKIEd, 2009); and (3) the computer-assisted testing system of the Hong Kong Examination and Assessment Authority (HKEAA) (2009). In addition, many local studies have reported on successful cases of AfL (see, for example, Au Yeung, 2009; Pang, 2008). However, despite the success of the reform agenda in promoting positive change, there needs to be more analysis of how AfL practices are affected by social and cultural factors. Teachers as 'doers' of the reform agenda are expected to have the knowledge, skills and resources to put this reform into action. However, many recent local studies have reported some concerns and difficulties voiced by teachers in trying to realize the AfL principles, including (1) the domination of summative, end-of-year examinations on schools' assessment culture (Kennedy, 2007; Kennedy, Chan and Fok, 2011; Pong and Chow, 2002); (2) an emphasis on student performance in public examinations among teachers, parents and students (Chan, 2007; Yu et al., 2006); and (3) a lack of support and understanding of AfL practices by principals, teachers and parents (Carless, 2005). Therefore, the present chapter, which discusses the influence of social and cultural factors on assessment, is critical to understanding AfL.

A few years ago, a team of researchers in a joint research project between HKIEd and South China Normal University, led by Professor Kerry Kennedy and Professor Gao Lingbiao, investigated the impact of social and cultural factors in the Chinese context on teachers' conceptions of assessment (TCoA). This work has expanded from the development of a cultural-specific model of TCoA (Brown, Hui and Yu, 2010; Brown et al., 2011; Gao and Kennedy, 2011) to a search for an additional meaning of assessment as supporting student learning (Hui, 2012) and for any hidden values that guide teachers' assessment practices (Hui and Brown, 2010). These studies inform the socio-cultural factors underlying Hong Kong teachers' conceptions and practice of assessment, which ultimately will have an effect on the success of the reform. Thus, the aim of this chapter is to examine the influence of accountability on learning improvement and to explore how the reform movement can be sustained.

ASSESSMENT FOR . . .

Assessment is a key part of teaching and learning. A commonly adopted definition of assessment is the systematic collection, review and use of information about educational programmes undertaken for the purpose of improving student learning and development (Palomba and Banta, 1999). The collection, review and use of assessment information involves not only the selection of evidence that is relevant to the set assessment criteria but also the selection of assessment strategies and any act to interpret and judge if the pre-set criteria have been met. By this definition, assessment is for learning; however, the socio-cultural background where the assessment is occurring and the corresponding practices used by teachers—the strategies that teachers use and the interpretation and judgement that they make— could divert assessment away from the purpose of improving student learning and development. Black and Wiliam (1998) listed some of the common mistakes in assessment: (1) students use rote and superficial learning for tests and examinations; (2) when there is no feedback on student performance, students strive only to achieve higher marks and not to understand how to improve their ability to learn; and (3) students view assessment as competition, since they are compared to one another in terms of marks or grades. Black and Wiliam's (1998) major recommendations to teachers were (1) to provide effective feedback to students; (2) to actively involve students in their own learning; (3) to adjust teaching methods to take into account assessment results; and (4) to allow self-monitoring and correction by students. Tests or examinations were not recommended at all.

For any assessment task that involves collecting and judging information or evidence of student learning, the concerns that arise are not only "What to assess?" "How to assess?" and "Who does the assessment?" but also "For what reason is the assessment done?" and "In what learning context does the assessment take place?" (Biggs, 1996). The first question—"For what reason is the assessment done?"—relates to the issue of accountability. As illustrated by Brown (2004), accountability is a major conception of assessment: "assessment can be used to account for a teacher's, a school's, or even a system's use of society's resources" and "students are held individually accountable for their learning through assessment" (p.304). Such a conception is twofold. Assessment results are used to demonstrate to the public, first, whether teachers and schools are succeeding in the prescribed job of educating students (school accountability), and, second, whether students are succeeding in their learning, as evidenced through proper certifications (student accountability). Accountability has a strong influence on teachers' beliefs and practices. Brown (2004) suggested a nexus of teachers' conceptions around the idea that "assessment for school accountability may lead to a raising of educational standards that will in turn lead to improved ability of students to receive qualifications and recognition of achievement" (p.313). Also, Brown and Harris (2009) reported that, in schools where

292 *Sammy King-Fai Hui*

school leadership had introduced a new policy of using assessment data primarily to inform school improvement initiatives, teachers more strongly endorsed the conception of school accountability as the dominant use of assessment, rather than school improvement. Therefore, we must look at the issue of accountability and examine how it affects the implementation of (new) assessment policies, ideas and practices, as much as we look at the issue of how students learn in the Chinese context.

The second question—"In what learning context does the assessment take place?"—relates to the nature of the assessment tasks and the generated situations in which students will use the knowledge they have obtained. Most educators, teachers and researchers agree that the best practice of classroom assessment is to make the assessment tasks authentic (Darling-Hammond and Snyder, 2000). As defined by Newmann, Brandt and Wiggins (1998), "'Authentic' refers to the situational or contextual realism of the proposed tasks" (p.20). Authentic assessment is realistic—real and true—in terms of its processes and products. It allows students to apply the knowledge they have gained in a bounded, but meaningful, real-world context and transfer that knowledge to a much wider context. Assessment tasks are authentic given that, for example, they (1) result in a knowledge product that has meaning or value beyond success in school (Wiggins, 2006); (2) emphasize a link between assessment, learning and real-world issues (Green, 1998); or (3) are being conducted in a context more like that encountered in real life (Diez and Moon, 1992). According to Frey, Schmitt and Allen (2012), the characteristic of "realistic activity or context" is the only characteristic that defines authenticity. However, after reviewing 47 scholarly publications, by 38 different primary authors, which provide a definition of authentic assessment for school-aged children, Frey, Schmitt and Allen (2012) found only 28 publications (59.6%) that indicated the presence of this characteristic. For the 19 publications that failed to address "realistic activity or context", they mistakenly suggested that authentic assessment necessarily requires "multiple indicators of performance" (13 publications) and "known or student developed scoring criteria" (10 publications), and that it involves "cognitively-complex tasks" (7 publications). Although Frey, Schmitt and Allen (2012) admitted that the best way to judge whether a definition of authenticity is useful is to consider "what is needed for the assessment approach to have value" (p.13), the backlash of failing to adequately address the realistic nature of assessment should not be underestimated, at least in the Hong Kong context, where the concern is making AfL possible (at the classroom level).

Assessment by itself is an insufficient condition for learning and improvement (Shavelson, 2007). It is not the assessment itself but how teachers use it that leads to improvement in student learning. If the aforementioned questions—"For what reason is the assessment done?" and "In what learning context does the assessment take place?"—are not addressed, there cannot be any claim of success in assessment reform. This is because a "one

Accountability and Improvement 293

size fits all" approach to AfL focuses on desirability (all about "for learning") rather than reality (the difficulties), and does not adequately address (1) whether the assessment tasks that teachers use in day-to-day classroom work are authentic enough to help students learn; (2) teacher concerns that assessment will be used to hold schools and students accountable; and (3) what teachers think assessment should achieve.

REVISITING THE TENSION

As articulated previously, it is widely recognized that a tension exists between two dominant forces for education assessment: teachers' goodwill and efforts to improve student learning, and the focus on accountability by various key stakeholders (Ewell, 2009). Accountability is a concept in ethics and governance with multiple meanings. In the field of education, it means more than the functioning and mechanism of school organizations. Accountability in education is performance-based and there are, as Volante and Jaafar (2008) suggested, at least two types of accountability: the ethical-professional (process of school improvement) and economic-bureaucratic (outcomes of school operations). The ethical-professional type of accountability emphasizes the measurement of student performance as the basis for improving student learning and improving schools, and the setting of standards on how student performance is compared and judged. The economic-bureaucratic type of accountability focuses on the use of systems and policies of rewards and penalties to ensure that performance-driven school improvement—the ethical-professional accountability—works and to enforce its stability.

Accountability should not be viewed as negative; rather, it is evaluative in nature. As illustrated by Andy Hargreaves in his preface to the book *Educational Accountability: Professional Voices from the Field* (Gariepy, Spencer and Couture, 2009, p.xv):

> The purpose of accountability, however, is not only to confront malpractice or even to prevent harm in the first place. It is also to improve performance by examining its impact, measuring quality and results and spurring people on to achieve even higher standards and greater improvement in the future.

In Hong Kong, school authorities (the EDB and various School Sponsoring Bodies [SSBs]) and parents are the major forces that push for high-performing schools. Since competition is keen and public resources are limited, these key stakeholders have a strong view that good schools make students smarter and that these schools should produce a high level of achievement in all kinds of assessment tasks (Biggs, 1996; Choi, 1999; Madaus, Russell and Higgins, 2009; Miller, 1998; Watkins and Biggs, 2001). A high level of

294 *Sammy King-Fai Hui*

achievement does not just indicate high ability; an individual's merit, worth and value are also ascribed through academic performance (China Civilisation Centre, 2007). Thus, assessment is believed to be a reliable tool to demonstrate to school authorities and the public that students learned and schools improved, and teachers tend to subscribe to the notion that assessment makes schools, teachers and students accountable.

This conception of assessment, according to Brown et al.'s (2011) study of 1,014 Hong Kong and 898 South China teachers, is represented in the form of a meta-factor of "accountability", which contains the sub-factors of "error" (teachers take into account measurement error when using assessments), "examinations" (examinations as assessment) and "teacher and school control" (assessment is used to control teachers and evaluate schools). "Accountability" in this study correlated strongly with another meta-factor of "improvement" ($r = 0.80$), which contains the sub-factors of "accuracy" (assessments are reliable), "help learning" (assessment helps students learn) and "student development" (assessment for student betterment or development). Together with the third meta-factor of "irrelevance" (assessment is fundamentally irrelevant to the life and work of teachers and students), which correlated weakly positive with "accountability" ($r = 0.28$) and weakly negative with "improvement" ($r = -0.22$), Brown et al. (2011) developed a tripartite model of how teachers conceived of assessment in the Chinese context. This model fit the responses of teachers from the two locations studied and is much more methodical when compared with previous attempts that used a translated version of Brown's (2004) TCoA questionnaire (for example, Brown et al., 2009; Li and Hui, 2007) to explore the specific effect of a Chinese culture on TCoA. A new survey instrument was developed and tested. Items were extracted from two qualitative studies that tapped into Chinese teachers' conceptions and practice of assessment (Hui, 2012; Wang, 2010); the authors assumed that "accountability" and "learning improvement" in the Chinese context were contextualized in a different way than was defined in the original TCoA questionnaire. Accountability, as referred to in Wang's (2010) study of Mainland teachers, is more about controlling student behaviours both inside and outside the classroom and preparing them for high-stakes and/or externally administered tests or examinations. Mainland teachers often question students in class and mechanically drill them with examination papers. Assessment therefore helps students avoid failure and gain good scores in examinations. On the other hand, learning improvement, as referred to in Hui's (2012) study of a group of experienced Hong Kong curriculum leaders (CLs), not only helps students improve their learning but also changes student attitudes towards learning, identifies their potential and prepares them for future challenges. These attributes are not only generic but also fundamental to learning and transferable from one learning situation to another. They better prepare students to fit in our knowledge-based society—which has a short knowledge cycle and demands a workforce that can continuously acquire

Accountability and Improvement   295

quick-changing knowledge and skills (UNESCO, 2010)—and they emphasize lifelong learning, that is, being "willing to participate in ongoing, not recurrent, education" (Online Education Database [OEDb], 2007). In this regard, assessment is used to provoke students' interest in learning, stimulate their thinking, foster their character, prepare them for lifelong learning and eventually help them succeed.

Brown et al.'s (2011) model highlights the three inter-correlated core purposes of assessment in the Chinese context: accountability, improvement and irrelevance. This model is more reality-congruent to what Chinese teachers think of assessment because it addresses the socio-cultural factors in which teachers' conceptions are based. This is evident in the strong positive association between accountability and improvement: under the influence of the long-standing "Chinese tradition of examination-merit decisions" (p.314), teachers tested students because they believed it was a powerful way to improve student learning and to help students achieve more in life. The strong force of accountability on learning improvement not only shapes TCoA but also affects how teachers put the assessment reform policy into practice in classroom contexts. Hui and Brown (2010) examined the judgement that experienced Hong Kong CLs gave to the use of a sample of self-selected classroom assessment tasks, which were supposed to be aligned with the policy of AfL. The study results indicated that although the selected assessment tasks were non-examination/test formats and exhibited many characteristics that support a formative, improvement-oriented purpose, these CLs strongly associated the tasks with improvement as well as accountability and examination purposes. In other words, when teachers think that the purpose of the assessment tasks is to improve learning, there is an intention embedded in teachers to hold students accountable and to better prepare them for high-stakes examinations, which in turn will help students be more successful in learning and make them better people. Again, accountability functions to improve learning. As Brown et al. (2011) suggested, "to the extent that assessment *for* learning policies advocate no testing or examinations, there will [be] difficulties in their adoption by teachers in Chinese contexts" (p.314; original emphasis). Table 17.2 lists the differences between the assessment purposes of accountability and improvement.

Based on the above analysis, accountability in the Chinese context is more like an external catalyst for learning improvement. Teachers are shaped with the need to hold students and themselves accountable, mainly to school authorities. This is evident in a strong positive association between the two conceptions of assessment and the way teachers use classroom assessment. Teachers' willingness to assess for learning and accountability, as well as to ensure these purposes happen as expected, is both 'ethical-professional' and 'economic-bureaucratic'. Therefore, policymakers and educators should not aim for a resolution to the accountability–improvement tension; rather they should pay more attention to helping teachers recognize that while each side has limits, both are worthwhile pursuits.

296 *Sammy King-Fai Hui*

Table 17.2 Differences between the Assessment Purposes of Accountability and Improvement

Assessment Purpose	Socio-Cultural Factors	Teachers' Conceptions
Accountability	Limited resources and keen competition in society Testing is a powerful way to improve learning	Always measurement error Examinations as assessment Assessment controls teachers and evaluates schools
Improvement	Students' future needs and the demands of a knowledge-based economy Assessment helps students do better	Assessments are reliable Assessment helps students learn Assessment for student development

AUTHENTICITY IS THE KEY

Assessment, as a process of documenting and judging evidence of student learning, demands that teachers take a cautious stand on the learning context and the kind of information that it collects. This measurement process rests on the assumption that assessment reveals some sorts of 'truths' that exist as characteristics—a constructed notion of understanding of knowledge or ability or skills—of an individual that can be accurately identified (Gottfredson, 2009). It is an epistemological issue of what counts as knowledge, how knowledge is acquired and how assessment extracts what students have learned from a personal cognitive domain to a public performative domain. As informed by Howard Gardner (1993), the essence of understanding is that it is performative; therefore, in order to demonstrate to others that one has learned, an individual has to perform that learning in terms of participation and response to set assessment tasks. Ultimately, student 'performances', no matter if they are scores in tests/examinations, or verbal answers to in-class questions, or written opinions to essay-type questions, or self-selected evidence and justifications to projects/portfolios, have to be judged by teachers as to whether they count as learning and how well that learning has been achieved. However, different from scores in tests/examinations, a particular 'performance' could be considered significant and meaningful if that performance was revealed from an assessment task that connected to the real world. An example could be reading this chapter on 'authenticity': if there is an assessment of what the reader has learned, the assessment task of writing a proposal to school management to recommend authentic assessment would better demonstrate that the reader understands than to just repeat the point in a paper or other decontextualized means. This is because, in the context of understanding and reforming assessment practice in schools, proposal writing is authentic (both real

Accountability and Improvement 297

and true) to every teacher and has value in the real world. Using the same logic, mathematics assessment tasks are authentic if "they involve finding patterns, checking generalizations, making models, arguing, simplifying, and extending-processes that resemble the activities of mathematicians or the application of mathematics to everyday life" (Stenmark, 1991, p.3). The argument here is that authenticity, as characterized by "situational or contextual realism" or "realistic activity or context", is a necessary condition for any assessment that claims to be epistemologically valid. If an assessment task does not involve realistic activity/context and does not reflect what students do and treasure in their real life, then it cannot provide valid information for teachers to judge a student on his/her learning; that is, it is epistemologically invalid.

In Hong Kong, the use of authentic assessment is acknowledged mostly on classroom levels, for example, engaging students in projects/portfolios and different classroom assessment tasks that elicit their learning performance. However, mostly because of the 'negative' influence of accountability on student learning, authentic assessment has not been considered as a change measure at school levels, at the least not evident in existing literature. Scholars who favour authentic assessment and tried it at schools and their classrooms are all in agreement that there is an innate relationship between authentic assessment and student learning. For example, Wong, Yung and Cheung (2008) experimented with a set of performance indicators (PIs) and different strategies, methods and tools for implementing authentic assessment with 15 preschools (13 kindergartens and two child care centres). They did two semi-structured focus group interviews with a total of 30 participants—two participants from each preschool—and documented their views on finding authentic assessment valuable to provide more thorough information of student development to further improve teaching and enhance teacher-parent communication. Another local study (Wu and Lee, 2009) reported the implementation of AfL in Mathematics in a local primary school. The authors noted the use of authentic assessment in students' activities; for example, asking primary 1 students to collect photos in their daily life that involve "lines" and "curves", and arranging primary 6 students to shop in the supermarket and then do the "four arithmetic operation". The authors found that these authentic assessment tasks were useful in helping students actively acquire Mathematics knowledge through direct, personal experience. In the same way, Lee (1998) made an interesting attempt to explore the positive effect of authentic assessment—portfolio assessment—on students' higher-order thinking skills and their conceptualization of learning. Interview findings indicated that the participating senior secondary school students eventually improved their learning strategies.

Authentic assessment functions within the domain of AfL (and assessment *as* learning), the learning improvement conception. Authentic assessment often involves interactions between teachers and students over

298 Sammy King-Fai Hui

the demands of the assessment tasks. As illustrated by Wiggins (1989), "Authentic tests are contextualized, complex intellectual challenges, not fragmented and static bits or tasks" (p.711). Authentic assessment is often used interchangeably with another assessment practice in the education literature—performance assessment. This is attributable in part to the lack of a clear definition of the two concepts, as "they are sometimes only vaguely defined and sometimes used without being defined at all" (Palm, 2008, p.1). Both concepts call for assessment tasks to elicit observable performance; however, authentic assessment emphasizes the fact that performance has to be generated from tasks that emulate real-life situations. In this regard, Oosterhof (2009) made it clear that authentic assessment is performance assessment, but the inverse is not true. Some practices of performance assessment do not belong to authentic assessment. Thus, it is unfair to judge authentic assessment with criteria specifically associated with performance assessment, such as the need for a specific format, indicators of acceptable performance, and cognitively complex tasks (Frey and Schmitt, 2007; Frey, Schmitt and Allen, 2012).

To answer the question "authentic to what?", Gulikers, Bastiaens and Kirschner (2004, 2006) suggested a five-dimensional framework (5DF), which listed the important criteria of authenticity: (1) task (what to do?); (2) physical context (where to do it?); (3) social context (with whom to do it?); (4) result (what is the result?); and (5) criteria (how is the result being judged?). Scott (2000) highlighted the necessary process of connecting, reflecting and feedback. 'Connecting' means requiring students to connect facts, concepts and principles together in unique ways to solve problems; 'reflecting' means helping students develop their self-awareness and reflective skills; and 'feedback' simply refers to providing feedback to learners related to significant objectives. In the process of reflecting, the idea of 'transfer' is worth noting. According to Fogarty, Perkins and Barell (1992), 'transfer' is defined as "learning something in one context and applying it in another" (p.ix; cited in Scott, 2000, pp.34–35). 'Transfer' is an important supplement to authenticity because transfer of knowledge and skills is a lifelong lesson for every student (UNESCO, 2010), and authentic assessment should be thought of as part of the learning process rather than simply a measuring device. Students learn through authentic assessment and therefore the designed tasks should embed learning by emulating real-life contexts.

In summary, authenticity is a necessary condition for assessment in order to collect epistemologically valid information of student learning for judgement. This is because authentic assessment tasks allow students to perform and transfer their constructed notion of understanding of knowledge and skills to a situation that emulates the real world. Authenticity is the key to the success of assessment reform in more strongly supporting student learning, and students do learn through actively engaging in well-designed authentic assessment tasks.

CONCLUSION

This chapter began with the premise that assessment reform in Hong Kong is an important reform area because it highlights the main aim of assessment is to support student learning. In order to judge the meaning of an assessment practice—that is, whether it is *of* or *for* (and *as*) learning—it is necessary to closely examine the questions "For what reason is the assessment done?" and "In what learning context does the assessment take place?" Research into Hong Kong TCoA highlighted the influence of socio-cultural factors on how teachers define the purposes of assessment and the way teachers implement assessment in school and the classrooms. The purposes of assessment for accountability and AfL improvement are strongly linked. Accountability drives schools to make a positive change and functions as an external catalyst for learning improvement; conversely, learning improvement demands collection and judgement of accurate and precise information of student learning. Also, it is necessary to assess students in a real-world context in order to collect epistemologically valid information to support student learning.

This chapter did not intend to judge whether assessment reform is successful in Hong Kong, a Chinese society that is strongly associated with a high regard of accountability as well as learning improvement; rather, it examined the meaning of the phrase 'assessment *for* learning' and presented the key arguments to those who want to achieve more success in assessment reform. The key arguments were:

- Assessment means to judge collected information of student learning against set criteria.
- Assessment by itself is an insufficient condition for learning and improvement.
- The strategies that teachers employ to collect information on student learning shape the assessment purposes.
- The primary areas of focus of assessment are supporting student learning and making schools, teachers and students accountable.
- Accountability policies initiate and drive change in schools.
- Assessment as a measurement process infers only an epistemological understanding of student learning.
- Authenticity is defined by the characteristic of 'realistic activity or context'.
- Authentic assessment that emulates real-life situations could retrieve more valid information of and support student learning.
- Authentic assessment allows students to learn through doing.

Finally, policymakers and educators should go beyond the '*for* learning' premise and foster an environment for teachers where they can critically examine the underlying purposes of existing assessment practices and at the same time put authentic assessment into test and practice.

300 Sammy King-Fai Hui

NOTE

The author is responsible for the choice and presentation of the arguments contained in this chapter, and the opinions expressed therein are not the opinions of The Hong Kong Institute of Education.

REFERENCES

Assessment Reform Group (2002). *Assessment for Learning: 10 principles.* London: Assessment Reform Group.

Au Yeung, Y.W. (2009). *Assessment for Learning: Establishing portfolio assessment in the Chinese language classrooms.* Hong Kong: Faculty of Education, Hong Kong University. (In Chinese)

Biggs, J. (1996). Assumptions underlying new approaches to assessment. In J. Biggs (Ed.) *Testing: To educate or to select? Education in Hong Kong at the crossroads* (pp.13–45). Hong Kong: Hong Kong Educational Publishing.

Black, P., Harrison, C., Lee, C., Marshall, B., & Wiliam, D. (2003). *Assessment for Learning: Putting it into practice.* Maidenhead: Open University Press.

Black, P., & Wiliam, D. (1998). *Inside the black box: Raising standards through classroom assessment.* London: King's College, School of Education.

Brown, G.T.L. (2004). Teachers' conceptions of assessment: Implications for policy and professional development. *Assessment in Education: Principles, Policy and Practice, 11*(3), 301–318.

Brown, G.T.L., & Harris, L.R. (2009). Unintended consequences of using tests to improve learning: How improvement-oriented resources engender heightened conceptions of assessment as school accountability. *Journal of Multi-Disciplinary Evaluation, 6*(12), 68–91.

Brown, G.T.L., Hui, S.K.F., & Yu, W.M. (2010). *Teachers' conceptions of assessment: Developing a model for teachers in Hong Kong.* Paper presented at the Seventh Conference of the International Test Commission, Challenges and Opportunities in Testing and Assessment in a Globalized Economy, Chinese University of Hong Kong, July.

Brown, G.T.L., Hui, S.K.F., Yu, W.M., & Kennedy, K.J. (2011). Teachers' conceptions of assessment in Chinese contexts: A tripartite model of accountability, improvement, and irrelevance. *International Journal of Educational Research, 50*(5–6), 307–320.

Brown, G.T.L., Kennedy, K.J., Fok, P.K., Chan, J.K.S., & Yu, W.M. (2009). Assessment for improvement: Understanding Hong Kong teachers' conceptions and practices of assessment. *Assessment in Education: Principles, Policy and Practice, 16*(3), 347–363.

Carless, D. (2005) Prospects for the implementation of Assessment for Learning. *Assessment in Education, 12*(1), 39–54. Retrieved 26 July 2013, from http://web.edu.hku.hk/staff/dcarless/Carless2005.pdf.

Chan, J.K.S. (2007). *We have various forms of assessments but only summative assessments count: Case studies of the implementation of an innovative assessment policy in Hong Kong.* Paper presented at the Redesigning Pedagogy: Culture, Knowledge & Understanding Conference 2007, Singapore, May.

China Civilisation Centre (2007). *China: Five thousand years of history and civilization.* Hong Kong: City University of Hong Kong Press.

Choi, C.C. (1999). Public examinations in Hong Kong. *Assessment in Education, 6*(3), 405–417.

Accountability and Improvement   301

Curriculum Development Council (2002). *Basic education curriculum guide: Building on strengths (primary 1—secondary 3)*. Hong Kong: Curriculum Development Council.

Darling-Hammond, L., & Snyder, J. (2000). Authentic assessment of teaching in context. *Teaching and Teacher Education, 16*(5–6), 523–545. Retrieved 26 July 2013, from http://www.jcu.edu/education/dshutkin/ed587/articles/Authentic_assessment.pdf.

Diez, M.E., & Moon, C.J. (1992). What do we want students to know? . . . And other important questions. *Educational Leadership, 49*(8), 38–41. Retrieved 26 July 2013, from http://www.ascd.org/ASCD/pdf/journals/ed_lead/el_199205_diez.pdf.

Earl, L.M. (2003). *Assessment as learning: Using classroom assessment to maximize student learning*. Thousand Oaks, CA: Corwin Press.

Education Bureau (2010a). *Assessment for Learning*. Retrieved 26 July 2013, from http://www.edb.gov.hk/index.aspx?nodeID=2410&langno=1.

Education Bureau (2010b). *Assessment for Learning Resource Bank*. Retrieved 26 July 2013, from http://www.edb.gov.hk/en/curriculum-development/assessment/assessment-for-learning/assessment-for-learning-resource-bank.html.

Ewell, P.T. (2009). *Assessment, accountability, and improvement: Revisiting the tension*. NILOA Occasional Paper No. 1, Urbana, University of Illinois and Indiana University, National Institute for Learning Outcomes Assessment. Retrieved 26 July 2013, from http://www.learningoutcomeassessment.org/documents/PeterEwell_005.pdf.

Fogarty, R., Perkins, D., & Barell, J. (1992). *The mindful school: How to teach for transfer*. Palatine, IL: IRI/Skylight Publishing.

Frey, B.B., & Schmitt, V.L. (2007). Coming to terms with classroom assessment. *Journal of Advanced Academics, 18*(3), 402–423. Retrieved 26 July 2013, from http://tebege.net/ar/Articles/Coming_to_Terms_With_Classroom_Assessment.pdf.

Frey, B.B., Schmitt, V.L., & Allen, J.P. (2012). Defining authentic classroom assessment. *Practical Assessment, Research & Evaluation, 17*(2). Retrieved 26 July 2013, from http://pareonline.net/pdf/v17n2.pdf.

Gao, L., & Kennedy, K.J. (2011). Teachers' conceptions of assessment in Mainland China: Categories, characteristics and implications. *Journal of Educational Studies, 7*(1), 39–47. (In Chinese)

Gardner, H. (1993). Educating for understanding. *American School Board Journal, 180*(7), 20–24.

Gariepy, K.D., Spencer, B.L., & Couture, J.-C. (Eds.) (2009). *Educational accountability: Professional voices from the field*. Rotterdam: Sense Publishers. Retrieved 26 July 2013, from https://www.sensepublishers.com/media/331–educational-accountability.pdf.

Gottfredson, L.S. (2009). Logical fallacies used to dismiss the evidence on intelligence testing. In R.P. Phelps (Ed.) *Correcting fallacies about educational and psychological testing* (pp.11–65). Washington, DC: American Psychological Association.

Green, J.M. (1998). Authentic assessment: Constructing the way forward for all students. *Education Canada, 38*(3), 8–12.

Gulikers, J.T.M., Bastiaens, T.J., & Kirschner, P.A. (2004). A five-dimensional framework for authentic assessment. *Educational Technology Research and Development, 52*(3), 67–86.

Gulikers, J.T.M., Bastiaens, T.J., & Kirschner, P.A. (2006). Authentic assessment, student and teacher perceptions: The practical value of the five-dimensional framework. *Journal of Vocational Education and Training, 58*(3), 337–357.

Hong Kong Examination and Assessment Authority (2009). *BCA/TSA*. Retrieved 26 July 2013, from http://www.hkeaa.edu.hk/en/bca_tsa/.

302 Sammy King-Fai Hui

Hong Kong Institute of Education (2009). *Assessment Research Centre.* Retrieved 26 July 2013, from http://www.ied.edu.hk/arc/.

Hui, S.K.F. (2012). Missing conceptions of assessment: Qualitative studies with Hong Kong curriculum leaders. *Asia-Pacific Education Researcher, 21*(2), 375–383. Retrieved 26 July 2013, from http://ejournals.ph/index.php?journal=TAPE R&page=article&op=view&path%5B%5D=5476&path%5B%5D=5641.

Hui, S.K.F., & Brown, G.T.L. (2010). *Contrasting teacher's espoused and enacted classroom assessment: Exploring Hong Kong Chinese teachers' conceptions of assessment.* Paper presented at the International Association for Educational Assessment (IAEA) 36th Annual Conference, Assessment for the Future Generations, Bangkok, Thailand, August. Retrieved 26 July 2013, from http://www.iaea.info/documents/paper_4d37c4.pdf.

Kennedy, K.J. (2007). *Barriers to innovative school practice: A socio-cultural framework for understanding assessment practices in Asia.* Paper presented at the Redesigning Pedagogy: Culture, Knowledge & Understanding Conference 2007, Singapore, May. Retrieved 26 July 2013, from http://conference.nie.edu.sg/2007/paper/papers/STUSY016A.pdf.

Kennedy, K.J., Chan, J.K.S., & Fok, P.K. (2011). Holding policy-makers to account: Exploring 'soft' and 'hard' policy and the implications for curriculum reform. *London Review of Education, 9*(1), 41–54.

Kennedy, K.J., & Lee, J. (2008). *Changing schools in Asia: Schools for the knowledge society.* London: Routledge.

Lee, Y.C.E. (1998). *Assessing and fostering senior secondary school students' conceptions and understanding of learning through authentic assessment.* Unpublished master's dissertation, University of Hong Kong. Retrieved 26 July 2013, from http://hub.hku.hk/handle/10722/27491.

Li, W.S., & Hui, S.K.F. (2007). Conceptions of assessment of Mainland China college lecturers: A technical paper analyzing the Chinese version of COA-III. *Asia-Pacific Education Researcher, 16*(2), 185–198. Retrieved 26 July 2013, from http://www.dlsu.edu.ph/research/journals/taper/pdf/200712/Li%20&%20 Hui.pdf.

Madaus, G., Russell, M., & Higgins, J. (2009). *The paradoxes of high stakes testing.* Charlotte, NC: Information Age Publishing.

Miller, S.A. (1998). Parents' beliefs about children's cognitive development. *Child Development, 59*(2), 259–285.

Newmann, F., Brandt, R., & Wiggins, G. (1998). An exchange of views on semantics, psychometrics, and assessment reform: A close look at 'authentic' assessments. *Educational Researcher, 27*(6), 19–22.

Online Education Database (2007). *The self-directed student toolbox: 100 web resources for lifelong learners.* 17 September. Retrieved 26 July 2013, from http://oedb.org/library/beginning-online-learning/the-self-directed-student-toolbox-100–web-resources-for-lifelong-learners.

Oosterhof, A. (2009). *Developing and using classroom assessments* (4th ed.). Upper Saddle River, NJ: Pearson Education.

Palm, T. (2008). Performance assessment and authentic assessment: A conceptual analysis of the literature. *Practical Assessment, Research & Evaluation, 13*(4). Retrieved 26 July 2013, from http://pareonline.net/pdf/v13n4.pdf.

Palomba, C.A., & Banta, T.W. (1999). *Assessment essentials: Planning, implementing, and improving assessment in higher education.* San Francisco, CA: Jossey-Bass.

Pang, N.S.K. (2008). *The practice of Assessment for Learning and metacognitive teaching in Hong Kong classrooms.* Hong Kong: Chinese University of Hong Kong.

Pong, W.Y., & Chow, J.C.S. (2002). On the pedagogy of examinations in Hong Kong. *Teaching and Teacher Education, 18*(2), 139–149.

Accountability and Improvement 303

Ross, K.N., & Jürgens-Genevois, I. (Eds.) (2006). *Cross-national studies of the quality of education: Planning their design and managing their impact.* Paris: UNESCO, International Institute for Educational Planning. Retrieved 26 July 2013, from http://unesdoc.unesco.org/images/0014/001470/147093e.pdf.

Scott, J. (2000). Authentic assessment tools. In R. Custer (Ed.) *Using authentic assessment in vocational education (ERIC Information Series No. 381)* (pp.33–48). Columbus, OH: ERIC Clearinghouse on Adult, Career, and Vocational Education. Retrieved 26 July 2013, from http://www.calpro-online.org/eric/docs/custer/custer5.pdf.

Shavelson, R.J. (2007). *A brief history of student learning assessment: How we got where we are and a proposal for where to go next.* Washington, DC: Association of American Colleges and Universities.

Stenmark, J.K. (Ed.) (1991). *Mathematics assessment: Myths, models, good questions, and practical suggestions.* Reston, VA: National Council of Teachers of Mathematics.

Stobart, G. (2008). *Testing times: The uses and abuses of assessment.* Abington: Routledge.

UNESCO (2010). *Lifelong learning.* Retrieved 26 July 2013, from http://uil.unesco.org/home/programme-areas/lifelong-learning-policies-and-strategies/news-target/lifelong-learning/9bf043146eaa0985e05daa9e12135f5b/.

Volante, L., & Jaafar, S.B. (2008). Educational assessment in Canada. *Assessment in Education: Principles, Policy and Practice, 15*(2), 201–210. Retrieved 26 July 2013, from http://www.tandfonline.com/doi/pdf/10.1080/09695940802164226.

Wang, P. (2010). *Research on Chinese teachers' conceptions and practice of assessment.* Unpublished doctoral dissertation, Guangzhou, South China Normal University. (In Chinese)

Watkins, D.A., & Biggs, J.B. (2001). The paradox of the Chinese learner and beyond. In D.A. Watkins & J.B. Biggs (Eds.) *Teaching the Chinese learner: Psychological and pedagogical perspectives* (pp.3–23). Hong Kong: University of Hong Kong, Comparative Education Research Centre.

Wiggins, G. (1989). A true test: Toward more authentic and equitable assessment. *Phi Delta Kappan, 70*(9), 703–713. Retrieved 26 July 2013, from https://my.parker.edu/ICS/icsfs/atruetest.pdf?target=6f96392f-5eda-43eb-8b2e-318a590f323b.

Wiggins, G. (2006). Healthier testing made easy: The idea of authentic assessment. *Edutopia.* Retrieved 26 July 2013, from http://www.edutopia.org/healthier-testing-made-easy.

Wong, N.C.M., Yung, Y.M.A., & Cheung, H.P.R. (2008). Empowering preschools in using performance indicators to assess children's learning and development. *Journal of Basic Education, 17*(1), 159–186. Retrieved 26 July 2013, from http://hkier.fed.cuhk.edu.hk/journal/wp-content/uploads/2010/04/jbe_v17n1_159–186.pdf.

Wu, S.W., & Lee, S.H. (2009). Assessment for Learning: The practice of mathematics subject in a primary school. *Hong Kong Teachers' Centre Journal, 8*, 165–171. Retrieved 26 July 2013, from http://edb.org.hk/HKTC/download/journal/j8/(5)HKTCJ08–Article3–5.pdf. (In Chinese)

Yu, W.M., Kennedy, K.J., Fok, P.K., & Chan, K.S. (2006). *Assessment reform in basic education in Hong Kong: The emergence of Assessment for Learning.* Paper presented at the 32nd Annual Conference of the International Association for Educational Assessment (IAEA), Singapore, May. Retrieved 26 July 2013, from http://www.iaea2006.seab.gov.sg/conference/download/papers/Assessment%20reform%20in%20basic%20education%20in%20Hong%20Kong%20-%20The%20emergence%20of%20assessment%20for%20learning.pdf.

Part VII

Quality Assurance and School Evaluation

18 The Role of Quality Assurance System in the Implementation of Curriculum Reform

Chi Chung Lam

INTRODUCTION

A new quality assurance (QA) system was introduced in the mid-1990s in line with other education reform initiatives. It not only provides an efficient mechanism for the government and administrators to monitor and improve the standard of school services but also contributed to the adoption and institutionalization of the curriculum reform introduced at the turn of the millennium. Compared with the failure of previous attempts of curriculum change from the 1970s to the 1990s, the wave of curriculum reform in the recent decade has been much more successful in terms of level of implementation. In this chapter, the impact of introducing the new QA system on facilitating the implementation of curriculum reform will be explained. The limitations of QA work in introducing genuine and sustainable curriculum change will also be discussed.

CURRICULUM CHANGES PRIOR TO 2000

Since the 1960s, after the Hong Kong government started to invest more into the education system, a series of attempts has been made to reform the school curriculum. In 1975, for example, a new integrated subject, Social Studies, was introduced to replace Economic and Public Affairs, Geography and History at the junior secondary level. On the cross-curricular side, the government introduced the *Guidelines on Moral Education* and the *Guidelines on Civic Education* in 1981 and 1985, respectively (Education Department [ED], 1981, 1985). In the late 1980s, sex education and environmental education were also introduced. In addition, the sixth form curriculum was reviewed in the late 1980s, resulting in changes like the introduction of a new compulsory subject of Chinese Language and Chinese Culture. Then the 1990s was marked by the introduction of a massive curriculum reform, Target Oriented Curriculum (TOC), which affected both the primary and the secondary sector (Lam, 1996).

308   *Chi Chung Lam*

Unfortunately, most of these curriculum reforms failed to be fully implemented. Moral education and civic education, for example, were found to be treated by teachers as add-on duties and schools did not take them seriously (Lam, 1995; Tang and Morris, 1989). Some curriculum changes such as Liberal Studies at the sixth form curriculum failed to attract a high rate of adoption despite the serious promotion efforts by the government. Morris (1996) summed up the implementation of curriculum reform as cosmetic change. The schools and teachers, because of bureaucratic control, might adopt the curriculum reform initiatives as instructed by the government, but they did not seem to really change their curricular or instructional practices. By 2000, school curriculum in Hong Kong schools was still found to be traditional and classroom teaching was very much teacher-centred (Education Commission [EC], 2000).

At the turn of the new millennium, a new wave of curriculum reform was introduced (Curriculum Development Council [CDC], 2001). The 21st-century curriculum reform was indeed very radical and large scale (Cheng, 2009; Lin and Zhang, 2006). The curriculum reform initiatives aimed at changing the curriculum from imparting knowledge to fostering whole-person development. To ensure the economic competitiveness of Hong Kong in the globalized world, nurturing generic skills such as problem-solving skills, communication skills and self-management skills became key educational aims (Cheng, 2009; EC, 2000). Reading to learn, moral and civic education, information technology and project learning were chosen to be the four key curriculum reform initiatives. Further, the reform had targeted all schools, from pre-primary to secondary. In light of the low level of implementation of curriculum reform in the 1970s, 1980s and 1990s, the chance of fully implementing such large-scale curriculum reform was slim. However, the implementation studies conducted by the government from 2003 to 2006 reported that the four reform initiatives had been incorporated into the school curriculum (EC, 2003, 2004, 2006). In contrast to the curriculum changes launched in the 1980s and 1990s, it was found that the culture of teaching and learning has changed. Teachers accepted the changes (Chan, 2008) and more interactive activities were used in classroom teaching. Life-wide learning and more school-based curriculum initiatives were evident (EC, 2006). What made such a difference? What facilitated the implementation of these reforms at the school level and the classroom level?

QUALITY ASSURANCE SYSTEM

The higher level of implementation of curriculum reform might be a result of many factors, such as the willingness of the government to invest huge amounts of resources. Among the various reasons, the introduction of a new QA system in the late 1990s has played an important role. In this chapter, the interplay of the QA system and curriculum reform will be discussed.

The Role of Quality Assurance System   309

When the government contemplated the education reforms in the late 1990s, the key consideration was how to enhance the quality of education in Hong Kong. In the mid-1990s, a number of reviews were conducted to identify the reality of teaching and learning in schools (see, for example, Board of Education, 1997). Moreover, the EC (2000) also analyzed the challenges Hong Kong was facing before deciding the aims of Hong Kong school education. Hong Kong, being an international cosmopolitan but without any natural resources, has been seen as facing fierce competition from many Asian cities, such as Singapore and Shanghai. To maintain and sustain the development of Hong Kong, it is of prime importance to ensure that the education system trains the educated young people appropriately (Ng and Chan, 2008). To do so, the school system must offer quality education experiences to all the young people. In light of the failure in bringing about deep-seated pedagogical and cultural changes in schools and among teachers, a more effective QA system seemed to be a crucial factor to the realization of the new vision of education.

Up to the early 1990s, the concept of QA was new to most teachers and schools. Schools did not need to report the performance of their students to the public. Teachers usually worked in isolation (Lam, 1995). Improving one's teaching through observing classroom teaching was rare (Lam, 2012). The government relied on subject inspectors' occasional visits to schools to monitor the quality of teaching and learning in schools. These visits were usually focused on the teaching of a subject rather than reviewing the quality of services of the schools.

In 1997, the EC released a report entitled *Quality School Education*, which marked the commitment of the government in introducing a new QA system. "Since then, a number of policy initiatives were introduced to put schools on track towards quality improvement. The most notable ones are the system-wide reform on school inspection and school-based management, the publication of school results for the public" (Tam and Cheng, 2001, p.48).

The QA system set up in the late 1990s and early 2000s is, in many ways, similar to those adopted in a number of Asia-Pacific countries (Mok et al., 2003). It comprises School Self-Evaluation (SSE) and External School Review (ESR). Each school is required to conduct its own self-evaluation. To monitor the quality of the services provided by the school, every school will go through an ESR every four to five years. A team of external members, made up mostly of government officials, with one external member who may be a principal, deputy head of other schools or academics from the tertiary sector, will inspect the school. They will observe lessons and meet stakeholders (including parents, students, teachers and school managers). Through the extensive data collection and sharing of the professional judgement of the team members, the school review team will formulate their judgement with reference to a set of performance indicators (PIs) set by the government. In the report, recommendations and suggestions on

310   *Chi Chung Lam*

improvement will also be included. As a rule, the ESR report has to be released to the stakeholders.

ENHANCING QUALITY THROUGH THE QUALITY ASSURANCE SYSTEM

The introduction of the new QA system changed the old system in a number of ways. In the past, the QA system was bureaucratic in nature. School inspectors were appointed to conduct classroom observation and monitor the curriculum work in schools. Normally, it was subject-based. The focus was on the products. The new QA system is more comprehensive in its scope. The three aspects, namely, inputs, processes and outputs, are covered (Mok, 2007). The dimensions of PIs cover not only teaching and learning but also school management (Quality Assurance Division [QAD], 2002, 2008). The structure and processes of the QA systems are, in a number of ways, much more effective in inducing schools to comply with the reform initiatives launched by the Government.

Aligning Aims of Education

People hold different views on aims of education and curriculum orientation (Schiro, 2013). One of the reasons for the low-level implementation in many educational and curricular reforms prior to the new millennium was the failure to align the views on what to accomplish through education and how these goals are to be achieved. For example, the TOC, introduced in the early 1990s, emphasized that all students could learn and it was possible for all students to achieve the learning targets. Formative and target-oriented assessments were proposed to be used as a means to help students achieve the targets. However, not all teachers and principals agreed with this value stance. They saw the importance of using norm-referenced assessment to induce competition among students, which, they believed, was a major motivating force to work hard. The usefulness of task-based learning (TBL), another key feature of the TOC, was also seen by many teachers as not practical. This 'cultural difference' between the reformers and school practitioners created serious implementation problems. The traditional 'research, development and dissemination' approach was simply ineffective (Lam, 1996).

The case of the TOC vividly illustrates the importance of aligning the educational goals held by the schools and the central curriculum development agency, if the implementation gap is to be bridged. The fact that 'quality' is a very ill-defined term and it may mean different things to different people (Tam and Cheng, 2001) underscores the importance of clarifying what quality education is. A set of 29 PIs, under four domains, has been developed for the new QA system (QAD, 2002). The four domains are: (1) management and organization, (2) learning and teaching, (3) student support and school ethos, and (4) student performance. The PIs not only state the learning outcomes but also enlist the educational means to achieve quality education. For example, on student support, whole-school approach to school discipline and counselling is listed in the PIs (QAD, 2002). This way of using multi-dimensional indicators broadens the focus of QA from inputs-outputs to inputs-processes-outputs (Mok et al., 2003).

With the alignment of the educational aims, the PIs and the curriculum reform goals and initiatives, schools are much more ready to design and adapt the curriculum reform initiatives in line with the government policy. The alignment of educational services at the school level and the central level is strengthened through two means. Firstly, under the QA system, schools have to face ESR once every four to five years. School development plan is one of the key documents to be submitted to the external review team; hence the direction of the development of the school has to be in line with the goals set. Secondly, the ESR team observes lessons of most of the teachers in the school during the external review. A classroom observation form specially designed for this purpose is used in the observation. The items and criteria included in the observation form reflect the spirit and the initiatives of the curriculum reform. For example, one of the observation items is whether the four curriculum initiatives (i.e., moral and civic education, IT, reading to learn and project learning) are evident in the session observed. Student-centred learning activities are expected to be found in the lessons, too. If schools want more positive comments and ratings in the ESR, they will have to plan, develop their curriculum plans and deliver their lessons according to these evaluation criteria and forms. In other words, these measures direct schools and teachers to put the curriculum reform initiatives into practice.

The government has also built assessment system to provide essential data for monitoring the achievement of the PIs. A set of instruments, known as APASO, was purposefully designed for measuring the affective learning outcomes (Mok, 2007). In order to monitor the academic performance of the primary and secondary students, the Territory-Wide Student Assessment (TSA) system was established in 2004. All primary 3, primary 6 and secondary 3 students are required to sit the test, which includes the three major subjects: English Language, Chinese Language and Mathematics. The data provide objective information for monitoring the academic standards of the students in a specific school and the system as a whole (Cheng, 2009).

If ESR reports are not important to school managers or teachers, the directive power of the ESR exercise may not be high at all. Before the introduction of the new QA system, schools were not required to release information about the school outputs, such as academic performance of the students. As part of the accountability movement and QA system, schools are required to release information of some of the key PIs, such as students'

312 *Chi Chung Lam*

achievements in pubic examination, the qualifications of the teachers and so on. In 1997, when the ESR was first tried out, the government required schools to post the report on their school website for access of all stakeholders (Mok, 2007). Even though this practice of releasing the school review report to the public was modified in 2005 because of the strong opposition from the schools (Cheng, 2009), the report has to be available to stakeholders, including the school management committee and parent–teacher association. School principals and teachers cannot ignore this high-stakes review. To ensure a positive review report, they must comply with the PIs as much as possible.

The pressure to work according to the PIs is intensified by the significant decrease in student numbers (Mok, 2007). Cheng (2009) reports, "The primary school enrolment dropped from 445,607 in 2000 to 366,531 in 2006 and the drop was 79,076 students, nearly 21.6 per cent primary school population. With this substantial reduction in student population, many schools and classes were closed due to insufficient numbers of enrolled students" (p.78). He further points out that under such a situation, school principals and teachers were very concerned with the survival of their school. Hence, they were "very sensitive" to education reform initiatives such as school reporting, SSE and ESR. In such a scenario, the schools would quite naturally comply with the government reform initiatives as reflected in the PIs.

Integrating School Self-Evaluation and External School Review

The QA system developed in the late 1990s was composed of SSE and ESR. As pointed out previously, the ESR has significant impact on the image of the schools, hence schools considering it a high-stakes evaluation. The ESR alone, however, may not be adequate to ensure that everyday educational services are of high quality as the review is only carried out once every four to five years. In between two external reviews, schools may lose the momentum to carry out the reform initiatives. The building in of SSE can sustain schools' efforts to monitor their own work and progress, and develop plans for improvement based on evidences collected in the self-evaluation process.

The QA system is also backed up by a new school management system. Like many other places, the majority of school places are provided by public-funded schools. However, most of the public-funded schools in Hong Kong are not directly managed and administered by the government. In the early 1990s, more than 85% of the schools were subsidized schools. They are run by religious bodies, voluntary agencies or NGOs, with full financial support from the government. For a long period of time, they enjoyed a very high level of autonomy. As long as they complied with a set of codes of practice, the School Sponsoring Bodies (SSBs) could decide all the school matters, including the school curriculum, the recruitment of

The Role of Quality Assurance System   313

staff, the deployment of resources and so on. The school governance was in the hands of the school bodies. Stakeholders such as parents and alumni were seldom involved in the running of the school. The conventional way of quality monitoring was provided by the school inspection work, which was very much a bureaucratic system. This system changed in the early 2000s. All subsidized schools had to set up an Incorporated Management Committee (IMC) which must comprise "representatives of the school sponsoring body, the school principal, independent social constituencies, and elected parents, teachers and alumni, responsible for the management of their schools" (Cheng, 2009, p.67).

With the participation of parents and independent members, the school management bodies would have to consider and respect the views and the preferences of parents. From the accountability point of view, parents could be seen as the 'customers' of educational services. They have a strong vested interest in guiding the schools to provide quality services. This structural change in school governance, coupled with the practice of SSE, institutes a system that will constantly monitor the standards of the services provided.

Building Up Evaluation Culture in Schools

Establishing a structure to evaluate school practices and monitor quality of services is an important step. The effective functioning of the QA system, however, relies on the building up of self-evaluation culture among teachers and principals. This involves changes of values towards evaluation by teachers and principals. Prior to the launch of the School Management Initiative (SMI) in 1991, the education system of Hong Kong was highly centralized (Ng and Chan, 2008). Sense of accountability was low in schools. Teachers and principals were strongly against the accountability movement, which involved releasing more school information to the public, the establishment of IMC and the release of the school review report (Cheng, 2009; Mok, 2007). Such opposition reflected the clashes between the QA culture and the values of teachers and principals.

By the late 2000s, the opposition of teachers and principals had mostly evaporated. They had accepted releasing school information, opening up schools to stakeholders' visits and setting up IMC. Nearly all schools had set up classroom observation system where teachers could learn from each other's lessons (Lam, 2012). This professional learning activity can help ensure and enhance quality of teaching and learning. Why have teachers and principals bought in and accepted the evaluation and monitoring practices?

The threat of dropping student numbers and the closure of schools had a significant part to play in this. School personnel, for survival, have to accept the practices. However, the building up of the evaluation and monitoring culture is also related to the implementation strategies of the QA system. The movement towards constructing a new QA system started in 1991 with the launch of the SMI. Under this initiative, schools were required to compile a school report and profile which should include information such as school aims, operating plans and students' performance (Education and Manpower Bureau & Education Department, 1991). The report and profile, after being submitted to the ED, "are published in public domains such as the internet" (Ng and Chan, 2008, pp.495). The release of school profile is to provide information for parents to choose schools (Ng and Chan, 2008). This request is reasonable as parents and students need the information for making informed decisions about school choice. Hence, schoolteachers and principals did find it difficult to argue against it.

After this first step was well established and with the successful experience of some schools in setting up a QA circle, the government moved to the next step of setting up SSE, which is the "internal quality assurance" process (Ng and Chan, 2008). The QA inspection, which was the external accountability prong of the QA system introduced in 1997 (Mok, 2007), was the most controversial initiative. The government did not force all schools to practice it. Instead, a group of schools were invited to do a pilot. In 2003, it was renamed ESR with its procedures simplified, and the report was to be accessible by a group of stakeholders rather than going public on all fronts. The QA system was further reviewed in 2007, resulting in the refining of PIs in 2008 (QAD, 2008).

The brief history of the development of QA shows that the government adopted an incremental approach. Instead of rushing through everything in a few years, it was developed step by step (Mok, 2007). The controversial elements were put in place after consultation with stakeholders, and some were piloted before full-scale implementation. Modifications were also made when it encountered strong opposition from the stakeholders. This incremental development process somehow made it easier for principals and teachers to accept the initiative.

Another important supporting measure in 'enculturating' the school personnel is the introduction of principal training and the extensive involvement of principals and deputy heads in carrying out an ESR. Up to the past century, training provided to school principals was confined to a basic course on administrative routines. "Prompted by the Hong Kong government's increasingly invasive reform agenda, particularly related to changes in school governance structures, and increased grumblings within the school leadership community, in 1999 the Education Department established a Task Group to look into the training and development of school heads" (Walker and Dimmock, 2006, p.128). This marked the first step in developing a principal training programme specially for Hong Kong. In the training programme, one of the areas is to help aspiring principals to prepare both a school plan and a personal development plan (Walker and Dimmock, 2006). This is closely linked to the QA processes promulgated by the government.

Another important channel for principals and deputy heads to understand the QA processes is through involving them in carrying out ESRs.

The Role of Quality Assurance System   315

Instead of only involving officials in the ESR work, the government sets the requirement of having one principal or deputy head from other schools in a review team. Training programmes on the design and delivery of ESR work are provided for school principals, deputy heads and professional educators who are interested in ESR. After qualifying as school reviewers, they will be invited to serve as unofficial members to help conduct reviews. Through this hands-on training and on-site practice, more school principals and deputy heads have deepened their understanding of the rationale, spirit and practices of QA. These helped build up their capacity for effective implementation of the QA system (Mok, 2007).

Utilizing the Mass Media

The QA system in Hong Kong is in many ways similar to their counterparts in the Asia-Pacific region (Cheng, 2009; Mok, 2007; Ng and Chan, 2008). It is part of the accountability movement adopted by the Hong Kong government and many other countries. Managerialism and the neo-right ideology swept through the education circle in many places (see, for example, Ball, 1999; Brauckmann and Pshiardis, 2010; Kyriakides and Campbell, 2004). But this does not mean that teachers and school principals would automatically accept it. Indeed, in the development process, inevitably there was opposition. Besides the factors discussed in the above sections, another factor was the success in using mass media to dominate the discourse in education reform.

Lin and Zhang (2006), after analyzing the implementation strategies of the reform in Hong Kong, point out that the government officials and the key policymakers launched an attack on the quality of educational services in Hong Kong in the late 1990s. The argument put forward was that Hong Kong was facing fierce competition in the globalized world. The conventional way of teaching and learning and the bureaucratic school management style were out of place to nurture the kind of young people the society needed (see, for example, EC, 2000). K.M. Cheng, one of the key players in education reform, wrote in 2002 that the Hong Kong government had used the mass media to promulgate the ideology. The government, along with the mass media, dominated the discourse of education reform. Under such circumstances, teachers and principals who were against the QA system found it difficult not to co-operate. They were expected to constantly improve their work to meet the rising expectation of the public. This helps build up the culture of self-evaluation in schools.

Financial Support

Another noteworthy factor accounting for the development and implementation of the QA system is the willingness of the government to invest. In 1998, the government set up the Quality Education Fund (QEF), an

316   *Chi Chung Lam*

endowment fund with HK$5 billion. The investment income from this fund is to support reform measures and educational quality enhancement work, including the implementation of school-based management (SBM) (Mok, 2007). Besides this, the public spending on primary and secondary education showed a 50% increase from the financial year 1996–1997 to 2003–2004 (Lin and Zhang, 2006). In the financial year 2006–2007, government expenditure on education amounted to 23% of the total government expenditure (see Mok, 2007, p.193). With the increase in funding, more resources were provided for the administrative offices, teacher and principal training, as well as human resources in schools.

DISCUSSION AND CONCLUSION

The setting up of the QA system and the building up of self-evaluation culture in schools have facilitated the implementation of curriculum reform initiatives launched in 2001. The annual school review reports and the series of implementation studies on curriculum reform have all found that most, if not all, schools have incorporated the four key curriculum initiatives (i.e., reading to learn, IT, moral and civic education and project learning). More school-based curriculum development (SBCD) is evident. Schools are more responsive to the views of parents.

Behind this success, however, is the question whether the present practices need further refinements or changes. Experiences in other places have shown that QA systems can bring about undesirable impacts (see, for example, Brauckmann and Pshiardis, 2010). In Hong Kong, Yeung (2010) conducted a qualitative study on how the views of 12 curriculum leaders (CLs) in primary schools on the QA system affected their work. The result shows that the QA system did exert pressure on them to carry out curriculum reform in school: "Schools are making greater efforts to ensure maximum congruency and alignment between the school plan and the official, planned curriculum" (p.200). Teachers and the school management had taken a number of measures, such as forming study groups to understand the requirements of school evaluation and classroom observation conducted in an ESR. However, Yeung's study also rings a cautious note. The CLs in her study reported that schools and teachers tended to take the QA measures as a "bureaucratic and managerial tactic" (p.199). They did, in fact, take a defensive approach to cope with this evaluation system such as "preparing substantial quantitative evidence. Many even put aside other essential duties (such as talking with students) and work, bowing to the expectation of the officials as well as the demand of parents" (p.199). This is very much like "teaching to the test" seen in the introduction of high-stakes examination as evident in Hong Kong (Morris, 1996) and the United States (Hargreaves and Shirley, 2009). Possible side effects could be schools and teachers losing their own drive to launch changes beyond the official framework. They might perceive themselves as technocrats to meet

The Role of Quality Assurance System 317

the goals set by the officials and/or the demands of parents, rather than as professionals charged with the responsibility of providing teaching and learning experiences best suited to their students.

To avoid these problems, the government would need to constantly review the whole system, including the goals of education, the PIs and the feedback loop of the school review results. In 2008, the Education Bureau (EDB) modified the PIs after an extensive consultation and review. The ESR was also simplified to cut down on the administrative paperwork. These moves have, in some ways, eased the pressure on principals and teachers. However, other components of the evaluation system, such as the TSA, still exert very high pressure upon some teachers and schools. As the culture of evaluation has taken root in many schools, it may be appropriate for a system which places more emphasis on SSE rather than external review. An improved SSE is more likely to achieve the 'overarching goals' of improving the organization and teaching and learning because it would move away from overly standardized evaluation system. Schools and teachers will be better placed to exercise their professional judgement. To achieve this more ideal practice, further strengthening the schools' capacity to implement SSE would certainly be essential.

REFERENCES

Ball, S. (1999). Perfomativity and fragmentation in 'postmodern' schooling. In J. Carter (Ed.) *Postmodernity and the fragmentation of welfare* (pp.187–203). London: Routledge.

Board of Education (1997). *Report on review of 9-year compulsory education*. Hong Kong: Government Printer.

Brauckmann, S., & Pshiardis, P. (2010). The clash of evaluations: In search of the missing link between school accountability and school improvement: Experiences from Cyprus. *International Journal of Educational Management, 24*(4), 330–350.

Chan, K.K. (2008). *Curriculum reform: Building on strengths for continuous intensification*. Retrieved 29 January 2013, from http://www.edb.gov.hk/index.aspx?nodeID=6400&langno=1.

Cheng, K.M. (2002). Reinventing the wheel: Educational reform. In S.K. Lau (Ed.) *The first Tung Chee-hwa administration: The first five years of the Hong Kong Special Administrative Region* (pp.157–174). Hong Kong: Chinese University Press.

Cheng, Y.C. (2009). Hong Kong educational reforms in the last decade: Reform syndrome and new developments. *International Journal of Educational Management, 23*(1), 65–86.

Curriculum Development Council (2001). *Learning to Learn: The way forward in curriculum*. Hong Kong: Curriculum Development Council.

Education and Manpower Bureau & Education Department (1991). *The School Management Initiative: Setting the framework of quality in Hong Kong schools*. Hong Kong: Government Printer.

Education Commission (1997). *Education Commission report no. 7: Quality school education*. Hong Kong: Government Printer.

318   *Chi Chung Lam*

Education Commission (2000). *Learning for life—learning through life: Reform proposals for the education system in Hong Kong.* Hong Kong: Education Commission.

Education Commission. (2003). *Progress report on education reform (2).* Hong Kong: Education Commission.

Education Commission (2004). *Progress report on education reform (3).* Hong Kong: Education Commission.

Education Commission (2006). *Progress report on education reform (4).* Hong Kong: Education Commission.

Education Department (1981). *General guidelines on moral education in Hong Kong.* Hong Kong: Education Department.

Education Department (1985). *Guidelines on civic education in schools.* Hong Kong: Education Department.

Hargreaves, A., & Shirley, D. (2009). *The fourth way: The inspiring future for educational change.* Thousand Oaks, CA: Corwin Press.

Kyriakides, L., & Campbell, R. J. (2004). School Self-Evaluation and school improvement: A critique of values and procedures. *Studies in Educational Evaluation, 30,* 23–36.

Lam, C.C. (1995). Teacher culture and micropolitics: The products and processes of curriculum implementation in moral education in Hong Kong. In F. Slater (Ed.) *Reporting Research in Geography Education* (pp.28–40). London: University of London, Institute of Education.

Lam, C.C. (1996). *Target Oriented Curriculum: An inaccessible ideal.* Hong Kong: Hong Kong Institute of Educational Research, Chinese University of Hong Kong. (In Chinese)

Lam, C.C. (2012). *The development and challenges of instructional supervision: The experience of Hong Kong.* Paper presented at Cross-Strait Conference on School Principalship, National Taipei University of Education, Taipei, Taiwan, November.

Lin, Z.Z., & Zhang, S. (2006). An analysis of the curriculum reform implementation strategies in Hong Kong. *Exploring Education Development, 12A,* 8–13. (In Chinese)

Mok, M.M.C. (2007). Quality assurance and school monitoring in Hong Kong. *Education Research for Policy and Practice, 6,* 187–204.

Mok, M.M.C., Gurr, D., Izawa, E., Knipprath, H., Lee, I.H., Mel, M.A., & Zhang, Y.M. (2003). Quality assurance and school monitoring. In J.P. Keeves & R. Watanabe (Eds.) *International handbook of educational research in the Asia-Pacific region* (pp.945–958). Dordrecht: Kluwer Academic.

Morris, P. (1996). *The Hong Kong school curriculum: Development, issues and policies* (2nd ed.). Hong Kong: Hong Kong University Press.

Ng, P.T., & Chan, D. (2008). A comparative study of Singapore's school excellence model with Hong Kong's school-based management. *International Journal of Educational Management, 22*(6), 488–505.

Quality Assurance Division (2002). *Performance indicators for Hong Kong schools: For secondary, primary and special schools.* Hong Kong: Education and Manpower Bureau.

Quality Assurance Division (2008). *Performance indicators for Hong Kong schools with evidence of performance: For secondary, primary and special schools.* Hong Kong: Education Bureau.

Schiro, M.S. (2013). *Curriculum theory: Conflicting visions and enduring concerns* (2nd ed.). Thousand Oaks, CA: Sage Publications.

Tam, W.M.F., & Cheng, Y.C. (2001). The management of education quality: Comparison of competing perspectives. *Education Journal, 29*(1), 47–70.

Tang, T.C., & Morris, P. (1989). The abuse of educational evaluation: A study of the evaluation of the implementation of the civic education 'guidelines'. *Educational Research Journal, 4*, 41–49.

Walker, A., & Dimmock, C. (2006). Preparing leaders, preparing learners: The Hong Kong experience. *School Leadership & Management, 26*(2), 125–147.

Yeung, S.S.Y. (2010). Using school evaluation policy to effect curriculum change? A reflection on the SSE and ESR exercise in Hong Kong. *Educational Research Journal, 25*(2), 187–209.

19 The Effectiveness of the Quality Assurance Mechanism for School Improvement

Eric Chi-Keung Cheng and John Chi-Kin Lee

BACKGROUND OF THE STUDY

In recent years there has been growing public interest in achieving the high-performance education system needed to cope with global competition. As public attention has become increasingly focused on the outcomes of the education system, politicians, policymakers and education practitioners have developed a quality assurance (QA) mechanism designed to improve the effectiveness of education in Hong Kong. This drive for quality has the twin purposes of educational development and increased public accountability by means of inspections and self-assessment by the schools. It is believed that the incentives of accountability and market competition will result in a higher performance of the education system. Similar concern about quality has become very evident in the educational discourse all over the world.

The education system in Hong Kong has been moving from quantitative to qualitative enhancement in recent years in order to create human resources that are capable of coping with global economic competition (Education Commission [EC], 1999, 2000). Under the compulsory education policy in Hong Kong, since 1978 all children have the right to receive a basic education. Since then, the education authorities have been striving to enhance the quality of school education. In order to pave a path leading to a QA mechanism, in 1991 the Hong Kong government introduced the School Management Initiative (SMI), which was designed to encourage management reform in Hong Kong aided schools (Education and Manpower Branch & Education Department, 1991). The SMI was premised on a school-based management (SBM) model, which gave the schools greater control over their finances and administration and made them more accountable to the public. In 1997, the SMI was modified and became SBM although the schools were not obliged to adopt this system. In order to encourage more schools to participate, the former Education Department (ED) made further changes to the policy in September 2000, providing extra grants and more flexibility.

In 1997, the Education Bureau (EDB) issued the EC's report no. 7, *Quality School Education*. The report suggested inculcating a culture of quality

The Effectiveness of the Quality Assurance Mechanism 321

in the school system and developing a comprehensive set of indicators to measure and monitor all aspects of a school's performance, educational standards and development. This report also recommended a two-pronged approach to QA: internal QA by the schools themselves, and an external QA mechanism. In accordance with this recommendation, the government established the Quality Assurance Inspectorate (QAI) to monitor the quality of education and also to encourage schools to achieve internal QA through self-evaluation using both external and internal means. This chapter explores the impact of this QA model on the improvement of the schools in Hong Kong.

QUALITY ASSURANCE MECHANISM

A QA mechanism for school systems is a systematic management, monitoring and evaluation procedure designed to ensure that the learning environment and the curriculum programme of the schools meet the performance standards needed to achieve the educational goals and to produce a human capital that will meet the expectations of society. External and internal reviews have been widely adopted in many countries as the tools to achieve QA, for example, Singapore (Ng, 2010); New Zealand (Sakura, 2007); Thailand (Pitiyanuwat, 2007); Scotland (Croxford, Grek and Shaik, 2009); and Australia (Gurr, 2007). The external review usually plays a monitoring role in the QA mechanism to complement the internal review. The external review is undertaken by government or independent external bodies using a set of pre-specified performance indicators (PIs) to assess the quality of the education provided. The internal review is commonly referred to as School Self-Evaluation (SSE). This is undertaken by the school itself and involves planning, implementation and evaluation. The use of SSE enables schools to collect information to help them in the systematic planning of the development process in line with the school development targets (Akpe and Afemikhe, 1991; Van Petegem, 1998). It assists the school administrators to identify the strengths and weaknesses of their schools and provides guidance on the best methods for school improvement (Akpe and Afemikhe, 1991). Its purpose is to develop schools by improving the students' learning abilities and the quality of the education provided. The development of a school depends mainly on the school's capacity for self-evaluation; an effective SSE would help schools to organize changes that would lead to improvement (Davies and Rudd, 2001).

Many countries have adopted SSE as a mechanism for internal reviews. For example, in Thailand schools are required to conduct an internal review and prepare an annual report dealing with the planning, implementation, monitoring and self-evaluation process (Pitiyanuwat, 2007). The SSE approach in New Zealand involves the preparations for the review, gathering information, analyzing the results, documentation and communication and

322   Eric Chi-Keung Cheng and John Chi-Kin Lee

making recommendations for action based on the findings (Sakura, 2007). Recently implemented SSE procedures in Scotland require schools to look at each aspect of their programme and to ask, 'How are we doing?' 'How do we know?' 'What are we going to do now?' (Croxford, Grek and Shaik, 2009). The SSE process in Hong Kong is based on a cycle that includes planning, implementation and evaluation stages, with monitoring of each stage. The schools are required to submit an SSE report to the EDB that is followed up for endorsement by an external review. The intertwined relationship between the internal QA by the schools themselves and the external QA mechanism could be articulated by the theory of loose-tight coupling.

THE LOOSE-TIGHT COUPLING THEORY

The concept of coupling has been used to describe the relationships between schools and the central district authority (Fennell, 1994). The theory of a loose-tight coupling provides a way of conceptualizing the internal and external reviews in the QA model in terms of the interrelatedness of support for professional development and the monitoring of educational quality between a school and the education authority. 'Loose coupling' refers to the weak tie between the various elements in a strongly disconnected education system (Weick, 1976) that maximizes the independence and professional autonomy of an individual school within the system (Weick, 1982; Ainley, Reed and Miller, 1986). It implies that the schools have a great deal of autonomy and can use their own discretion in carrying out their educational functions, using mostly their own professional judgement. Conducting a SSE is in effect the expression in practical terms of the spirit of professional accountability. The professional identities and competence of the school leaders and teachers are recognized and respected, and support by the education authority is reflected in a relationship of interdependence between the education authority and the schools. 'Tight coupling' refers to the existence of more centralized and official hierarchical structures and quality control that are designed to facilitate and enhance the achievement of the national educational goals. In a school system it operates by means of education directives and External School Reviews (ESRs) that direct the behaviour of school leaders and teachers. Loose coupling and tight coupling often overlap and are applied to varying degrees depending on the local circumstances.

In loose coupling, the education authority may provide resources to support the institutionalization of the SSE mechanism and to enhance the professional development of in-service teachers, for example, by inviting experts to provide school-based support services. Tight coupling reflects an official policy of enforcing education ordinances, formulating education policies and exercising QA control to maintain the quality of education. School inspections, which embody the idea of tight coupling, are conducted

The Effectiveness of the Quality Assurance Mechanism 323

by an education authority to evaluate the overall performance of a school and present recommendations for improvement. The development of a set of evaluation tools is indispensable in a QA mechanism for an education system (Fitz-Gibbon, 1996), so the school leaders will be guided by these indicators in their self-evaluation exercise and the formulation of a school plan (Cheng, 2011).

An SBM policy was introduced in Hong Kong in 1991, extended in 1997 and changed again in 2000. The latest policy reflects a greater degree of support for the process of decentralization, moving from tight coupling to loose coupling in the aided schools in Hong Kong. However, a school becomes more accountable for quality in line with the decentralization of power. A QA mechanism in the form of SSE and an ESR has been introduced into the Hong Kong school system with a view to enhancing the performance of that system (Education Commission, 1997). SSE helps the school to collect the information needed to plan its development effectively and systematically in line with the overall aims for school development (Akpe and Afemikhe, 1991; Van Petegem, 1998). The QA process starts at the school level—the school carries out a SSE and produces a report towards the end of the year. The EDB conducts an inspection in the form of an ESR of the performance of the school as a whole. It can also be used to assess the self-evaluation capacity demonstrated by the school. The performance in each area is assessed using four levels: excellent, good, acceptable and unsatisfactory. The first cycle of External School Reviews (ESRs) was completed in 2007 and the second cycle will cover the six years from 2008 to 2014. The key differences between the two ESRs are highlighted in Table 19.1. The ESR exercise complements the school's self-evaluation and contributes to maintaining a balance between public accountability and professional accountability (Cheng, 2011). Each school's performance is monitored, and objective recommendations are presented for improvement.

The process of conducting SSE in Hong Kong also adopts a cyclical approach that includes planning, implementation and evaluation, with monitoring at each stage. The schools are required to submit an SSE report for endorsement by an external review. Nonetheless, some tensions may arise from the use of a combination of SSE and external inspection and other challenges (Lee, 2009; Ngan, Lee and Brown, 2010). Macbeath (2008) conducted an impact study on the effectiveness of an ESR for enhancing school improvement following an SSE in Hong Kong. He reported that the implementation of an SSE and an ESR as complementary processes had served as a significant catalyst for change and school improvement. However, the post-ESR support and the embedding of the SSE in routine work still left room for improvement. A recent review of school inspection experiences in high-performing education systems reveals that while the inspecting body in Hong Kong and Singapore is a government department, in Scotland and the Netherlands it is an executive agency (Whitby, 2010, p.6). In addition, in terms of the key areas and indicators used in the self-evaluation, the SSE

324 *Eric Chi-Keung Cheng and John Chi-Kin Lee*

Table 19.1 Comparing the Key Characteristic of First and Second Cycle ESR

	First ESR Cycle	*Second ESR Cycle*
Focuses of the Review	• Standard-based orientation Standardized indicators focused mode	• Improvement-oriented • School specific and focused mode
Arrangement	• Standardized and rigorous	• Flexible and tailored
Measures Taken	• Relativity: compare the performance indicators, stakeholder questionnaires and key performance measures to initiate starting points for review	• Longitudinal: follow up the suggestions made in the previous Quality Assurance Inspection (QAI), ESR or Comprehensive Review (CR) report
Performance Indicators	• 4 areas, 14 domains • PI version 2003	• Four areas, eight domains • PI version 2008
Duration and Schedule	• Duration of the ESR visit and schedule of the ESR were fixed at four days	• Duration of the ESR visit and schedule of ESR will be flexibly tailored
Documents to Be Prepared and Submitted	• Schools are required to compile a school self-assessment (SSA) report containing school plans, school reports, a stakeholder Survey, Key Performance Measures (KPM)	• Schools need not compile a school self-assessment (SSA) report, or specifically administer the Stakeholder Survey (SHS) or collect the key performance measures (KPM) data for the ESR
Lesson Observation	• Observed without post-lesson sharing	• Observed with post-lesson sharing
Publication of ESR Report	• ESR reports for schools at an earlier stage were uploaded to the EBD web	• ESR reports are not uploaded to the EDB web • Report to the key stakeholders

in Hong Kong covers most of the indicators, but does not cover specific subject contents in the key area of the teaching-learning process and internal communication in the key area of management processes (p.9). Moreover, it is notable in Hong Kong that 'external evaluation is used to complement schools' self-evaluation process' (p.15). It is interesting, therefore, to examine whether the scrutiny of the SSE report by the ESR does in fact facilitate or diminish the process of school improvement in Hong Kong.

CASE STUDIES

In Hong Kong around 85% of the schools are aided schools. One aided primary school and one aided secondary school were selected for case studies

The Effectiveness of the Quality Assurance Mechanism   325

to investigate the effect of SSE and ESR on school improvement. An aided school receives financial support from the government but is managed by a non-government organization which is the School Sponsoring Body (SSB). Around 85% of the schools in Hong Kong are aided schools. The principals in both of the schools have served in their current positions since the school started. They have led their schools into adopting the SSE mechanism and participating in the two cycles of ESRs of the QA mechanism in Hong Kong. Both schools are located in rural areas of Hong Kong and their student intake is of average academic ability. In-depth interviews were conducted with both of the principals to investigate the influences of SSE on their school, including management effectiveness, teacher participation, organizational communication, formulation of a school development plan and changes in the SSE mechanism over the past 12 years.

A Primary School Case

The selected primary school was established in 1991. It moved to a new campus in 2002 and now provides whole-day primary schooling in 30 classes to around 1,000 students with 50 teachers. The school had participated in different modes of inspection, including QA inspection with respect to the management and organizational domain, and the ESR. The school was selected for QA inspection in 1998, following the enactment of the EC's report no. 7, which was designed to assess the quality of education. The QA inspection was a comprehensive inspection model in which all the performance domains prescribed in the PIs framework would be scrutinized by an EDB inspection team consisting of about seven members who were teacher experts from various key learning areas (KLAs). The major recommendation in the QAI report for the school in that year was the creation of a school development committee (SDC) to design a strategy and direction for the school development and to co-ordinate the teams and departments which would implement the plans. There was a follow-up inspection in 2007 to scrutinize whether the school had followed the recommendations of the QA inspection and it was found that the school had not yet set up the committee for school development.

QA Enhances School Management Capacity

The SDC was eventually established in 2007, immediately after the completion of the focus inspection. It was mandated to formulate a school development plan and to oversee its implementation. The SDC is chaired by the principal. He has appointed seven senior teachers with the rank of assistant master (AM) and primary school master (PSM) as the members to work with him. The SDC has become the think-tank of the school with respect to curriculum development and the professional development of the staff. Each member of the SDC is in charge of a team of front-line teachers,

326   Eric Chi-Keung Cheng and John Chi-Kin Lee

observes their lessons and makes suggestions on how they can improve their teaching and administration. Their comments are also submitted to the principal for consolidation and the principal will then pass them on to their respective appraisers of the school. Since the members of the committee may not be teachers of the subject of the lesson being observed, the teachers being observed will be given an opportunity to practice how best to explain to laymen the rationale of their teaching strategies. This can be useful and serve as a mock class observation, such as might be done by external reviewers from the EDB. In addition the committee members can give the teachers their objective opinions. The principal considered that the above mechanism had the benefit of promoting the development of both the school organization and the teachers:

> *Changes were most obvious at the managerial level, for example, my vice principal(s) and subject heads. Our teachers always have opinions about the curriculum and teaching, and our managerial level learnt how to handle such opinions and analyze situations by utilizing the data/information from the School Self-Evaluation report, and to make a judgement and take appropriate action. This is what we have learnt from the QA in the past ten years.*

SSE Improves Communication and Collegiality

The EDB informed the school one year ahead of time that an ESR would be conducted in 2011. The school was informed that the eight performance domains prescribed in the PIs for Hong Kong schools (version 2008) would be applied to review the school performance. They were requested to submit their self-evaluation documents, school development plans and annual school reports ahead of the ESR. The school held several internal meetings to consolidate all the work that they had done in the eight performance domains and to review their performance. At that time, they had formulated their school plans collectively, and the collaborative process of compiling the school report from different committees and departments enhanced the organizational communication and staff collegiality since the process provided chances for colleagues to give advice on areas of concern. The principal considers that the ESR gave him an opportunity to identify differences amongst his colleagues in their perceptions of the school's mission and to reconcile them with that mission:

> *Some colleagues considered that students hopping around was a sign of a pleasant learning atmosphere, while other colleagues viewed this as a sign of disorder. This example alerted me to the fact that not all the colleagues understand the rationale of the school's mission, and this needed to be dealt with in order for our mission to be achieved effectively. In conclusion, the ESR provided us with a platform for communication on school planning, and also provided a platform for*

identifying disagreement amongst the staff and the resolution of it, which was useful in school planning.

Conducting an SSE requires the school to collect, discuss and evaluate the evidence that is related to the achievement of the major concerns listed in the school plans. Before the practice of SSE was introduced, many teachers often had no opinions about the school policies and performance, and, even if they did, they did not dare to express their opinions during school meetings. The school now encourages them to express their concerns and opinions by a series of SSE meetings during which opinions from various channels can be collected to improve the communication and consultation among the staff. These meetings gradually became the major channel of communication to encourage teacher participation, to improve their decision making and in turn to transmit the benefits to the student learning process. One example that illustrates how this improved communication resulting from the SSE can improve teaching and learning is a proposal submitted to the principal by the Department of English to streamline the assessment arrangements:

> *In the past, there were mid-term and final exams in each semester for primary 1–3 students, and the teachers of the Department of English proposed to replace the mid-term exam with a formative assessment. That was a bold proposal that was based on their thorough understanding of the students' learning pattern, the school's development direction and considerations of resources.*

Following the introduction of this system, the communication between the principal and the Department of English has been enhanced; the department often finds new ideas to bring up to the principal. Similarly, more ideas were received from the teachers of different subjects once the channels for collecting opinions increased. This indicated that they had become more eager to present innovative ideas as a result of the enhancement of their knowledge, leadership and resources:

> *After co-ordinating their opinions, the head of the Department of English and the native English teacher would come to the principal's office and make suggestions on teaching and learning, and they would then relay the ideas, together with my feedback, to their panel for discussion. The panel chair would then further discuss with me; this is just the way the English team communicates with me.*

ESR Provides the Direction for Strategic Planning

The ESR report recommended to the school that it formulate a detailed development plan to enhance student self-learning ability. Although Small Class Teaching (SCT) was prioritized as a major concern in the triennium

328   Eric Chi-Keung Cheng and John Chi-Kin Lee

school development plan, the ESR report commented that the school should also state concretely and specifically what were the strategies for each year to deal with this major concern. The principal made the following responses:

> I understand the intention of the ESR recommendations. However, in drawing up such detailed plans, there were difficulties in clearly distinguishing the procedures step by step, as three years is quite a long period for changing the school's internal and external environment.
>
> We also have to consider the situation of the school when revising the plan. In the past, our school focused on the development of generic skills in the students. This is a big challenge for many schools, and the EDB did recognize our efforts and the performance of our students. On the other hand, they recommended that we develop the self-learning skills of students, which is an even more challenging task, especially for junior grade students, and it requires much help from the teachers. However, it's good that we have a new and a more challenging mission to strive for.

Standardization Overrides Contextualization

It is essential to consider the school background and context when interpreting the data and comments reflected in the SSE report in order to have a fact-based authentic ESR report. In the course of preparing for the ESR and drafting the SSE report, the ESR officials recommended that the school follow the template provided by them and that they remove all the routine items and include only the items of major concern. However, the routine items in fact reflected the effective pedagogical practices that were based on past successful experience and that helped the school to deal with the major concerns raised in the school development plan. These routine items provided the background information on what was being done in the school. They should also be taken as evidence that supports the school's achievements. If the data and figures collected for evaluation are interpreted without taking into consideration the overall school background and the reasons underlying the routine items, the ESR report would not be in a position to support the planned school development and may even create confusion. The principal gave the following three examples to illustrate the importance of considering the school background:

> For example, some improvement plans require an in-depth investigation into the school context rather than just simply looking at the scores to make a judgement. For example, on some items we scored 4 in the stakeholder survey, like 'parents' perception of the school'. So what else can be done for improvement on this item? It's already

The Effectiveness of the Quality Assurance Mechanism   329

so high that nothing else can be done to achieve an even higher score. However, if you talk to some parents a lot of different opinions could be collected for the plan. Another example was that the score for 'teachers' self-perception of their performance' was also high. However, it's very normal for teachers to score themselves high, no matter what their actual performances were. Does this mean there is no need for me to follow up on this item? Absolutely not. The last example is that we scored low on 'students' self-perception of their performance'. This was due to the fact that few of our students got high grades in test and examinations as our standard is very high. Again, it's normal for them to grade themselves low.

These three examples show that although these figures provided a reference for the school management to understand the school's situation, it cannot give them the whole story of what is happening in the school. Therefore, the ESR should take into account a school's background when referring to the data and figures, and seek more information from other sources, in order to make a subjective and observational analysis.

A Secondary School Case

The selected secondary school has been operating since 1998. It now has 28 classes, around 1,000 students and 72 teachers. In the first ESR, The school scored three to four points for most of the items. The teachers were satisfied with the results and therefore kept to the same practices in their teaching. In the second ESR, there were no statistics presented or specific comments about the school's performance. But the summary of the holistic performance of the school showed that it had not made much improvement, except in the area of National Education in which there was a great improvement. In general, the school performed very well in the area of Organizational Management (graded 4) and performed well in the areas of teaching and learning (graded 3). For Student Support, the school still needed to work on ways to reinforce the students' self-learning skills and confidence. Since the school had a good starting point, and the performance in every aspect was not bad, the ESR did not put much pressure on the school as the school could easily met the basic requirements of the ESR. However, new ideas may be needed if it is to achieve 'excellent' performance.

SSE Enhances Co-Ordination and Collegiality among Departments

Before the implementation of QA (ESR), each subject department would have their own ways of teaching students to achieve good performances. Co-ordination between departments seldom occurred and the single simple mission of the school was to teach students to enable them to achieve higher grades. But now it has changed. For each ESR, the school is required to

330   Eric Chi-Keung Cheng and John Chi-Kin Lee

conduct an SSE and formulate a three-year plan. All subject departments and committees have to work together to respond to the areas of concern. Co-ordination between the subject departments and committees was strengthened as a result. The ESR also aligned the senior management of the school and the subject departments in both a structural alignment and a functional alignment. The cohesion and level of participation in shared decision making by the middle management was also strengthened. The principal made the following comments:

> One of our major concerns was to solve the problem of learning differences, so all subject departments and committees worked together towards this goal. This had a positive influence on our team spirit and teamwork building. In the coming triennium, the mission of our school will be to cultivate peer lesson observation. In the past, lesson observation would only be conducted by peers within the same subject area. But now we are promoting inter-subject lesson observation by implementing co-operative learning as the teaching strategy. Therefore, all subject teams now share a common goal and concept and this is good for the school.
>
> When a major concern is raised by the senior management, all subject departments worked towards overcoming that major concern, and this is shown in their respective subject department proposals. This also means that the central and individual subjects are aligned structurally. Once a major concern is raised, it must be discussed in staff meetings. Though not all staff would be involved in the discussion, at least those at the management level would discuss plans on how to deal with the major concern. In the past, major concerns might be different across subject areas. But now, to deal with a central major concern, at least those subjects in the same stream, say the Science stream, or the Arts stream, would discuss the common major concern together. This reflects the functional alignment and the increase in communication resulting from the SSE/ESR.

SSE Enhances Planning Capacity

The planning capacity of the school improved after the implementation of the QA mechanism. In the past, the subject plans and agenda items of subject meetings were mainly drafted with reference to those of the previous years. After the implementation of ESR/SSE, the plan was formulated according to the students' needs and the evaluation of the items in the previous years. The teachers began to conduct surveys to collect data. In addition to using the surveys provided by the EDB, the individual subject teams would also design their own surveys. In this way the data collected could also be used for school development. Through this data-driven reflection process, the planning competence of the teachers was improved. The principal made the following comment:

Firstly, 'reflection' of the past year's performance provided an important insight for use in drafting the upcoming subject plan. The reflection was not only subject-based but also whole-school-based. Therefore, the subject plans and evaluations were drafted according to the needs of the students and the development of the society. Secondly, with the implementation of the different indicators of the QA mechanism, like HKAT for S1, TSA for S3 and performance indicators for S6–S7, the different subject teams had to draft subject plans in response to those evaluation items.

ESR Provides the Direction for School Improvement

The comments from the two ESRs were generally positive and reflected the situation of the school, and the school agreed with the recommendations in the report. In the current three-year plan, they are focusing on improving the areas of concern raised in the reports, and they are tackling the problem of learning differences. Since their students ranged from band 1 to band 3, and not all teachers know how to accommodate students from different bands, it was suggested that more time be taken to tackle learning differences. The ESR reports also commented that the teachers did not have the skills needed to ask questions that provoked higher-order thinking among the students. The principal made the following comment:

In general, the ESR report showed that we have no problems in organizational management, and we also scored 6 or above on many value-added indicators. What was suggested was that the teachers' questioning skills be strengthened to enable them to ask higher-order-thinking questions and learn to deal with learning differences effectively. To improve this area, our three-year plan focused on teacher development on the above two items, such as training on questioning skills to stimulate higher-order thinking, promoting the teaching of co-operative learning, and adjusting the curriculum and assessment mechanism for junior grades in order to address the problem of learning differences.

Since most of the students are drawn from the northern, more rural, area, their confidence and higher-order thinking are also areas that need improvement. In order to enhance the students' confidence, more work was done on enhancing the students' personal growth and more programmes were run by the career planning unit. The three-year school plan was drafted to take into account the comments of the ESRs, which dealt with concerns that had already been spotted by the school. In this way, the ESR reinforced what the school had observed and this reduced any resistance to enforcing the school policy for improvement:

332   Eric Chi-Keung Cheng and John Chi-Kin Lee

Teachers might not be willing to accept training or to implement co-operative learning if the current situation shows no obvious evidence of problems in student learning and student conduct. Therefore, the findings from the SSE, ESR or other student surveys provided support and were a driving force for improvement.

Generality Overrides Individuality

It is essential to provide comments and suggestions to individual teachers on ways to improve their teaching skills, in addition to providing overall feedback and comments to the school management in the performance domain of teaching and learning. The existing ESR practices for class observation do not involve a post-lesson conference to provide comments and suggestions to the teachers being observed. The inspectors are simply asked to grade each of the performance items on the lesson observation form and then submit the forms, which are used to calculate the overall performance of the school in the teaching and learning domain. On the other hand, comments on the school performance on management and organization, student support and student achievement will be fed back to the principal and senior teachers through some meetings. This failure to hold post-lesson observation dialogues with individual teachers represents a lost opportunity to enhance their professional development. Therefore, it is not surprising that the teaching and learning domain has been reported as the worst performing domain ever since the publication of the first QA report. Since the class observation occupies most of the ESR time in the school, it would be more effective if the inspectors were to dialogue with individual teachers in a post-lesson conference and in this way support their professional growth. The principal commented:

We were only given figures, like the mean scores of all schools and our scores as feedback. However, the absence of discussion following class observations did not help in developing the teachers' professionalism. The inspectors only provided a written or spoken comment in which they say or write something very basic, based on limited facts, that is partly or sometimes true, but not always. They generalize, so using such statements is not beneficial for individual teachers. We cannot use their statements to identify problems and advise the teacher for follow-up support. We were given some general comments like 'a lack of higher-order thinking' and 'room for improvement in accommodating learning differences'. However, 'who' was the one lacking higher-order thinking? Without knowing who that was, the teacher who lacked higher-order thinking might think that s/he is already performing well in this respect and would never know s/he had problems. A scoring with general comments and communication without dialogues cannot help in developing the professionalism of teachers; so it was a waste of time and resources were wasted.

The Effectiveness of the Quality Assurance Mechanism   333

Schools which used to be rated 'good' might already be aware of their own problems even without an ESR. For example, they may like to know what else can be done to perform even better on good items such as 'management and organization'. Just listing the good items and the problems without giving in-depth feedback from the experts from the ESR does not contribute to the professional development of teachers. Putting too much stress on scoring, giving feedback without discussion and dialogue, and failure to tackle specific problems are all major obstacles that prevent the ESR from enhancing the education system in Hong Kong to the 'excellent' standard. If no improvement is made to the ESR feedback loop mechanism, it will not contribute to enhancing the teachers' professional development.

What Next for the ESR?

Enhancing the Developmental Function of the ESR

Too much stress on scoring without a good feedback loop is the main drawback of the ESR. Finding a balance between accountability and development is critical for school sustainability. The principal of the secondary school recommended that the EDB should enhance the developmental function of the ESR by requiring more specific comments and feedback to individual teachers. This could improve the school performance especially in the teaching and learning domain:

> Currently, for almost 90% of the schools ranked around 3 in the ESR, and the schools which are graded especially low, like 2, the ESR team could focus on diagnosing their weakest areas, rather than covering all areas, with a view to making the improvement more specific. For schools with good performance in general, the ESR could advise them to identify one area in which they could strive for 'excellence'—that is, the best in Hong Kong. This is what is really meant by 'supporting' a school, namely, to reinforce their strengths and improve their weaknesses, and not merely 'scoring'.

Continuity and the Need to Be More Specific and Focused

Following the two completed cycles of ESR, the EDB is very well aware of the performance of a school. Currently, the ESR reviews the school in all its aspects, and this is time-consuming. The secondary school principal suggested that in the future the focus of the evaluation should be specific and focused:

> If a school reports that their students lack confidence and self-directed learning skills, the ESR team could then observe and analyze the causes of the problems, give advice to the school on how to improve

334 Eric Chi-Keung Cheng and John Chi-Kin Lee

the situation and arrange to revisit the school after three years for evaluation. The same could be done on subject-specific problems, for example, by analyzing the reasons for the low standard of the students in English, give them advice on improvement and then revisit them after three years for evaluation. By concentrating on a small area of specific weakness, the school can concentrate on it and be motivated to improve it. Such specific weaknesses could also be identified as areas of concern in the school plan for improvement. The current ESR gave us few comments on how to deal with the areas of concern in the school plan.

IMPLICATIONS

To summarize the case study findings, it seems that both the SSE and the ESR contribute to school improvement in the area of school management and organization. The SSE enhances communication, collegiality, co-ordination and planning capacity. This finding is similar to Macbeath's (2008) study that an SSE creates collaboration within schools and enhances a sense of team spirit. The SSE is a management process that involves teacher participation in decision making and planning, communication and co-ordination to prepare for the ESR. Another finding is that the ESR indicates the directions for school planning. However, in spite of the emphasis in the second ESR cycle on school specific and focused characteristics, both of the case study schools in this chapter still consider that it is over-standardized and should be more specific and focused. Table 19.2 provides a summary of the findings from both cases.

The case studies reveal that the effects of an SSE on school improvement are notably greater than those contributed by an ESR, but without an ESR to monitor the SSE process and to endorse the direction of development, schools may not be eager to conduct an SSE for development planning and the power of the SSE will be limited. Because SSE and ESR have been adopted in Hong Kong as a QA model and complement each other (Macbeath 2008; Whitby, 2010) they are mutually dependent as means of supporting school development in Hong Kong. The coupling relationship between the SSE and the ESR could be explained by the theory of a loose-tight coupling in terms of professional accountability and state accountability. If the professional accountability of the schools in Hong Kong is strong enough to sustain the SSE for school development, the state accountability in the form of an ESR to exert an influence on the school system could be reduced. Therefore, it is critical to identify the point of balance between professional accountability and state accountability if the aim is to optimize school improvement.

The theory of a loose-tight coupling of internal and external reviews may provide insights for government officials, policymakers and educators

The Effectiveness of the Quality Assurance Mechanism 335

Table 19.2   Summary of the Findings from the Case Studies

	Primary School Case	*Secondary School Case*
SSE	• Enhances school management capacity • Improves communication and collegiality • Enhances planning capacity	• Enhances co-ordination and collegiality amongst departments
ESR	• Provides direction for strategic planning	• Provides direction for school improvement
Comments on ESR	• Standardization overrides contextualization	• Generality overrides individuality • Should be more specific and focused

for the formulation of a policy to maximize school improvement. Schools are now increasingly expected to assume part of the responsibility for the development and guaranteeing of educational quality and are required to undertake self-evaluation. For this, they should be given more space to conduct their own school policy. In addition, the ESR has only limited power to maintain a school at a good quality level and to identify areas of concern since improvement of a school depends on the willingness and initiative of teachers. Regarding the accountability of the QA mechanism, the ESR can respond to the state accountability by ensuring that the performance of a school reaches a 'good' standard. However, anything above 'good' depends on the professionalism of the teachers. Those subject teams which produce an 'excellent' performance are reinforced by their own professionalism and self-evaluation, and they would still work towards 'excellent' even if there were no ESR. This reflects the professional accountability of the teachers, who are not driven by considerations of state accountability alone.

CONCLUSION

The impact of the QA mechanisms in Hong Kong on school improvement is promising. The two case studies indicate that institutionalizing a SSE mechanism within a school can enhance the capacity of the school management. They both report better communication and collegiality, co-ordination between departments and planning capacity as a result of SSE. The significance of the ESR of the QA mechanism in Hong Kong is its power to reinforce the self-evaluation capacity for school improvement. Providing more training for teachers on how to conduct SSE is recommended if the policymakers really want to improve school education using the QA model.

336   Eric Chi-Keung Cheng and John Chi-Kin Lee

If SSE is embedded into the strategic planning process, the capacity of the school management to achieve the school objectives for sustainable development could be enhanced.

REFERENCES

Ainley, J., Reed, R., & Miller, H. (1986). *School organization and the quality of schooling*, ACER Research Monograph, 29. Hawthorn, Vic: Australian Council for Educational Research.

Akpe, C., & Afemikhe, O. (1991). School Self-Evaluation: An examination of the state of the art in Nigeria. *Studies in Educational Evaluation, 17*, 117–127.

Cheng, E.C.K. (2011). An examination of the predictive relationships of self-evaluation capacity and staff competency on strategic planning in Hong Kong aided secondary schools. *Education Research for Policy and Practice, 10(3)*, 211–223.

Croxford, L., Grek, S., & Shaik, F. (2009). Quality assurance and evaluation (QAE) in Scotland: Promoting self-evaluation within and beyond the country. *Special Issue of Journal of Education Policy, 24(2)*, 179–193.

Davies, D., & Rudd, P. (2001). *Evaluating School Self-Evaluation: LGA educational research Programme*. London: Local Government Association.

Education and Manpower Branch & Education Department (1991). *The school management initiative—setting the framework for quality in Hong Kong schools*. Hong Kong: Government Printer.

Education Commission (1997). *No. 7 Report: Quality school education*. Hong Kong: Government Printer.

Education Commission (1999). *Review of education system—framework for educational reform: Learning for life (consultation document)*. Hong Kong: Government Printer.

Education Commission (2000). *Review of education system-reform proposals (consultation document)*. Hong Kong: Government Printer.

Fennell, H.A. (1994). Organizational linkage expanding the existing metaphor. *Journal of Educational Administration, 32(1)*, 23–33.

Fitz-Gibbon, C. (1996). *Monitoring school effectiveness: Simplicity and complexity*. In J. Gray, D. Reynolds, C. Fitz-Gibbon & D. Jesson (Eds.) *Merging traditions: The future of research on school effectiveness and school improvement* (pp.74–90). London: Cassell.

Gurr, D. (2007). Diversity and progress in school accountability systems in Australia. *Educational Research for Policy and Practice, 6(3)*, 165–186.

Lee, J.C.K. (2009). Educational evaluation in Hong Kong: Status and challenges. In S.S. Peng & J.C.K. Lee (Eds.) *Educational evaluation in East Asia: Emerging issues and challenges* (pp.61–71). New York: Nova Science Publishers.

Macbeath. J. (2008). *The impact study on the effectiveness of External School Review in enhancing school improvement through School Self-Evaluation in Hong Kong*. Retrieved 13 January 2013, from http://www.edb.gov.hk/FileManager/EN/Content_6467/final_report_of_impact_study_english_0708.pdf.

Ng, P.T. (2010). The evolution and nature of school accountability in the Singapore education system. *Educational Assessment, Evaluation and Accountability, 22(4)*, 275–292.

Ngan, M.Y., Lee, J.C.K., & Brown, G.T.L. (2010). Hong Kong principals' perceptions on changes in evaluation and assessment policies: They're not for learning. *Asia Journal of Educational Research and Synergy, 2(1)*, 36–46.

Pitiyanuwat, S. (2007). School assessment in Thailand: Roles and achievement of ONESQA. *Educational Research for Policy and Practice, 6(3)*, 261–279.

The Effectiveness of the Quality Assurance Mechanism 337

Sakura, F. (2007). School monitoring and quality assurance in the New Zealand school system. *Educational Research for Policy and Practice, 6(3)*, 229–234.

Van Petegem, P. (1998). *Forming school policy: Effective school research as an inspiration for School Self-Evaluation.* Belgium: Leuven ACCO.

Weick, K.E. (1976). Educational organizations as loosely coupled systems. *Administrative Science Quarterly, 21*, 1–19.

Weick, K.E. (1982). Administering education in loosely coupled schools. *Phi Delta Kappen, 63*, 673–676.

Whitby, K. (2010). *School inspection: Recent experiences in high performing education systems.* Reading, United Kingdom: CfBT Education Trust and NFER. Retrieved 13 January 2013, from http://www.cfbt.com/evidenceforeducation/pdf/schoolinspections2.pdf.

20 Curriculum and Teaching Reforms
Challenges and Prospects

John Chi-Kin Lee

TRENDS AND CONTEXTS OF CURRICULUM AND TEACHING REFORMS IN HONG KONG

The previous chapters have offered discussions on issues related to educational reforms in Hong Kong as one of Asia's high-performing education system. After the introduction of more than ten years' curriculum and teaching reforms in Hong Kong, what can we learn from the experience? Based on the literature review and insights from previous chapters, challenges and potentials of curriculum reforms are identified and discussed. Since the end of the 1990s, the government has encouraged the creation of curriculum space through some priority tasks, such as "trimming and restructuring the curriculum", "reducing excessive tests, examinations and dictations" (Curriculum Development Council [CDC], 2001, pp.6–7). In addition, the government has advised the promotion of four key tasks (moral and civic education, reading, project learning and using information technology) as vehicles for curriculum reforms; emphasis of students' mastery of "basic competencies in Chinese, English and Numeracy", as well as the cultivation of nine generic skills and priority be given to "critical thinking, creativity, and communication skills" (CDC, 2001, pp.6–7).

Chan, Kennedy and Fok (2008) remark that Hong Kong tends to adopt both "hard policies" and "soft policies" in curriculum policy implementation. 'Hard' policy instruments usually refer to regulations and rigid directives that are formal requirements and tend to be characterized by centralized control. 'Soft' policy instruments are exemplified by guidelines or professional development opportunities and tend to highlight process, flexibility and context (Fok, Kennedy and Chan, 2010, p.3). During the colonial period in Hong Kong, there was a dominance of 'hard policies' when teachers tended to be technicians, implementing mandated syllabuses and adopting officially approved instructional materials. With gradual decentralization and encouragement of school-based curriculum development (SBCD), Hong Kong authorities have tended to adopt 'soft policies' since the new century such as the use of government guidelines (e.g., CDC, 2001), the recommended textbooks and the adoption of school-based curriculum in which teachers are expected to assume an expanded role of being "professionals, academic(s) and leaders at classroom level, collaborative partners at school and community levels" (Chan, Kennedy and Fok, 2008, p.149). Such a drastic shift from using 'hard' policy instruments to adopting 'soft' policy instruments has generated challenges for curriculum reform and its success hinges on teachers' professional identity and competence to serve as professional practitioners in Hong Kong community (Chan, Kennedy and Fok, 2008). Nonetheless, the government still employs 'hard' policies or measures such as Territory-Wide System Assessment (TSA) and school-based assessment (SBA) as well as School Self-Evaluation (SSE) and External School Review (ESR), which are seen as sources of teachers' increasing workloads and pressure. Schools with a small number of classes are particularly under threat of closure when there has been a continuous decline in school population. Apart from the impact of declining population and policies calling for accountability, the school sector seemed to be affected by performativity and inter-school competition. Using project learning as an example, even 'soft' policies or measures such as application for Quality Education Fund (QEF) funding and sharing and provision of curriculum resources might be interpreted as instruments that "encouraged competitions for funding and performances among schools" (Fok, Kennedy and Chan, 2010, p.9). While the curriculum reform in Hong Kong has achieved substantial success, Yeung, in Chapter 4 of this volume, calls for a reconceptualization of curriculum ideologies which may emphasize a social reconstructionist approach in combination with features of critical pedagogy. On the other hand, the city state's role in curriculum policy making remains strong despite the fact that curriculum development in Hong Kong has not only been shaped by globalization but also affected by political and socio-economic factors in local settings. Lee and Gopinathan (2012, p.63) remarked that "in Hong Kong, there has been a need to put more emphasis on making students more patriotic and become more familiar with the political, economic and social developments of China and the relationship between China and Hong Kong". However, there has been resistance in the implementation of the proposed Moral and National Education (MNE) curriculum. Kennedy and Kuang, in Chapter 7 of this volume, analyze the issues of national identity and patriotism in Hong Kong's educational reform. They point out a possible 'soft' approach that integrates ideas of national identity into formal, informal and non-formal curriculum experiences for students.

Barber, Donnelly and Rizvi (2012) refer to the examples of Korea, Singapore, Shanghai and Hong Kong in the Pacific Asian systems and highlight the high values attached to the teaching profession and quality of teacher creating "a virtuous cycle with families" in these systems (p.44). For Hong Kong, like other Pacific Asian systems, the government has adopted a long-term technocratic and strategic approach to educational improvement, but "to Michael [Barber], looking at this approach to reform back in the year

340 John Chi-Kin Lee

2000, it seemed painfully slow, but as a means of taking a high-performing system and making it better still, it has proved to be exemplary . . . The necessary change is now happening in every classroom, and affecting every teacher and student in Hong Kong rather than remaining simply as words in a policy document, as so often happens with reform in other countries" (p.46).

The outstanding results of the Programme for International Assessment (PISA) in Hong Kong and/or the commendations of the Hong Kong education system in some international consultancy reports could have been influenced by the socio-cultural context, which is partly related to the Confucian Heritage Culture (CHC) and the long history of competition through Imperial examination (Barber, Donnelly and Rizvi, 2012). Lam (2011, p.24) elaborates succinctly:

> Chinese education is commonly seen as relying solely on rote learning with little understanding . . . This can be seen as a result of the overemphasis on studying for examinations and the high level of compliance to authorities demanded by the Chinese culture . . . Teachers often 'teach for the test' and concentrate on drilling students to attain the best results for entry to universities.

During the late 1990s when the Accelerated Schools Project (ASP) was introduced to Hong Kong, Levin (2004, pp.48–49), the founder of the ASP, remarked:

> Perhaps the most important cultural factor operating against change and risk-taking at the school site is the importance that Hong Kong authorities and parents place on examination rankings. Even if the Hong Kong government broadens its own assessment of schools, the memorization-examination process is so deeply embedded in Hong Kong education and Chinese history that school culture may be unwilling to yield its importance, even it is modified by official policy.

As regards the influence of examinations on teaching and learning, Hong Kong has been promoting Assessment for Learning (AfL) and some achievements have been made in connection with the implementation of Target Oriented Curriculum (TOC), the Basic Competency Assessment (BCA) and SBA (Berry, 2011). Nonetheless, assessment tends to be perceived as relatively high stakes, and many schools in Hong Kong still adopt traditional assessment practices. Berry, in Chapter 15 of this volume, suggests that both the content or hardware aspects such as models, frameworks and guidelines in connection with AfL would be essential, while the process or software aspect involving teachers' empowerment with support from the educational contexts is equally important. Yan, in Chapter 16 of this volume, proposes that to enhance future implementation of SBA, in addition to teacher training and support, more attention should be given to the

Curriculum and Teaching Reforms 341

development of common assessment criteria and performance standards as well as moderation. Moreover, Hui, in Chapter 17 of this volume, promotes the notion of authenticity as the key to assessment both as a measuring device and as a process of learning. There is also a call for new forms of assessment that address not only knowledge but also thinking, leadership and ethics (Barber, Donnelly and Rizvi, 2012, p.57).

On the other hand, under the influence of CHC, hard work and efforts are valued (Lee and Dimmock, 1998). In a recent review of the National Curriculum in the United Kingdom, the expert panel made reference to examples of some high-performing countries/places, including Hong Kong, and remarked, "Meanwhile, Hong Kong uses within-school rank ordering vigorously but, as with South Korea and Singapore, also operates with a curriculum model focusing on 'fewer things in greater depth' which all pupils are expected to attain. They also emphasise effort rather than ability" (Department for Education, 2011, p.46).

IMPLEMENTATION OF CURRICULUM AND TEACHING REFORMS

As remarked by Marsh (2009, p.170), "Despite the enthusiasm that can be generated by new reforms it is important to remember that making reform proposals is only part of the process and that there are many problems in getting reforms implemented".

For assessing implementation of curriculum and teaching reforms, success or failure often hinge on criteria such as effectiveness (e.g., students' learning outcomes), popularity or spread and survival or longevity of innovation as well as the perspectives of implementation (fidelity versus mutual adaptation) (Cuban, 1998; Lee, 2006). For the curriculum reform in Hong Kong, the mid-term report issued by the Education Bureau (EDB) (2008), as well as the study by Yuen, Cheung and Wong (2012), reveals positive effects and outcomes. Nonetheless, their findings advise that more professional training in the areas of fostering students' critical thinking skills, managing student diversity and handling assessment could be provided to teachers (Yuen, Cheung and Wong, 2012, p.724) and the development of validated instrument of assessment that could be used in schools was needed (p.725).

As regards popularity of the reform, while the media is included in the reform process to enhance "perception management" (Organisation for Economic Co-operation and Development [OECD], 2011, p.104), there was a local resistance or grievances against both the process and outcomes of the educational reforms (Hallinger, 2010, p.404; Cheng and Walker, 2008).

The government tends to facilitate a mutual adaptation approach of curriculum implementation through 'soft' policy instruments about which the OECD (2011, p.104) asserts that "with the pulling force of the public and university entrance exams, schools have developed rather diverse approaches to implementing the reform. Nonetheless, because of the change

342 John Chi-Kin Lee

led by the reform, schools across the board have developed their own mechanisms of collective decision making and division of labour which respect their individual school cultures". School practitioners are encouraged to develop their school-based curriculum. Nonetheless, Marsh, Morris and Lo, in Chapter 3 of this volume, suggest that SBCD might still take time for the central government and local schools to enact a transaction approach which embraces negotiation and promotes teacher professionalism.

In Hong Kong, there are substantial experiences on school–university partnerships that facilitate schools wishing to, or being encouraged to, undertake curriculum and teaching changes. For example, a team of researchers led by Mun-ling Lo (2009) at the Hong Kong Institute of Education adopts Ference Marton's theory of variation (Marton and Booth, 1997) in a number of projects designed to help teachers plan lessons for better teaching and learning. Teams of school development officers and researchers at the Chinese University of Hong Kong have also undertaken a number of large-scale school improvement and curriculum development projects that promoted a whole-school approach to school improvement (e.g., Chiu and Mak, 2011; Lo and Ho, 2010) and an action-research approach to curriculum development (e.g., Lee, 2006, 2010a, 2010b).

Successful implementation of curriculum and teaching reforms across different parts of the world has never been easy. Since 2000, there have been critical comments on the pace of reform in Hong Kong and other challenging issues, such as "the problem of designing curriculum targets, the implementation of curriculum integration, school-based curriculum development, and the resource support for curriculum reform" (Lam, 2001, p.131). In addition, three major limitations on curriculum reform in Hong Kong are addressed by Fok and Ip (2010): the excessively large scale of the reform-generating difficulties in co-ordination; heavy teacher workloads; and the backwash effect of the examination culture. Chan and Fok, in Chapter 13 of this volume, highlight the challenges of implementing project learning as one of the four key tasks in curriculum reform: subject-trained teachers having difficulty coping with cross-disciplinary project learning; a lack of appropriate professional training; a lack of teaching resources; and heavy workload for teachers. Moreover, the findings of another study suggest that increasing student diversity, partially associated with the inclusive education policy, is perceived as a hindering factor to successful implementation of the curriculum reform (Cheung and Wong, 2012). Leung, in Chapter 5 of this volume, summarizes critical teacher concerns, such as having diversified interpretations of the key initiatives of the curriculum reform, being uncertain about managing their multiple roles in curriculum implementation, lacking teacher collaboration in some schools, having limited resources and expressing varied concerns on school-based professional development. Taking the teaching of critical thinking skills in a secondary school as an example, despite the success of the project, teachers found it was not so easy "to break away from their old habit of a teacher-centered way of teaching . . . Additionally, there was a great constraint of time and resources" (Fok, 2002, p.90). This raises a call for teacher education programmes to consider enhancing thinking and meta-cognitive skills for student-teachers' learning. In a similar vein, Lam, in Chapter 6 of this volume, advocates, in the case of Liberal Studies, the teacher education programme to incorporate elements of "self-reflexivity, collaborative and dialogical examination of worldviews and critical discourse" (p. 96). Reduction of class size to facilitate teacher–student and student–student interactions has been advocated to address the pressing problem of catering for student diversity. Lai, Chan and Lee, in Chapter 9 of this volume, argue that successful implementation of Small Class Teaching (SCT) necessitates a school-based policy of SCT that highlights principal leadership, curriculum leadership, teacher leadership and student leadership, as well as support from various stakeholders.

While this book attempts to cover many pertinent topics in curriculum and teaching reforms, the chapters are no means exhaustive. There have been some discussions on how to sustain educational innovations and how to nurture more creative talents in the educational system in Hong Kong as a knowledge-based society. van Damme (2012) suggests that education systems should cultivate three types of individual skills for innovation-driven societies: technical skills including know-what and know-how; behavioural and social skills comprising self-confidence, energy, perseverance, passion, leadership, collaboration and communication; and skills in thinking and creativity, such as critical thinking, capability to make connections, curiosity and imagination. Nonetheless, this is easier said than done. Based on Carless's (2013) analysis of innovation in language teaching and learning, there are teacher-related, system-related and school-related barriers and facilitating conditions. It is essential to ensure the organizational and support conditions conducive to innovations, which are cultural contexts and celebrations of early, small-scale success based on less ambitious targets, as well as an emphasis of teachers' ownership of changes and inclusion of change management strategies. In addition, there may be potentials for using information and communication technologies for implementing creative classrooms and promoting students' creative learning. Innovation of assessment for students' creativity and building up a public vision of education of all creative talents in a knowledge-based society with due regard to quality and equality could also be possible levers of future reform. These suggestions partly echo the third wave of educational reforms, which highlight students' "contextualized multiple intelligences (CMI)—triplized Learning" and involve features such as self-actualization, how to learn, networked and world-class learning and so on (Cheng, 2011, p.262).

ADDRESSING ISSUES AND PROSPECTS OF CURRICULUM AND TEACHING REFORMS

For future curriculum development, a number of major and interrelated suggestions are presented below. Firstly, based on past experiences and

344   John Chi-Kin Lee

the incident of shelving MNE curriculum guides (primary 1 to secondary 6), it is sensible to gauge teachers' and even public receptivity to existing and future curriculum and teaching reforms and to teachers' emotions and fears as they engage in implementing reforms (Lee, 2000; CDC, 2012). As regards receptivity to change, Hallinger (2010, p.413) pointed out that in Asian societies with a large power distance, there was a tendency to have passive or superficial receptivity change because of respect for authority but a possible lack of engagement and translation into classroom and school practices. It is also notable that even within and across schools, there could be different levels of receptivity to curriculum reforms. While a study in Hong Kong reveals that local school heads' and teachers' agreement with and support for curriculum reform tend to reflect good progress in the reform items on teaching and learning (Cheung and Wong, 2011), different views on various aspects of the reform are found between senior management and front-line teachers in primary and secondary schools, suggesting the need to enhance communication and collaboration among curriculum leaders (CLs), teachers and school heads (Cheung and Wong, 2012).

The second suggestion is to enhance trust building and foster partnerships not only between groups and individuals at various levels but also between various influential stakeholders in the education sector. For trust, we need to respect the professional judgement of school leaders and teachers. Lam, in Chapter 18 of this volume, argues that while the establishment of a quality assurance (QA) system and SSE culture have boosted the implementation of curriculum reform initiatives, it may be desirable to place more emphasis on SSE and teachers' professional judgement rather than external reviews. Cheng and Lee, in Chapter 19 of this volume, echo that for schools to move from good to excellent, it depends mainly on the professional accountability of teachers rather than the state accountability through ESR. As regards partnership within schools, Chow, in Chapter 14 of this volume, refers to the example of English Language and suggests that the success of medium of instruction (MOI) and Language across the Curriculum (LAC) policies hinges on transformation of academic cultures and practices through partnership and interdisciplinary collaboration at different levels, as well as continuous professional development of teachers.

For partnership between various key stakeholders, Law, in Chapter 12 of this volume, points to the importance of school–university partnership for SBCD as university faculties could be able to provide stimulation, advice and support for school practitioners, while schools need to provide an infrastructure that fosters pedagogical innovations and teacher learning conducive to student learning. Stewart (2012, pp.166–168) advocates an international partnership for school education and proposes a "partnership development matrix for interactions with Chinese schools" with the involvement of leaders, faculty and students in which technology is used to enhance connection.

As regards parental involvement, the findings of two case study schools by Ng (2011) reveal that there appears to have been teacher Balkanization and the success of change depends on school leaders' personal beliefs to support parental involvement and provide professional development for teachers.

The third suggestion is to pay more attention to student voice, which has been an increasingly important agenda in educational policy and research. While there are diverse definitions and understanding of student voice, student voice is often associated with notions of student participation, active citizenship, youth leadership, youth empowerment and youth–adult partnership (Mitra, 2009, p.819). There are many ways that student voice can contribute to educational change: "students as *data sources*, as *collaborators in learning communities*, and as *co-leaders of change efforts*" (Mitra, 2009, p.821; original emphasis). A study of student voice in an educational centre in Hong Kong shows that there are differences between teachers' and students' perceptions of student voice, and teachers might have different attitudes towards the promotion of student voice (Cheng, 2012). Cheng (2012, p.363) argues from a cultural perspective that Confucius "valued student voice, using open dialogue to enable his students to share their views with their teacher". This is noteworthy for Hong Kong, and the government and other stakeholders listening to student voices has the potential to improve curriculum development.

The fourth suggestion is that for sustaining reforms, it is imperative to conserve the heritage and preserve the merits in the educational system (Hargreaves and Fink, 2006). Under the context of curriculum reform, where many ideas and concepts originated from the Western world, a serious question about whether there should be a complete paradigmatic change from the traditional Chinese pedagogical practices that emphasize lecturing rote learning to progressive pedagogy and student-centred learning is raised. Or could there be a preservation of the merits and essence of Chinese pedagogy and exploration of ways of assimilating with those Western approaches to teaching and learning after careful evaluation of its desirability and feasibility in a Chinese context? From a practical perspective, any attempts towards blending of Western and Chinese approaches should take into account the deep-seated influence of the Chinese traditional examination and competitive culture. This is in line with the remarks made by Ryan (2011, pp.3–4): "The reforms are overlaid on conventional teaching and learning practices in ways that sometimes make for 'hybrid' models that draw from Western models but have 'Chinese characteristics', or at other times in ways that can cause tensions and challenges, especially in relation to 'student-centred' versus 'teacher-centred' classroom".

Marton (2000, p.288) also reminds us not to discard but to enhance the pedagogy practiced in Hong Kong as it "is surely an offspring of Chinese pedagogy, the oldest and maybe the most efficient pedagogy (in its more advanced forms) of which we know". One study shows that as long as teacher beliefs and practices as well as student participation allow it, there can be the potential of co-existence of teacher beliefs sharing a combination of preparation for examination and knowledge-building enquiry

346 John Chi-Kin Lee

as well as an integration of cognitive enquiry and values formation, and students' transformed adaptation of their learning by combining memorization and understanding as well as individual and collaborative learning (Chan, 2009).

Ko, in Chapter 8 of this volume, comments that the research lesson using the Learning Study approach cannot use the terms 'teacher-centred' or 'student-centred' as the majority of whole-class lesson episodes, on the one hand, are well controlled. On the other hand, the majority also has active teacher–pupil and pupil–pupil interactions. In another study, Lam, Law and Shum (2009) found that despite the advocacy of student-centred approaches in education reform, two teacher interns still adopted a traditional direct instruction in lower secondary writing classes. These studies seem to suggest that while either teacher-centred or student-centred approaches might not dominantly affect educational outcomes of students, the use of motivating strategies, less classroom management problems and the utterance of higher cognitive demand in student learning tasks might be more conducive to students' learning outcomes.

Lau (2012), in a study of instructional practices and self-regulated learning in Chinese-language classes, has found that "explicit instruction and modeling of strategy use, prompts to guide strategy use and systematic arrangement of teaching sequences" (p.437) are seen as effective forms of teacher support for enhancing students' reading ability and motivation. Nonetheless, there is still a dominance of teacher-centred instruction, which might affect students' self-regulatory strategies (p.446). A study exploring the classroom environment of junior secondary schools and its relationship with students' motivation and use of self-regulated learning strategy reveals that while high teacher support and involvement are salient features of the classroom environment in Hong Kong, it is the teachers displaying teacher-centredness in the classroom rather than student-centredness who tend to be more impactful on students' self-regulated learning. In addition, compared with student collaboration, the factor of classroom order and student involvement in the classroom may be a more significant predictor of self-regulated learning. From a Chinese perspective, Lee, Yin and Zhang (2009, p.229) propose that "teacher-centredness" does not necessarily imply a negative cultural connotation, even when teacher authority or exclusive control is highlighted in classroom activities. It is argued that the teacher-centred approach can create a respectful and comfortable working relationship between teachers and students, though it may seem hierarchical in the eyes of Western researchers (Biggs and Watkins, 1996; Ho, 2001).

While acknowledging possible cultural influences on teaching and learning in Chinese classrooms, it is thus postulated that higher priorities could be accorded by policymakers and educators to the following measures to enhance teacher involvement and support for student learning (e.g., Braine, 2003; Lau and Lee, 2008; Lee, Yin and Zhang, 2009; Schuh, 2004; Young, 2005; Lee, 2011):

Curriculum and Teaching Reforms 347

- Providing motivating learning tasks with diversity, variety and meaning; arranging activities with more student choices; and enhancing tasks and autonomy support for planning and application of appropriate strategies
- Highlighting mastery orientation and enhancing positive, formative feedback to students; cultivating better connections between teachers and students
- Addressing and catering for individual student needs

In the future, more studies could be conducted to assess the effectiveness of student-centred pedagogy in Hong Kong classrooms in the context of curriculum reform and to develop ways of adopting different forms of structured and interactive, as well as both didactic and constructivist Chinese, pedagogy (Lee, Lam and Li, 2003, p.61; Chan, 2009).

The OECD (2009) published the results from Teaching and Learning International Survey (TALIS). The conclusions in the executive summary highlighted:

> Teachers' reports of unmet demand for professional development, particularly in areas relating to catering for increasingly heterogeneous learning groups, the effective use of information and communication tools and student behaviour, signal that teachers themselves often do not feel sufficiently prepared to meet the challenges which they face . . . TALIS also shows that there is generally much greater scope for teachers to learn from other teachers, with teachers reporting relatively infrequent collaboration of the teaching force within the school beyond a mere exchange of information. (p.25)

Stewart (2012, pp.95–96) suggested ten important lessons from the world's top performing and improving education systems. These lessons include fostering long-term vision, providing sustained leadership, setting ambitious standards, having commitment to equity, cultivating high-quality teachers and school leaders, securing alignment and coherence, achieving intelligent accountability, using resources effectively, enhancing student motivation and engagement and emphasizing global and future orientations.

Amongst these important lessons from other education systems, more support is needed for the professional development of principals and teachers, and especially to the promotion of professional learning communities (PLCs) or communities of practice in schools. The study in Hong Kong by Lee, Zhang and Yin (2011) showed that the PLC factor of collective learning and application and faculty trust in colleagues could significantly and positively affect teachers' collective efficacy on student discipline. These findings also revealed that better management of student discipline, which is partly associated with obedience to and respect for authority, could be enhanced in the Chinese classroom. The sharing of

348 John Chi-Kin Lee

good practices of classroom management and catering for student diversity is emphasized in PLCs.

In the context of Hong Kong, relatively low levels of efficacy in classroom management and student engagement among both pre-service and novice teachers have been noted (Chan, 2008), which signals the possible need for strengthening teacher development activities and teacher education programmes. In Hong Kong, Primary School Curriculum Leaders (PSCLs) have been formally established to assist the school principal in leading and implementing whole-school curriculum development. While there are remarkable achievements by PSCLs, Tsui, in Chapter 11 of this volume, remarks that PSCLs have moderate satisfaction with their performance in "[promoting] a professional exchange culture". More could be done to train PSCLs to become change agents and facilitators of PLCs within and across schools. In a recent study on Liberal Studies student-teachers' decision making in lesson planning, Lai and Lam (2011) suggest that more attention could be given to novice or beginning teachers by facilitating in schools a professional culture that supported collaboration and enquiry and providing school-based mentoring programmes.

Another suggestion is to pay heed to teachers' workload and resource support. The journey of educational and curriculum reforms is inevitably embedded with a cost, and teachers' workloads and extra-school and intra-school resource support must be considered. In Chapter 10 of this volume, the results of Ko and Walker's study paradoxically illustrate that teacher workload seems to be heavier and the resource capacity lower in schools with stronger leadership than their counterparts with weaker leadership.

As regards external support, it is desirable to consider offering additional support to students from lower-class families, where there may be a lack of parental care, financial support to life-wide learning and project learning activities and access to information and communication technology (Leung, 2008). Teachers' workload has been an issue of concern particularly in the local educational sector. The Committee on Teachers' Work (2006), established by the Hong Kong government, published a report with 18 recommendations. Amongst these recommendations there were suggestions for boosting the professional image and status of the teaching profession and adopting a whole-school approach to teacher well-being; an emphasis on self-management and personal growth in teacher education programmes; a provision of additional administrative support; and a suggestion of a possible increase in the teacher-to-student ratio to reduce teachers' workloads and enhance teachers' work. While some measures have been taken to reduce teachers' workloads, according to a recent study on teacher stress, recommendations are made to slow down SBA and stop ESR, increase teacher-to-student ratio, consider division of work between administrative and teaching staff, provide professional support services and emphasize teacher autonomy (Fung, 2012, pp.211–212).

In future curriculum and teaching reforms, ways of enhancing students' socio-emotional learning and self-directed learning could be further explored. There have been different approaches and supporting strategies to enhancing students' socio-emotional learning, such as peer and adult emphasis on high expectations and support for academic success, caring teacher–student relationships, proactive classroom management and co-operative learning, as well as safe and orderly classroom environments (Durlak et al., 2011, p.418).

Using a revised Chinese version of the Motivated Strategies for Learning Questionnaire (MSLQ) in Hong Kong has identified the importance of extrinsic learning and peer learning in the learning strategy. In addition, the relatively high correlation of extrinsic and intrinsic motivations might be partly explained by the influence of the Chinese context, where education is perceived to be important for both personal development and social mobility (Lee, Yin and Zhang, 2010; Lee, 1996). Moreover Lau and Lee (2008, p. 359) use "perceived instrumentality"—an individual's understanding of the future instrumental value of a present behaviour—to explain partly the prevalence of extrinsic motivation in learning in the context of Hong Kong (Lau and Lee, 2008). The findings of Zhu and Mok's (2012, p.24) study show that the effect of academic goal orientation on academic achievements of secondary school students is stronger than either academic planning or goal setting, and if there is an alignment between a student's academic goal orientation with his/her mastery goals, this orientation will be positively associated with achievement. It seems plausible to emphasize a balanced approach to providing praise and external rewards to students and cultivating students' intrinsic quest for meaning and joy of learning (Lee, Yin and Zhang, 2010, p.161).

The last but not least suggestion is that in terms of curriculum studies research in Hong Kong, there has been a tendency to adopt Western paradigms and concepts as well as to adapt studies undertaken in the Western world. As regards SBCD, Kennedy (2010, p.15) poses two questions: "Can SBCD be sufficiently indigenized as a tool to meet the diverse cultural requirements of different education systems? How can SBCD ensure that the curriculum of schools is consistent with local cultural values but capable of drawing on other traditions where desirable?"

It is thus suggested that more efforts could be devoted to conceptualize and build up a distinctive Hong Kong and Chinese approach to curriculum planning, curriculum implementation and curriculum studies through integrating cultural, professional and theoretical perspectives. As regards pedagogical and learning research, more could be done to analyze students' voices and students' experiences in the formal curriculum decision-making and hidden curriculum, as well as to track students' longitudinal changes in teaching and learning effectiveness through self-evaluation and peer and external evaluation (Lee, 2009; Lee, Lu and Huang, 2009).

350　John Chi-Kin Lee

In conclusion, it is argued that at the policy level, priorities should be given to relieve teachers' workload and anxiety, enhance an engagement process in which the languages of appreciation for teachers' efforts and teachers' ownership, as well as a synergy of self-evaluation and external support, are emphasized. At the practice/implementation level, it is desirable to contemplate issues such as planning for principal and teacher leadership succession and developing school capacity, enhancing student learning with special reference to emotional and high-order skills development, nurturing PLCs and adopting incremental changes with consideration of the traditions of educational systems under the influence of Chinese culture.

These suggestions hopefully provide some important but not exhaustive pointers for future curriculum reform and implementation in Hong Kong. The realization of these suggestions necessitates theoretical explorations and practical experimentations of blending Chinese and Western thought in curriculum and pedagogical reforms and empirical studies to tease out the critical conditions for sustaining educational innovations and to identity practical and contextual solutions for local adaptations of reform features and overcoming the challenges. The realization of these suggestions also necessitates 'curriculum settlement' for future strategies of curriculum development, as well as a compromise of goals and negotiation among various stakeholders (Kennedy, 2005, p.46; Morris and Adamson, 2010).

It also underscores a partnership approach which capitalizes trust and teachers' positive receptivity to change, provides support to teachers, facilitates the contribution of other stakeholders and focuses on student learning and their whole-person development in a changing and globalized world.

ACKNOWLEDGEMENT

The author would like to thank all contributors to this book as a tribute to our late beloved friend and renowned curriculum expert, Professor Colin Marsh. Part of the content in this chapter is based on the author's presentation *Curriculum and Teaching Reforms: Contexts, Implementation and Sustainability*, on 19 November 2011, in the Chair Professors Public Lecture Series, Hong Kong Institute of Education.

REFERENCES

Barber, M., Donnelly, K., & Rizvi, S. (2012). *Oceans of innovation: The Atlantic, the Pacific, global leadership and the future of education*. London: Institute for Public Policy Research.
Berry, R. (2011). Educational assessment in Mainland China, Hong Kong and Taiwan. In R. Berry & B. Adamson (Eds.) *Assessment reform in education: Policy and practice* (pp.49–61). Rotterdam, The Netherlands: Springer.

Curriculum and Teaching Reforms 351

Biggs, J., & Watkins, D. (1996). The Chinese learner in retrospect. In D.A. Watkins & J.B. Biggs (Eds.) *The Chinese learners: Cultural, psychological and contextual influences* (pp.269–285). Hong Kong: Comparative Education Research Centre and the Australian Council for Educational Research.

Braine, G. (2003). From a teacher-centred to a student-centred approach: A study of peer feedback in Hong Kong writing classes. *Journal of Asian Pacific Communication, 13*(2), 269–288.

Carless, D. (2013). Innovation in language teaching and learning. In C.A. Chappelle (Ed.) *The encyclopedia of applied linguistics.* Oxford: Wiley-Blackwell Publishing. DOI: 10.1002/9781405198431.wbeal0540. Retrieved 8 September 2013, from http://web.edu.hku.hk/staff/dcarless/Carless_2013_innovation.pdf.

Chan, C.K.K. (2009). Classroom innovation for the Chinese learner: Transcending dichotomies and transforming pedagogy. In C.K.K. Chan & N. Rao (Eds.) *Revisiting the Chinese learner: Changing contexts, changing education* (pp.169–210). Hong Kong: Springer and Comparative Education Research Centre, University of Hong Kong.

Chan, D.W. (2008). General, collective, and domain-specific teacher self-efficacy among Chinese prospective and in-service teachers in Hong Kong. *Teachers and Teaching Education, 24*, 1057–1069.

Chan, J.K.S., Kennedy, K., & Fok, P.K. (2008). 'Hard' and 'soft' policy for the school curriculum: The changing role of teachers in the "Learning to Learn" reform. In J.C.K. Lee & L.P. Shiu (Eds.) *Developing teachers and developing schools in changing contexts* (pp.135–153). Hong Kong: Chinese University Press and Hong Kong Institute of Educational Research.

Cheng, A.Y.N. (2012). Student voice in a Chinese context: Investigating the key elements of leadership that enhance student voice. *International Journal of Leadership in Education: Theory and Practice, 15*(3), 351–366.

Cheng, Y.C. (2011). Towards the 3rd wave school leadership. *Revista de Investigacion Educativa, 29*(2), 253–275.

Cheng, Y.C., & Walker, A. (2008). When reform hits reality: The bottleneck effect in Hong Kong primary schools. *School Leadership and Management, 28*(5), 505–521.

Cheung, A.C.K., & Wong, P.M. (2011). Effects of school heads' and teachers' agreement with the curriculum reform on curriculum development progress and student learning in Hong Kong. *International Journal of Educational Management, 25*(5), 453–473.

Cheung, A.C.K., & Wong, P.M. (2012). Factors affecting the implementation of curriculum reform in Hong Kong: Key findings from a large-scale survey study. *International Journal of Educational Management, 26*(1), 39–54.

Chiu, C.S., & Mak, K.W. (2011). The influence of Quality Improvement Project in Hong Kong education reform: School leaders' perspectives. *Education Journal, 39*(1–2), 39–65. (In Chinese)

Committee on Teachers' Work, The (2006). *Final report.* Retrieved 1 August 2011, from http://www.legco.gov.hk/yr06–07/english/panels/ed/papers/ed0212cb2–1041-6-e.pdf.

Cuban, L. (1998). How schools change reforms: Redefining reform success and failure. *Teachers College Record, 99*(3), 453–477.

Curriculum Development Council [CDC] (2001). *Learning to learn: Life-long learning and whole-person development.* Hong Kong: Printing Department.

Curriculum Development Council [CDC] (2012) *Moral and National Education curriculum guide (primary 1 to secondary 6).* Hong Kong: Printing Department. Retrieved 3 September 2013, from http://www.edb.gov.hk/attachment/en/curriculum-development/moral-national-edu/MNE%20Guide%20(ENG)%20Final_remark_09102012.pdf.

352 John Chi-Kin Lee

Department for Education (2011). *The framework for the national curriculum: A report by the expert for the national curriculum review.* London: Department for Education. Retrieved 8 October 2013, from https://www.education.gov.uk/publications/eOrderingDownload/NCR-Expert%20Panel%20Report.pdf.

Durlak, J.A., Weissberg, R.P., Dymnicki, A.B., Taylor, R.D., & Schellinger, K.B. (2011). The impact of enhancing students' social and emotional learning: A meta-analysis of school-based universal interventions. *Child Development, 82*(1), 405–432.

Education Bureau (2008). *Improving learning, teaching and the quality of professional life in schools: A mid-term report on curriculum reform to school heads and teachers.* Retrieved 8 October 2013, from http://www.edb.gov.hk/FileManager/EN/Content_2396/english_professional_report_final_v3.pdf.

Fok, P.K., & Ip, W.H. (2010). The decade review of Hong Kong curriculum reform: An analysis of contextual perspective. *Journal of Curriculum Studies, 5*(1), 1–37. (In Chinese)

Fok, P.K., Kennedy, K.J., & Chan, J.K.S. (2010). Teachers, policymakers and project learning: The questionable use of 'hard' and 'soft' policy instruments to influence the implementation of curriculum reform in Hong Kong. *International Journal of Education Policy and Leadership, 5*(6). Retrieved 8 October 2013, from http://journals.sfu.ca/ijepl/index.php/ijepl/article/view/198/93.

Fok, S.C. (2002). Teaching critical thinking skills in a Hong Kong secondary school. *Asia Pacific Education Review, 3*(1), 83–91.

Fung, W.W. (Ed.) (2012). *Teachers' stress.* Hong Kong: Hong Kong Professional Teachers' Union. (In Chinese)

Hallinger, P. (2010). Making education reform happen: Is there an 'Asian' way? *School Leadership and Management, 30*(5), 401–418.

Hargreaves, A., & Fink, D. (2006). *Sustainable leadership.* San Francisco, CA: Jossey-Bass.

Ho, I.T. (2001). Are Chinese teachers authoritarian? In D.A. Watkins & J.B. Biggs (Eds.) *Teaching the Chinese learners: Psychological and pedagogical perspectives* (pp.99–114). Hong Kong: Comparative Education Research Centre and the Australian Council for Educational Research.

Kennedy, K.J. (2005). *Changing schools for changing times: New directions for the school curriculum in Hong Kong.* Hong Kong: Chinese University Press.

Kennedy, K.J. (2010). School-based curriculum development for new times: A comparative analysis. In E.H.F. Law & N. Nieveen (Eds.) *Schools as curriculum agencies: Asian and European perspectives on school-based curriculum development* (pp.3–18). Rotterdam, The Netherlands: Sense Publishers.

Lai, E., & Lam, C.C. (2011). Learning to teach in a context of education reform: Liberal Studies student teachers' decision-making in lesson planning. *Journal of Education for Teaching: International Research and Pedagogy, 37*(2), 219–236.

Lam, B.H. (2011). The contexts of teaching in the twenty-first century. In S.N. Phillipson & B.H. Lam (Eds.) *Learning and teaching in the Chinese classroom: Responding to individual needs* (pp.1–30). Hong Kong: Hong Kong University Press.

Lam, C.C. (2001). The proposed curriculum reform of Hong Kong—full of contradictions, short of professionalism. *Educational Research Journal, 16*(1), 131–158. (In Chinese)

Lam, S.F., Law, Y.K., & Shum, M.S-K. (2009). Classroom discourse analysis and educational outcomes in the era of education reform. *British Journal of Educational Psychology, 79*, 617–641.

Lau, K.L. (2012). Instructional practices and self-regulated learning in Chinese Language classes. *Educational Psychology: An International Journal of Experimental Educational Psychology, 32*(4), 427–450.

Curriculum and Teaching Reforms   353

Lau, K.L., & Lee, J.C.K. (2008). Examining Hong Kong students' achievement goals and their relations with students' perceived classroom environment and strategy use. *Educational Psychology, 28,* 357–372.

Lee, J.C.K. (2000). Teacher receptivity to curriculum change in the implementation stage: The case of environmental education in Hong Kong. *Journal of Curriculum Studies, 32*(1), 95–115.

Lee, J.C.K. (2006). Hong Kong: Accelerated Schools for Quality Education Project (ASQEP) experiences. In J.C.K. Lee & M. Williams (Eds.) *School improvement: International perspectives* (pp.159–174). New York: Nova Science Publishers.

Lee, J.C.K. (2009). The landscape of curriculum studies in Hong Kong from 1980–2008: A review. *Educational Research Journal, 24*(1), 95–133.

Lee, J.C.K. (2010a). Asian curriculum studies, continental overview. In C. Kridel (Ed.) *Encyclopedia of curriculum studies (volume 1 A–K)* (pp.54–58). Thousand Oaks, CA: Sage Publications.

Lee, J.C.K. (Ed.) (2010b). *School-based curriculum development, teacher development and partnerships.* Beijing: Educational Science Publishing House. (In Chinese)

Lee, J.C.K. (2011). *Curriculum and teaching reforms: Contexts, implementation and sustainability.* Chair Professors Lecture Series, Hong Kong Institute of Education.

Lee, J.C.K., & Dimmock, C. (1998). Curriculum management in secondary schools during political transition: A Hong Kong perspective. *Curriculum Studies, 6*(1), 5–28.

Lee, J.C.K., Lam, W.P., & Li, Y.Y. (2003). Teacher evaluation and effectiveness in Hong Kong: Issues and challenges. *Journal of Personnel Evaluation in Education, 17*(1), 41–65.

Lee, J.C.K., Lu, J., & Huang, X. (2009). A review of twenty-year curriculum and instruction research: Perspectives from Hong Kong and the Chinese Mainland. *Journal of Southwest University (Social Sciences Edition), 4,* 66–74. (In Chinese)

Lee, J.C.K., Yin, H.B., & Zhang, Z.H. (2009). Exploring the influence of the classroom environment on students' motivation and self-regulated learning in Hong Kong. *Asia-Pacific Educational Researcher, 18*(2), 219–232.

Lee, J.C.K., Yin, H.B., & Zhang, Z.H. (2010). Adaptation and analysis of Motivated Strategies for Learning Questionnaire in the Chinese setting. *International Journal of Testing, 10,* 149–165.

Lee, J.C.K., Zhang, Z.H., & Yin, H.B. (2011). A multilevel analysis of the impact of a professional learning community, faculty trust in colleagues and collective efficacy on teacher commitment to students. *Teaching and Teacher Education, 27*(5), 820–830.

Lee, M.H., & Gopinathan, S. (2012). Global or glocal? Roadmaps for curriculum development in Singapore and Hong Kong. *Curriculum and Teaching, 27*(1), 43–65.

Lee, W.O. (1996). The context for Chinese learners: Conceptions of learning in the Confucian tradition. In D.A. Watkins & J.B. Biggs (Eds.) *The Chinese learners: Cultural, psychological and contextual influences* (pp.25–41). Hong Kong: Comparative Educational Research Centre and the Australian Council for Educational Research.

Levin, H.M. (2004). Learning from school reform. In J.C.K. Lee, L.N.K. Lo & A. Walker (Eds.) *Partnership and change: Toward school development* (pp.31–51). Hong Kong: Hong Kong Institute of Educational Research and the Chinese University Press.

Leung, W.L.A. (2008). Teacher concerns about curriculum reform: The case of project learning. *Asia-Pacific Education Researcher, 17*(1), 75–97.

354 John Chi-Kin Lee

Lo, L.N.K., & Ho, B.B.Y. (2010). The meaning of the change agents' action: An exploration of its impact on capacity enhancement for school improvement. *Education Journal, 38*(1), 1–31. (In Chinese)

Lo, M.L. (2009). The development of the Learning Study approach in classroom research in Hong Kong. *Education Research Journal, 24*(1), 165–184.

Marsh, C.J. (2009). *Key concepts for understanding curriculum.* London: Routledge.

Marton, F. (2000). Afterword—the lived curriculum. In B. Adamson, T. Kwan & K. Chan (Eds.) *Changing the curriculum: The impact of reform in primary schooling in Hong Kong* (pp.277–292). Hong Kong: Hong Kong University Press.

Marton, F., & Booth, S. (1997). *Learning and awareness.* Mahwah, NJ: Lawrence Erlbaum Associates.

Mitra, D.L. (2009). Student voice and student roles in education policy and policy reform. In G. Sykes, B, Schneider, D.N. Plank & T.G. Ford (Eds.) *Handbook of educational policy research* (pp.819–830). New York: American Educational Research Association and Routledge.

Morris, P., & Adamson, B. (2010). *Curriculum, schooling and society in Hong Kong.* Hong Kong: Hong Kong University Press.

Ng, S.W. (2011). Managing teacher Balkanization in times of implementing change. *International Journal of Educational Management, 25*(7), 654–670.

Organisation for Economic Co-operation and Development [OECD] (2009). *Creating effective teaching and learning environments: First results of TALIS Executive summary.* Paris: OECD. Retrieved 8 October 2013, from http://www.oecd.org/edu/school/43044074.pdf.

Organisation for Economic Co-operation and Development [OECD] (2011). Shanghai and Hong Kong: Two distinct examples of reform in China. In OECD (Ed.), *Strong performers and successful reformers in education: Lessons from PISA for the United States* (pp.83–115). Paris, France: OECD Publishing. Retrieved 1 August 2011, from http://www.pisa.oecd.org/dataoecd/32/50/46623978.pdf.

Ryan, J. (2011). Introduction. In J. Ryan (Ed.) *Education reform in China: Changing concepts, contexts and practices* (pp.1–17). London: Routledge.

Schuh, K.L. (2004). Learner-centred principles in teacher-centred practices? *Teaching and Teacher Education, 20*(8), 833–846.

Stewart, V. (2012). *A world-class education: Learning from international models of excellence and innovation.* Alexandria, VA: ASCD.

van Damme, D. (2012). *Educating for innovation-driven societies.* PowerPoint presentation. Retrieved 8 October 2013, from www.oecd.org/edu/ceri/50435473.pptx.

Young, M.R. (2005). The motivational effects of the classroom environment in facilitating self-regulated learning. *Journal of Marketing Education, 27*(1), 25–40.

Yuen, T.W.W., Cheung, A.C.K., & Wong, P.M. (2012). A study of the impact of the first phase of the curriculum reform on student learning in Hong Kong. *International Journal of Educational Management, 26*(7), 710–728.

Zhu, J., & Mok, M.M.C. (2012). Effect of academic goal orientation, goal setting, and planning on academic achievement of secondary students in Hong Kong. *Assessment and Learning, 1,* 11–30.

Contributors

Rita BERRY has been an Associate Professor and an Honorary Associate Professor in the Department of Curriculum and Instruction, Hong Kong Institute of Education. She has led many externally and internally funded research projects and writes books and book chapters published by prestigious publishers as well as international peer-reviewed journal articles. She edits books, externally examines academic work and provides consultancy services. Her interests include linking assessment to teaching, learning and curriculum development. Her email is rsyberry@gmail.com or rsyberry@friends.ied.edu.hk.

Jacqueline Kin-Sang CHAN is Associate Dean (Research and Development) in the Faculty of Education and Human Development, and Associate Professor in the Department of Curriculum and Instruction, the Hong Kong Institute of Education. She is research active in areas of curriculum reforms and innovations, curriculum policy implementation and teachers' beliefs and professional development. She can be contacted at jaclo@ied.edu.hk.

Kam-Wing CHAN is an Assistant Professor of the Department of Curriculum and Instruction and Director of the Centre for Small Class Teaching, Hong Kong Institute of Education. He has co-ordinated different types of professional development programmes on Small Class Teaching and has authored a number of publications, such as research papers, books and book chapters with a focus on Small Class Teaching and co-operative learning.

Eric Chi-Keung CHENG earned his Doctor of Education in Education Management from the University of Leicester. He currently serves as an Assistant Professor of Department of Curriculum and Instruction, the Hong Kong Institute of Education. Eric's research interest covers the areas of school management, knowledge management, lesson and Learning Study. His publications include quality assurance in education, management strategies, teacher leadership, teacher collective learning,

356   Contributors

teacher emotional competency, teacher personal knowledge management, communities of practice, self-regulated learning and knowledge strategies.

Alice W.K. CHOW is an Associate Professor in the Department of English Language Education of the Hong Kong Institute of Education. Her research interests include English-language curriculum and pedagogy, teacher preparation and school-based teacher development. Dr. Chow has published in leading international journals, such as *International Journal of Leadership in Education, ELT Journal, Language Teaching Research* and *Teaching and Teacher Education.*

Ping-Kwan FOK is Assistant Professor in the Department of Curriculum and Instruction, the Hong Kong Institute of Education. He is interested in research areas such as curriculum policy, curriculum implementation, critical thinking and Liberal Studies curriculum and teaching. He can be contacted at pkfok@ied.edu.hk.

Sammy King-Fai HUI is an Assistant Professor of the Department of Curriculum and Instruction at the Hong Kong Institute of Education. He worked before in different higher education institutions in Hong Kong, focusing on postgraduate-level educational research and data collection and analysis methods. His current areas of research include outcomes of learning at post-secondary education level, Chinese teachers' conceptions of assessment and curriculum leadership.

Kerry J. KENNEDY is Research Chair Professor in Curriculum Studies at the Hong Kong Institute of Education. He was the 2012 co-winner of the IEA Richard M. Wolfe Memorial Award.

James KO is Assistant Professor of Department of Education Policy and Leadership, Hong Kong Institute of Education. He has worked for various large-scale research projects funded by the RGC in Hong Kong, and by the ESRC and DSCF in the UK. He does mixed-method research and his research interest is now focusing on educational leadership and effectiveness, including their assessments and improvement.

Po-Yuk KO is Associate Professor of Department of Curriculum and Instruction and Director of Centre for Learning Study of the Hong Kong Institute of Education. Her research interests include classroom research, teacher professional development and Chinese Language education. She is a leading figure in Learning Study—a pioneering area of classroom research in Hong Kong. She has authored or co-authored many books and journal articles and served as regional editor and reviewer for a number of international journals.

Contributors 357

Xiaoxue KUANG is a PhD candidate in the centre for Governance and Citizenship at the Hong Kong Institute of Education.

Kwok-Chan LAI was the founding Director of the Centre for Small Class Teaching (CSCT), Hong Kong Institute of Education, and is currently its Honorary Co-Director and Adjunct Associate Professor. He has published numerous monographs and papers on SCT and has extensive experience in providing professional training on SCT to officials and teachers in Hong Kong, Macau and Mainland China. He has been invited to deliver keynote addresses and serve as advisers on SCT to education bureaus in Shanghai and Nanjing, China.

Chi Chung LAM is a Professor at the Department of Curriculum and Instruction, Chinese University of Hong Kong. He has extensive working experience in secondary schools and the university sector. During the past two decades, he has been active in research work on the curriculum change and reform in Hong Kong. His research interests include curriculum reform and implementation, geographical curriculum changes, mathematics curriculum and teachers' beliefs.

John Tak-shing LAM is an Assistant Professor at the Hong Kong Institute of Education, Department of Curriculum and Instruction. Formerly he was an English-language teacher in Hong Kong secondary schools. His academic expertise lies in curriculum studies, Action Research, teachers' thinking and school-based curriculum development. His latest academic interests are in citizenship education, Liberal Studies and school-based curriculum development. He has published a number of academic books, book chapters, refereed international and local journal articles on these topics.

Edmond Hau-Fai LAW is Associate Professor in Curriculum and Instruction Department, Hong Kong Institute of Education. He specializes in curriculum leadership and activity theory. His recent publications include 'In Search of a Diverse Curriculum: Toward the Making of Postmodern Hong Kong in the 21st Century' (in *International Handbook of Curriculum Research*, Routledge, 2014) and 'Impact of Leadership Styles on Communication Networking in Subject Teams: A Hong Kong Perspective' (in *International Journal of Leadership in Education,* 2014).

John Chi-Kin LEE is Vice President (Academic) and Chair Professor of Curriculum and Instruction, Hong Kong Institute of Education. He is also Changjiang Chair Professor at Southwest University, China. He serves as Regional Editor (Asia-Pacific) of *Educational Research and Evaluation*, Associate Editor of *Teachers and Teaching* and *Journal of Teacher Education and Educators*. He has published and co-edited many books

358 Contributors

in education, including *Changing Schools in an Era of Globalization* (Routledge, 2011) with Brian Caldwell. His email is jcklee@ied.edu.hk.

Anthony Wai-Lun LEUNG is an Assistant Professor at the Department of Curriculum and Instruction, Hong Kong Institute of Education. He teaches and consults in the areas of curriculum reform and change, curriculum organization and integration, curriculum implementation, project learning, Liberal Studies and Small Class Teaching. One of his recent publications is a co-authored book entitled *Curriculum Change and Innovation* (Hong Kong University Press, 2012).

Joe Tin-yau LO is an Adjunct Associate Professor at the Department of Social Sciences, HKIEd. He has published extensively in the areas of social education, citizenship education, comparative education, China and Hong Kong Studies. He has recently co-edited a book (with David Grossman) entitled *Social Education in Asia: Critical Issues and Multiple Perspective* (Information Age Publishing, 2007). In addition, he has been engaging in an oral history publication project on the education and heritage in Hong Kong and China.

Colin MARSH was an Adjunct Professor at Curtin University, Perth, Western Australia. He had a wealth of experience teaching in areas such as teaching and learning, curriculum, evaluation, implementation, humanities. He was the former editor of *Curriculum Perspectives* and had published many books in education, including *Curriculum: Alternative Approaches, Ongoing Issues* (4th Ed., with George Willis, Pearson, 2006) and *Key Concepts for Understanding Curriculum* (4th Ed., Routledge, 2009). He passed away in August 2012.

Paul MORRIS is currently a Professor of Education at the Institute of Education, University of London. From 1976 he worked at the Faculty of Education at HKU and from 2000 to 2007 he was the Deputy Director/President of the HKIEd.

Kwok-Tung TSUI is an Associate Professor at the Hong Kong Institute of Education. His research interests include curriculum leadership, teacher leadership, teacher effectiveness and professional development. He had been appointed by the World Bank as international consultant for the School Education Quality Assurance Program in Vietnam in 2008–2009 and Primary Teacher Project in Vietnam in 2000. Dr. Tsui has been commissioned by the Education Bureau of the Hong Kong government to lead a team to train local primary school curriculum leaders since the inception of this scheme in 2002 and conduct a large-scale survey on curriculum leadership and management in primary schools contracted in 2010.

Contributors 359

Allan WALKER is Joseph Lau Chair Professor of International Educational Leadership and Dean of Faculty of Education and Human Development, Hong Kong Institute of Education.

Zi YAN is an Assistant Professor in the Department of Curriculum and Instruction at the Hong Kong Institute of Education. He is currently the Deputy Chair of the Pacific Rim Objective Measurement Society, which is dedicated to promote objective measurement. He obtained his PhD at James Cook University, Australia, with a specialization area in Educational Measurement. His main research interests are in school-based assessment, Rasch measurement, scale development and large-scale assessment.

Shirley Sze Yin YEUNG is an Assistant Professor in the Department of Curriculum and Instruction at the Hong Kong Institute of Education. Her research areas include curriculum change and implementation, school curriculum evaluation, curriculum integration, infusing higher-order thinking across the school curriculum and teachers' belief and conception of the curriculum. She has published book chapters, including 'Curriculum Change and Innovation' (Hong Kong University Press, 2012) and 'Teaching and Learning of Higher-Order Thinking' (Contemporary Development, 2012).

Index

334 academic structure, 3

A

academic rationalism, 52–54, 59
accountability, 10, 20, 39, 44, 57, 61, 64, 77, 79, 155, 157–59, 161–62, 205, 215, 274, 288, 290–99, 311, 313–15, 320, 322–23, 333–35, 339, 344, 347
action research, 6, 26, 41, 91, 119, 120, 127, 181–86, 197, 203, 342
activity approach (AA), 54, 133–35, 146
Advisory Committee on Teacher Education and Qualifications (ACTEQ), 4
alignment, 42, 76, 86, 155–56, 158, 160, 163–64, 196, 226, 229, 274, 311, 316, 330, 347, 349
Asian, 23–25, 28–31, 89, 110, 117, 128, 175, 196, 199, 200, 204, 206, 309, 339, 344
assessment
  as learning, 289, 290, 297
  for Learning (AfL), 7–9, 19, 23, 27–29, 34, 41, 71, 181, 230, 249, 255–56, 259, 280, 288–90, 292, 295, 340
  for selection, 9, 23, 27
  methods/strategies, 63, 74–75, 80, 96, 145–46, 201, 212, 255, 258, 260–61, 264, 268, 289, 291
  of learning, 9, 34, 249, 288–90
authentic assessment, 285, 292, 296–99
authenticity, 292, 296–99, 341
awareness of social and global issues, 86

B

balance, 3, 8, 17–21, 23–26, 28, 39, 56, 84, 107, 289, 323–34, 349
Basic Competency Assessment (BCA), 233, 237, 257–58, 265, 340
basic curriculum, 8, 22, 70
basic education, 2–3, 26, 132–33, 181, 225, 236, 288, 320
Beijing, 33, 111, 128, 141
Board of Education, 39, 135, 309
British, 1, 3, 17–18, 24, 57, 89, 221, 223, 230, 233
broadening of one's horizon, 86

C

capacity enhancement, 239
catering for learner diversity, 74–75, 80, 142, 144
central development, 8, 23, 25
centralization, 8, 23, 33, 25, 34–35, 78
Centre for Small Class Teaching (CSCT), 138–39, 141–43
centre periphery approach, 223
Chief Executive, 19, 38, 70, 109, 135, 137, 176, 243 (*see also* Donald Tsang)
Chinese
  classroom, 9, 26, 117–18, 126, 346–47
  culture, 10, 26, 188, 270, 294, 307, 340, 350
  Language, 3, 5, 9, 26, 71, 122, 137, 199, 233–34, 237, 257, 259, 265–66, 276, 278–80, 307, 311, 346
  pedagogy, 10, 345, 347
  teacher, 117, 294–95, 117
citizenship education, 20, 24, 66, 103, 106

362   Index

class size, 28, 93, 132–38, 144, 146, 167, 202, 343
class size reduction, 132, 134–36
classical humanist approach, 223
classroom environment, 138, 140–41, 145, 346, 349
co-curricular activities, 108
coherence, 85, 155–56, 158–60, 163–64, 347
collaborative research and development, 40, 72, 211, 214, 237–38
collegiality, 168, 326, 329, 334–35
Colonial, 17–19, 21, 35, 55, 57, 111, 118–19, 212, 221–23, 229–30, 233–34, 338
Colony, 1, 17, 24, 89
Committee on Professional Development of Teachers and Principals (COTAP), 4
communication network, 204
communicative language teaching (CLT), 224
Communist, 33, 35, 104, 109
community of philosophical hermeneutic enquiry, 84
Confucian Heritage Culture (CHC), 21, 29, 117–18, 340–41
constructivist, 95, 139, 226, 347
context, 8–10, 17–20, 22, 24–27, 35–36, 39–30, 43, 53, 59, 70, 84, 87–91, 97, 103–4, 111, 118, 127, 132, 139, 143, 152–53, 155, 164–67, 170–71, 185, 188, 195, 203, 207–8, 214, 218, 221, 223–24, 226–27, 229, 231, 237, 239–40, 244, 246–49, 256, 270, 274, 277–78, 284, 290–92, 294–99, 328, 338, 340, 343, 345, 347–50
contextualization, 328, 335
continuous professional development (CPD), 78, 119, 182, 243, 344, 4, 238
cooperative learning, 142, 332, 349
criterion-referenced, 233
critical thinking, 19, 24, 53, 56, 61, 71, 212, 228–29, 280, 338, 341–43
cultivating one's critical mindedness, 86
culture building, 178
curriculum as technology, 52–53, 60, 62–63
curriculum conceptions, 51–52, 55
Curriculum Development Council (CDC), 3, 8, 17, 19, 21–28, 36,
38–39, 54–55, 56–60, 62, 64, 70, 71–72, 77–79, 82, 86, 90, 102, 108–9, 118–19, 136, 175, 181, 185, 209, 211–12, 214–15, 221, 224, 226–28, 230, 238, 244–45, 257, 288, 308, 338, 344
Curriculum Development Institute (CDI), 24, 39–40, 86, 92, 95, 214–15, 223, 230, 237–38
curriculum
  development team, 188, 197, 204
  evaluation, 178
  guides, 3, 20, 34, 58, 62, 65, 78, 93, 109, 181, 203, 209–10, 214–15, 224, 227, 248, 288, 344
  implementation, 24, 26, 38, 72, 74–75, 79–80, 82, 91, 96, 177, 207–8, 341–42, 349
  integration, 54, 109, 217, 342
  leadership, 9, 21, 89, 143, 175–79, 181–83, 189, 196, 343
  planning, 24, 53, 72, 139, 178–82, 188–89, 196, 216, 238, 268, 349
  reform, 3, 7–10, 17–22, 24–29, 33, 36, 39–44, 55–56, 59–60, 63–64, 70–75, 80, 82–84, 80–90, 107, 136, 171, 175–186, 207–9, 213–18, 222, 227, 237, 239, 256, 285, 307–8, 311, 316, 338–39, 341–42, 344–45, 347–48, 350
  space, 87, 89–90, 111, 338

D

decentralization, 8, 23, 25, 29, 33–35, 37–38, 41–44, 78, 175, 323, 338
deep learning, 9, 202
delegation, 33–34, 40, 152
democratization, 65–66
development of cognitive processes, 52–53, 59–61, 63–64
didactic, 9, 88, 95, 126, 200, 239, 347
discourse style, 200
distributed leadership, 143, 169, 199, 204

E

economic-bureaucratic, 293, 295
Education and Manpower Bureau (EMB), 3, 8, 19, 39, 41, 56, 60, 85, 135–37, 176, 215, 314
Education Bureau (EDB), 3–7, 21, 26–28, 33, 35, 40–41, 43,

55, 57–62, 73–75, 79, 86, 90, 94–95, 97–98, 108–9, 136, 138–40, 146, 176–183, 185–188, 215–17, 222, 230, 234, 265, 281, 289, 293, 317, 320, 322–26, 328, 330, 333, 341,
Education Commission (EC), 2–3, 17–20, 36–38, 56–57, 59, 70, 108, 118, 134–36, 225, 227, 230–31, 233, 235, 237, 241, 257, 308–9, 315, 320, 323
Education Development Fund (EDF), 20, 41–42
education reform, 3, 7, 19–20, 25, 29, 41, 118, 127–28, 135–36, 175, 177–79, 225, 257, 271, 289, 307, 312, 315, 346
e-learning, 55, 59–60, 62–64, 56, 71, 137
empowerment, 33, 39, 42, 152, 168, 271, 340
enhancement grant, 238, 239
English language, 3, 9, 26, 221–27, 229–30, 232–34, 236–38, 240, 242–45, 248, 257, 259, 265–66, 276, 311, 344
English language teaching (ELT), 223–24, 237–38, 244
ethical-professional accountability, 293
expansive learning, 197
expert judgment approach, 283
external communication, 155, 157, 159, 161–62
External School Review (ESR), 7–8, 55, 57, 60–62, 64, 73, 75, 77, 79, 90, 151, 215–17, 309–12, 314–17, 323–35, 339, 344, 348
external school review (ESR) cycle, 324, 334

F

fine-tuned, 233
formative assessment, 9, 28, 139, 230, 249, 255, 257–58, 262–63, 269, 271, 274, 282, 327
fusion of horizons, 84, 87, 91–94, 97–98

G

generality, 332, 335
generic skills, 41, 56, 61, 70–71, 73, 75, 118, 201, 203, 212, 215–16, 228–29, 248–49, 308, 328, 338

globalization, 8, 19, 21, 23–24, 29, 51, 56, 63–64, 66, 70, 85, 175, 228, 339
goal setting, 178, 280, 349
Grattan Institute, 89, 90
group work, 80, 122, 126–27, 138, 146

H

hard policy, 90, 213–16, 218, 338–39
high-performing, 1, 4, 6, 89–90, 293, 323, 338, 340–41
high-stake, 230, 255–56, 258, 274–75, 277–78, 284–85, 294–95, 312, 316, 340
historical, 8, 17, 33, 36, 43, 95, 111
Hong Kong Diploma of Secondary Education (HKDSE), 3, 22, 27, 44, 229, 239–41, 258, 275–76, 278–80, 283
Hong Kong Examinations and Assessment Authority (HKEAA), 21, 26–28, 55, 86, 97, 230, 258, 276, 279, 283–84, 290
Hong Kong Professional Teachers' Union, 86
Hongkonger, 103–4
humanistic approach, 52–53

I

ideology, 8, 18–19, 51–54, 59–67, 221, 223, 315
ideology improvement, 6–7, 10, 17–18, 26, 42–43, 73–74, 77, 79, 81–82, 119–20, 123, 126, 128, 132–33, 135, 139, 142, 144, 152, 154–55, 158, 160–61, 165, 168, 171, 184, 196, 203, 233, 236–38, 243, 256, 263, 266, 271, 288, 290, 292–97, 299, 310, 312, 320–21, 323–25, 328–29, 331–35, 339, 342
inclusive, 28, 151–52, 201, 234, 342
Incorporated Management Committee (IMC), 4, 313
Independent Education Study (IES), 86
individualized support, 153
individuality, 332, 335
information technology for interactive learning, 22, 72, 214
information technology in education (ITEd), 19
Institute of Language in Education (ILE), 225, 235

364　Index

Instructional leadership, 152, 158, 171, 177

intellectual stimulation, 153

International Study of Civics and Citizenship Education (ICSS), 103

irrelevance, 10, 294–95

K

key learning areas (KLAs), 40, 56, 71, 75, 108, 189, 212, 214, 233, 325

key tasks, 17, 22, 71, 78, 108, 214–15, 228, 338, 342

knowledge construction, 228

L

laissez-faire policy, 233–34

Leadership style, 9, 199–200, 204

learner-centred, 9, 52–53, 54, 59–61, 63–64, 239, 243

learning
circle, 132, 137, 139, 142–45
communities, 10, 42, 94, 138, 145, 181, 184, 186, 189, 248, 264, 270, 345, 347
context, 291–92, 296, 299
for achievement, 25
outcomes, 34, 84, 86, 98, 121, 127, 166, 201, 216, 257, 261–63, 274–75, 282, 311, 341, 346
study approach, 42, 117, 119, 121, 126–28, 346

Learning to learn, 3, 8, 17, 22, 39, 70, 72–83, 175, 178–79, 185, 210, 214, 216, 227–28, 257

Legislative Council, 86, 136, 137, 139

Liberal Studies (LS), 3, 8, 9, 23, 26, 55–57, 60–61, 65, 67, 84–87, 91–98, 108, 212, 276, 278–280, 308, 343, 348

lifelong learning, 2–3, 17, 29, 36, 41, 60, 70, 72, 74, 82, 119, 179, 196, 212, 226, 228, 248, 274, 295

life-wide learning, 3, 20, 25, 143, 212, 308, 348

Llewellyn Report, 35–37, 195, 201

localization, 8, 23–24, 225

M

McKinsey & Company, 5, 73, 89, 186

medium of instruction, 60, 134, 151, 225, 344

Medium of instruction (MOI) language policies, 6, 55, 57

memorization, 27, 97, 224, 340, 346

meta-cognitive, 343

moderation, 240, 280, 283–85, 341

moral and civic education, 22, 45, 56, 71, 75, 189, 214, 308, 311, 316, 338

moral and national education (MNE), 8, 20, 33, 55, 58, 60, 62, 65–66, 102, 104, 109, 334, 339

N

national identity, 58, 62, 102–4, 107–12, 339

nationalism, nationalistic, 20, 62, 66, 110

Native-speaking English Teacher (NET), 237–38

neoliberal, 23, 36, 43

new progressivism, 19, 21

New Senior Secondary (NSS), 3, 7–8, 22, 25–28, 55, 56, 59–61, 64, 70, 85, 151, 212, 229, 235, 237, 239–41, 243, 248, 275, 278–81

normative-re-educative, 9, 222–23, 225

norm-referenced examination, 256

O

Organisation for Economic Co-operation and Development (OECD), 5, 19, 21, 29, 133–34, 140, 184, 211, 341, 347

P

participation style, 200

partnership, 9, 72, 78, 82, 89, 95, 97–98, 119–20, 137–41, 134–44, 146, 205, 209, 223, 242–43, 342, 344–45, 350

patriotism, 58, 62, 66, 102–5, 107, 110, 339

pedagogy, 7, 9, 10, 26–28, 34, 44, 60, 65–66, 126, 134, 145, 184, 189, 201, 235, 239, 255, 257, 339, 345, 347

peer lesson observation, 264, 330

performance indicators, 57, 209, 297, 309, 321, 324, 331

Physical Education (PE), 9, 56, 71, 275–76, 280

planning capacity, 10, 330, 334–35

policy environment, 154–60, 162, 164

power hierarchy, 168, 196

Index 365

power-coercive, 199, 222–23
Primary School Curriculum Leaders (PSCLs), 9, 176, 178–79, 180–88, 348
Primary School Masters/Mistresses (Curriculum Development) (PSM(CD)), 40
principal leadership, 9, 143–45, 151, 153–54, 160, 177, 343
problem-solving, 60–61, 64, 71, 222–23, 226, 228, 308
professional development, 4–6, 21, 41, 44, 71, 74, 76, 78, 80, 82, 90, 93, 118–21, 127–28, 132, 134, 137–39, 142–45, 151, 154, 158, 171, 179–89, 209–13, 217, 235, 237–39, 243, 249, 259–60, 267, 271–72, 289, 322, 325, 332–33, 338, 342, 344–45, 347
professional learning community (PLC), 10, 186, 347–48, 350
Programme for International Student Assessment (PISA), 4–6, 23, 72, 89, 117, 128, 184, 340
Progress in International Reading Literacy Study (PIRLS), 4–7, 72, 241
project learning, 22, 25, 71, 73, 119, 214–18, 308, 311, 316, 338–39, 342, 348

Q

quality
assurance, 7, 10, 24, 55, 57, 77, 155, 157–59, 161–62, 171, 178, 205, 213, 215, 307–310, 314, 320–21, 324, 344
education, 20, 211, 309–11
Quality Education Fund (QEF), 6, 20, 26, 196, 213–14, 235–36, 315, 339

R

rational-empirical, 9, 222–23, 230
reading to learn, 22, 71, 214, 228, 237–38, 241, 308, 311, 316
redistributive, 209–11
reform syndrome, 7, 20
religious/political orthodoxy, 52, 54
resource capacity, 155, 160, 163–64, 348
resource management, 152, 155, 157–62, 165–66
restructuring, 165, 338

rote learning, 21, 117–18, 126, 255, 340, 345

S

school
condition, 158–59, 163–64
curriculum, 8–9, 51–54, 59–61, 64–66, 70, 77–79, 84, 89, 95, 103, 107, 109–12, 118, 176, 178–79, 181, 185–86, 188–89, 201, 212, 227–28, 241, 307–8, 312, 348
improvement, 6, 18, 26, 61, 79, 83, 144, 154, 160–61, 168, 171, 216, 233, 243, 292–93, 320–21, 323–25, 331, 334, 342, 335
School management Initiative (SMI), 35, 313, 320
School Self-Evaluation (SSE) policy, 2, 7, 8, 10, 24, 55, 57, 60–62, 64, 74, 79, 151, 215, 309, 312–14, 317, 321–30, 332, 334–36, 339, 344
School Sponsoring Bodies (SSBs), 4, 33, 154, 293, 312–13, 325
School-based
assessment (SBA), 9, 27–28, 44, 97, 229–30, 232, 235, 240, 243, 249, 257–59, 274–85, 339–40, 348
curriculum development, 3, 7, 9, 24, 33, 39, 71, 89, 119, 175–76, 181, 196, 200, 210, 248, 316, 338, 342
Curriculum Project Scheme (SBCPS), 37–38,42
curriculum support teams, 38
Curriculum Tailoring Scheme (SBCTS), 38, 43
management (SBM), 4, 7, 20, 29, 151, 309, 316, 320, 323
school-university partnership, 95, 97–98, 146, 342, 344
seed projects, 40, 72, 209–11, 214, 238
self-regulated learning, 26, 59, 346
Shanghai, 6, 21, 89, 136, 141, 185, 222, 232, 243, 309, 339
Singapore, 6, 23, 89, 120, 186, 204, 222, 243, 309, 321, 323, 339, 341
small class teaching (SCT), 9, 21, 121, 132–33, 136–47, 166, 327, 343
Smart Classroom, 141
social efficiency, 8, 52–53, 60–64

366 Index

social reconstruction, 51–53, 60–61, 66, 339
socio-cultural, 17, 21, 25, 199, 277, 290–291, 295–96, 299, 340
socio-emotional learning, 10, 349
socio-political, 8, 17–18, 20
soft policy, 208–9, 211, 213–16, 338–39, 341
soft approach, 108–9, 232–33, 339
stakeholders, 21, 23, 28–29, 57, 65, 73, 85–87, 95, 98, 221–23, 257, 280, 285, 293, 309–10, 312–14, 324, 428, 343–45, 350
standardization, 240, 284, 328, 335
Standing Committee on Language Education and Research, 236
statistical approach, 283
strategic direction, strategic planning, 10, 154–60, 162, 164, 167, 171, 327, 335–36
student
  leadership, 143, 170, 343
  outcomes, 9, 151, 153–54
student-centred, 22, 60, 63–64, 118, 136, 145–46, 227, 235, 248, 311, 345–47
summative assessment, 230, 349, 263, 274, 282
sustainability, 10, 76–77, 81, 128, 223, 269, 333
sustainable development, 10, 44, 74, 81, 336

T

Targets and Target-related Assessment (TTRA), 18, 226–27, 231–33, 235, 243
Target Oriented Assessment (TOA), 255–57
Target Oriented Curriculum (TOC), 18–19, 36, 146, 226–27, 232–33, 235, 243, 255–57, 307, 310, 340
task-based learning (TBL), 127, 227, 235, 243, 310
teacher-centred, 27, 54, 117–18, 126, 235, 342, 345–46

teacher
  collaboration, 342, 168
  growth/development, 9, 39, 42, 59, 80, 144, 151, 154, 157–60, 162, 167, 169–70, 177, 182, 189, 199, 217–18, 271, 331, 348
  leadership, 143, 168, 177, 196, 343, 350
  learning, 91, 128, 139, 205, 264, 344, 199–200
  learning communities (TLCs), 264, 269
  stress, 348
  workload, 28, 160, 348
Teaching Research Office (TRO), 118
team spirit, 2, 79, 167, 170, 200, 204, 330, 334
tension, 24, 36, 91–92, 106, 293, 295
Territory-wide System Assessment (TSA), 211, 233, 257, 311, 339, 213, 239, 258–59, 265, 317, 331
textbooks, 35, 37, 44, 59, 63–64, 66, 72, 78, 117, 127, 145, 210–11, 249, 256, 338
top-down approach, 18–19
traditional classroom, 195
transactional leadership, 158, 165
transformational leadership, 152
Trends in International Mathematics and Science Study (TIMSS), 4–5, 72, 89, 117
trust, 21, 144, 152, 155, 160, 163–64, 169, 232, 259, 277, 344, 347, 350

V

values and attitudes, 26, 36
Variation for Improvement of Teaching and Learning (VITAL), 42, 120
Variation theory, 120–22, 126–27
vision, 3, 44, 54, 118, 145, 151–53, 156, 158, 160, 164–67, 170–71, 208, 264, 309, 343, 347

W

whole-person development, 3, 8, 17, 22–23, 26, 36, 56, 70–72, 74, 119, 179, 308, 350